Come Fly with Us

Outward Odyssey
A People's History of Spaceflight

Series editor
Colin Burgess

Come Fly with Us

NASA's Payload Specialist Program

Melvin Croft and John Youskauskas

Foreword by Don Thomas

UNIVERSITY OF NEBRASKA PRESS • LINCOLN & LONDON

Library of Congress Cataloging-in-
Publication Data
Names: Croft, Melvin, author. |
Youskauskas, John, author.
Title: Come fly with us: NASA's
Payload Specialist Program / Melvin
Croft and John Youskauskas;
foreword by Don Thomas.
Description: Lincoln: University
of Nebraska Press, [2019] | Series:
Outward odyssey: a people's history
of spaceflight | Includes bibliographical
references and index.
Identifiers: LCCN 2018003953
ISBN 9780803278929 (cloth: alk. paper)
ISBN 9781496212245 (epub)
ISBN 9781496212252 (mobi)
ISBN 9781496212269 (pdf)
Subjects: LCSH: United States. National
Aeronautics and Space Administration.
Payload Specialist Program—History.
| Payloads (Aerospace engineering)—
United States—History.
Classification: LCC TL521.312 .C76 2019
| DDC 629.4500973—dc23
LC record available at
https://lccn.loc.gov/2018003953

Set in Garamond Pro by
Mikala R. Kolander.

Dedicated to the unsung heroes of NASA's payload specialist program, who dared to dream of flying in space, then turned that dream into reality. This is your story.

Contents

Illustrations

Foreword

Along with the lunar module that landed astronauts on the moon during the Apollo program, the space shuttle is arguably one of the most iconic flying machines of the twentieth century. Besides launching satellites into Earth orbit and others to distant planets, the space shuttles also brought astronauts and supplies to the Russian *Mir* space station and were a major workhorse for the delivery of components and construction of today's International Space Station. The space shuttle carried the Hubble Space Telescope to space, where five servicing missions took place to repair the Hubble and upgrade its many sensors and cameras. Far eclipsing the science returns of the *Skylab* space station, the space shuttle was all about science with twenty-seven Spacelab missions, twenty-two Spacehab missions, and many others dedicated to astronomy, the microgravity and life sciences, and studying Earth. In fact, there probably wasn't a single space shuttle that launched from the Kennedy Space Center that didn't have middeck lockers filled with additional science experiments from researchers across the United States and around the world.

Besides the wealth of scientific data returned to Earth, the space shuttle was instrumental in opening up space to a large and diverse group of individuals. While a few science astronauts were selected during the Apollo program with one of them (Jack Schmitt) walking on the moon, not until the shuttle era did NASA begin selecting large numbers of mission specialist astronauts to support the science objectives. Both men and women were recruited from a wide range of backgrounds. Medical doctors, scientists, engineers, astronomers, geologists, and later in the program, even school teachers were selected to fly as mission specialists.

Beginning with the launch of the first Spacelab mission during STS-9 in 1983, NASA started flying a whole new category of noncareer astronauts called payload specialists aboard the space shuttle. Initially, as documented by the authors of this book, payload specialists were professional scientists with unique skills and backgrounds that helped maximize the scientific return from the missions, but soon NASA opened it up to fly engineers from some of its industry partners, with Charlie Walker representing McDonnell Douglas Corporation, Robert Cenker from RCA, and Greg Jarvis from Hughes Aircraft.

International participants were also invited to fly as payload specialists with Ulf Merbold from Germany, Marc Garneau from Canada, Patrick Baudry from France, Prince Sultan Salman Abdulaziz Al-Saud from Saudi Arabia, Rodolfo Neri Vela from Mexico, Mamoru Mohri from Japan, and Ilan Ramon from Israel just a few of the many international participants. The military also selected payload specialists to support some of their Department of Defense space shuttle missions, including Gary Payton and William Pailes from the air force and Thomas Hennen from the army. Even politicians were invited to fly as payload specialists, such as Bill Nelson from the House of Representatives and Jake Garn from the Senate. Teachers were invited to join the ranks, with Christa McAuliffe being the first to launch aboard *Challenger*. And John Glenn was able to return to space as a payload specialist aboard space shuttle *Discovery* in 1998. While proposals made to fly celebrities—such as journalists, artists, poets, singers, and actors—and even regular citizens into space were never realized, the breadth of experience and diversity in backgrounds of the payload specialists who flew on the space shuttle is truly amazing.

Although this book mostly covers the early years of that particular program, I had the great pleasure to fly with three payload specialists on three of my four flights and worked and socialized with many more of them at the NASA Johnson Space Center during my seventeen-year career as an astronaut. Sharing my very first mission with Chiaki Mukai, the first woman from Japan to fly in space, made the experience even more special by providing me with the opportunity to visit her country and learn about her customs and traditions. I'll never forget the amazing experience I had eating fugu in a small restaurant in Hiroshima along with fellow crew member Leroy Chiao and our backup payload specialist Jean-Jacques Favier or sampling eel gall bladder soup at a local restaurant in Tokyo!

Orbiting Earth 692 times during my four missions, I was able to see much of our planet from above, and the experience forever changed my perspective of where I fit in on Planet Earth. Being born in Cleveland, Ohio, I grew up identifying primarily as a Clevelander. But after my trips to space, today I identify myself more as an Earthling, just one of over 7 billion fellow passengers traveling through the cosmos on Spaceship Earth. Flying with Chiaki on STS-65 helped broaden my cultural experience, so I not only saw other countries down below but was able to experience some of their cultures as well, just one of the great benefits that the payload specialist program brought to the rest of the Astronaut Office. It was truly an enriching experience!

Don Thomas

NASA mission specialist, STS-65, STS-70, STS-83, and STS-94

Acknowledgments

This chronicle of NASA's payload specialist program would not have been possible without the contribution of many individuals and institutions. Foremost, the payload specialists and crews that shepherded them into space deserve heartfelt thanks for their role in advancing America's space program. We are indebted to university archivist Lauren Meyers and her staff at the University of Houston–Clear Lake Archives for providing unlimited access to their wonderful JSC History Collection. The kind folks at this library accommodated our every request, which lead to a treasure trove of NASA records that document the genesis of the payload specialist and more. The NASA Oral History Project provided tremendous insight from many of the crew members and support personnel for each of the missions, adding colorful commentary to our account of this pioneering program.

We are most gracious to a number of individuals who were willing to take the time to describe these missions. Dr. Rick Chappell provided a wonderful explanation of the beginnings of the payload specialist program and how they were selected. Loren Acton described in detail his journey into space. Michael Lampton was kind enough to share his experiences as a backup payload specialist and his own quest to make it into outer space.

Payload specialists Bob Cenker and Rodolfo Neri Vela and manned spaceflight engineers (MSEs) Frank Casserino, Gary Payton, and Brett Watterson contributed immensely with their personal time for extensive interviews. Special thanks to Bill Pailes and Eric Sundberg for going above and beyond to help make this project a success. We are greatly indebted to astronaut Don Thomas, a successful author in his own right, for penning a forward to this incredible story.

Others who were kind enough to answer questions include astronauts Bo Bobko, Brian Duffy, Fred Gregory, the late Hank Hartsfield, Rick

Hauck, Charlie Walker, Paul Scully-Power, Jerry Ross, Brewster Shaw, Loren Shriver, and Bill Thornton. Larry Gooch and Don Hard lent valuable insights into the early days of the Manned Spaceflight Engineer Program, and Paul Bellia of the Secretary of the Air Force Special Projects (SAFSP) Alumni Association continues to keep the history of Special Projects alive through this organization of U.S. Air Force veterans. Thanks to Munro Wood for allowing us to learn what an accomplished, talented, and determined person his father was. NASA engineer Ed Rezac was also extremely helpful in providing operational insights about the orbiters. And a final special thanks to astronaut Jack Fischer, who took the time to approve the use of his photo, even though he was in Russia at the time, just days away from his first mission into space.

Special thanks go to Colin Burgess, series editor of the fascinating and informative Outward Odyssey book series, for offering us the opportunity to write the story of the payload specialists. He graciously edited our first draft—often adding information from his vast library of space knowledge—and was always willing to provide sage advice as we conducted our research and put pen to paper.

Of course, without the incredible support of our families, this book could never have come to fruition. A heartfelt thanks to Heather, Robin, Wil, and Katherine, who heard "I'll be working on the book" a few times too often while life went on without the authors' presence.

We'd like to thank the University of Nebraska Press, senior editor Rob Taylor, and his incredibly talented staff for guiding us through the complicated process of turning our manuscript into a finished product that we hope will allow the reader to walk in the footsteps of the payload specialists. The incredible detailed editing and challenges by Jeremy Hall improved the manuscript tremendously.

Lastly, while many of the stories told here are based on the recollections of those involved, any factual errors are ours alone.

Come Fly with Us

Introduction

Ships and sails proper for the heavenly air should be fashioned.
Then there will also be people, who do not shrink from
the dreary vastness of space.

Johannes Kepler

At the conclusion of space shuttle *Columbia*'s fourth mission in July of 1982, NASA's orbital flight test program was deemed complete and the Space Transportation System was declared operational. The crew of STS-4, commander Thomas "Ken" Mattingly and pilot Henry "Hank" Hartsfield, undertook a worldwide tour to celebrate the important milestone and to begin the outright promotion of the shuttle as a commercial, profit-making vehicle for the rapidly expanding world launch market of military, communication, weather, and Earth-monitoring satellites.

Over the course of dozens of speeches, including one at the internationally attended Paris Air Show, Mattingly and Hartsfield would tout the benefits of the shuttle to the United States in terms of opening the space frontier to commercial interests, national security, and national prestige. At the conclusion of his remarks, Mattingly would always end with an invitation: "Come fly with us!"

It not only was an enticement to potential customers seeking launch services but also served to inspire the thousands of young people in the crowds to pursue careers in science and engineering and perhaps someday come to work for the country's space program. It would also indicate the sea change that was coming with the space shuttle and perhaps a future space station. NASA, an agency birthed to undertake a short-term exploration program of the Earth-moon system, was transitioning to an Earth-orbiting research and development operation. This new direction would require experts in a diverse range of disciplines, from researchers in biology to materials processing, astrophysicists to satellite engineers. And these people would not necessarily need to be professional astronauts.

Between November 1983 and January 1986, a new breed of space traveler flew aboard America's fleet of four space shuttle orbiters. Twenty-two men and women, designated "payload specialists," would join NASA's professional cadre of pilots and mission specialists on thirteen space shuttle flights. These brave space travelers were comprised of scientists, engineers, military officers, and foreign representatives. NASA would find it appropriate in this new age of space transportation to invite influential politicians who had oversight of their programs and budget, and even private citizens such as teachers, journalists, and artists.

The shuttle was conceived as all things to all people. Not only would it be an orbiting platform for fundamental research; it was also a space truck—a satellite delivery vehicle with seats! And one or more of those seats would serve as an incentive to potential customers in the highly competitive satellite-launch business. *Fly your spacecraft on the shuttle, and you can send along one of your own people to look after it!* Although far cheaper, the space shuttle's main competition, Europe's Ariane rocket, could never offer that. Nor could it offer another benefit unique to the space shuttle orbiter—if something went wrong with one of those complex, expensive spacecraft prior to deployment, it could even be brought back home.

Launch rate and a steady stream of customer payloads were critical to the shuttle's future, one that promised lower costs and airline-like schedules. Each orbiter was designed to fly one hundred missions, and the four-ship fleet was to fly up to twenty-four missions per year. NASA had entered into a partnership with a European consortium to build Spacelab, a manned research module to be used in the shuttle's payload bay. This program brought research scientists from Germany, the Netherlands, and the United States along with it. Participants from countries such as Canada, France, Mexico, and Saudi Arabia were offered flights not only to attract satellite-deployment business but to show the world that the United States had superior technical prowess to the Soviet Union.

The Department of Defense (DOD) would be a major customer, whose requirements for payload size, polar-orbiting missions, and cross-range landing distance would dictate the very shape of the shuttle we know today. They too would fly handpicked specialists on highly classified missions to further the national security interests of the United States, in the darkest days of the Cold War.

The shuttle had to be sold to the industry and the public as being not only reliable enough to replace all the expendable boosters in the U.S. inventory but safe enough to transport ordinary citizens to and from space. No longer would spaceflight be a realm limited to steely-eyed military test pilots, but rather it would be open to select participants through a citizen-in-space program, giving the public the impression that spaceflight for the common person was within reach.

Each person selected for a seat on the shuttle had a unique story. They came from many different parts of the world and many different walks of life. Some had dreamed of flying in space since childhood, while others either never considered it or thought it impossible for any of a number of reasons. Those who got to join NASA astronaut crews had spent their life-times, in some cases unknowingly, preparing for the opportunity to fly in space. Many had entered fields of study that naturally led them to be qualified in performing the scientific and microgravity research that the space shuttle would enable. Others had virtually no connection to the aerospace or scientific world yet by happenstance found that they met newly developed criteria allowing them to be considered.

Aside from John Glenn or perhaps Christa McAuliffe, none of these men and women were household names. Without formal introduction, be it at a professional conference or hotel lounge, they might be overlooked as just another businessman, lawyer, or consultant. They would face adversity in many forms, from the challenges of selection and training to overcoming the fear of sitting atop a fragile winged aircraft bolted to millions of pounds of volatile liquid and solid rocket fuel. They would find some in the ranks of NASA's astronaut corps and management to be ambivalent toward their place aboard the missions. The military payload specialists would have to overcome a decades-long debate within their own services over the necessity to fly astronauts in space at all while simultaneously contending with the unenviable task of flying top secret payloads on a very visible civilian-operated spacecraft.

For each payload specialist, it was a unique experience, one they would take with them for the rest of their lives. However, spaceflight was but a brief moment in many of those lives. After the reporters, cameras, and cheering crowds went away, they returned to their everyday jobs and continued doing what it was that got them there in the first place. And many of them had quite exceptional careers following spaceflight, some allowing the experience to define them, while others never looked back. Some openly embrace the astronaut image, sharing the wondrous memories of space publicly for decades after, while others avoid the limelight altogether.

One payload specialist of this first era of space shuttle operations would fly safely three times, while two others would lose their lives before even reaching orbit. At the time of the *Challenger* tragedy, many more were trained and ready to carry out their missions. The accident would put the entire program on hold for two and a half years and forever changed the thinking about sending non-NASA astronauts aboard what was an inherently dangerous launch vehicle with no practical means of crew escape. But in the years prior to the loss of *Challenger*, there were no signs of NASA's recruitment of payload specialists slowing down.

In Los Angeles, California, a satellite designer would find a posting on a bulletin board seeking candidates that read like an all-expenses-paid adventure cruise. In East Windsor, New Jersey, an aerospace engineer who had twice been rejected as an astronaut by NASA would receive an unforgettable phone call. In Washington DC a young congressman would receive a letter from NASA's administrator that almost casually asked if he had room on his calendar for a flight into space. And a schoolteacher from Concord, New Hampshire, selected from thousands of applicants, would be told she was to be the first private citizen to go into orbit. They were all offered the same invitation that Ken Mattingly had so simply stated as he traveled around the world in that summer of 1982: "Come fly with us!"

America's space shuttle was open for business, and the possibilities were limitless.

1. The Genesis of the Payload Specialist

I believe that it is also important to insure that provisions are made
to fly individuals assigned as mission specialists from the Astronaut
Office at JSC as payload specialists.

Christopher Kraft

It was a hot and humid Florida afternoon on 29 July 1985 as space shuttle *Challenger* stood poised and pointed to the deep-blue skies on Kennedy Space Center's (KSC) launchpad 39A, fueled and ready for a planned
seven-day scientific mission to low Earth orbit. Spacelab 2 was the primary
mission for STS-51F, although this was the third Spacelab mission due to
delays in critical hardware. Unlike the previous two Spacelab missions,
which carried a pressurized module where the payload crew performed
scientific experiments, Spacelab 2 consisted of a series of open pallets situ-
ated in *Challenger*'s payload bay. The thirteen instruments for astronomical observations located on the pallets would be operated from the flight
deck inside the orbiter.

The crew was already nestled inside the sleek orbiter awaiting the planned
5:00 p.m. launch. Several hours earlier the crew, on their way to the eleva-
tor that would carry them up to the orbiter crew cabin, had walked past the
gigantic hissing, creaking, and sputtering shuttle as the supercooled oxygen
and hydrogen fuel in the external fuel tank dueled with the laws of physics, desperately craving to revert back to their natural gaseous state. The
machine was seemingly alive as it was being readied for launch—a grim
and not-so-subtle reminder that this was not just another training simulation. Once inside the orbiter, the astronauts were seated in their prearranged
seats, facing upward and harnessed to the beast in preparation for the wild

ride into the heavens. Commander Gordon Fullerton and pilot Roy Bridges were seated in the cockpit, with mission specialists Karl Henize and Story Musgrave sitting behind them on the flight deck. Mission specialist Tony England and two scientists called payload specialists—John-David Bartoe and Loren Acton—were seated in the middeck of the orbiter. The four crewmen on the flight deck were busy preparing for the upcoming Armageddon known as launch, whereas the three astronauts positioned in the middeck had few official duties during this time; they were along for the ride until they reached orbit.

Bartoe, a scientist, was very anxious for the launch to occur, but he was not apprehensive. The training that NASA had provided him was very thorough, albeit short, and had prepared him for this moment. He described his mindset about launch during an Astronaut Encounter event at the Kennedy Space Center Visitor Complex in 2014: "Just push the button and let this thing go." Acton, another scientist and noncareer astronaut, was equally excited to reach orbit, where he would perform the experiments that he had spent years training for.

Those listening over the airways to the events taking place this day heard the NASA public affairs officer (PAO) Jim Ball relate, "We have a go for auto sequence start. *Challenger's* four redundant computers now have primary control of critical vehicle functions. T minus twenty seconds; everything is go. T minus twelve . . . ten . . . We have go for engine start. Five . . . four . . . three . . . two . . . one . . . ignition, and liftoff. We have liftoff of *Challenger* and Spacelab 2. The shuttle has cleared the tower," came Ball's excited words.

"Houston now controlling; they'll be throttling down to 65 percent throttle on their main engines," the Houston PAO Brian Welch reported. Control of the shuttle had been passed from the KSC Launch Control Center to Houston's Mission Control Center (MCC) following liftoff. The space shuttle main engines were throttled back for a short time as the vehicle with its live cargo negotiated its way through max Q, a short duration when the aerodynamic stresses on *Challenger* were at its greatest due to the thick and sticky atmosphere. As *Challenger* climbed higher, the atmosphere thinned and the stresses on the vehicle waned to the point where the main engines could be returned to full power. At a distance downrange of 2 miles and an altitude of 4.1 miles, mission control instructed *Challenger*, "You're go at throttle up."

"Engines now back up to 104 percent," reported Welch. *Challenger* was looking great. A mere ninety seconds had elapsed since launch, and the vehicle velocity was already 3,200 feet per second and the rate of climb a blistering 2,000 feet per second. "Standing by for SRB sep," Welch conveyed; shortly after, he stated, "Good SRB sep confirmed." The depleted solid rocket boosters (SRBs) had done their job and were promptly separated from *Challenger* by explosive charges and were cast away to lessen the weight of the vehicle.

Shortly after five minutes of mission elapsed time, the crew were told, "Press to ATO," which, as public affairs officer Welch explained, meant "that they should be ready to dump any remaining fuel should an engine go down anytime in the next forty-five seconds. ATO stands for 'abort to orbit,' should that be necessary." ATO is not a scenario the crew hoped for or remotely expected, but it's a contingency that they had planned for religiously, although no shuttle had ever had to abort to orbit before.

Coming up on five minutes and thirty-six seconds into the mission, and with the external fuel tank still attached, *Challenger* was screaming along at a velocity of eleven thousand feet per second at an altitude of 58 nautical miles and 275 nautical miles downrange. *Challenger* had successfully negotiated its way to the edge of space, and if all continued to go well, it would reach its planned orbit in about three minutes.

Then the call came that no one wanted to hear: "Mission Control Houston, we have a center engine down on the *Challenger*. The crew has been instructed to abort to orbit." It was time to see if the myriad of simulations that the crew had been painstakingly subjected to over the years was going to pay dividends. Fortunately for the crew, mission control reported that "two engines are up and running, and they are stable."

Three minutes and thirty-one seconds after liftoff, a temperature sensor in the center engine failed, followed two minutes and twelve seconds later by the failure of a second sensor that caused the center engine to shut down. The shuttle could still make it to orbit with only two good engines, albeit into a slightly lower orbit than planned. Mission control was already planning for the contingency of another engine failure, which unknown to the astronauts at the time was dangerously close to happening. The crew was informed that they had "single-engine TAL capability." TAL stands for "transatlantic abort landing," which would have led to a return to Earth with a gut-wrenching and tricky landing in Europe. The crew was able to relax a little when mission control confirmed that they could "still get to Zaragoso [Spain] should they lose another engine." Fortunately for the crew, they averted disaster. At nine minutes and forty-one seconds mission elapsed time, the remaining two engines were shut down, and *Challenger* was in orbit for the eighth time.

Many at NASA held grave concerns about how a superficially trained payload specialist would react to an emergency situation on a real flight—not a simulation—and the shutdown of a main shuttle engine during launch definitely qualified as a bona fide potential disaster. How did the STS-51F payload specialists sitting in the middeck react to the ATO? After all, they were not career aviators or astronauts and had only trained for several months with the entire NASA crew. Bartoe quietly enlightened a room full of lunch guests at the Kennedy Space Center Visitor Complex in 2014, explaining confidently that he was never too concerned for his safety as they had performed simulations many times for this exact failure. Once in orbit, Bartoe, a solar physicist, was going to study the sun and the stars with a cadre of exotic telescopes, some which he had helped design. And this was his primary concern; because they were now in a lower orbit, all premission planning for his work on when and where to point his precious telescopes at the preselected objectives was no longer applicable. "Sun and star sightings were out the window," he mused.

Acton, an astrophysicist, had a different concern. "First of all, there was the thought of when we lost the engine of doing an emergency landing and NASA would take two years to get the whole thing put back together, and I wasn't sure my wife would put up with it," Acton quipped to the authors. Fortunately for Bartoe and Acton, ground control quickly came up with a new sighting plan.

Although not selected by NASA or trained as NASA astronauts, Bartoe and Acton remained calm throughout the near disaster. Both were part of a special program that saw twenty-two scientists, dignitaries, and other noncareer astronauts launch on the shuttle through the twenty-fifth shuttle mission. The first of a brand-new breed of astronaut—the payload specialist—would fly aboard Spacelab, carried in the payload bay of the orbiters. But events that would lead to the payload specialist astronauts flying into space had been underway well over a decade before space shuttle *Columbia* made its maiden voyage in April 1981.

1. Payload specialists John-David Bartoe and Loren Acton engrossed in training for their upcoming Spacelab 2 mission on *Challenger*. The crew successfully negotiated the first and only abort-to-orbit in the thirty-year span of the space shuttle program. Courtesy NASA/Retro Space Images.

NASA was able to convince Congress to approve funding of the shuttle in 1972 for a variety of reasons. One of their biggest selling points was that the shuttle was going to be the vehicle to help the Department of Defense (DOD) fight the Cold War by launching top secret military satellites and possibly even performing orbital reconnaissance. Very early in the program it was proposed that the military would fly their own people on the shuttle to carry out these missions.

The space shuttle was also going to be NASA's platform for the continued human exploration of space for the foreseeable future, and management of the shuttle was assigned to the Johnson Space Center (JSC). But NASA also touted that it would have the capability to provide low-cost access to space for scientists without requiring them to become career astronauts. NASA, attempting to divide work equitably among its major centers, then chose the Marshall Space Flight Center (MSFC) located in Huntsville, Alabama, as the lead center for Spacelab.

Competition between the major NASA centers, including JSC and MSFC, was common, and although MSFC was given control of Spacelab, it wasn't clear who would interface with the academic world that would develop the experiments destined to fly aboard NASA's new research facility. The role of choosing astronauts had been in JSC's job description since the center was opened, so naturally they believed they should be the organization to work with the customers and their experiments, including deciding who would operate those experiments once in orbit. After all, JSC had already selected scientist-astronauts into their corps and flown America's first space station—*Skylab*—so they had experience working with the academic world.

Andrew J. Dunar and Stephen P. Waring, in *Power to Explore: A History of Marshall Space Flight Center, 1960–1990*, believe that MSFC won the contest because they governed Spacelab and it simply made more sense for them to work directly with the customers. They would also work closely with the academic institutions that would select the science payload specialists who would fly on the Spacelab missions.

Dr. Rick Chappell explained the beginnings of the payload specialist concept in a July 2015 interview with the authors. Chappell—the chief of the Solar Terrestrial Division, Space Laboratory at Marshall Space Flight Center in Huntsville—served as the mission scientist for Spacelab 1, flown in 1983 on STS-9. He retired from NASA as the chief scientist at MSFC. "When NASA was beginning to develop the shuttle and looking around for support from the science and engineering community, one of the things NASA wanted was to pull from the science community," he recalled. "The scientists asked, 'If we decided to do science on the space shuttle, would scientists get to fly?'" Qualifying his next remark as being secondhand, Chappell continued the story:

> *The science community made a deal and said, "Okay, we'll look positively at the potential of what can be done on the space shuttle, but we want scientists to fly to carry out these experiments." And so there was a deal in there that brought about a reasonable amount of support from the science community for the potential of space shuttle in exchange for flying some of their folks.*
>
> *I don't know if it was ever written down, but it [the agreement] was there. . . . The concept was that people who had spent their life doing research on a given subject would take that extra piece and go fly in space and be a part of the experiment.*

They would not be expected to become professional astronauts like NASA's mission specialists. Chappell admitted that "the mission specialists were extremely talented. . . . Some of them were engineers but a whole lot of them were scientists." They could be trained to carry out most of the planned experiments, but they "would have to be taught some of the specifics of the research. Since we could take passengers, why not take at least a couple of passengers who had spent their whole career doing the kind of research they were going to do in space?"

Well before the shuttle had been approved in 1972 and they had been awarded Spacelab, MSFC called for industry proposals in 1970 to develop a science lab that could fit inside the payload bay of the planned shuttle. One concept, the Research and Applications Modules (RAM), precipitated from a study carried out in 1971–72 by the Convair Division of General Dynamics. RAM consisted of payload modules that could be transported to Earth orbit inside the orbiter payload bay and then returned to Earth on the same or subsequent missions. These modules could hold a variety of scientific instruments and experiments and remain in space for extended periods of time. Shuttle flights carrying RAM would be called sortie missions, but RAM could also be used for scientific studies attached to a space station, if and when one existed.

A similar concept, the Sortie Can, originated from a study performed by the Preliminary Design Office at MSFC, also in the 1971–72 time frame, relying partially on the RAM design. A low-cost module twenty-five feet long and fifteen feet in diameter, the Sortie Can would have barely fit inside the orbiter payload bay for short-duration crewed missions. Its open-truss pallet and internal rack mount were both intended to allow experiments access to the vacuum of open space. The concept included the capability to extend the Sortie Can from the shuttle payload bay, offering better viewing capabilities for asteroid and near-Earth observations. A shorter fifteen-foot-long version was also considered.

Meanwhile, the European Space and Research Organization (ESRO) were assessing options for building their own capability to carry out space-based scientific investigations in cooperation with NASA. Studies assessing a variety of potential experiments and capabilities were conducted by ESRO contractors in 1971. According to Douglas R. Lord in *Spacelab: An International Success Story*, the Sortie Can concept became the focus of ESRO, which they renamed the Sortie Laboratory. The name soon evolved to Space Laboratory, then to Space Lab, and finally to Spacelab.

Following protracted negotiations, NASA and the Europeans reached an agreement whereby a space laboratory capable of flying inside the shuttle's cavernous payload bay would be developed and built by ESRO. James Fletcher, NASA administrator, and Alexander Hocker, ESRO director general, signed the Spacelab Memorandum of Understanding (MOU) on 14 August 1973. The MOU spelled out the backbone of the Spacelab program, including its objectives, responsibilities, and funding.

By 1975 ESRO and its sister organization, the European Launcher Development Organization (ELDO), had merged to become the European Space Agency (ESA). Under the agreement, ESA would take on responsibility to fund, develop, and build Spacelab. Ten European nations participated in the Spacelab venture. West Germany took the lion's share of the commitment, funding 53.3 percent of the cost. Italy and France combined for an additional 28 percent, with the remainder covered by the United Kingdom, Belgium, Spain, the Netherlands, Denmark, Switzerland, and Austria.

NASA held a space shuttle sortie workshop from 31 July to 4 August 1972 at the Goddard Space Flight Center that was sponsored by the Offices of Space Science and Applications (supported by the Office of Manned Space Flight). It's not clear when or who coined the term *payload specialist*, but Dr. John E. Naugle, NASA associate administrator, referred in his opening comments to "the capability the shuttle has of carrying substantial amounts of equipment into orbit [and] . . . up to seven . . . payload specialists. Furthermore, these payload specialists can be scientists, engineers, technicians, doctors. . . . These people need not be astronauts or even scientist-astronauts requiring several years of training. Rather, they can be healthy scientists or engineers who will have had a training and conditioning course of a few months."

The duties of the payload specialist were loosely defined at this workshop as "responsible for the applications, technology, and science payload/instruments operations. This specialist has detailed knowledge of the payload/instruments, operations, requirements, objectives, and supporting equipment. More than one payload specialist may be included in the crew." They would not have an active role in the operation of the shuttle. The activities expected of the payload specialist were broadly outlined from prelaunch through postlaunch activities.

Dr. Hans Mark wrote in *The Space Station: A Personal Journey* that NASA established the Seitz Committee in September 1973 to assess what kind of work could be done in orbit by citizens not trained to be NASA astronauts and to determine the associated risks. Mark and Christopher Kraft, director of JSC, were both members of the Seitz Committee. Some committee members, including Mark, supported less strenuous standards for this new type of astronaut, whereas others, especially Kraft, resisted the relaxation of flight standards. Mark recalled that committee members eventually reached a compromise; Kraft relented at the time but would spend the next decade arguing against it.

Beginning in 1973 the payload specialist selection and training process began to take shape. A plethora of memoranda and working documents from JSC, MSFC, and NASA Headquarters managers and workers paint a picture of a long and slow process, often heated, in deciding how the payload specialist would fit into NASA's future. Scientist-astronaut Bill Thornton weighed in on the process in January 2017, explaining to the authors some of the difficulties encountered. He began by saying that "you can't afford to bring all this up . . ." and then changed his train of thought midsentence: "There was a huge fight going on between some of the remainders of the old school . . . because NASA was being totally reshaped." Thornton spoke with passion about dogfights between the centers—battles won and battles lost.

Just a little over one year after geologist and scientist-astronaut Dr. Harrison (Jack) Schmitt spent three days traipsing across the surface of the moon on the *Apollo 17* mission in December 1972, he was a member of a group of four who expanded the job descriptions and training outlines for the payload specialist. Astronaut Karl Henize, who himself would go on to fly on the Spacelab 2 mission in 1985, penned an internal JSC memorandum on 23 January 1974 that set forth preliminary flight training for payload specialists. In addition to Henize and Schmitt, NASA engineers Samuel Nassiff (design and project engineer) and Frank Van Rensselaer (Spacelab operations director) participated in this informal discussion. The memorandum heading read, "Minimum Flight Requirements for Payload Specialists Not Previously Designated as Astronauts."

Henize prophetically wrote that it was assumed a payload specialist was "a scientist or technician from the institution which developed the payload instruments" who would be selected by the institution, with NASA concurrence, approximately six to twelve months prior to launch, and who had a comprehensive understanding of the experiment and its objectives before being selected. Henize's assumptions were pretty close to what eventually came to fruition, except that a small group organized by MSFC called the Investigators Working Group (IWG) were heavily involved in selecting the Spacelab payload specialists based on recommendations from the academic institutions that developed the scientific experiments to be flown. Astronaut and medical doctor Joe Kerwin, a member of the Skylab 2 crew, who eventually became intimately involved in defining the payload specialist role, explained to the authors in 2015 that writing the job description was "difficult, because we had to attempt to define the payload specialist role before we knew what we were going to fly." Few expected at this time that the position would one day morph to include persons who weren't scientists or engineers.

Henize and his small working group recognized that although the primary role of the payload specialist was to carry out scientific research in outer space, they acknowledged that the payload specialist "will wish to undergo considerable final training in instrument operation during the final six months before flight (probably in conjunction with the mission specialist), but this is taken to be the responsibility of his parent institution and payload center." The amount of necessary operational training would become a hot topic within NASA years later, but Henize and his group seemed to grasp that the shuttle would not be the equivalent of a modern-day airliner where one could buy a ticket and climb aboard with only a short safety briefing.

Henize and his working group advocated that NASA conduct physiological and psychological screening of the payload specialists to determine if they were suitable for spaceflight. The group also recommended that a total of 120 hours of training should be adequate for the payload specialist to safely fly on the shuttle.

The team recommended twenty-four hours of flight-safety training, including procedures for survival equipment, inflight emergencies, rescue, and emergency pad egress. Eight hours of training were planned to learn how to survive in space—how to sleep, eat, exercise, stow gear, perform personal hygiene, and become familiar with onboard lighting. These training activities seem rather straightforward, but some proved challenging. Henize and his group could not have anticipated the complexity of the shuttle toilet and how many hours of training would be required to learn its many vagaries. Some of the difficulties involved in toilet training were explained to the authors in 2009 by astronaut Hank Hartsfield. As he suggested, the biggest problem was that the astronaut needed to be perfectly centered on the toilet seat, otherwise things could rapidly get smelly and very messy. Hence NASA trained its astronauts on a toilet mock-up fitted with a video camera, including crosshairs, ensuring the astronaut's rear end—especially the serious part of it—was perfectly centered, while their training mates watched the exercise on live video. With a wry smile, Hartsfield shared that when the trainee laughed, the "old sphincter could be seen making some very funny gyrations." How embarrassing when the rest of your training chums were surely trying to make you laugh at your expense for their own enjoyment! Years later the toilet would truly haunt one payload specialist.

Another twenty-four hours of training were required to understand orbiter subsystems operation and characteristics, communications, life support, electrical power, attitude control, and data management. Forty-eight hours for simulation and flight operations familiarization and twelve hours in the centrifuge, T-38 jet training aircraft, or zero-g flights were proposed. And of course there was the physiological conditioning that meant time in the altitude chamber and possibly conditioning against motion sickness.

Henize and his team also inferred that mission specialists, nonpilot astronauts whom NASA selected and trained, would be involved in these scientific missions on the shuttle. The selection and training of payload specialists and perhaps more importantly their roles would be topics of prolonged discussion and differences of opinion between JSC and MSFC for the next half decade. MSFC saw the opportunity to select a full complement of payload specialists to run the Spacelab missions, whereas JSC believed their mission specialists were fully qualified and capable of performing most of the scientific investigations.

In his book, Douglas Lord (NASA Spacelab director) states that many at JSC felt the mission specialists should crew the Spacelab missions. Veteran astronauts such as Story Musgrave, Joseph Allen, and Robert Parker had worked in the NASA trenches for years without the opportunity for a ride into space. Many of the mission specialists had scientific backgrounds, and all were highly intelligent and surely could have been easily trained to carry out any experiment that the academics could invent. And they were already fully trained NASA astronauts. On the other hand, Lord pointed out that NASA had promoted the shuttle as an opportunity for scientists to fly their experiments into space without requiring them to go through years of astronaut training. Moreover, the Spacelab MOU guaranteed the Europeans a position on the initial Spacelab flight, and this seat would surely be awarded to a scientist.

Shortly after Henize's memorandum, Robert C. Kohler from JSC's Mission Training Section made it clear in an internal memorandum dated 11 March 1974 that the center and MSFC had not reached an accord over the direction of the payload specialist. Kohler had conferred with Lee Weaver from MSFC (Crew Operations, Space Lab Program Office) on 7 March 1974 regarding payload specialist training and admitted, "It was mutually recognized that the responsibility for providing and managing Payload Specialist training (JSC versus MSFC) has not been agreed to." Weaver suggested to Kohler that the Convair 990 Program might be analogous to the upcoming Spacelab missions and may apply to shuttle crew operations.

NASA had acquired a CV-990 retired airliner in 1964 that was used as an airborne observation and research platform. The airliner could carry thirty scientists and was outfitted with a wide variety of equipment necessary to carry out scientific observations and research, including the observation of solar eclipses and atmospheric research. Later in 1975 and 1977 NASA successfully carried out two Spacelab simulations aboard the CV-990 *Galileo II* aircraft.

Kohler also suggested that each center attempt to decide what they should do regarding the payload specialist training but confided that top management would likely make the final decision. He outlined three areas that needed to be addressed prior to the next meeting in April: crew makeup and duties, training requirements, and the role of the mission specialist.

Weaver's suggestion to use the Convair 990 Program proved to be a valuable tool in preparation for the Spacelab missions. The program would take place in an aircraft flying missions of duration similar to that expected of Spacelab missions and carrying a variety of sophisticated experiments.

Four relatively simple simulations were carried out in the 1972–74 time frame, followed by a more complex mission on the Convair 990 aircraft. A principal investigator (PI) from the organization responsible for each experiment participated in the first four missions. The last of these initial tests employed individuals with backgrounds similar in description to that of a payload specialist.

Lord cites that ESRO and NASA, building on these early trials, agreed to a more involved simulation called the Airborne Science/Spacelab Experiments System Simulation (ASSESS), which took place on the Convair 990 *Galileo II* aircraft. A crew representing both ESRO and NASA completed a six-day mission on 7 June 1975. Simulation objectives were to assess the Spacelab design and operational concepts and to actually carry out scientific tests. The aircraft flew five days in a row (but not continuously), and while on the ground the crew lived in quarters adjacent to the aircraft. Dr. John E. Beckham and Nicholas Wells represented ESRO as crew members, and Dr. Kenneth A. Dick and Dr. Robert A. Parker stood in for NASA. Parker, selected as a NASA scientist-astronaut in 1967, would go on to fly on Spacelab 1 in 1983 as a mission specialist.

In his 2002 NASA Oral History interview with Jennifer Ross-Nazzal, Parker recalled that "[the project] lasted on and off for four to six months. In retrospect, I don't know why we did it, except [that perhaps] Ames [or perhaps Marshall] wanted to be . . . doing some [payload ops] stuff." However, Lord believed it was a valuable yet inexpensive program; significant lessons were learned that were directly applicable to the real Spacelab missions that would begin flying eight years later.

A second simulation, ASSESS II, was carried out in May 1977. This was a longer-duration simulation consisting of nine flights over ten days. Four payload specialists and a mission specialist made up the crew; the mission specialist on the flight was NASA's own scientist-astronaut Dr. Karl Henize.

A NASA executive summary titled *ASSESS II Mission* cited numerous lessons learned. For instance, "Payload specialist candidates should be subjected to some type of stress." It was also determined that the mission specialist played a vital role in the training mission and recommended them for Spacelab missions. The inclusion of a NASA mission specialist as part of the crew of specialist scientists portended the future of the Spacelab program.

Dr. Christopher Columbus Kraft cut his teeth in NASA's Mercury program in the early 1960s and was a veteran flight director by the time the Gemini program came of age in the mid-1960s. Kraft moved over to the Apollo program into a management position and eventually to the position of center director at JSC. Kraft was exceptionally experienced and savvy in NASA ways, and on 19 July 1974 he penned a letter to George Low, acting associate administrator for center operations at NASA, offering JSC's "recommended selection criteria and training requirements for payload specialists." Kraft emphasized the European payload specialist scheduled to fly on Spacelab 1 by agreement in the Spacelab MOU, making it clear that "crew functions provide for the assignment of primary duties with payload operations to the mission specialist."

Kraft included an enclosure outlining selection "criteria and screening techniques" based on NASA's experience selecting astronauts. This enclosure provided much more detail than the 1974 memorandum composed by Karl Henize. Kraft believed that JSC should have some control over payload specialist selection—including the Europeans—offering that he would be "glad to provide additional comments to ESRO upon our experiences with previous astronaut selections." He was very suspicious of this new position that MSFC was pushing, and he was just gearing up to thwart them from taking control of anything that had to do with selecting and training payload specialists.

The enclosure from Kraft is a thirty-page document on the selection and training of payload specialists. The commander, pilot, mission specialist, and payload specialist positions were broadly defined with respect to payload operations. The commander and pilot's responsibilities provided that they "support/perform specific payload operations if appropriate and at the discretion of the payload sponsor." The mission specialist would clearly be a career astronaut who may help out in the management of payload operations and possibly "serve as the payload specialist." Kraft's message was crystal clear: JSC really didn't need MSFC's astronauts; Kraft's pilots and mission specialists could do the job.

The enclosure further defined the job description of the payload specialist: They were responsible for ensuring that payload objectives were met. They would be an expert and proficient in the experiments they were assigned, with "detailed knowledge of the payload instruments (and their subsystems), operations, requirements, objectives and supporting equipment [and] will be responsible for the management of the payload operations and for the detailed operation of particular instruments or experiments." Additionally, they had to understand the basic orbiter systems, including "accommodations, life support, hatches, tunnels, caution and warning systems."

The language used in the enclosure defining crew duties is a bit softer than the memorandum from Kraft to George Low. The guidelines in the enclosure show that payload operations duties for the commander, pilot, and mission specialist would be determined by the payload sponsor. However, Kraft made it clear in his memorandum to Low that his mission specialists would be involved in any payload operations. Period!

The enclosure also dictated that the payload sponsor would provide the selection criteria for the payload specialist, or it may be provided by JSC if necessary. JSC would also dictate medical and other standards. The level of education would be at the discretion of the payload sponsor, but it should be commensurate with the requirements of the experiments to be carried out in orbit. They had to be fluent in English.

The first Spacelab mission was slated to carry a payload crew of four, including a single European payload specialist—to be selected by ESA—as specified in the Spacelab MOU. The payload sponsor would compensate NASA for training costs. The recommendation was that five or six candidates be screened for a second payload specialist position and two go through flight training. Presumably one would be chosen to fly aboard Spacelab 1, and the other would act as a backup. JSC was tasked with the responsibility to ensure that the candidates met medical standards and also "screen for operational suitability."

The general health of the candidates was to be "equivalent to civil aviation standards," and they had to be at least twenty-one years old and no older than sixty. There would be no sexual discrimination, so women were eligible. Pregnant candidates were to be disqualified. Any candidates exhibiting a propensity to motion sickness would also be excluded. Demonstration flights in high-performance aircraft were required, to assess how the candidate would adapt to the flight environment. JSC had the right to reject any candidate for "medical, training or any other problems arising during [the] training period."

Initially, about fifty hours of background training were required for all payload specialists, some carried out during the screening process. This phase of training included participation in aerobatics and an introduction to the dizzying, crushing effects of a centrifuge as well as the physiological-altitude chamber. The candidates were also slated to receive briefings in shuttle orientations, flight operations, and survival equipment and techniques.

The shuttle training for the payload specialist was bumped up to approximately two hundred hours of flight training required at JSC for the initial Spacelab mission or one carrying new hardware. Repeat missions required only 120 hours of training. They needed to know emergency egress procedures on both the launchpad and runway. The flight plan, procedures, rescue, and intravehicular activity were other areas in which the payload specialists needed to be familiar. Other training exercises included the shuttle mission simulator, the full-scale shuttle one-g trainer, Spacelab trainers and simulators, launchpad and altitude chamber training, and integrated simulations combining all crew members.

During this time there was much optimism over the potential operability of the shuttle, reflected in the anticipated number of missions per year and necessary complement of payload specialists in Kraft's enclosure. From 1980 to 1983 there were twenty-four, thirty-six, thirty-eight, and forty flights expected per year, respectively. Each flight carried one payload specialist and excluded any DOD astronauts (who would also be called payload specialists). Therefore, based on the JSC plan, forty-eight to eighty payload specialists, including backups, were required to be trained for the years 1980–83. The rub with Kraft was that he was adamant his mission specialists were qualified to fly these missions, so it wasn't clear how many payload specialists were required.

MSFC had a slightly different concept of the role of the payload specialist. They developed a model for the first twenty missions that called for up to three payload specialists on each flight designated for science, and they would select those payload specialists. Naturally, non-science flights would carry no payload specialists based on the thinking at the time, although that would change rather quickly once the shuttle was certified to be operational.

On 5 April 1976 Kraft sent John Yardley, associate administrator for spaceflight, an updated and abbreviated version of his of 19 July 1974 memorandum that was far more direct. Kraft assumed that payload operations training would be completed well before they jumped into shuttle training as "full-time participants in integrated team sessions at JSC starting at T-3 months [prior to launch]." Kraft continued to build his case that mission specialists were capable and available to contribute to the science missions. He also introduced the concept of two-shift operations, which would require only one payload specialist on board; a mission specialist would assist with payload operations to ensure the science objectives were met. Kraft acknowledged that some flights might have two or three payload specialists on board, but later in the same communication to Yardley, he stressed again that "onboard scientific expertise is also available from a career astronaut designated the mission specialist."

The same optimism of the shuttle flight schedule was being carried in an updated model sent to Yardley, assuming that twelve payload specialists would be selected in 1978, with eighty required for each subsequent year, an unrealistically optimistic scenario. The revised model also required the prime payload specialist be designated by the payload sponsor, with NASA's approval, no later than sixty days from launch. JSC would retain the right to accept or reject the recommendation from the sponsoring organization.

JSC revised the definitions of crew positions, and perhaps the most significant change was for the mission specialist. The new definition now required that mission specialists have "a detailed knowledge of the payload instruments . . . operations, requirements, objectives, and supporting equipment." Additionally, the mission specialist was given responsibility for management of payload operations as well as "overall orbiter operations in the areas of flight planning, consumable usage, and other activities affecting payload operations." JSC was slowly evolving the role of the mission specialist to take on payload responsibilities; no longer was their role at the discretion of the payload sponsor, at least in the eyes of those at JSC. The training requirements necessary for payload specialists to become familiarized with shuttle operations were also revised to a total of 159 hours in three major categories: basic, advanced, and flight specific.

Although there remained differences in opinions over the roles of the payload and mission specialists and subsequent training requirements, progress was being made in other areas. Robert Aller, deputy associate administrator for aeronautics and space technology at NASA Headquarters, weighed in on the issue on 12 May 1976 in a memorandum to Robert Wilson focused on preparing a plan to address the selection of payload specialists. Wilson held the position at NASA Headquarters of special assistant to the assistant administrator for planning and program integration. He offered up several guidelines, some similar to what had already been discussed, but stressed that this was an interim response. His thinking was that the payload spon-sor would determine the education and training requirements necessary to make one eligible and conduct a preliminary physical examination as established by NASA. The candidates should be able to pass a class III flight physical and be "psychologically qualified to fly in space in a closed envi-ronment." The director of the Life Sciences Office and the JSC Flight Oper-ations Directorate would establish weight and height standards. Years later in an April 1981 *New York Times* article, William K. Stevens quoted Jim Bilodeau, the director of crew training at JSC, as saying, "Basically . . . we'll be able to take everybody but the walking wounded." While Bilodeau may have exaggerated a bit, the payload specialists were clearly going to be held to lower medical standards than their counterparts.

Many decisions remained to be made, some of the same questions con-tinued to be asked, and new ones were conceived. Robert Wilson wrote a letter to selected JSC and MSFC employees in May 1976 informing them that Dr. John Naugle of Headquarters, NASA associate administrator, had established an action plan that would help decide how to select and train payload specialists and that addressed the method of their employment.

Wilson also wanted to know if there was "proper differentiation between the responsibilities of the payload specialist versus the mission specialists." Most of the remaining decisions that needed to be made before payload spe-cialists could be selected, trained, and fly missions seemed straightforward. However, the distinction between the roles of the payload and mission spe-cialists remained elusive. Perhaps Wilson's comments were aimed at bring-ing JSC and MSFC together on this contentious issue. Wilson anticipated a NASA management instruction (NMI), a documentation process, would be prepared from the results of the action plan, and later in September 1976 Philip B. Culbertson, then head of the Advanced Manned Missions Plan-ning Group in the Office of Manned Space Flight, sent the draft NMI to JSC.

Kraft expressed his interest in the selection of payload specialists in a memo to John Naugle regarding his action plan on 28 July 1976: "Since the Johnson Space Center (JSC) is responsible for the selection and train-ing of the commanders, pilots, and mission specialists that will fly on the Space Shuttle. JSC is, of necessity, very interested in the policy and pro-cedures for selection of payload specialists as members of the flight crew." His opinion was that the payload specialists would receive training from JSC but not the same that the NASA astronauts received. They would be given "basic space flight indoctrination" and would "participate with the rest of the crew [in training]." Years later some in the astronaut corps would bristle at this shortened training program for the payload specialists.

Kraft took the opportunity again to make JSC's position clear that his mission specialists were qualified to fly as payload specialists. He cited that the astronaut office had "9 outstanding individuals in the scientist-astronaut group and are in the process of selecting 15 more mission specialist astronaut candidates who are expected to be equally capable and from whom payload specialists could be selected." The nine scientist-astronauts active at this time whom Kraft was likely referring to were: Owen Garriott, Ed Gibson, Joe Kerwin, Don Lind, Joe Allen, Karl Henize, Story Musgrave, Robert Parker, and Bill Thornton. All held PhDs in science or medical fields, and three—Garriott, Gibson, and Kerwin—had already flown into space on *Skylab* missions. Kraft advised that those developing the payload "be made aware of the advantages of using trained NASA MSs [mission specialists]" and offered further discussion if necessary.

Joe Kerwin cut to the chase in early August 1976 in a scintillating internal JSC memorandum to the director of flight operations on the development of the payload specialist training plan, or perhaps the lack of a well-defined plan. Kerwin stressed that the responsibilities and functions for the payload and mission specialists "have been going on for some time," clarifying that JSC's "position has not changed significantly since 1974." Unfortunately, he noted that "neither has it been accepted by the Agency as a whole." Kerwin was concerned that the mission specialist was being denied a "role as experiment operator" and that his role was being preempted "in scientific decision-making." Kerwin continued, "At the same time, the role of the mission specialist in managing payload support systems (such as Spacelab) has been preempted by the commander and pilot, in order to make efficient use of their inflight time. The result . . . is that the only defined role of the MS is EVA [extravehicular activity]." Kerwin claimed that the mission specialist was "charged with the vague duty of coordinating . . . in the areas of flight planning, consumables usage . . . Etc.," but he added that it "has been anathema [to] say that he is responsible (onboard) for overall payload operation." Not mincing words, Kerwin then wrote, "It is hard to tell a MS from a PS [payload specialist] in the current definition."

Kerwin emphasized that this uncertainty and confusion "has [led] to such concepts as the 'lead payload specialist,' who assumes the MS's role. . . . These concepts tend to be depressing to our current MS cadre." Kerwin held that critical decisions needed to be made in the near term regarding training plans for mission and payload specialists, qualifications for new mission specialist candidates, and "astronaut participation in payloads."

The planning for Spacelab 1 was already underway at MSFC, and Kerwin used this as an example of why the role of the mission specialist had to be determined, and soon. MSFC was already selecting experiments for Spacelab 1, scheduled to be completed by early 1977. The selection of payload specialists and preliminary flight planning would follow. He pointed out the complexity of the first Spacelab mission by citing a multitude of experiments to be carried out, which entailed "five crew members including two payload specialists, one of which would be a European, and two-shift operations." Kerwin emphasized the need for a mission specialist on this difficult first Spacelab mission, which he cited as inconsistent with MSFC's plan.

MSFC wanted to select the payload specialists early in the process and subject them to two full years of training on orbiter systems. As Kerwin emphasized, they also planned to have payload specialists "cross-trained on all experiments" with no payload training being "planned for the career crew, including the MS." Kerwin expressed grave concern, because simulations were planned "at the end of the training flow, but MSFC doesn't know what they're for. Their total recognition of STS training for PS's is the 150 hours of 'mission independent' training they got from us."

Two training categories had been developed that applied to the payload crew—those doing the experiments. Mission-independent training did not vary with the payload and applied to training on operational aspects of the shuttle or Spacelab. Mission-dependent training is defined in NASA's STS-9 press kit as "the training associated with Spacelab 1 experiments and payload operations."

Kerwin was just getting warmed up. The MSFC plan included "no inflight time on payloads allocated to the MS, only the PS's will operate payload experiments." Lastly, he asserted that "MSFC would like to know what the MS does, so we do have a problem."

To Kerwin the solution was clear: "You could say that the PS is responsible for experiment operations, while the MS is responsible for payload operations. But the distinction has got to be made, because *somebody* in the spacecraft has got to be in charge." He also felt it was imperative that the mission specialist "operate payload equipment inflight." While there was a clear need for the mission specialist to have the responsibility for payload operations, that job was not terribly time consuming, and "he won't just float around being responsible."

Kerwin further reiterated that mission specialists "are supposed to be trained scientists and engineers [and] are a resource for STS users which ought to be utilized . . . before an additional PS is added to the crew."

Continuing to build his case, Kerwin confessed that some, if not all, payload developers would struggle with the concept of their payload being managed by NASA astronauts instead of their own payload specialist. He then astutely added, "Maybe the answer is that it's not strictly 'their' payload. It's NASA's payload."

Kerwin ended by philosophically pointing out that MSFC wanted to turn their payload specialists into mission specialists and then asked, "Will PS's become career astronauts or should they continue to be 'visiting scientists' who fly only a few times to operate equipment in which they are experts?"

One lesser detail that was not finally settled until 1983 was the placement of the various patches on the payload specialist flight uniforms. NASA Headquarters memorandum E-6, issued by the Public Affairs Office and titled *Spacelab 1 Payload Specialist Uniforms*, outlined an agreement between NASA and ESA on where to place patches and other identification media on the payload specialist jackets and shirts. The exact locations for the ESA badge, name plate, IWG patch, ESA logo, American flag, NASA logo, and Spacelab symbol were all clearly delineated. A handwritten comment on the memorandum, scribbled by veteran astronaut John Young, poked fun at the effort. "This means the mission patch will have to be worn on the PS's *rear*. It's the only place left," he wrote, and then added, "I'm not wearing any purple patch." Young may have been referring to the ESA Spacelab 1 patch, which carried shades of purple. Astronaut Brewster Shaw chimed in: "Right on. This thing is obviously too political for me. Let's let the P.S.'s wear the official designated P.S. patch and we'll wear the STS-9 patch. Do you suppose we should leave their names *off* the STS-9 patch?" By the time Spacelab 1 flew in 1983, the payload specialists' names would indeed find their way onto the official crew patch.

In spite of the continued disagreement over the roles of the mission and payload specialists, progress—albeit slowly—was being made to finalize and formalize the position. For instance, the draft NMI that Philip Culbertson sent to JSC on 29 September 1976 described the procedure for the selection and employment of payload specialists, including backups. There were also detailed procedures to ascertain when a payload specialist was required. But it did not mandate the number of payload and mission specialists per science mission; it made that decision flight dependent. Support that mission specialists could provide was given full attention. Once a plan had been developed, the IWG would then assess the plan to verify it or revise the number of payload specialists necessary for the mission. This decision seems to have been a compromise between the wants of MSFC and JSC.

The IWG would then recommend that two of the surviving candidates be trained for each payload specialist position. Both candidates would be trained in mission-dependent duties necessary to carry out the planned scientific investigations. Candidates who met the mission-independent training requirements were then to be certified by the JSC Flight Operations Directorate, followed by the designation of primary and backup payload specialists by the IWG.

Chris Kraft continued to make his case for flying mission specialists as payload specialists. Kraft penned a letter to NASA administrator James C. Fletcher on 12 October 1976 emphasizing that payload and mission specialists as well as pilot astronauts must all be utilized for payload operations in order "to efficiently maximize the return from the shuttle payloads." Kraft admitted that some payloads would require a payload specialist, but in his opinion "most experimenters will find the talents within our career astronaut office adequate and even optimum for the conduct of their research, but I realize this viewpoint is not accepted by all." He further suggested, "We should work to develop and clarify the relationship of mission specialist[s] to the investigator community so that it is clear that he will be their representative inflight and that he will not be unduly constrained from acting in their best interests, both preflight and inflight."

Kraft contended that the experience and knowledge of his NASA astronauts gave them an edge and therefore they would be much more efficient at carrying out the scientific work than a payload specialist who had received accelerated training, ultimately improving the efficiency of the scientific work. He cited lessons learned from *Skylab* that "made it very clear that increases of up to 50% in experiment time are possible as experience is gained." Kraft reasoned, "The [*Skylab*] crewmen were given substantial responsibility in operations planning and worked with the PI [principal investigator] groups to optimize the conduct of their experiment. We believe similar responsibility, both before and during flight, will develop the necessary broader competence and lead to an equally good performance in Shuttle." He added, with some emphasis, "We should build upon this experience for Shuttle."

Kraft had all the answers, contending that if JSC identified and assigned the NASA crewperson to a specific payload early in the queue, the payload training could be spread over a longer time frame, reducing the number of hours per month required, which would allow the mission specialists to maintain their proficiency on orbiter systems. He also asserted that if the IWG selected one of his astronauts to be a payload specialist, it would "encourage interdisciplinary training, where selection was based originally on his expertise in a specialized discipline."

Kraft then shot to the heart of the matter. "Unfortunately, in my opinion, some centers seem to be making premature plans to hire and train payload specialists. I believe this is wrong organizationally." Arguing that the payload specialist was going to be nothing more than "a passenger . . . to perform a specific function in space," he reaffirmed that the tasks could easily be accomplished by the NASA crew in most cases. Kraft believed that payload specialists would "understandably experience anxieties and, perhaps, sickness. We cannot ignore the situation that a passenger onboard the shuttle poses a special kind of problem, and we should not be willingly planning for payload specialists when mission specialists are available with adequate to expert technical ability in payload research areas."

Kraft went so far as to offer up a volunteer—an astronaut—who could be assigned to a "given center" so they could be trained in the necessary scientific payload operations. If a mission specialist was not up to performing the needed task, "then we should plan to take a passenger" but should not "hire, train, and fly passengers and ignore the capabilities of the crew, as there seems to be a desire to do this."

Kraft summarized, "I hope it is clear that I support the idea of payload specialists when and where they are needed; I support the idea of passengers of all types. However, I request that you become satisfied that our NASA planning for selecting and training payload specialists is consistent with the need."

Neil Hosenball, serving at that time as NASA's general counsel, proposed changes in the NMI to NASA Headquarters regarding the employment of payload specialists in February 1977. He believed that it was not practical for NASA to hire payload specialists, nor would hiring them "be very appealing to the expert or scientist who is established in his/her academic or other environment outside of NASA." Hosenball recommended a simple solution based on the Ames Airborne Science Program. Essentially, if the payload specialist was a NASA or other federal employee, NASA could negotiate the particulars of their assignment with the proposers. If not, the proposers would be responsible for making arrangements with those payload specialists from a private establishment and also be responsible for the appropriate arrangements for salary. Thus the payload specialists would not be hired or paid by NASA, but they might be a NASA or federal employee. Hosenball took this opportunity to remind Headquarters that "NASA will make available mission specialists to act as payload specialists in appropriate cases." Kraft had laid a broad network of supporting allies.

There was some concern raised by Hosenball about how non-NASA employees would be supervised. He wasn't concerned with day-to-day supervision during preparation for the flight, as NASA worked with contractors on a regular basis, and any problems that might come up could be handled by going through the contractor employer. But he was concerned that once the crew were in orbit, supervision might become an issue. Nevertheless, Hosenball held that the National Aeronautics and Space Act of 1958 sufficiently covered this situation by clearly emphasizing that "the Shuttle commander's orders are to be followed by all."

Gerald Mossinghoff, then NASA's deputy general counsel, also expressed concerns regarding liability with carrying non-NASA personnel on the shuttle. In a July 1977 memorandum, he wrote that although no liability policy regarding payload specialists had been adopted, his office was reviewing a policy that it planned to propose to the NASA administrator. His position was that the U.S. government would not hold payload specialists or their employers liable due to their negligence for damages to the shuttle or Spacelab or any injuries they caused. Conversely, users of the shuttle would agree to not bring legal action against the United States or other payload specialists.

Many of the NASA astronauts were highly skeptical of the role and training of the payload specialists for the Spacelab missions. Handwritten comments on a 2 February 1978 MSFC Spacelab 1 draft memorandum provides the view of some of the JSC astronauts involved in the mission. The JSC routing slip for the memo contains a succinct comment from John Young that summarized his opinion: "Written proof that this thing is going to fall on its _ _ _!" Veteran astronaut Ken Mattingly chimed in, "This is so far from what's required I don't know whether to cry or get drunk. How do you offer comments on this when the entire concept is out to lunch?" The word "milestone" in the first sentence of the memo was crossed out and changed to "millstone," and "Impossible" was written alongside the entire first paragraph. MSFC recognized the "unique, ambitious, and historic nature of the SL-1 mission." *Skylab* astronaut Ed Gibson noted that "the Titanic was also historic." Above the word "historic," Young wrote, "For God's sake!" and Gibson added, "Barf!" The professional cadre of the European payload specialists was stressed, stating they were analogous to the NASA mission specialist astronauts, only to be countered with, "They are not PS(s) but a poor man's MS." That statement also received a "Ha!" while the suggestion that they would be considered for multiple flights garnered a "Ha double." The recommended heavy travel schedule for training at the investigator facilities to learn the science experiments commanded a "guarantee all crewpersons will be single by launch day." These comments are not surprising given the lack of support for the payload specialist program by JSC management. Regardless, the program was moving forward.

The astronauts were taking some good-natured potshots at the NASA bureaucracy, but there was substance behind many of their comments. William R. Bock, Spacelab 1 training coordinator, prepared a Spacelab Payload Crew Training Report in May 1979 summarizing the results of one of the training tours. He described the CHIT (Crews' Honest Input to Training), which "was developed to provide a mechanism for the crew to make inputs to the program." The CHIT identified numerous areas for improvement while the crew was traveling to the various institutions to learn the vagaries of the equipment they would be using once in space.

NASA published its NMI "Payload Specialists for NASA or NASA-Related Payloads" in the 10 March 1978 *Federal Register*. For the most part, it is consistent with the February 1977 revised NMI. However, a statement was added that finally addressed the roles of the mission specialists and payload specialists. The IWG was directed to consider "any support which can be provided by the flight crew" when determining the number and qualifications of payload specialists.

Specifically, the sponsoring Program Office would request that the director of JSC supply the names of qualified mission specialists capable of serving as payload specialists for the flights under consideration, and the IWG would consider them as viable candidates. It appears Kraft's insistence that his scientist-astronauts be considered for payload specialist duty had not fallen on deaf ears.

The selection of the payload specialists for Spacelab 1 was underway in early 1978, and even with a published definition of the payload specialist's role, there remained uncertainty. The Spacelab MOU provided ESA one payload specialist slot on Spacelab 1, but the additional slots to carry out the planned scientific experimentation on the first two Spacelab missions had not been filled. Chris Kraft wrote to Alan Lovelace, NASA deputy administrator, on 10 May 1978, again expressing concerns with the selection process. "I have reviewed the payload specialist (PS) selections in progress for Spacelabs 1 and 2," he stated, "and I have a number of concerns about what we are doing." Kraft held to his guns, insisting that a payload specialist was needed only if they possessed "unique knowledge or capability concerning that experiment"; otherwise his mission specialists were up to the job.

Kraft alleged that "we are becoming too enamored with the public relations aspects of such selections without properly considering what we are doing practically and operationally." Kraft admitted that JSC personnel may not completely understand the marketing of the shuttle, but he emphasized, "We do have an appreciation for how to make a shuttle mission successful and safe." Understanding that marketing the shuttle and operations were "not necessarily compatible factors," he claimed that "promises are being made now that cannot be kept when we fly."

Therefore, Kraft strongly recommended that Lovelace take the appropriate actions so that the operational, scientific, and marketing groups could come together and align themselves to ensure "a safe flight with all scientific objectives accomplished at the lowest possible cost to the user."

George Abbey, director of flight operations, hints in a 7 September 1978 letter to ESA's Johannes (Han) de Waard that the JSC stance on the roles of the payload and mission specialist was winning the day, informing de Waard, "Since two mission specialists (MS) will be available for experiment operations during SL-I, we suggest the training plan include statements concerning their use in the ESA-sponsored experiments."

Robert A. Kennedy, director of the Spacelab payloads program at NASA Headquarters, distributed a draft memorandum on 29 May 1979 suggesting changes to the NMI, focused on the determination of the need for payload specialists. Simply put, unique requirements were required to warrant the selection of a payload specialist; otherwise, the sponsoring office (of experiments) would request from JSC "the names and qualifications of appropriate Mission Specialists who are available to serve as Payload Specialists for the flight under consideration."

It had taken five years of sparring between JSC and MSFC to determine who would select the astronauts to fly on Spacelab missions. It's not clear who made the final decision, but the scheme was a compromise. MSFC would finally progress beyond a center that just designed rockets; it would work with the institutions chosen to select astronauts—payload specialists—to fly into space. JSC's scientist–mission specialists looked to get plenty of opportunity to utilize their extensive academic training in space. Joe Kerwin put it all into perspective during a private discussion of the payload specialist with one of the authors in 2015: "It just worked itself out."

The Marshall Space Flight Center's Charles (Rick) Chappell, as associate director for science, agreed with Kerwin in a 2015 interview. He explained that MSFC developed a strategy in the early 1970s that would "increase their case for managing shuttle payloads." He asserted that the strategy was to hire scientists to work at MSFC in varied scientific disciplines "and then using that as an underpinning of their case to NASA Headquarters that they should be managing science payloads on the shuttle." He also believes that this strategy gained critical support from the scientific community, which encouraged NASA Headquarters to assign MSFC science payload support on the Spacelab missions. Chappell, hired by MSFC in 1974 as one of those bright scientists necessary to expand their role in NASA's crewed space program, maintained, "That ended up working pretty well because Marshall ended up managing the science operations for Spacelab 1, Spacelab 2, Spacelab 3, the microgravity flights, and to a lesser extent the life sciences flights."

While NASA was struggling to define the duties of civilian researchers and engineers aboard space missions throughout the 1970s, the DOD was concurrently pursuing its own integration with the nascent program. The relationship between NASA, the U.S. military, and the various clandestine entities of the country had always been somewhat of a forced marriage of organizations with competing priorities and budget requirements. When the space shuttle was first conceived, it was thought that most major payloads destined for low Earth orbit would ride aboard a vehicle that had yet to be designed to accommodate any single type of cargo.

During the shuttle's development, the vision of it becoming the sole launch vehicle of the United States relied on a number of factors, most important being the flight rate. By keeping the orbiters flying regularly and spreading the operational costs over a greater number of customers, the price of taking payloads into orbit would, in theory, drop exponentially. In order to produce the required demand for launch services, the DOD, with its wide range of surveillance, communications, and weather satellites, was targeted as a prime user of the space shuttle.

In the late 1970s, the undersecretary of the U.S. Air Force, Dr. Hans Mark, pushed to move all Defense Department satellites onto the new space shuttle, and the Carter administration agreed, making it the policy of the United States to phase out all existing expendable launch vehicles. In August 1977 Mark was appointed director of the supersecret National Reconnaissance Office (NRO), an organization that would not even be officially acknowledged until 1992. The NRO was responsible for the country's fleet of spy satellites operating electronic-optical imaging, radar imaging, eavesdropping, and secure-communications spacecraft. This policy decision, challenged by many in defense circles, would not only influence the design requirements of the shuttle but also take a huge leap of faith that it would be reliable enough to carry the large number of government payloads then planned.

In an internal NRO 1997 interview with Gerald Haines, declassified in

2012, Mark would recall the mindset of those in the national security services of the time:

> *I was very anxious to get the military involved in the shuttle because it was in fact the most capable launch vehicle that we were building at the time. Remember that the Titan 34-D was not as capable as the shuttle and that was the thing that was coming in the military. It had to do with the capability of the bird. The things we have done since then—repair on-orbit, and checkout on orbit before you deploy a satellite and all that capability with human beings I thought was a very valuable capability to have. My military friends don't agree with that to this day.*

But the grandiose plans for space in the minds of some air force planners would be severely scaled back over time, as budget cuts and defense priorities shifted. A once-proposed fifth orbiter would not be built, and even some of the on-orbit servicing of spy satellites was deemed too complex and expensive to pursue. The DOD, along with its partners in the covert worlds of the NRO and other intelligence agencies, would continue to play a major role in the development and early operations of the shuttle, but never to the extent envisioned in the early 1970s.

All these decisions were taking place during an intense heating up of the Cold War between the United States and the Soviet Union. With so much riding on the successful integration of the military's space program with the space shuttle, the decision was made to select a cadre of engineers, primarily from the U.S. Air Force, to oversee the classified spacecraft that would fly aboard the orbiter. This group, selected in 1979, would comprise the first corps of manned spaceflight engineers, who would potentially serve as payload specialists aboard the missions that would launch or perhaps service DOD payloads.

With the demise of the X-20 Dyna-Soar and the later Manned Orbiting Laboratory programs, it is likely that the air force would have had no use for having men in space for the foreseeable future. But as the shuttle program got started and the decision was made to bring the military in as a prime customer of NASA, various ideas began to be floated around as to how military astronauts could be useful aboard the orbiter.

In a July 1972 internal CIA report, declassified in 2012, several potential missions requiring human interaction were offered, some of which would,

in fact, come to be realized. These included the use of astronauts "conducting extravehicular activities" and "the possibility of rendezvous with a failed
or partially failed U.S. spacecraft and conducting repair operations." The
report also examined the "unique role man might play in expanding the
reconnaissance activities that could be performed from space platforms,"
but those details remain redacted.

While these secretive missions were being studied, the desire for the shuttle to launch critical NRO payloads brought a host of challenging issues for
program managers and engineers to consider. Photo-reconnaissance satellites typically operated in polar orbits, circling high over the geographical
north and south poles as Earth spun below, allowing for near-complete coverage of almost any point on the planet. As the orbiter's design was being
contemplated, two main issues were of concern to the military—the size of
the payload bay and the unique challenges associated with launching space
shuttles into orbit from the West Coast of the United States.

The largest military payloads of the time were ten feet in diameter, having been designed to fly atop the Titan III booster. While the NRO had,
at the time, drawn up larger spy satellites that might require a large cargo
hold on the shuttle, the orbiter's originally intended mission also had significant influence on the orbiter's design. The space station modules that
it might one day haul into orbit would also need to be large enough to live
in for months at time.

Once the fifteen-by-sixty-foot payload bay dimensions had been established, the next hurdle was to figure out how to return the orbiter, with a
large payload presumably still aboard, from orbital velocities back down
through the atmosphere to a runway landing. Beyond that, the DOD requirement for polar-orbiting flights from the West Coast's Vandenberg Air Force
Base would add an important complication—the launch and landing site
would rotate on the order of one thousand miles to the east before the shuttle completed its first trip around the world.

Astronaut Ken Mattingly, who was deeply involved in the development
of the shuttle and would eventually find himself in command of the first
classified NASA mission, related to Kevin Rusnak of NASA's Oral History
project, "The polar mission was really shaped after a DOD requirement.
The original mission, as I recall, was a one-rev [revolution] mission. You
launched, got in orbit, opened the payload bay doors, deployed a satellite,

[or] rendezvoused with an existing satellite, retrieved it, closed the doors, and landed. And this was all going to be done in one rev so that—or maybe it was two revs, but it was going to be done so that by the time anyone knew we were there, it was all over."

This demanding mission profile would have had the ground track of the shuttle remain over the open Pacific Ocean for the brief duration of the flight. In this manner, the clandestine missions could be carried out without overflying the Soviet Union and remain out of sight from the prying eyes of its ground-based optical and radar tracking assets. More than any other requirement, the DOD-driven need to achieve this cross range produced the iconic delta-winged space shuttle shape we know today.

By 1979 the maiden voyage of the space shuttle was still years away, but this was also the year in which several key events occurred that brought the air force's long-dreamed-of goal of putting a military man in space closer to reality. *Columbia*, atop the 747 Shuttle Carrier Aircraft, finally left her birthplace in Palmdale, California, for testing and launch preparations in Cape Canaveral, Florida. Modifications began on the sprawling Space Launch Complex 6 (SLC-6, pronounced "Slick 6") to accommodate the orbiters among the coastal hills of Vandenberg Air Force Base in California. And the U.S. military called on qualified candidates to apply for up to twenty slots as manned spaceflight engineers. They were all told that they were competing to become astronauts.

The selection of this cadre of military spacemen was conducted under great secrecy. Not only did the air force want to keep their identities hidden; it wanted the entire existence of the team to remain unknown to those outside the military and NASA. The generals of the Air Force Special Projects Office, however, did want to take advantage of the civilian agency's experience in selecting suitable candidates. In a 14 June 1979 memo to John Yardley, Kraft explained the military's plan and offered his own concerns about how this program might affect the organization:

> *We are providing, at the request of the Air Force, assistance in the selection of about twenty officers to perform a "payload specialist" function at SAMSO [Space and Missile Systems Organization located at the Los Angeles Air Force Station]. As you know, we are concerned about how these people are to be trained and if their training will eventually impact*

the facilities at JSC. We fully agree though, that what SAMSO does in its sandbox is its business, and we will cooperate until it is apparent that their business is also our business. At that time, we may require further guidance, more equipment and money, or all three.

It is our understanding that the Air Force will select about twenty engineers who will work on certain payloads and then they may be given as opportunity to fly as payload specialists on the shuttle. The selection activity is to begin next week and end sometime in July. We have been asked to provide Jay Honeycutt to assist in the selection process.

During his visit to JSC, [NASA administrator] Dr. Frosch expressed some concern about how these payload specialists might be trained, identified, and employed. We have the same reservations. But unless you feel differently, Honeycutt will help them to the extent that he can.

Yardley replied in agreement on 26 July but also left open the possibility of using all-NASA crews to fly the classified missions: "As I mentioned to you on the phone, General [Jack] Kulpa seemed receptive to explore the ideas we discussed concerning NASA mission specialist utilization."

As this secretive team of military officers was thrown into the tumultuous relationship between NASA and the DOD—particularly the U.S. Air Force—they would be faced with the challenges of integrating their covert world of launching military space reconnaissance satellites with the civilian government space agency and its civilian workforce. They would also come to realize that not only were those requirements seemingly at odds with one another, but the very launch vehicle the DOD had reluctantly bought into was less than ideal for accomplishing their mission.

Despite Kraft's campaign, no NASA mission specialist ever flew as a payload specialist on a space shuttle mission, although they would be an integral part of the scientific experiments flown on Spacelab. Four Spacelab missions carrying nine payload specialists would fly by the end of 1985, and a variety of scientific investigations were successfully carried out by the payload crew, including both mission and payload specialists.

The DOD would forge ahead with its plans to fly its own engineers in the mid-1980s, with ambitious plans to expand their operations on the space shuttle in the years ahead. There would be more tweaks to the payload specialist program in its early stages, as a wider range of people were considered as candidates for space missions.

As NASA management solidified the payload specialist concept in the late 1970s and the first crew members began working together, a new challenge would come as these outsiders sought the acceptance of the NASA astronauts they would be flying with.

2. Integrating the Payload Specialists

Anyone is eligible to become a payload specialist.

NASA, *Role of the Payload Specialist*

NASA selected its first scientist-astronauts in astronaut group 4 in June 1965. Prior to group 4, only hotshot aviators were eligible to become astronauts. Owen Garriott, Edward G. Gibson, Duane E. Graveline, Joseph P. Kerwin, F. Curtis Michel, and Harrison H. Schmitt were chosen to become astronauts based on their research and academic backgrounds. Schmitt, a geologist, was the only one to fly into space during the lunar program, while Garriott, Gibson, and Kerwin crewed *Skylab* missions. Graveline and Michel never made it into outer space, both departing the space agency without being assigned to a mission.

Kerwin and Michel both had experience flying military aircraft prior to their selection, but all the scientists of group 4 were different from the existing astronauts. Initially they were treated as outsiders by their astronaut peers just as surely as the payload specialists of the shuttle program were treated differently when they arrived on the scene.

Three-time shuttle astronaut Mike Mullane claimed in his popular memoir *Riding Rockets* that during the early years of the shuttle program those astronauts with military backgrounds had an intrinsic distrust of the scientist- and civilian-astronaut candidates when they first arrived in 1978 in NASA's astronaut group 8. They were different. Could they be trusted, and did they have the "right stuff"? Fortunately, NASA's regimented astronaut training program provided ample opportunity for the academicians and civilians to prove their mettle. According to Mullane, after two years of training together, including rides in T-38 jets and stints in altitude cham-

bers, the NASA astronauts came to trust their civilian and academic counterparts. The extended length of the training program was a key factor in
gaining their trust.

Payload specialists, on the other hand, did not go through the same
rigorous training process developed to mold them into crackerjack astronauts. Some of the payload specialists were selected by organizations hosting
experiments and hardware to be delivered into space on the shuttle. Several
were chosen by the military. It was often unclear how others came to be
payload specialists. All received an abbreviated training program on basic
shuttle operations. NASA performed medical and psychological evaluations
on each candidate to ensure they were fit to fly into outer space, but nothing near the level of evaluation required by the NASA astronaut candidates.

Integrating the payload specialists into the mission crews was not going
to be a walk in the park. Many, if not all, of those in the astronaut office
in the early shuttle days were fully aware of JSC management's opposi-
tion to the payload specialist position. Ulf Merbold, payload specialist
on STS-9, remembers that he received a warm welcome from the folks at
MSFC in Huntsville, Alabama, when he first became involved in the program. He was excited about being one of the first non-Americans to be
considered for spaceflight on the shuttle. MSFC, as lead center for the ESA
design and development of Spacelab, was excited to have him participate
in their program-related activities. But the atmosphere was different when
he reached Houston; the welcome mat was not rolled out. Merbold said he
was treated like an intruder.

Additionally, many astronauts felt that flying crew members with minimal mission-independent training was inappropriate; without the rigorous
training that the NASA astronauts received, they simply could not fully com-
prehend the dangers of launching into space on the equivalent of a lethal
bomb, adapting to the vagaries of microgravity, and the searing temperatures of reentry the orbiter had to endure before it could safely land. Mike
Mullane writes in *Riding Rockets* that it was an immoral program driven
by public relations.

The brief mission-independent training that was afforded to the payload specialists led to another anxiety for the NASA astronauts; if you didn't
know someone extremely well, then how could you be absolutely certain
how they would react in the alien environment of outer space? Further-

more, they weren't trained to handle emergencies during the mission, so it is doubtful they could have helped resolve any problems that might have occurred. It's conceivable that they might have made the problem worse.

These concerns were certainly valid reasons why many NASA astronauts balked at flying the outsiders, but they were intangible concerns. Payload specialists would never be allowed to fly the orbiters, thus the pilots were immune from being replaced by a payload specialist. On the other hand, mission specialists losing seats on the shuttle—taken by payload specialists—was a reality.

Payload specialists have often been unfairly maligned and treated differently by their peers, likely due to the disparity in training. A NASA pamphlet that announced the new position of payload specialist in the late 1970s called for volunteers and clearly stated, "They [payload specialists] are not professional astronauts," reinforcing the perception that they would be different from the regular NASA astronauts. Astronaut Mike Massimino, in his 2016 autobiography *Spaceman*, writes that there were seven crew members on *Challenger* when it broke apart shortly after launch in January 1986; only five were NASA astronauts. Massimino referred to the remaining two crewpersons as a payload specialist (Greg Jarvis) and a school teacher (Christa McAuliffe), perpetuating the notion that payload specialists were not real astronauts.

The idea of a scientific specialist was not invented by NASA. The concept has been successfully deployed in many scientific endeavors, such as the exploration of deep ocean basins. Scientists carrying out research on the drill ship *Glomar Challenger* provide a close analogy to the payload specialist position on the space shuttle. The ship was designed in the late 1960s to sample rocks and sediments beneath Earth's ocean basins as part of the Deep Sea Drilling Program. Core samples were taken from the deep ocean floor along the Mid-Atlantic Ridge between South America and Africa to better understand the geology, and many significant discoveries were made as a result of this work. The ship was retired after fifteen years of operations and replaced by the JOIDES (Joint Oceanographic Institutions for Deep Earth Sampling) drill ship *Resolution*. Visiting scientists on both ships were tasked with describing rock and sediment cores recovered during the drilling process. These scientists were trained in emergency procedures and how to use the ship's facilities, but they were not trained to operate the ship or drilling rig. They were specialists, similar to the NASA payload specialists.

Former NASA astronaut Kathy Sullivan, who holds a doctorate in geology, was a crew member on three space shuttle missions, and in March 2014 was appointed as undersecretary of commerce for oceans and atmosphere and as administrator of the National Oceanic and Atmospheric Administration. Dr. Sullivan compared the payload specialist position to her experiences on oceanographic ships. She explained that as a visiting scientist on these expeditions, she didn't need to know how to operate the ship in order to accomplish her mission. "I was scientific party," she explained. "I sure didn't know how to handle the ship like the chief mate, and I didn't know how to work the deck like the boatswain, and I sure didn't know all the ship's wiring and tolerances for system loads like the chief engineer." Her job was primarily in support of scientific research; she didn't need to know how to operate the ship.

The conundrum is whether the space shuttle was operational and ready to carry specialists who may not have fully understood the stupendous risks involved in flying on the shuttle. Veteran NASA astronaut John Young wrote in his autobiography *Forever Young* that it wasn't until the fatal breakup of *Columbia* in 2003 that NASA finally accepted that the shuttle was not operational and was still essentially an experimental vehicle.

Jerry Ross offered similar comments about the shuttle while discussing his first space mission on orbiter *Atlantis* in 1985. "Eighteen years later (after STS-61B), the space shuttle is not an operational vehicle in a normal sense. It's still very much a research and development experimental vehicle." Five-times-flown astronaut Hoot Gibson recalled that after four shuttle missions, President Reagan declared the shuttle operational and that many astronauts were skeptical and smiled at the concept. Some felt that it was unfair and misleading to those without an intimate understanding of the shuttle and its intrinsic risks, to naively launch into space aboard an unproven spacecraft and launch system.

Not surprisingly, some of the payload specialists believe they fully understood the risks involved in riding an unproven 4.5 million–pound, fire-belching behemoth into space. Oceanographer Dr. Paul Scully-Power, payload specialist on STS-41G, recently confided to the authors, "Yes, you can calculate the number of single point of failure nodes." He placed the risk of flying his mission at about one in one hundred. It's unclear how he came up with that number, but he clearly understood that there was some probability that once the launch sequence began, the crew might not make it to the end of the mission alive. One chance in one hundred that you might be killed is worthy of contemplation. For comparison, a NASA study showed that sport parachuting—which many consider to be very hazardous—carries a one in five hundred chance of loss of life, much less risky than what Scully-Power attributed to flying on the shuttle.

One veteran astronaut admits he did not fully grasp the inherent risks during his time in the program. Thrice-flown shuttle astronaut Rick Hauck, a graduate of the Naval Test Pilot School with over five thousand flight hours, is well versed in the risk associated with flying high-performance jet aircraft. Hauck informed the authors in January 2017, "Prior to STS-1, I had seen a PRA [probability risk analysis] estimating the risk of loss at 1/280 or so. But in its most simplistic terms, given a loss on flight 25 [*Challenger*], if I knew in advance that one in twenty-five would fail, I would probably think twice about flying three (as I did) out of the first twenty-six flights." On the other hand, Scully-Power put it in perspective in 2015: "It depends on the individual. Remember that it is perhaps the only binary decision you will make—you either survive or not."

Hauck believed that NASA should not have placed payload specialists at risk until they had achieved "an indication of very high confidence in the risk level." NASA had considered establishing a minimum Mission Operations Control Room (MOCR)—essentially an MOCR with a much smaller staff—which would have allowed two flights to be controlled simultaneously (from two MOCRs). In Hauck's view, implementation of the minimum MOCR concept would have been a clear indication that NASA had gained a high level of confidence in the risk associated with flying on the shuttle.

Ultimately, the full risk of flying on the shuttle was not realized until many years later in hindsight. While the payload specialists may not have had the background to fully grasp the risk as soundly as the NASA astronauts, they undoubtedly understood that launching into space on the shuttle was a very risky proposition and that loss of life was not an unrealistic outcome. Still, for a variety of reasons—science, service to their country, or thrill—they were willing to take that risk.

Mike Massimino asserts in his book *Spaceman* that one does not become an astronaut by flying into space. Instead, one trains on the ground to become an astronaut, so they are prepared when they eventually fly into space. For the NASA astronauts of the shuttle era, the initial training flow for an astronaut candidate lasted about two years, where they learned the details of the shuttle system, plus a myriad of emergency procedures. Once an astronaut was assigned to a mission with a specific objective, there was additional training with their crew, which lasted from months to over a year. Often the crew participated in formal team-building exercises. By launch day, everyone on the crew knew one another intimately and knew what to expect of one another once the mission began. They were a team! The concern that some of the NASA astronauts had about inadequate training—bonding time—with the payload specialists held merit; they simply didn't know the payload specialists well enough to understand how they would respond to an inflight crisis. Granted, the payload crew (mission and payload specialists in charge of the experiments) on each of the Spacelab missions had ample opportunity to get to know one another during mission-dependent training, which lasted much longer (six years on Spacelab 1) than the mission-independent training. Still, the entire crew—pilots and the mission and payload specialists—had not spent a significant amount of time training together as a team.

Hank Hartsfield expressed his concern by asking, "If you had a problem on orbit, am I going to have to babysit this person, or are they going to be able to respond to an emergency situation and take care of themselves like the crew has to?" He was concerned that a payload specialist could easily become a liability to the crew, explaining, "You could wind up having a person that wasn't used to that kind of conditions to endanger the rest of the crew because you have to attend to them."

Hartsfield also believed that the NASA selection process gave astronauts confidence that they could trust one another. "They've had a thorough psychiatric evaluation before they even got selected," he stated. "We put them in hazardous situations." Although the payload specialists were given a psychiatric evaluation by NASA, many were selected by their host organizations and did not go through the same thorough, regimented vetting process as NASA astronauts (although several European payload specialists went through the regular astronaut training program).

Hartsfield carried a soft voice but could be very passionate about his beliefs. He stressed the value of the T-38 jet in assessing the mission specialist's reaction to adverse conditions. The pilot astronauts regularly flew the T-38 trainer as a mode of transportation from Ellington Field, located just southeast of Houston, to the cape and other destinations. It also served as a chase plane during shuttle launches and landings; plus, it provided them ample opportunities to maintain their flight proficiency and, no doubt, time to blow off a little steam on occasion. It also gave the mission specialists a lot of time in the back seat, where they learned how to react to what Hartsfield called "contingencies." Hartsfield believed that "if you fly long enough, you're going to have some contingencies, and you see how they react to that." Furthermore, he believed that observing the mission specialists over the course of years flying in the back seat of a high-performance aircraft allowed the pilots to assess the pluck of the mission specialists. As he explained, "You get to watch them. . . . You're building the database that this is a good, reliable person and you can count on them." The payload specialists spent limited time in the back seat of the T-38s during their condensed training cycle, inadequate time for the pilots to adequately assess how they might react to adverse conditions.

Not all astronauts shared the same apprehensions of Hartsfield and Mullane. Veteran astronaut Bob Crippen, John Young's pilot on the very first space shuttle mission, STS-1, was a bit more accepting of the payload specialists. But Crippen made it clear that he didn't consider payload specialist Marc Garneau a regular crew member, telling him, "Hey, stay on the middeck till I tell you it's okay to come on the flight deck, and do your thing."

Crippen continued, "Then we added Paul D. Scully-Power, an Australian that worked for the United States Navy." Crippen knew Scully-Power prior to his being named to the STS-41G mission. "I sat down and explained to him, 'Hey, we'd love to have you up there.' Now, his mission, he needed to be on the flight deck, looking out the windows. So we had to pick out periods of time where that was going to be acceptable, and it ended up working out just fine."

John-David Bartoe and Paul Scully-Power believe that they spent enough time training with their respective crews and that they were fully prepared for any anomalies or contingencies. Scully-Power said he had spent six months training with his crew, but he was also already part of the Astronaut Office briefers, so he was fully prepared for any anomalies that might have occurred. Bartoe only spent about two months training with his crew, but he said that the simulations fully prepared him to deal with any problems. During the hair-raising abort to orbit during his launch on STS-51F, Bartoe claimed that he knew what was happening and was never alarmed.

What might a payload specialist have done once on orbit to jeopardize the lives of the entire crew? Bob Crippen told a small group of space buffs at an *Apollo 16* fortieth anniversary celebration that he always made his crewmates remove their boots once in orbit, mostly so they wouldn't hit any switches and damage them. Payload specialist Bartoe admitted that initially he was a "real klutz in the microgravity [environment]," and it took a while for him to grow accustomed to his new surroundings, supporting Crippen's concerns about boots.

Perhaps an inexperienced payload specialist might have flipped a switch or pressed a critical button—accidentally or intentionally—without any of the crew knowing. Or opened the hatch to the orbiter? Except for planned EVAS, no one actually opened a hatch while on orbit, but a rumor that a payload specialist thought about it has made the rounds and has been discussed, or gossiped, by many space aficionados over the years.

A number of astronauts have spoken of a payload specialist who showed a lot of interest in the side hatch of the orbiter on one of the early shuttle missions. Several commanders, early in the history of flying payload specialists, padlocked the hatch out of fear that one of the payload specialists whom they did not know very well might attempt to open the hatch once in orbit. Several of these commanders locked the hatch because it had been done on a mission prior to theirs and not because of any specific concerns with members of their crew.

Two shuttle astronauts told the authors the incident was a serious anomaly that gave the crew grave concern. Payload specialist Fred Leslie (STS-73) shared on the online group sci.space.shuttle that the commander of the mission on which this incident supposedly first occurred was seriously concerned and thus took action to ensure that the payload specialist could do no harm.

Fred Gregory—pilot on STS-51B, which carried Spacelab 3 and two payload specialists—shared with the authors in November 2016 that Taylor Wang was the payload specialist likely referred to in this account. Gregory readily admitted that commander Bob Overmyer secured the hatch due to concerns about Wang's psychological condition after he discovered that his experiment in fluid physics failed to work and mission control would not give him the time to attempt to troubleshoot and, if successful, make appropriate repairs. However, Gregory believes that Overmyer overreacted. Wang had spent five years of his life developing his specialized apparatus and thus experienced a meltdown when he discovered that it didn't work. Wang also had difficulty using the finicky orbiter toilet. No doubt he was having a bad day.

However, there was no lock used to secure the hatch as rumored. Gregory confirmed to the authors that Overmyer secured the side hatch of the orbiter with ordinary duct tape. He just wanted to be sure that a despondent payload specialist could not open it, thereby exposing the entire crew to the deadly vacuum of space.

There were other plausible explanations for the need of the padlock. At least two payload specialists who flew during the program were told that its genesis went all the way back to the very first shuttle flight. The lavatory was located immediately adjacent to the orbiter hatch on the aft left side of the middeck. It was used both for waste management as well as hygiene. With as many as eight crew members using that same area throughout weeklong missions, a steady line of crew members would bathe, shave, and clean up right next to the hatch.

As the story was related to some payload specialists by experienced astronauts, it takes a few days in space to unlearn many of the earthly encumbrances that space flyers have lived with since birth. In microgravity, one does not need to set something down or hang it up—it can simply be released to float until needed again. But when new to this environment, early shuttle crews found that the first instinct after toweling off in the waste compartment was to find a convenient place to "hang" the cloth. The most obvious hook was the knobbed hatch handle. As it was told, the concern was that sooner or later a crew member pulling a towel off of the knob would result in it being inadvertently rotated to the open position. It took several of the early shuttle crews making the same observation before program managers agreed that there was a potential issue. Ross, who was selected to be an astronaut in 1980 and wound up flying seven times, supports this story, recalling in November 2016 that using the hatch as a towel rack was a concern during the early shuttle days.

During the shuttle program, operational setbacks resulted in fewer flights than were originally planned, which meant there were many more astronauts prepared to fly than there were seats available on shuttle flights. Following the successful launch of the first shuttle mission, STS-1 in April 1981, NASA projected there would be twelve flights in the year 1984, fourteen in 1985, seventeen each in the years 1986 and 1987, and twenty-four in 1988, utilizing both Kennedy and Vandenberg, California, launch complexes. That estimate proved to be wildly optimistic, as there were only five flights in 1984 and nine in 1985—the most missions the shuttle would ever fly in a single year in the entire span of the program.

The positioning between JSC and MSFC over the role of the payload and mission specialists continued well into the operational shuttle program. Many of the NASA astronauts wondered why the mission specialists couldn't perform the scientific experiments to be carried on the orbiter, just as Kraft had advocated back in the middle 1970s. After all, NASA selected many astronauts with PhDs who had specialties in the required fields of interest—such as oceanography, physics, and astronomy—who were capable of carrying out complex experiments and performing specialized research on shuttle missions. Even if the experiment or investigation was not their trained expertise, they were intelligent, creative, driven people and surely could have been trained to do the job. Mike Mullane certainly agreed with this logic: "We felt a little bit like the payload specialists were outsiders, and a lot of us, I think, felt like, hey, if they're flying, that's a slot one of us could be flying. So there was some friction there."

Years later after payload specialists began launching into space, Kathy Sullivan shared Mullane's logic: "We were giving away seats, is the way we kind of saw it, to nonprofessional astronauts, when we thought that the [NASA] astronauts could do the jobs if properly trained." There were twenty-four slots filled by payload specialists (one flew three times) on the first thirteen shuttle missions carrying payload specialists. Eight of those slots were taken by passengers not critical to carrying out the primary objective of the mission—the mission would have likely proceeded without them—so there would have been no need for a mission specialist to take their place. Only sixteen mission specialists lost seats to payload specialists during just over two years (late 1983 to early 1986) of shuttle operations. That may have been deemed too many by the NASA astronauts, but neither they nor JSC management had the authority to decide if payload specialists were going to fly. NASA Headquarters held that power. Regardless, once payload specialists were assigned to missions, the professionalism of the NASA astronauts prevailed; the outsiders were welcomed by the crew members, treated respectfully, and given the support they needed to carry out their objectives. In many cases, the NASA astronauts became close friends with the payload specialists and developed long-term relationships that continued long after they left the astronaut corps.

NASA has an impressive track record for selecting astronauts who are professional, intelligent, and driven, and who are also team players. Astronauts are not all created from the same mold, and it's probably unfair to make blanket statements about them. But all things being equal, astronauts want to fly into outer space, and they want to fly before their peers, regardless of how much they respect them. Shuttle astronaut Kathy Sullivan's aspiration to make her first flight was preempted by another astronaut—a payload specialist! Sullivan, now a veteran of three spaceflights, eventually flew on STS-41G, STS-31, and STS-45 and holds the distinction of being the first American woman to conduct an EVA, or space walk. But she was rather blunt about her feelings toward payload specialists taking seats on the shuttle, specifically one flying before her. As she recalled, "One of the guys who was a payload specialist was an American who had not cut the mustard in our selection. . . . He goes and flies before almost anybody in our class. He flew on STS-9. Some [of] our guys had flown, but a whole bunch of us hadn't."

Although Sullivan politely didn't mention the name of the payload specialist she was referring to, the only American payload specialist who flew on STS-9 was Byron Lichtenberg, one of the first two payload specialists to fly on the shuttle. Sullivan's resentment of Lichtenberg at the time is understandable; she had followed the conventional NASA path to outer space and wanted to fly first. Lichtenberg applied for astronaut groups both 8 and 9 but was not selected. Lichtenberg wanted to fly too, and in spite of NASA's rejection, he followed his childhood dream—via the payload specialist path—all the way to launchpad 39A, where he rocketed into outer space aboard space shuttle *Columbia* in 1983.

Curiously, Sullivan didn't mention another payload specialist who flew before her on STS-41D. Charlie Walker was also unsuccessful in his quest to become a NASA astronaut. He was turned down for the 1978 astronaut class. Sullivan conceded, "You can tie yourself into knots over, 'I won out over him in the heat to be an astronaut, but he gets to go fly before me.'" Sullivan wanted to "fly first . . . fly soon . . . fly a lot." She felt that because she had worked hard and competed hard, it was unfair for a payload specialist to "go in front of me, really," which she claimed were "very natural human reactions."

By 1983, when the first payload specialists were assigned to the STS-9 mission, there were just under eighty active astronauts qualified for shuttle missions. Some were in management positions and perhaps not on the prime list for mission assignments; over thirty were pilots. That left approximately forty-five mission specialists looking for a seat on one of the five shuttle flights scheduled to launch in 1984. During the first three years of shuttle operations, no more than three mission specialists had flown on any single mission, so the expectations for an aspiring mission specialist to garner one of those fifteen seats for 1984 were slim—fifteen seats being sought by three times as many driven and highly competitive astronauts.

The three seats taken by payload specialists on STS-41D and STS-41G in 1984 would have made the odds only slightly better for the mission specialists' chances of securing a ride into space. But NASA was ready to step up their number of flights scheduled for 1985, trying to prove that their lofty flight predictions made to justify the building of the reusable shuttle were realistic. Nine missions flew in 1985, and eight of them carried a total of fifteen payload specialists (Charlie Walker flew twice that year), the same number of mission specialists that flew in 1984. Mission specialists looking toward their chances of securing one of the coveted seats must have been concerned, perhaps furious, about payload specialists taking more and more seats.

Surely the NASA astronauts understood the reasons for adding payload specialists—experts in a particular area of investigation—to flight crews and endorsed their inclusion. For example, the nine Spacelab payload specialists who flew from 1983 to 1985 were all authorities in their respective scientific fields. Charlie Walker was an expert in electrophoresis, a technique that separates molecules based on size and charge. Hartsfield commanded STS-41D, which was Walker's first mission, and was generally very critical of the payload specialist position. However, he was extremely complimentary of Walker, saying, "In fact, I worked hard to integrate Charlie into the crew because I felt that was essential for our success. He was a good student. He was going into a strange environment, and he wanted to learn, and he gave it his full attention."

Mike Mullane stated in *Riding Rockets* that Spacelab astronauts, other scientists, and Charlie Walker made legitimate contributions to the missions they flew on. But then there were the passengers, or part-timers as Mullane called them, cloaked as payload specialists whose reasons for flying were circumspect at best. Make no mistake about it; their flying on the shuttle was more than sour grapes to the pilots and mission specialists. Mullane even placed the honorable and much-adored late John Glenn into this category. Glenn was the first American to orbit Earth and overnight became an American hero, but he also flew many years later aboard *Discovery* as a seventy-seven-year-old senior citizen payload specialist on the STS-95 mission. Also included in this passenger-junket category were a U.S. senator and representative, a Saudi Arabian prince, a Frenchman, a Mexican, an engineer, and a school teacher.

Were all the NASA astronauts leery of this new breed of astronaut? There are a handful of responses from astronauts captured in NASA's Oral History program regarding payload specialists and more specifically the so-called passengers. Many astronauts were publically supportive of the program, but some were critical, especially of those they perceived as merely passengers thrust on them and taking up valuable flight seats. Many astronauts who were not supportive of payload specialists flying on shuttle missions were more critical about NASA management allowing them to fly than they were about the individual payload specialists. Regardless, it's difficult to criticize someone who jumped at the opportunity of a lifetime to fly into outer space.

Jeff Hoffman, who flew over 21 million miles on five shuttle missions, initially thought the idea of carrying a passenger aboard the shuttle was a crazy idea, but eventually he flew with Republican senator Jake Garn on STS-51D. Although skeptical during training, he was very complimentary of Garn years later, but he admits, "He [Garn] told me afterwards, he said, 'Jeff, don't ever play poker.' He said, 'It took you a while to disguise your initial skepticism about this whole thing.'"

Rumors abounded that NASA was considering flying other dignitaries on shuttle missions, including the popular news anchor and space enthusiast Walter Cronkite. The popular musician John Denver also campaigned strongly for a ride. At first glance this may seem preposterous, but NASA had considered flying nonprofessional astronauts on the space shuttle years before the first payload specialist flew on STS-9 in 1983. In a memorandum dated 7 October 1976, to NASA administrator Dr. James Fletcher, Chris Kraft wrote, "Also, there may be requirements to carry flight observers, pilot trainees, political or media representatives, a physician, or any other person one would normally find in a routine operation. All of these people, including payload specialists, I call the passengers." There it was; NASA had given thought to, perhaps even intended, flying passengers way back in 1976. Kraft noted later in the same memorandum, "There may be some doubt in others' minds about how responsive the mission specialist will be to the requirements and desires of the sponsoring investigators." Kraft seemed clairvoyant!

Rick Hauck recollected in January 2017, "Sometime in the 1983–85 time frame, astronauts were solicited for their thoughts on the subject [of payload specialists]. Recall that because some were of the opinion that astronauts weren't very good at conveying the excitement, the grandeur, the thrill of rocketing into space, there was talk of flying journalists, poets, artists, congressmen (oh, we did that, didn't we?)." Hauck believed that NASA shouldn't put those folks at risk until the space agency had adequate experience to understand that they had a "very high confidence in the risk level achieved by that point."

Following his first flight, Mullane's position on flying payload specialists softened, admitting that he became a little more tolerant of the "outsiders" once he had his first mission behind him. In fact, he was quite complimentary of payload specialist Charlie Walker. Scully-Power believes the program was "very successful. It enabled subject matter experts to join the crew to enhance specific missions. I think the balance was about right between the career astronauts and the payload specialists."

Following the breakup of *Challenger* in January of 1986, the passenger program ended. Payload specialists did not fly again until late 1990 when Samuel Durrance and Ronald Parise joined the crew of STS-35 on a Spacelab mission dedicated to astrophysics. Payload specialists then continued to fly regularly on the shuttle for the next thirteen years until construction of the International Space Station became the primary focus for the shuttle. The last payload specialist to launch on the shuttle was Ilan Ramon from Israel, on the ill-fated STS-107 mission flown by shuttle *Columbia*.

Kathy Sullivan summarized, "I think the reaction [to payload specialists] was probably about as varied as folks in the astronaut corps. It's not homogeneous by any means." While a few astronauts have been forthcoming in their assessment of the program, both positive and negative, we know very little about what the majority of them think of the experiment. The first payload specialists flew in late 1983 on the very first Spacelab flight, a highly successful mission focused on scientific research. By the end of 1985, twenty payload specialists had made a total of 1,289 revolutions of Earth and traveled over 30 million miles. Science, national security, and goodwill were served on twelve fascinating missions that brought forth a new era in American spaceflight.

3. Spacelab, a New Era in Spaceflight

Pursuant to the offer of the Government of the United States
of America to Europe to participate in the major
U.S. space programme.

Spacelab Memorandum of Understanding

Spacelab 1 payload specialist Ulf Merbold slowly inserted a long needle into a small glimmering sphere of water that was floating inside the Spacelab module. He gently injected a tiny air bubble inside the water globule and then observed how the laws of physics peculiar to orbiting Earth governed the movement of the air within the bubble. He was awestruck at the variety of oscillations the water bubble made once it had been excited by the injection of the air. The globule of water shimmied and danced directly in front of his eyes, all while he floated effortlessly inside Spacelab. "It's very spectacular, and if you leave it on its own, it is really an ideal sphere," he enthused following his 1983 voyage to space. "I think it is impossible on the ground to make a sphere like that." Merbold's keen observational skills, honed to perfection by virtue of his years of training to become a materials scientist, led to him being selected to carry out advanced scientific research in space, the kind of investigation that often leads to unexpected discoveries.

The first mission carrying payload specialists flew in 1983 with high hopes of fulfilling one of the shuttle's primary objectives—to provide access to outer space for scientific research by scientists with limited astronaut training. The shuttle had been declared operational after *Columbia* landed on the STS-4 flight eighteen months earlier; scientists were eager to exploit the launch system capability to ferry large and groundbreaking payloads into orbit and to carry out scientific research on them. Spacelab 1 flew on the

STS-9 mission and carried two payload specialists—Drs. Byron Lichtenberg and Ulf Merbold.

Marshall Space Flight Center's Rick Chappell recently recalled that "*Skylab* was sort of the jumping-off point for Spacelab. It was an activity in which science and human spaceflight was merged in a much more significant way." Each of the three manned *Skylab* flights carried a scientist along with two pilots, signaling an increased focus on science over the early spaceflights. The *Skylab* pilots were very well trained to carry out scientific observations and research, but they didn't have the academic pedigree that the scientific community expected. On the other hand, the scientist-astronauts on the *Skylab* missions had strong academic backgrounds in the sciences and were trained researchers.

Spacelab 1 carried four full-fledged scientists with PhDs who comprised the payload crew—two mission specialists and two payload specialists. The pilots flying *Columbia* on STS-9 often participated in experiments, usually as test subjects for life sciences experiments. Pilot Brewster Shaw recalled in November 2016 that he and Commander John Young occasionally ventured into Spacelab but were greeted by the payload crew with ambivalence— "Don't touch that" or "Get out of the way."

Columbia launched from KSC on 28 November 1983 and settled into a near-circular orbit of 155 nautical miles, inclined fifty-seven degrees to the equator. Inside the cargo bay, *Columbia* carried the first Spacelab module into orbit. The STS-9 press kit offered several primary objectives for its maiden voyage: to ensure that the system performed as advertised, to obtain scientific data, and to "demonstrate to potential users of the Shuttle/Spacelab system the broad capability of Spacelab for scientific research." Later Spacelab missions would have a narrower scientific focus, but the first mission needed to verify the capability of Spacelab to carry out scientific investigations over a wide variety of disciplines. Hence, it was planned to conduct more than seventy separate experiments in five broad areas of scientific research: life sciences, atmospheric physics and Earth observations, astronomy and solar physics, space plasma physics, and materials science and technology.

The veteran John Young commanded this mission, with the pilot Brewster Shaw making his first journey into space. Drs. Owen K. Garriott and Robert A. R. Parker were the mission specialists and part of the payload

2. Ulf Merbold, operating the gradient heating facility located in the Spacelab module in support of a materials-processing experiment. Courtesy NASA/Retro Space Images.

crew, both of whom had impressive scientific credentials. Parker was making his maiden voyage into space, while Garriott was a veteran of the Skylab 3 expedition. Garriott earned a PhD from Stanford University in electrical engineering (1960) and taught electromagnetic theory and ionospheric physics at Stanford from 1961 to 1965 prior to being selected in 1965 as a scientist-astronaut. Parker held a doctorate in astronomy from the California Institute of Technology (1962).

Payload specialist Dr. Ulf Dietrich Merbold was born in Greiz, Germany, on 20 June 1941. He earned a degree in physics in 1968 and his doctorate in natural sciences in 1976, both from Stuttgart University. Following completion of his doctorate, Merbold worked at the Max Planck Institute for Metals Research located in Stuttgart, where his focus was on solid-state and low-temperature physics, concentrating on crystal lattice defects. He joined ESA in 1977, was selected for the Spacelab 1 mission in 1982, and became the first European and non-American to fly on an American spacecraft.

Dr. Byron Kurt Lichtenberg was born on 19 February 1948 in Stroudsburg, Pennsylvania. He received a bachelor of science degree in aerospace

3. A happy and animated Byron Lichtenberg floats inside the Spacelab 1 module.
Courtesy NASA/Retro Space Images.

engineering from Brown University, Rhode Island, in 1969. Following his undergraduate work, Lichtenberg served in the U.S. Air Force from 1969 to 1973 and completed a tour of duty in Vietnam, flying 238 combat missions for which he was awarded ten Air Medals and two Distinguished Flying Crosses. Following his military accomplishments in Vietnam, he attended the Massachusetts Institute of Technology (MIT), where he received his master of science degree in mechanical engineering in 1975 and his doctorate in biomedical engineering in 1979. He continued to fly jet aircraft from 1975 to 1992 in the Massachusetts Air National Guard. Lichtenberg applied for NASA astronaut groups 8 and 9 but was not selected. He carried outstanding credentials both as a scientist and military aviator, and his missing the cut is testament to the astronomical odds of being selected by NASA to be an astronaut.

Lichtenberg belonged to an MIT biomedical engineering research group that wanted to better understand the causes of what is now termed space adaptation syndrome (SAS) and how to prevent it. When he was selected to be a payload specialist, this group was designing an experiment to be flown on a shuttle mission that would investigate the vestibular organ. This organ, located in the inner ear, governs equilibrium of the human body and is largely responsible for detecting change of speed and the direction of body movement. In space, some astronauts had become unexpectedly and violently ill, which was believed to be related to the vestibular organ. The mystery illness was causing deep concerns for NASA, as no one could predict who would fall victim once in orbit or why.

Lichtenberg's alternate for Spacelab 1 was Dr. Michael Logan Lampton. Born 1 March 1941 in Williamsport, Pennsylvania, Lampton received his bachelor of science degree in physics from Caltech in Pasadena, California, in 1962 and his PhD in physics from the University of California–Berkeley in 1967. Prior to receiving his undergraduate degree, Lampton earned his first claim to fame as one of the "Fiendish Fourteen," who perpetrated the Great Rose Bowl Hoax in 1961, an ingenious prank that received national attention in the United States. This group of devious Caltech students devised a plan that tricked the opposing fans to recognize Caltech at half-time instead of their own team as previously planned. Following Lampton's backup role on STS-9, he was assigned as the prime payload specialist on STS-51H, another Spacelab mission.

Dr. Wubbo Johannes Ockels was the alternate for Merbold on Spacelab 1. Ockels was born 28 March 1946 in Almelo, Netherlands. He earned his undergraduate degree in 1973 and PhD in 1978, both in physics and mathematics from the Nuclear Physics Accelerator Institute (KVI) in Groningen in the Netherlands. He was selected to be a payload specialist along with Merbold and Claude Nicollier of Switzerland by ESA in 1978.

Both backup payload specialists participated in mission-dependent and mission-independent training just like the prime crew members. Lampton recently responded to a query about his mission independent training:

Yes indeed, about 20 percent of my STS-9 training was mission independent. Firefighting school (with a real fire to put out!), launch tower emergency escape, toilet training, food prep, stowage, hatch operations, launch and landing ops including the use of the personal egress air pack (PEAP of course), comm[unications], electrical power distribution systems, data systems including the high-rate multiplexer (HRM, of course) through which just about all the science live data was downlinked. But also, since the payload specialists who do not fly (me: a backup) serve as crew communicators and science team communicators, there is a bunch of ground training in how to be an effective CAPCOM.

Lampton recalled his mission-dependent training:

At the time, it seemed to us that the mission-dependent training was like going back to graduate school but majoring in everything. STS-9 was Spacelab 1, and it was a demonstration mission showing how versatile the Spacelab systems could be. We did all kinds of research stuff: medical, metallurgical, remote sensing, astronomy, microgravity, lots more. My training started in late 1979, and the mission flew in late 1983—longer than anticipated. But then this was the first Spacelab, and there were a bunch of preparation delays on all sides.

Just like NASA's pilots and mission specialist astronauts, Lichtenberg, Lampton, Merbold, and Ockels went through an extensive vetting process before they were selected for the opportunity to fly aboard Spacelab. It had already been decided that two of the four payload crewmen operating Spacelab 1 would be mission specialists, leaving only two remaining slots for payload specialists. Chappell recalled in July 2015 that Kraft sent a list of mission specialists to MSFC, testing the waters to see if they would select one, or more, of them to fly as payload specialists on Spacelab 1. "My recollection is that he sent the list, we looked at it, and we said the people we're talking about nominating and selecting are a lot more familiar with the science we want done than any of the people on Kraft's list. So we sort of said thanks for the list, but [no thanks]."

Chappell explained that by 1976 everyone had pretty much agreed on the definition of the payload specialist, and with the first flight of the shuttle approaching, it was time to give consideration to how to select and train them. The Spacelab payload specialists would be selected by an IWG and would be "drawn from the scientific and technical community—domestic or foreign—having a specific interest in that mission." The IWG would consist of "the principal investigators or their representatives who have been selected for a particular mission."

MSFC had given a lot of informal thought about how to select the payload specialist as far back as 1975. But once the Spacelab 1 payload configuration had been decided in late 1976 and early 1977, NASA asked the IWG for their payload specialist selection process. As chief scientist for Spacelab 1, Chappell remembered that a working group of fifty to sixty people was required due to the large number of microgravity experiments from Europe: "We used to meet in Von Braun's conference room at Marshall, and there would be people almost sitting out in the hall. We had to figure out how to organize that many people so they could have meaningful discussions and make meaningful decisions. We did that by discipline." Chappell explained that they began with a clean sheet of paper and developed a process that would ensure harmony within the scientific community. There was a lot of back and forth with the MSFC, JSC, and Headquarters managers. The process took at least six months to develop, after which they let the principal investigators nominate candidates.

Chappell clarified that the Europeans' selection process was different from that used by the United States for Spacelab 1. ESA selected its astronauts and made them members of its organization, similar to NASA's astronaut corps, whereas NASA's Spacelab payload specialists were selected by the academic community and were not part of NASA's cadre of astronauts. David Shapland and Michael J. Rycroft wrote in *Spacelab: Research in Earth Orbit* that ESA received several thousand applications from its member organizations for aspiring payload specialists, following the release of the announcement of opportunity in March 1977. By September that list had been culled to fifty-three hopefuls who were then evaluated for their scientific and engineering skills and medical condition. Four survived this cut: Ulf Merbold (Federal Republic of Germany), Franco Malerba (Italy), Claude Nicollier (Switzerland), and Wubbo Ockels (the Netherlands). Chappell recalled that he was not involved with ESA in the process up to this point: "The IWG didn't pick them [the ESA candidates], although my guess is that ESA got input from the different European investigators that they then used to put their pool of applicants together."

The French were not pleased with the selection process. Jean-Loup Chrétien, who would become the backup payload specialist to Frenchman Patrick Baudry on STS-51G in 1985, was in the running for a spot on Spacelab but was not selected. Chrétien believed "that was a very strange first selection for the Spacelab mission that no French people were selected, and the French president was very upset." It was a blessing in disguise for Chrétien; he went on to become the first western European in space, as a crew member on the Russian *Soyuz T-6* mission launched on 24 June 1982, well over a year before STS-9 flew.

According to Chappell, the American payload specialists for Spacelab 1 were chosen by a subset of the IWG, the Payload Specialist Selection Group (PSSG). Scientists from all the various disciplines that were involved in Spacelab 1 comprised the PSSG, and they selected the candidates they would recommend. Chappell remembered, "We probably had twenty, thirty, maybe forty American nominees that came from the science disciplines represented on the mission."

A September 1977 NASA news release from MSFC reported that there were eighteen American payload specialist candidates being considered for Spacelab 1. Interestingly, William (Bill) Thornton, a NASA scientist-astronaut and mission specialist, was also a candidate for the payload specialist slot on Spacelab 1. Thornton confirmed to the authors in January 2017 that NASA submitted his name to the working groups for consideration. He then explained, "To make a long story short, NASA put me in as a very logical person to occupy the payload [specialist] position. It was one of the bitterest fights to select their own people," referring to the MSFC working groups. Thornton was adamant that "they wanted their own people and there was no way in the world the boards and things were going to say I was qualified to do it." According to Thornton, he was already well versed in the operation of the available equipment designed to provide answers to key questions about SAS. His medical background made him an excellent choice for the life sciences experiments scheduled for Spacelab 1. Thornton confessed, "Well, yes, but not in the dogfight that was going on over a lot of things." Thornton was steadfast that he could have made a strong contribution to understanding SAS, having flown on STS-8 in August–September 1983, the mission prior to Spacelab 1, where he conducted biomedical experiments on the space malady. Although he lost out on the chance to fly on Spacelab 1, he told the authors with a hint of modesty and a healthy dose of satisfaction, "I got to fly first after all."

This list of eighteen was narrowed down to six American candidates in December 1977, along with the four ESA nominees. Craig L. Fischer, Lampton, Lichtenberg, Robert T. Menzies, Richard J. Terrile, and Ann F. Whitaker were the Americans still in the mix, along with Merbold, Ockels, Malerba, and Nicollier from ESA. NASA announced in June 1978 that Lichtenberg and Lampton were the winners of the American competition; one of them would be selected as the prime American crewman for Spacelab 1.

Delays in getting the shuttle ready to fly prompted NASA to offer ESA's payload specialists the opportunity to train alongside its mission specialist astronauts. Prior to selecting ESA candidates for the mission specialist program, NASA administrator Robert A. Frosch made it clear to Erik Quistgaard, ESA director general, that Spacelab took priority over the mission specialist training.

Nicollier and Ockels began training with NASA astronaut group 9 in 1980, making them the first non-Americans to participate in NASA's mission specialist training. According to the ESA website, Merbold would have joined Nicollier and Ockels in the mission specialist training, but he could not meet the medical requirements to become a mission specialist. But due to the relaxed medical standards, Merbold still qualified to be a payload specialist.

Unfortunately, according to Nicollier, as the group 9 training progressed, the preparation for Spacelab 1 was suffering. In a JSC 24 September 1981 memorandum, Nicollier informed the Spacelab 1 investigator community that Ockels was going to leave mission specialist training to concentrate on

Spacelab 1. Nicollier withdrew from the Spacelab training to continue training as a mission specialist in Houston. Chappell told the authors in August 2016 that this was likely Ockels's way of ensuring his inclusion on a later mission, the upcoming Spacelab D1. It may have even been ESA's attempt to get both Ockels and Nicollier on the D1 flight. ESA hoped that Nicollier would secure a seat on the upcoming Spacelab D1 flight as a mission specialist. Ultimately, Nicollier was not assigned to that mission but remained at JSC until 2005, flying four shuttle missions as a NASA mission specialist.

Some of the career NASA astronauts were not enamored with the training plans set forth by the academics, reflected in an MSFC draft memorandum dated February 1978 and titled *Spacelab Payload Crew Training Plan Coordination Draft*. The 1978 memorandum clarified that "NASA does not require that investigators provide special hardware to accommodate payload crew training. It is the investigators' option (along with his sponsors) to conduct training wholly in classrooms on breadboard systems, on flight hardware, on specific training hardware, or on some combination of the above." That statement prompted a handwritten sarcastic "Oh boy!" from John Young, whereas Ed Gibson highlighted the entire paragraph and scribbled, "This is [a] very *improbable approach*. It makes failure of many exp[eriment] objectives highly probable. At $20M a launch, this is not cost effective." While these comments may seem harsh, they appear to have been effective in pointing out areas of concern that were eventually addressed prior to the mission.

Following a long period of training, NASA announced in October 1982 that Byron Lichtenberg had been chosen as the prime NASA payload specialist and that Michael Lampton would serve as his alternate. According to Chappell, ESA selected Merbold as their prime crewman, with Ockels as his backup, about the same time. Chappell believes the IWG was involved in the selection of the ESA prime and alternate payload specialists. "I remember that the ESA candidates were interviewed by the PSSG, and a recommendation from that group was made to ESA and NASA. But I do know that we voted on the final two [and] we ended up picking the same two they picked. We didn't tell them what to do, but there had been enough coordination going on that everybody knew where everybody was headed."

In 2015 Chappell recalled the selection process and compared the STS-9 payload specialists to the mission specialists:

Byron was just finishing his PhD at MIT *in space life sciences, but he hadn't spent his whole life in it. Owen [Garriott] was an electrical engineer but knew a lot about the atmosphere and the ionosphere and the aurora— that was a big area of Spacelab 1 also. I would say they were the equivalent but in different disciplines. Owen knew a lot more about spaceflight although Byron was a fighter pilot, but Owen knew both spaceflight and ionospheric and atmospheric physics very well, but Byron knew life sciences very well. Bob Parker was a solar physicist; had not done research in a while, but he was incredibly well experienced with* Skylab *because he was sort of the project scientist on* Skylab. *So he was the interface between the scientists [and] he and Owen were ideal mission specialists to be on Spacelab 1. They represented two different disciplines, and they'd been through a lot of science operations. Ulf Merbold was 100 percent scientist; he was a materials science guy [and] there was a lot of materials science on Spacelab 1, and Ulf understood most of that before he ever started training. Ulf was the quintessential person to be a payload specialist.*

Chappell believes that Garriott's and Parker's experience and backgrounds made them excellent choices for the Spacelab 1 mission. Parker explained that regarding the science on Spacelab 1, the mission specialists often deferred to the payload specialists, who were much more current in their field of expertise, and often "did get in and stir the pot a little bit about what kind of science was done." Describing his and Garriott's role, Parker explained, "Hey, we're the eyes and ears and hands of the guys on the ground. So if they want us to turn that switch and do this thing this way, we'll do it for them."

Garriott and Parker had no backups; NASA did not select backups for the NASA astronauts on shuttle crews. The authors asked Chappell if there was ever any consideration given to one of the alternate payload specialists filling in for one of the mission specialists if they couldn't fly due to medical or other reasons. He confirmed that there had been informal talk and speculation. But he reasoned that Chris Kraft would have likely suggested they find another mission specialist: "We would have just had to have double-timed to train that person, and that kind of makes sense because the mission specialists also have a lot of knowledge and responsibility for shuttle systems."

Lampton reminisced about the selection process, "What fun to remember these issues. There was a roomful of us applicants. I do not recall their names. We all thought of ourselves as **WINNERS**. Byron and I won out. But there were plenty of other routes, so no one was worried, then."

Once *Columbia* had achieved orbit on 28 November 1983, the crew worked in twelve-hour shifts, just as Chris Kraft had recommended in 1976. For this flight, Young, Parker, and Merbold comprised the Red shift, whereas Shaw, Garriott, and Lichtenberg were designated the Blue shift.

This first Spacelab mission also promised to vastly improve ground-to-spacecraft communications. Previously, astronauts had experienced periods of communications blackout due to the lack of a sufficient number of ground stations to provide constant communication. NASA had intended to place two tracking and data relay satellites (TDRS) into geostationary orbits—one on STS-6 and another on STS-8—so that communications and data from Spacelab would be available to scientists on the ground in real time. Unfortunately, the STS-6 mission encountered problems deploying the first TDRS into its proper position. Eventually NASA was able to coax the satellite into its proper trajectory, but the launch of the second TDRS was delayed until NASA could address the problems encountered on the first TDRS deployment. The single TDRS was adequate for most of the experiments on STS-9 and far better than the communications capabilities on all previous flights.

Prior to the STS-9 mission—with only a few exceptions—any communication from mission control to the spacecraft was conducted through the CAPCOM, another astronaut trained in how to best communicate with those in orbit. The ground-based scientists were adamant that one-on-one conversations with the payload crew were imperative to mission success. Thus, they had their own scientific equivalent of the CAPCOM—the alternate payload specialist. Chappell believed strongly in the new communication process. Both Lampton and Ockels provided much-needed support during the flight in the Payload Operations Control Center (POCC) located at JSC. Scientists and technicians provided ground support at the POCC for the Spacelab experiments, much like the shuttle was governed out of the MCC. Chappell explained, "From the Marshall point of view we thought that *by God* the scientists ought to be able to talk to the crew." He steadfastly believed that if an instrument developed a problem on orbit or there appeared to be uncertainty about a measurement, the payload crew needed to talk directly to the person who knew the machine inside and out. "If Byron were running the television [and] looking at the *aurora* and describing things, then he needed to be talking to Stephen Mende, whose camera it was that was making the *aurora* imagery."

Spacelab 1 proved to be an extremely versatile laboratory, including a pressurized module where the astronauts worked and an unpressurized pallet that sat in the orbiter's payload bay adjacent to the module. A tunnel led from the middeck of *Columbia* to the Spacelab module, nestled into the aft end of the payload bay. The module and pallet could be flown together or individually. Two versions of Spacelab were developed, a long module and a short module. The long module was flown on the Spacelab 1 mission, along with one pallet.

Included on Spacelab 1 was a scientific air lock that allowed up to 220 pounds of scientific equipment to be exposed directly to raw space. The equipment was placed on a small table inside the module, which could be raised until it was in the vacuum of space, courtesy of the air lock, and then lowered back into the module by the crew once the experiments had been completed. The air lock was a much-needed addition that vastly increased Spacelab's scientific capability. However, it did add an element of risk to the mission. A 17 November 1982 informal memorandum titled "Spacelab Scientific Airlock EVA Contingency Tasks" addressed one potential scenario. If the experiment table failed to retract or the outer hatch refused to close, the cargo bay doors of the orbiter could not be closed. And upon reentry the aerodynamics of *Columbia* would be compromised; it could not land with open payload doors. Under this scenario, an EVA would be required to remedy the situation.

EVA procedures were relatively simple, but R. T. Adams explained in the memorandum that there were inadequate restraints to allow an astronaut to easily access the air lock from the outside. Assuming the EVA crewman were able to translate over to the outer hatch, he would first attempt to remove the jam, but if that didn't work, then a measured jolting force might have triggered the table to respond. This procedure would likely have required the assistance of an internal vehicular activity crewman inside Spacelab, which would have necessitated Spacelab to be isolated from the orbiter in case of a breach of pressurization. Consideration was even given to having one EVA crewman restrain a second EVA crewman by holding onto his legs. If all else failed, the table and experiment could be jettisoned. If an emergency required a space walk, it would not be performed by either of the payload specialists. EVAs fell under the job description of the mission specialists. Fortunately, no EVA was ever necessary to free a jammed air lock on Spacelab.

There were approximately seventy experiments aboard Spacelab 1, depending on how one counted them up. Harry G. Craft Jr., Spacelab 1 mission manager at MSFC, joked in *The Spacelab Accomplishments Forum*, "We used to have fun counting them. ESA wanted to count it up into the hundreds or two hundreds and NASA wanted to count it to be the lower numbers." According to *Spacelab—International Cooperation in Orbit*, Spacelab 1 carried seventy-two experiments, requiring forty different instruments, but other sources cite slightly more or less. There were eighteen instruments on the pallet and nineteen in the module; three had elements in both the module and the pallet. Some instruments were capable of performing more than one experiment. Thirteen of the seventy-two experiments were sponsored by NASA, and fifty-nine came from the ten European states comprising ESA, which at first seems overwhelmingly lopsided in favor of the Europeans. However, in *The Spacelab Accomplishments Forum*, ESA engineer Werner Riesselmann pointed out that ESA-built multiuser facilities could accommodate many experiments. Considering the number of racks available in Spacelab and the mass and energy usage of each organization's experiments, the split was fairly equitable between ESA and NASA.

Spacelab 1 weathered the jaw-breaking launch on 28 November and reached orbit in great shape. The hatch to the tunnel connecting Spacelab to the orbiter middeck proved to be a bit problematic, as the crew had extreme difficulty opening it, but once inside, the crew began the first experiments within the first few hours.

There were only a few significant problems encountered during this mission. One of these related to one of the fourteen remote acquisition units (RAUs), which managed data coming from experiments and subsystems. The cold plate for RAU 21, necessary to keep the unit from overheating, was cooled using Freon but regardless warmed above the planned twenty-two degrees Celsius (seventy-two degrees Fahrenheit), apparently causing the RAU to sporadically malfunction. The ground crew was able to develop a work-around, and though the unit continued to be problematic throughout most of the flight, it did its job.

Several sources, including a 1988 MSFC book titled *Science in Orbit: The Shuttle and Spacelab Experience, 1981–86*, contend that about half of all space travelers suffer from SAS. Some medications moderate the symptoms—believed to be related to the mechanism of the inner ear—but as yet there is no remedy that cures the problem. Nor is there anything that can be done prior to launch to prevent SAS. Early in the shuttle program, NASA was very concerned and keen to figure out how to overcome the dire effects of SAS. Hence, three of the life sciences apparatuses on STS-9 were focused on the poorly understood syndrome. Some of the vestibular experiments were designed to make the astronauts sick in hopes of learning more about SAS. NASA called these experiments "provocative tests."

Dr. Chappell enlightened a group of reporters on the second day of the mission, explaining the vestibular studies that scientists hoped would help them understand why astronauts become sick in space and then what to do about it. Scientists had developed a handful of reasons that might explain the causes of SAS, yet there remained much uncertainty. In space the vestibular organs do not function as they do on Earth due to the lack of gravity. Regardless, the eyes still try to tell the brain which way is up. Chappell informed the reporters, "So the way to study this is to look at reflexes like changes that the eyes make when the body is actually moved—it's called counter-rolling or nystagmus adjustments that the eye makes as the body moves, which are driven directly by the vestibular organs."

In one experiment, the crew member placed "his head inside a rotating drum decorated with a random dot pattern for visual stimulation," a device designed to disorient the astronaut and hopefully cause the onset of SAS to help pin down what kick-started the illness. Lichtenberg explained this experiment after the mission. "The small box that we've had on our heads is an accelerometer package," he pointed out. "Here we are showing a rotating dome which is trying to investigate the visual-vestibular interaction that occurs either on the ground or in space. You can see the reflection of the rotating dome actually in the person's eyeball. It's [a] very impressive thing to put your head inside this rotating dome, and contrary to early predictions it is not provocative in space as long as your head is fixed."

The hop-and-drop experiment (*Spacelab 1 Experiments*) was designed to "investigate the effects of weightlessness on spinal reflexes and posture." The experiment employed the use of a bungee cord, causing the astronaut to fall or drop toward the floor of Spacelab in order to assess "acceleration forces which stimulate the vestibular-otolith organs." Byron Lichtenberg described the experiment being administered in his postmission narrative. "Here is Owen being a subject in one of the many life sciences experiments that we've done," he explained. "This is called the hop-and-drop experiment. It's designed to look at the influence of the vestibular organs on the postural reflexes. We measure the muscle signals in the lower leg. If you look at Owen's left leg, you'll see electrodes and cables down in his lower calf. Another part of that experiment entails hopping. Again we are looking at the muscle responses, primarily generated by the vestibular system." The purpose of the electrodes in Garriott's lower calf was to stimulate nerves—NASA's way of saying "being shocked by an electrical current"—in his lower leg, which were recorded and evaluated and added to the growing database in hopes of understanding SAS. These experiments were the first clinical case histories directed at understanding the debilitating space illness.

At a change-of-shift briefing on 29 November, the day after launch, a reporter asked how the crew was feeling. Harry Craft responded, "I asked the question before I came over. I haven't any reports at all on any problems unless John has." Flight director John T. Cox (known within NASA as "Granite Flight") agreed. NASA's policy was to protect the privacy of the astronauts and not make public the identity of those who became ill in orbit. The reporters would have understood this, likely prompting them to continue to press for information about sick astronauts, knowing this would sell more newspapers than writing about vestibular organs.

At a science briefing the same day, reporter Mark Kramer from CBS noted that the first day in space for the payload crew had not been all roses. "There seems to have been a few instances overnight when one could detect, what could [have] been interpreted as [a] little testiness on the part of the crew, [which] might have been caused by them being pushed, and in fact there were a few remarks which said . . . along the lines of we don't do things instantly here." The comments from the crew reminded Kramer of the Skylab 4 mission when that crew believed they were being pushed too hard; their frustrations were eventually resolved via a frank discussion with mission control. Unfortunately, the briefing transcripts do not indicate any response to Kramer's remarks.

Later that same day, Carlos Byars, with the *Houston Chronicle*, inquired at a briefing if anyone had gotten sick? Chappell took the question and replied that none of the payload crew had fallen ill. Reginald Turnill, with the British Broadcasting Corporation (BBC), wanted to know at the 29 November change-of-shift briefing, "If the payload specialists failed to make themselves spacesick with these [vestibular] tests, I mean can one consider the tests a failure in that they won't have succeeded in finding out what causes space sickness?" Chappell explained that the experiments were designed to study how the body adjusts to microgravity, and it's those adjustments that were being studied, not particularly whether the subject became sick. "If the crewman doesn't get sick that's marvelous," he responded. "He will still adjust to the microgravity environment and those adjustments are the things that are being measured."

Most reporters are persistent and have good noses for getting a story. Lee Dembarten, from the *Los Angeles Times*, inquired at the 30 November change-of-shift briefing, "How ill was Byron Lichtenberg?" John Cox answered that Lichtenberg was feeling great and was ready to go back to work. Dembarten continued his inquiry: "How about yesterday?" Cox explained that Lichtenberg had been working on the life science experiments, which were developed to be provocative. Mission rules stipulated that if an astronaut became uncomfortable as a result of the experiment, he was supposed to stop, which is what Lichtenberg did. Not yet ready to give up a potential story, Dembarten then asked, "Did he vomit?" Cox responded, "I don't have any idea."

Turnill need not have worried whether the vestibular experiments were working. In a paper titled "M.I.T./Canadian Vestibular Experiments on the Spacelab-1 Mission: I. Sensory Adaptation to Weightlessness and Readaptation to One-G: An Overview," a group of scientists, including Lichtenberg, evaluated experiments that were conducted on human spatial orientation by four of the STS-9 crew members, which included pre- and postflight experiments. The four participants were Garriott, Parker, Lichtenberg, and Merbold. Three of the four participants developed symptoms of space sickness early in the mission, which lasted for two to three days. The symptoms were suggestive of prolonged motion sickness.

Merbold recalled how his body reacted to the microgravity environment, following the mission: "It wasn't really so bad. I had two occurrences when I threw up and was bad off for a few seconds, but afterwards you feel much better."

Lichtenberg noticed the first signs of sickness at fifty-one minutes mission elapsed time: "I had this for about the first three or four days [and] it was like everything in my stomach was up underneath my sternum." Going slowly was the best medicine he could find. Bob Parker also had problems with SAS, remembering, "Closing my eyes did not really help, it only made things worse." He felt best when he could wedge himself into a corner, eyes open staring straight ahead. Garriott recalled that after taking a Reglin pill to thwart space sickness, "I thereupon got sick and proceeded to get sick several times that afternoon. I took a second one some four hours later and again threw up." Laughing, he concluded, "So it could be that it promoted sickness!"

When asked in July 2015 if the sickness experienced on Spacelab 1 occurred naturally or was the result of the provocative vestibular experiments, Chappell responded that he believed it was some of both. Clearly the provocative vestibular experiments made life on the shuttle more difficult than under normal conditions. The protocol for the experiments was to do them at the beginning of the mission and then at the end of the mission, after the brain had time to adapt to the new environment. Chappell said, "They found a lot of really neat things." And in layman's terms, he then explained their scientific understanding, at that time, of the possible cause of SAS to the reporters:

The brain begins to depend on the eyes for which way is up. The problem that causes motion sickness has to do with where the brain is confused, because there are three ways for the brain to tell which way is up and in space two of those don't work. Your eyes tell you where the ceiling and the floor is; so that is up and down. The muscles in your legs and back and stomach tell you where the force is; there are nerves in those muscles which are feeding information to the brain saying . . . activate the muscles in the back because we are getting pulled down or activate these mus-

cles in the arm so I can lift it against gravity. These nerve signals match what the eyes are saying. But the third thing is the otolith organ, which is inside the bone behind your ear. The otolith organs . . . they are little hollow tubes that have hairs and have little rocks in them—some kind of calcium compound. If you lean your head over, the little rocks will run down the tubes and touch the hairs. and the brain can interpret that; it's an accelerometer basically. Our brain uses that information when you're sitting in your office. But in space the rocks float around in those tubes as you move your head. So the otolith organ does not work in space. The nerves (in the muscles) aren't helping either because there is no weight holding you in the chair. So the brain figures out over a course of two to three days that the eyes are the only thing you can depend on. It's important for there to be a ceiling and a floor.

The astronauts on this mission reacted differently to space; some became sick, while others didn't. Sleep patterns varied; some catnapped, whereas others slept soundly throughout their sleep period. Merbold had his own philosophy regarding sleep: "Well, there is an emotional aspect to sleep. My strategy was that I might sleep a lot for the rest of my life, and I did not want to waste any minute to sleep more than necessary, so that's what I did. I think the average hours of sleep during the entire mission was between four and five hours [per sleep shift]."

There was a tremendous amount of enthusiasm and expectation for the rest of the mission from Chappell, with his enthusiastic proclamation at the end of the first day: "So, we've been able to see in this first shift the use of the Spacelab as an observing platform, the use of the Spacelab as a microgravity laboratory for life sciences and material sciences investigations, and the Spacelab as a base for active investigations, active stimulation of the ionosphere environment. So, even though we are only at the end of the first day, it's been a very exciting day so far."

Video of the payload crew performing their work clearly showed their enthusiasm for the scientific research they were conducting in the multifaceted laboratory. Merbold exemplified his passion while providing postmission commentary of the flight video, describing one of the materials science experiments. You could still hear the enthusiasm in his voice well after the mission had ended.

The fluid physics module is a machine to study the behavior of liquids under weightless conditions. . . . It looks a little bit like a fiat engine. The idea is to understand liquids, because all the material science experiments like growth of single crystals or the production of new alloys deal with liquid materials, with liquid metal. That machine allows us to use silicone oil as a model. We heat one side of the silicone oil, and you see a flow pattern inside. And that phenomenon is called Marangoni convection. It can be observed only in space, because it is met on the ground by the standard convection, which is gravity driven. Marangoni convection is driven by a difference in surface tension.

Announced on 3 December NASA and ESA managers had mutually decided to lengthen the mission by an additional day. Allan Thirkettle, then ESA manager at KSC, explained in *The Spacelab Accomplishments Forum* that Spacelab used less power than expected, which meant the fuel cells had extra capacity. All was going extremely well on the first Spacelab mission, in spite of a variety of minor problems.

That same day, Craft described several problems that the crew was dealing with. Several experiments were having some problems, what he called "demonstrating anomalies." Two furnaces from the material sciences double rack were not functioning, but the scientists on the ground in the POCC were working diligently on ways to get them up and running again. The metric camera had a film jam on the second magazine. The crew had already captured over five hundred exposures on the first magazine, so even if they could not make the repair, they could still count this experiment as a success.

Between the ingenuity of the payload crew and the help from the POCC, especially the capability to talk directly to one another, the schedule was folding out just as planned in spite of the equipment problems. For example, Dr. Earl Knott, ESA project scientist, reported on the science activities during shift 9, which occurred on 3 December. First, he stated that all was going well with the crew's work in the fluid physics module of the material science experiments. Then, he praised the interaction between the crew and the POCC, which resulted in investigators overcoming problems with several experiments. Chalk one up for those who believe humans are absolutely necessary for performing great science in orbit; a machine could not have repaired the faulty equipment.

"The Red shift [Parker and Merbold] is certainly building a strong reputation on their ability to repair things," Chappell reported. "They're repair men extraordinaire." Parker had repaired the high-data-rate recorder when it encountered problems a few days earlier. Merbold had to remove the front panel on the mirror heating facility, redirect several critical wires, and then test the system—and it worked! The materials scientists were blessed with additional data from the mirror heating facility, courtesy of the fix-it-all crew.

At a 5 December media briefing, MSFC's Chappell shared a spectacular example of great teamwork between those in the POCC and the orbiting astronauts to repair the metric camera.

Mounted in Spacelab's optical window, the camera held the potential to vastly increase the number of high-resolution photographs taken of Earth's surface between fifty-eight degrees latitude north and south over what could be taken aerially by aircraft. A kaleidoscope of fascinating features could be quickly mapped in only ten days, including agricultural patterns, land use, rivers and waterways, geological formations, historical sites, and buildings.

The situation was that the cassette had jammed after taking about twenty-five pictures out of approximately five hundred, so they spent a lot of time, Wubbo, Joe Engle. They found a camera similar to it here. They spent a lot of time working on procedures on how to improvise a darkroom in the middeck so that they could guide Bob Parker through this repair—none of the crew had seen the inside of that cassette—so Wubbo was act-ing sort of [as] the CAPCOM . . . and he had a telephone on one ear where he was talking to the . . . people in Germany in German and his head-set on the other ear, where he was talking to Bob Parker in English, and he had a screwdriver in the one free hand . . . and a set of procedures all over the desk in front of him, and it was just a phenomenal sort of thing that went on for about thirty minutes to an hour with intermittent oppor-tunities for communications. It was just a fantastic thing to watch. Bob took the camera down into the middeck, got into one of the bunks, taped one of the orbiter curtains over the air duct where there was a lot of light leak. They turned off all the lights on the tunnel and in the middeck. Bob took the camera apart, took some scissors and cut the film, pulled it off of the roll that was jammed . . . took the film out, stored that, brought the camera out, figured out what the problem was. Went back in and put the film back into the roll, put the cassette back in the camera, then they mounted the camera back on the window. Bob had the camera working, and he just said it [was a piece] of cake, so that Parker continues to do these phenomenal repair jobs, and this one was a really great one.

Jules Bergman of ABC News asked the mission leaders on 4 December to briefly summarize the flight to date. "How would you say it's going?" he enquired. Harry Cox was very upbeat about the results so far, describing it as "an outstanding success from both the science and national transportation system capability to support science," stressing that the MSFC folks would not be reveling in this great success without those at JSC providing a remarkable platform to place their prized Spacelab into orbit. In spite of the disagreement between JSC and MSFC on how payload specialists were selected and trained, they were working together as a close-knit team once in orbit.

During the mission, the backup payload specialists and a gaggle of scientists and principal investigators manned the POCC at JSC. Chappell shared that there were around twenty people sitting at consoles in the POCC, including the payload operations director (POD); the alternate POD; and data, consumables, and replanning personnel, "and then [there] were back rooms for each one of those individuals." Most experiments were followed in real time at the POCC via audio or video communications with the payload crew.

Lampton and Ockels remained very busy in the POCC during the mission. The authors asked Lampton if he was able to talk directly to the astronauts during the STS-9 mission. "Yes, my role was the science-team communications guy," he responded. "It is analogous to CAPCOM, who is central to the commander-pilot communications with the many ground services." But the alternates did more than just talk to and advise the payload crew; they routinely worked as a high-performance team and helped solve complicated problems experienced by the payload crew.

The scientists trapped on Mother Earth seemed no less excited about the mission than those circling the planet. Chappell described the atmosphere surrounding the scientific community regaling in the superfluity of data raining down on them from the heavens. As more and more data became available, the scientists began to paste it on the walls and doors, similar to what takes place "around Christmas time when all the kids on the block

4. Spacelab 1 backup payload specialists Michael Lampton and Wubbo Ockels pose for a preflight photograph. Ockels would go on to fly on the Spacelab D1 mission in late 1995. Unfortunately, Lampton never made it to orbit due to medical issues and the loss of *Challenger*. Courtesy NASA/Retro Space Images.

get new toys." They were "collaring each other with the new results, and within the Mission Control Room you find them quite frequently in there with their data showing it to each other. It's very clear that we are at an exciting stage of the mission."

MSFC managers were already claiming the mission a complete success by the ninth day, having already exceeded premission expectations. The crew was allowed some say in their activities for the bonus day in orbit. They performed a couple of vestibular experiments, the linear threshold and chloric experiment, fluid physics module work, and the master discrimination experiment; they also used the rest of the metric camera film, photographing the United States and Europe, before it was time to pack up and head for home.

Columbia and Spacelab returned to Earth on 8 December 1983, having orbited the planet 167 times and traveled 4.3 million miles. The orbiter weighed over 220,000 pounds when it kissed the dry lake bed runway 17 at Edwards Air Force Base, just a little under 27,000 pounds lighter than when it left KSC ten days earlier. The mission did not end for the payload crew once they were home; they would spend a little over a week in postflight tests in support of the extensive life sciences research that began even before *Columbia* left the ground.

Merbold recalled his first reaction to returning to Earth. "When I got up from the seat for the first time, I think there were two things; one was the weight. It felt like standing up [in] 2.5 g's." But even more startling was the feeling of rolls; he compared the experience to walking on a ship rolling in an ocean storm. "I was trying to get my foot, trying to make it walk. I was walking with a wide gait, a little bit unsteady and weaving back and forth." Everything began to return to normal by the next day, but when he arose the next morning, the heady sensation had returned.

The Europeans had finally dipped their toes into the puddle of human space exploration, with two spaceflights under their belts—one on a Soyuz spacecraft and another on *Columbia*. One of their own astronauts had flown into space and carried out complex scientific research in a laboratory that they had built, albeit at a mammoth cost of close to a billion dollars. MSFC was no longer just a supplier of hardware. They were acutely involved in the science being carried out on Spacelab 1, and they had helped select their own astronauts to fly on this historical mission. The teamwork between MSFC, JSC, and ESA had been exceptional, beginning what many believed would be a new era in scientific research in outer space.

Shapland and Rycroft assessed the success rate of the experiments on the Spacelab 1 mission; almost 75 percent of them were 100 percent successful! Just over 14 percent achieved at least three-quarters of their goals, and less than 5 percent were a bust. Lt. Gen. James Abrahamson, associate administrator in the Office of Space Flight at NASA Headquarters, had nothing but praise for the mission, exclaiming, "First of all, I assume that there is nobody that doesn't think that this was a fabulous mission." He believed the international cooperation "was just a fabulous success" and heralded "the tremendous start for the science and operational phase of this Spacelab program."

Abrahamson shared some comments from a former flight director who was instrumental in bringing home the *Apollo 13* astronauts in 1970 after an explosion damaged their spacecraft on the way to the moon. "Gerry Griffin, the center director at Johnson, offered a complimentary perspective. He said that the way the whole team was working out problems today made him think back to some of the real challenges that the Apollo program and the Mercury and Gemini had. Said it really made him feel good because he saw that that team was not only still there but more polished and more oiled than before, so, this whole thing is a very human program."

Gene Kranz, another flight director involved in the Apollo 13 mission, was initially skeptical of whether the scientists could operate the POCC in the same professional and efficient fashion as the MCC was operated. Harry Craft, in *The Spacelab Accomplishments Forum*, shared that Kranz confessed to him following the mission, "I expected any day to have to pick you guys up off the floor. You did a fantastic job, and you're a tribute to the agency."

Dr. Burton I. Edelson, NASA associate administrator in the Office of Space Science and Applications, put the debate from the 1970s regarding the roles of the mission and payload specialists into perspective: "We had two mission specialists, we had two payload specialists, each of those were PhDs, scientists. They were not merely mechanics or adjusters or manipulators in some minor degree. They were behaving as scientists, performing scientific experiments in space."

Chappell remarked on the differences between the payload and mission specialists: "So it was a little gray in there, but I think it worked out nicely." Spacelab had come of age and would host more scientific expeditions on future missions.

Byron Lichtenberg flew again in 1992 on STS-45, another Spacelab mission. Rick Chappell made it to the threshold of space, serving as the alternate payload specialist on that flight but unfortunately would never make

5. Backup payload specialist Rick Chappell smiles for the camera during a terminal countdown demonstration test for STS-45 at Kennedy Space Center. Astronaut Jim Newman sits in the orbiter side hatch. Courtesy Rick Chappell.

it to space himself. STS-45 pilot Brian Duffy shared with the authors in November 2016 that although Michael Lampton did not get to fly on that mission, he and Chappell made huge contributions working out of the POCC.

Ulf Merbold flew into space twice more, first on Spacelab mission STS-42 and then in 1994 with a Russian crew aboard *Soyuz TM-20*, which linked up with the orbiting *Mir* space station. He spent a total of forty-nine days, twenty-one hours, and thirty-eight minutes in space during his three missions. ESA kept its promise and assigned Ockels to a later Spacelab mission, flying his first and only time on STS-61A (Spacelab D1).

Michael Lampton was not as fortunate, for like Rick Chappell, he never flew into space. When asked how disappointed he was to not have flown after coming so close, he responded, "Not painful at all. I was promptly put back on to flight status for the upcoming EOM-1 mission [Earth Observation Mission] aboard *Atlantis*, where Byron and I were comanifested. But that mission was cancelled in the aftermath of the *Challenger* disaster. But that was okay; I got reassigned to STS-45 ATLAS-1, aboard *Atlantis*, which *did* fly in March 1992. Unfortunately, I was diagnosed with kidney cancer in 1991 and had to bail out. My backup Dirk Frimout flew in my place. The cancer was the sad thing." The eventual good news for Lampton was that his medical treatment was successful, and he later became heavily involved in the SNAP (Supernova Acceleration Probe) project, part of the ongoing Joint Dark Energy Mission (JDEM)—a cooperative venture between NASA and the U.S. Department of Energy.

4. Mission to Planet Earth

Okay, Houston. You suppose you could turn the Earth a little bit so
we can get a little bit more than just water?

Michael Collins

For the twenty-four men who traveled to the moon from 1968 to 1972,
there was never any doubt upon their return that they had indeed landed
on the right planet. Bobbing and rolling in the waves of an endless sea of
blue, these twentieth-century lunar explorers found themselves surrounded
by the most identifiable feature of Earth, which they had just marveled at
from deep space. It is a very watery planet. "It's good to be back, and what
better place to end our journey than on the ocean?" Collins recalled of that
triumphant 24 July 1969 day, in his book *Carrying the Fire*.

For anyone who had been out on the waters of the Pacific Ocean, the
color was a startling, deep royal blue. Collins remembered thinking how
nice it would have been to remove the visor of his biological isolation gar-
ment and splash some of the cool water on his face. But of most immediate concern was getting out of the moonship *Columbia* and aboard a more
seaworthy vessel, for he was not here to explore this gorgeous body of liquid water, just having explored the barren surface of the moon. For Collins,
this ocean merely represented his first welcomed contact with the planet
he had left behind eight days before—home.

More than fifteen years later, 218 miles above that same deep-blue Pacific
Ocean, a payload specialist from Sydney, Australia, floated across the flight
deck seats of the space shuttle *Challenger*. A civilian oceanographer now
employed by the U.S. Navy, Paul Scully-Power was placed aboard the thir-
teenth shuttle mission specifically to study the world's oceans from orbit.

Anchoring himself belly-up in the cockpit, in what he referred to as the "gondola mode," Scully-Power utilized the six wraparound windows to provide himself a panoramic view of the Earth below. Much as the dirigible passengers of the 1930s could view the ocean and clouds sliding slowly by as they crossed the Atlantic, Scully-Power used this vantage point to observe, among other things, the phenomenon of spiral eddies both large and small. Like the loops and whorls of fingerprints pressed down on the waters by some giant hand, these phenomena promised new insights into the mechanisms of Earth's watery surface and how it interacted with the planet's other, gaseous ocean—our atmosphere.

Unfortunately, on this first day in space after years of studying Earth's waters from both on and below their surface, Scully-Power was dismayed to find much of the blue planet covered in bright, white clouds. "One is really impressed by the amount of cloud cover that is around the world," he dictated into a small tape recorder. "It's not solid, it's broken up, but boy, there's a lot of cloud." But before long, his audiotape, notebook, and hundreds of frames of camera film would begin filling up with priceless observations taken through his trained eye.

For the first time in spaceflight history, a dedicated scientific observer was placed aboard a shuttle mission whose sole purpose was to observe Earth from space.

Bob Crippen was one busy astronaut in the early 1980s. After serving as pilot on the historic maiden space shuttle flight with John Young in April of 1981, he moved immediately to command of STS-7, whose crew included Dr. Sally Ride, America's first woman to fly in space. He was then assigned to command STS-41C under NASA's new numbering scheme, flying in April of 1984 and successfully repairing the Solar Max satellite in orbit. Before he even launched on STS-41C, Crip, as he was known around the Astronaut Office, was assigned as commander of the five-member team that would crew STS-41G that October.

Fortunately, in addition to pilot "Big Jon" McBride and mission specialists David Leestma and Dr. Kathryn Sullivan, his crew once again included Ride. Having flown with Crippen previously and knowing his preferences, Ride would fill the role of coordinating training activities until Crippen completed his STS-41C duties and could join the rest of his team in the simulators. "Our crew started training without a commander, and I was the only one on the crew who had flown before," Ride explained to NASA's Rebecca Wright. "During the first couple of months, I tried to give the rest of the crew some indication of the way that Crip liked to run a flight and run a crew."

When Crippen and Ride first flew together on STS-7, it marked the first time that the orbiter's remote manipulator system—its robotic arm—would release a small satellite and later retrieve it. The remote manipulator system, dubbed Canadarm, was developed and built by SPAR Aerospace of Canada, after NASA in 1974 sought out the expertise of the robotics firm. That collaboration led to a further proposal to fly Canadian astronauts aboard the shuttle as well. The only problem was that there were no Canadian astronauts.

So in early 1983, Ottawa's National Research Council (NRC) announced its first recruitment for potential astronauts to fly on the American shuttle. More than four thousand hopefuls filed applications in response to the announcement, and after exhaustive interviews and medical and psychological exams, the council selected twenty finalists. They were then brought to Ottawa for one final test—how suitable they were to handle the fame that was bound to come their way and their ability to communicate to their countrymen the importance of space to their future. One by one, the twenty candidates faced yet another selection panel, interacted with engineers at a satellite production facility, and were scrutinized in various social settings organized by the committee, all while being subjected to the constant attention of the press.

On 5 December 1983 the NRC held a press conference introducing the six astronaut selectees to their nation: Dr. Roberta Bondar, a neurobiologist and medical doctor; Dr. Steve MacLean, a laser physicist; Dr. Ken Money, a physiologist and air force fighter pilot; Dr. Robert Thirsk, an MIT engineering graduate and medical doctor; and Bjarni Tryggvason, an engineer, meteorologist, and pilot. But even before the final selections were announced, the press had zeroed in on Marc Garneau, a sharply uniformed naval officer with a doctorate in electrical engineering.

Garneau, born in Quebec City in February 1949, came from a military family. He had crossed the Atlantic Ocean twice as a young boy and became enamored with the powerful beauty of the high seas. His romantic

6. Canada's Marc Garneau on the flight deck of the space shuttle cabin trainer at the Johnson Space Center. Courtesy NASA/Retro Space Images.

memories of those voyages would compel him to join the navy, receiving his bachelor of science degree in engineering physics from the Royal Military College of Kingston in 1970. Earning his doctorate three years later, he was assigned as a combat systems engineer from 1974 to 1976.

Earning a reputation as an authority in naval communications and electronic warfare systems, he was also an adventurer; in late 1969 into early 1970, Garneau rekindled his love for the open ocean, sailing across the Atlantic in a fifty-nine-foot boat with twelve other crewmen.

The NRC and NASA had plans to fly two members of the Canadian astronaut group—one in late 1985 and one the following year. But in January 1984, just as President Reagan was committing the United States to building the space station, Donald Johnston, the Canadian minister of state for science and technology, made a surprise announcement that Canada would send their first astronaut aboard the October shuttle mission. NASA's *News Roundup* quoted administrator James Beggs as saying, "NASA's offer at this time is in recognition of Canada's contribution to the space shuttle—in particular the delivery of Canadarm, the robot arm now part of the space shuttle."

Garneau would learn of his selection just a month later. Recalling his reaction to being chosen as Canada's first astronaut over his five teammates, Garneau says he was "absolutely bowled over." As he would admit candidly to Canadian interviewer Peter Mansbridge in December 1985, he "didn't know all that much about [space]" prior to his selection as an astronaut, but the program would come to dominate the next two decades of his life.

Paul Scully-Power spent many of his college days at the University of Sydney on the beach working on his assignments and studying . . . and surfing. Born 28 May 1944, he had breezed through high school as a gifted athlete, being coached by his father in running and tennis. His time spent in the surf and the mesmerizing effect of watching the crashing waves on the beach somehow blended with his natural ability in understanding mathematics and physics. He found himself gravitating to the study of the oceans, writing his thesis on the applied mathematics of oceanography.

Following a devastating accident in the surf that left him with a badly broken ankle, Scully-Power would leave his championship-winning athletic days behind when he earned his degree in oceanography in 1965 and went on to pursue a graduate degree in education. In 1967 he joined the Royal Australian Navy (RAN) and helped to introduce a new oceanography unit at Rushcutters Bay in Sydney. As a young naval officer, he qualified as a compressed air diver in 1969.

Scully-Power would often give oceanographic lectures throughout the RAN and took on a professorial appearance with his signature short-cropped red beard, three-piece suits, and the requisite smoking pipe. In 1972 his reputation as the section head of the service's research laboratory earned Scully-Power an opportunity that would set him on an uncharted course to space, when he was designated by his command as an exchange scientist with the U.S. Navy.

Working at the Navy Underwater Systems Center (NUSC) at New London, Connecticut, he became reacquainted with his former colleague Dr. Robert Stevenson, who had pioneered the observation of oceanographic phenomena during the Gemini program of the 1960s. Stevenson had trained many of the astronaut crews since that time to look for and photograph ocean features, but given the multitude of tasks for which early crews were responsible, they could only devote so much time to the subject.

Working with Stevenson, Scully-Power became increasingly involved in space-borne remote sensing projects and the manned spaceflight program. During *Skylab*, Scully-Power would serve as part of the Earth-observations support team at Houston. "Skylab 4 provided the first real time demonstration that the observations and photographs of the ocean by the astronauts were indeed representative of the real ocean dynamics," Scully-Power later wrote.

The RAN granted Scully-Power an extension on his exchange duty in 1973, and given his desire to continue space-based orbital observations with NASA, he began to consider staying in the United States permanently. With twenty-three scientific cruises at sea under his belt, the U.S. Navy wanted to keep the Australian, too, and offered Scully-Power a permanent position with NUSC. While it was a difficult decision, he chose to immigrate to America with his young family and work as a civilian oceanographer for the U.S. Navy, continuing his advisory role with NASA.

Scully-Power spent several days during the joint U.S. and Soviet Union Apollo-Soyuz docking mission aboard the HMAS *Bombard* research vessel in July 1975. Using specialized equipment, he and the crew located an ocean eddy about one hundred miles southeast of Sydney that was calculated to be seventy miles in diameter. The *Bombard* radioed their finding to mission control in Houston, and over the next five orbits, the astronauts were able to photograph the area using a 3D stereoscopic camera from space. Ocean eddies at that time were thought to be relatively small, isolated features, yet understanding them showed promise for benefitting the fishing industry—the eddy's warmer average temperature was very attractive to large ocean fish like tuna.

One of the greatest results of the Apollo-Soyuz observations was the first photography of solitons, by astronaut Vance Brand. Solitons are large-scale subsurface waves that move in packs of as many as ten and appear from space as long parallel bands of rough water but can reach as high as one hundred meters in depth. Ever since Brand's observation of these ocean features, they have been ubiquitously referred to as V-Brand waves around the Astronaut Office.

By 1978 Scully-Power was invited with Stevenson to JSC to brief new astronauts on oceanography for the upcoming shuttle missions. He was earning himself a reputation with the astronauts and was often present in mission control during the flights. Stevenson had been pressing for a dedicated oceanographic observer to be placed aboard a shuttle flight for some time, and following STS-2, astronaut Richard Truly went to George Abbey himself and suggested that either Stevenson or Scully-Power be placed aboard STS-8, which Truly was to command.

NASA and the U.S. Navy undertook some informal discussions at that time to fly the two oceanographers on upcoming back-to-back missions. However, with the increasingly common occurrences of SAS, or space sickness, with early shuttle astronauts, NASA decided to assign medical doctors Norm Thagard and Bill Thornton on STS-7 and STS-8, respectively. But in May 1984 the mission then designated as STS-17 that was to be flown on *Columbia* was shifted to the orbiter *Challenger*. The switch to *Challenger*, configured with more seats than its older sibling *Columbia*, opened the possibility for one of the oceanographers to fly that coming fall. The one issue of concern, though, was that NASA had never flown a seven-member crew, and with Garneau already assigned to the flight, the addition of another payload specialist would be an experiment in itself.

It was an ideal mission for an oceanographer—the first that was to go to a highly inclined fifty-seven-degree orbit, allowing Earth observations over a much larger swathe of the planet than ever before. In addition to the Earth Radiation Budget Satellite (ERBS), which was to be deployed on the first day of the mission, *Challenger* would also carry a larger, more advanced shuttle imaging radar payload (SIR-B) than its predecessor on STS-2. With the addition of a tilting mechanism, the radar could map surface and subsurface features—day or night and regardless of cloud cover—with incredible resolution.

Leestma and Sullivan were to conduct a space walk late in the mission to test on-orbit satellite refueling techniques utilizing hydrazine. Fuel is the most life-limiting consumable of most satellites, and it was hoped that future shuttle missions might be able to prolong their usefulness by replenishing the vital yet volatile fuel. The test apparatus mounted in the payload bay was an exact reproduction of a Landsat fueling panel, providing an accurate assessment of the viability of the procedure. "Hydrazine is very much like water," explained Leestma, "but it's got a lot of different properties, one of which is that it blows up if it's not handled right."

With Bob Stevenson's wife terminally ill, he elected to take himself out of contention for the flight, and so on 1 June 1984 Scully-Power was informed by George Abbey that he was to fly aboard STS-41G, with training to begin in Houston in just two weeks. The news swept across his home country, and as with Canada, Australia would claim rights as a spacefaring nation in celebrating its first native-born to travel into orbit.

Dr. Kathryn Sullivan, who was to be the first American woman to conduct a space walk during the STS-41G mission, noted years later to NASA historian Jennifer Ross-Nazzal that while the scientific community lobbied hard to fly payload specialists in the early 1980s, one of the most influential people at NASA, Abbey, was not too keen on the idea: "George, in particular, at that point was just really trying to bar the door against that. You can see a trend in several of the '83, '84, '85 flights. 'Match Jeff [Jeffrey A.] Hoffman up with an astronomy payload, match Kathy Sullivan off with a geology payload, and demonstrate the argument that we've hired the mission specialist corps to be able to bridge that for you, so your guy doesn't get to go.'"

With the prime crew already assigned and Crippen now integrating himself into training sessions following his return from 41C, all seemed to be set in stone, until the orbiter swap happened and Scully-Power was added. In Sullivan's mind, this change upset the balance of the crew due to the fact that several of the payload specialists responsibilities—Garneau's medical experiments and Scully-Power's oceanographic observations—were added only when they came along. This would require cross-training on the part of the NASA crew members to back up the payload specialists, should they not be able to function well once in orbit.

Just when they were nearing the end of a long, arduous training cycle, Sullivan recalls, "Here's two new guys, a list of stuff that's got to get done, and nothing is taken off the rest of the crew obligation list." The payload specialists also came along at a time when the science-oriented mission specialists were still trying to solidify their own reputation as key players within the astronaut corps and the scientific community at large. Having two "outsiders" added to a crew to perform tasks the mission specialists felt should be their responsibility was not an ideal situation for them. "It was disruptive. It was uncomfortable," Sullivan remembers.

Crippen took the news that he would be taking on two additional crew members in stride. A consummate professional and experienced commander, he accepted what the payload specialists were on board to do and set out to establish a clear set of rules for how they would operate in orbit. "Marc was Canadian Navy and military, so I had no problem with Marc coming on board. He had his own set of experiments," Crippen explained to NASA's Rebecca Wright. "Then we added Paul. We'd worked with Paul a lot before on doing Earth observations, or ocean observations—he was a little bit of a loose cannon, and I knew that about him."

While it was easy for Crippen to just have Garneau stay below in the middeck to conduct his experiments, Scully-Power needed the panoramic view of the flight deck windows to perform his observations. "So we had to pick out periods of time where that was going to be acceptable, and it ended up working out just fine," Crip recalled. The choreography of having seven crew members aboard a ship without the additional room of a Spacelab module was to become a well-rehearsed part of the crew's training, but it paid off handsomely once the mission was underway.

As the seven began training, socializing, and eventually bonding, all the early concerns were left behind as they focused singularly on the mission ahead. "Marc Garneau, early on, put it best of all. He was just, as Marc is, clear and candid but gracious about it," remembers Sullivan. "He could imagine if he were sitting in our seats (the professional astronauts), it would be upsetting and disconcerting, and that he'd be annoyed at least to have to deal with this disruption. He couldn't change any of that, he hadn't created it, and he couldn't make it go away." Garneau would tell his crewmates, "I don't know what else I can say other than I've got things to do for my country, too, and that's what I'm going to try to do."

Scully-Power had never seen Earth from so high up. Sealed tight in a bright-orange full-pressure suit and closed-helmet visor, he glanced out the window and could take in a remarkable stretch of the West Coast and far out into the Pacific Ocean. But he was not yet in space. Ten miles above California's Edwards Air Force Base, he was undertaking a training evolution that he alone had requested—a flight in NASA's B-57 to an altitude of sixty thousand feet.

The flight allowed Scully-Power to work with his suite of photographic equipment from a perspective that closely represented what he might see from orbit. Aside from the practice, though, he would later write, "It brought home to me at least that we're operating in a very alien environment, and that's a message we as [payload specialists] could very easily lose, because the orbiter is a shirt-sleeve environment." Much like the strict regimen of working with his equipment and crewmates beneath the oceans as a navy diver, Scully-Power would come away from the flight recognizing that "we have to be very careful and very safety conscious; otherwise, one small mistake could create problems for everyone."

He and Garneau would spend many hours in the air during their training. Supersonic, high-g flights in NASA's sleek T-38s would be followed by zero-g flights aboard the KC-135. Scully-Power would also take training hops with Jon McBride aboard the Shuttle Training Aircraft (STA), simulating the orbiter's steep, high-speed approach to landing, on occasion with veteran astronaut John Young acting as McBride's instructor. At some point, the Australian native would acquire a nickname during his run-up to the STS-41G mission. NASA test pilot Joe Algranti had noted that Scully-Power's initials—PSP—were the same as the abbreviation for "pierced steel planking," an innovative temporary-runway material used on unimproved strips during World War II. The name stuck, and before long many of Scully-Power's flight suit name tags were stamped simply with "PSP."

Scully-Power would coordinate his in-flight observations using an exhaustively compiled plan from the Navy Space Oceanography Committee. The areas of highest interest would be covered not just by his direct visual and photographic studies but by additional infrared and color sensors aboard the NOAA-7 satellite, as well as the SIR-B radar in *Challenger*'s payload bay. The major features he would be looking for were the solitons observed during Apollo-Soyuz, oceanic spiral eddies, coastal fronts, and island wakes. The entire observation plan was organized into a list that denoted target, mission elapsed time (MET) it was to be viewed, orbit number, and proper camera settings for photography.

The key to being able to see and photograph many of the ocean features was sunglint—the sharp reflection of the sun's glare on the surface of the waters. Having the sun directly overhead in relation to the orbiter did him no good; as the shuttle raced around the globe and the sun transited overhead, he would seek out the lower sun angles that would briefly reveal—somewhat like a desert mirage—the dynamic structures he was tasked with studying.

7. Marc Garneau (*left*) and Paul Scully-Power, both naval officers, shared a love of the oceans that would be studied from orbit during sts-41g. Courtesy nasa/Retro Space Images.

Garneau was to be responsible for a suite of medical and engineering experiments known collectively as canex. The Space Vision System was an experimental device used in conjunction with the Canadarm to provide more precise guidance for approach, capture, and berthing of satellites. The medical experiments would relegate Garneau to the middeck for much of the flight, with Scully-Power assisting during night passes or when flight deck activities precluded him conducting observations.

Scully-Power did have one final hurdle to overcome prior to flying to space—nasa wanted him to shave his trademark red beard. No astronaut had ever flown with a beard, and their rationale was that it would interfere with the donning of his helmet and possibly compromise the airtight face seal. PSP had been an accomplished diver for most of his life, was quite accustomed to getting bulky helmets over his head, and had no trouble with

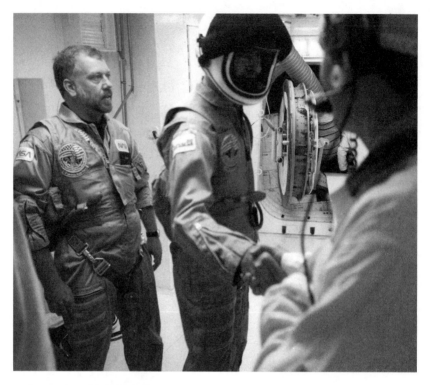

8. Garneau (*center*) bids farewell to a closeout crew member before boarding *Challenger* as Scully-Power looks on. Courtesy NASA/Retro Space Images.

it in the full-pressure suit he wore on the high-altitude WB-57 missions. Once he proved to NASA managers that it was a nonissue, they relented, paving the way for another first for the space program.

On 5 October 1984 *Challenger* lit up the predawn sky as it rolled around to an unprecedented direction up the eastern coastline and was quickly swallowed up by a low-altitude shelf of clouds. Punching out from the top of the overcast into the twilight above, the shuttle arced out over the Atlantic and climbed quickly into the brightening sky. Commander Crippen told his crewmates that *Challenger* would give them "the ride of your life," but immediately upon getting into orbit, Scully-Power seemed less than impressed.

"The launch was very smooth," he dictated into his tape recorder. "I think the biggest vibration was with the gimbaling of the nozzles of the three main engines prior to flight." Scully-Power was not prone to excitement or anxiety by nature, and the dynamic ascent that many others would describe with words like "shocking" or "frightening" would leave him somewhat underwhelmed. "I think the hardest thing on launch was the 3 g's acceleration," he reported. "It wasn't hard in itself; it was just the fact that you had to hold this three-g configuration for quite some minutes."

Attending to their first order of business, the environment-monitoring satellite was soon lifted from its moorings in the payload bay by Ride and held high above the orbiter at the end of the remote manipulator system. Problems began almost immediately when the crew commanded the two large solar panels to deploy, and they remained firmly locked in their stowed position. Ground controllers suspected that either the latches or hinges had frozen, so with the deployment delayed for several orbits, they had Crippen and McBride flip the orbiter to face the satellite toward the sun to warm the satellite.

The flight deck was a crowded, busy place with five NASA astronauts, some still in their launch and entry coveralls; the large-format IMAX camera; and now Scully-Power and Garneau. While the ERBS satellite baked in the sunlight, Crippen turned on a television camera to show the ground how the cabin looked with the full complement of crew members and gear floating throughout. "We just wanted to prove that we really can fit seven people in here," he radioed down. Even then, Scully-Power was seen taking his first opportunity to evaluate the view from the cockpit windows.

Seven hours into the mission, Scully-Power was still frustrated by his inability to see what he had come to space to study. "We have just finished a pass down the entire Atlantic, both north and south," he reported. "There was an extreme amount of cloud. There were patches of clear, but mostly you'd have to say the whole Atlantic was scattered cloud." While he was able to view some surface features with gyrostabilized binoculars, the clouds hid the big-picture perspective he was looking for.

Scully-Power had a full suite of cameras—35 mm Nikons, 70 mm Hasselblads, and a large-format Aero-Linhoff—at his disposal, but up to this point there wasn't much for him to photograph. Two orbits later, the satellite had yet to be deployed, and Scully-Power was at the side hatch window still attempting to get his research started. The ERBS was filling the viewport, though; "So close it almost seems to be tucked under the port radiator, and we have the earth below at an unusual attitude," he recorded as *Challenger* slipped into another sunset.

9. Scully-Power takes a break from his oceanographic observations to assist Garneau with his CANEX experiments in the middeck of *Challenger*. Courtesy NASA/Retro Space Images.

Warming the satellite worked, as they suspected, and the ERBS solar panels were finally deployed, revealing the golden body of a blue-winged butterfly being held at the end of the shuttle's arm. Ride gently released the robotic hand's grasp on the satellite, and Crippen pulsed the smaller vernier thrusters to begin separating the spacecraft from it. The IMAX camera captured dramatic views of the deployment that would later captivate audiences in the movie *The Dream Is Alive*.

By the second day of the mission, Marc Garneau was well into the ten experiments sponsored by the NRC of Canada. OGLOW was a study of the "orbiter glow" phenomenon—a little understood faint red glow that emanated from the shuttle's surfaces as it traversed through the extremely thin upper atmosphere. Garneau used a series of filters and an image intensifier in an effort to photograph the glow at the various altitudes at which the mission would operate.

His medical experiments focused on SAS, which included vision tests, sensory function in limbs, various vestibular illusions, and even taste. As

Crippen had planned, when the shuttle was on the dark side of its ninety-minute orbit of Earth, Scully-Power would suspend his observations and assist Garneau in the middeck as a test subject for many of the experiments. The two were also tasked by Crippen to do the majority of the meal preparations for the crew and to take care of various housekeeping duties such as filter cleaning and changing out the air-scrubbing lithium hydroxide canisters.

Scully-Power was finally able to see the surface waters, as he excitedly dictated his notes. "Just came over the Mediterranean with Italy in the background, shooting south—superb spirals and fronts in the central Mediterranean," he recorded. "Tremendous ship wake in the Gulf with just incredible spirals and contorted structure. Spectacular spiral eddies throughout this whole region, just spectacular!" As he looked down at the great sea, the sun's glint revealed a vast, complex waterscape of the huge whirlpools, with shocking clarity.

And at last just an hour into the second flight day, he saw for himself from orbit the solitons on the open waters of the Red Sea. He counted off ten waves and noted, "The normal soliton packet with two crests right close together . . . definitely a double-humped soliton for each wavelength. As we've come down the Red Sea, the specular point [sun reflection] has kept on tracking straight down the middle of it; just one spectacular pass."

Crippen and McBride lowered *Challenger*'s altitude from the high perch required to deploy the ERBS satellite to 170 miles, allowing a better vantage point for the SIR-B radar, the large-format camera mounted in the payload bay, and for Scully-Power's study of the oceans. The following day, they would lower it farther to 140 miles.

He immediately found that his "gondola position" in the forward cockpit was ideal because he could look out ahead, in the direction of travel, and see what was coming. He preferred the orbiter flying nose first but found the tail-leading attitude worked well too. The thirty-five-foot wide SIR-B radar antenna was deployed in *Challenger*'s payload bay in three large leaves that would fold on top of one another when stowed. The radar swept over a wide band of Earth below and recorded data that would later be transmitted to the ground.

Unfortunately, the K_u-band antenna that handled all the orbiter's high-speed data suffered a failure that left it spinning wildly on its motorized gimbal mounts at the forward right corner of the cargo hold. Mission control sent up instructions to disable the steering commands, but with the antenna now locked in position, the crew would have to point the entire ship at the TDRS high overhead. Rather than regular science return to the ground, investigators would have to resort to recording much of the data on board for later analysis.

Scully-Power now found that his carefully plotted observation plan was all but useless. He did the best he could viewing from the windows he had available, but with the payload bay facing up toward space for long periods to communicate with the TDRS, it was a challenge to photograph his scheduled targets. But still the next several days were like a dream to the oceanographer, with every orbit of the planet bringing fascinating new images and discoveries.

For hundreds of miles, seemingly arranged connected spiral eddies stretched out in lines like the swirling clouds of Jupiter. Scully-Power photographed the Black Sea, the Strait of Hormuz, and the Gulf of Oman and spotted burning oil wells in the Persian Gulf spewing black smoke high into the atmosphere. Immense dust storms that blotted out the tan deserts swept sand far out into the neighboring seas. The wakes of ocean-traversing cargo ships trailed behind them for over one hundred miles, all just momentarily highlighted as the sun flashed across the shiny blue surface below.

In the middle of the Sahara Desert, the crew spotted on several occasions an immense impact crater with multiple concentric rings within it. The Aorounga crater of Chad, spanning twelve miles and formed more than 345 million years ago, is one of three craters formed when a huge asteroid broke up and slammed into the barren landscape. But another surface feature would fool even this crew of highly educated scientists. "Dave Leestma and I saw in southern Sumatra what looked like a spectacular lava flow, approximately thirty-five miles in diameter," Scully-Power noted. "You could even see the rivers of lava as a spiderweb throughout the flowing area." Several days later, as they came up on the same site and eagerly pressed their noses to the windows to see it again, they came to realize it wasn't a volcano at all but the lights of Singapore.

On the sixth day of the mission, Leestma and Sullivan exited the air lock into the payload bay to begin their experimental work with the orbital refueling system. While television stations followed the historic first EVA for one of America's female astronauts, Scully-Power took advantage of the now far roomier cabin to continue his observations. "We're just right in the middle of the EVA, but coming over the Gulf of Mexico and looking south into the sunglint," he reported. In between the scattered puffball cumulus clouds, he could pick out the Gulf Loop Current in the shimmering reflected sunlight.

Sailing past the emerald islands of the Bahamas and out into the deep southern Atlantic Ocean at the lowest altitude of the mission, Scully-Power felt as if he could almost touch the surface of the waters himself. Reaching the extreme southern point of their fifty-seven-degree orbit and approaching the terminator between South America and Southern Africa, he caught sight of fine white threads on the deep-blue waters below. "It's the first time I've seen ice in the water," he recorded. "It's long, curly streamers of ice, quite similar to the ice photographed by John Young on STS-9."

After Leestma and Sullivan completed their simulated on-orbit refueling experiment, they were tasked with some unplanned activities to address several in-flight anomalies that had cropped up. Sullivan peeked in between the folded panels of the SIR-B to see what might be causing them to not latch firmly in the stowed position. It appeared that the thermal blankets of the payload had puffed out somewhat, preventing them from folding completely. Later in the mission, Sally Ride would use the Canadarm to gently press the panels down for a firm latch. The pair also stowed the dish-like K_u-band antenna at the front of the bay in a position safe for the eventual closing of the payload bay doors for landing.

Of great personal interest to the Australian native was the opportunity to view his home country from orbit, but with the complex interaction of *Challenger*'s orbit and the crew's timeline, it seemed that every pass over the continent would occur during their scheduled sleep period. So the evening following the EVA, Scully-Power defied Crippen's desire to have everyone sleep at the same time and silently floated up to the flight deck windows to observe his home from space.

Flying high over the Great Barrier Reef and the "turquoise gems" of Curtis and Fraser Islands, he couldn't see any ocean dynamics but was still transfixed. Crossing through the heart of Australia, he found that the country looked "strikingly different from any other country from space." Yellow-orange deserts and reddish-brown central highlands yielded to green fertile coastal areas as *Challenger* left the continent behind over Spencer's Gulf and Kangaroo Island.

Having spent most of the night halves of the orbits on the middeck with Garneau, Scully-Power also took the opportunity to enjoy the stars and the twinkling city lights in the darkness below. To his surprise, he found that the intricate patterns within the oceans revealed themselves in the blue-white light of the moon almost as well as in the sun. "Moon glitter does work," he noted. "I saw a front in the ocean in moon glitter."

On the day that the crew was to return to Earth, the middeck was a bee-hive of activity. Garneau took a few precious moments to enjoy his last taste of zero gravity, unbagging a fresh carrot and spinning it in front of his face before snatching it up in his mouth from midair. He too would spend some time admiring the beauty of the planet after spending so much of the mission in the virtually windowless room, working on his experiments.

Scully-Power floated in the middle of the deck, somersaulting in the weightlessness he would not likely ever experience again. "I was not amused at the time because he was having a ball hovering himself out in the middle of the middeck and doing flips and tumbles, which is terribly fun to do, but he was right in the middle of everywhere I needed to be," recalled Sullivan. "He seemed totally unaware of the fact that there actually were things to do that day." Just when she had about enough of the payload specialist's antics, one of *Challenger*'s big 870-pound thrusters fired and shook the orbiter with a thunderous cannon blast: "Paul went rigid in the middle of middeck, and his eyes were eighteen inches diameter. He thought the vehicle was coming apart, and he shouted out, 'What the hell was that?' It was probably between clenched teeth that I said something like, 'It's a primary thruster, Paul. We're going home today.'"

Sullivan and Leestma helped the payload specialists strap into their seats with their harnesses and helmets in place for reentry. Leestma then joined Crippen, McBride, and Ride on the flight deck for the trip home. *Challenger* would return from her highly inclined orbit on a first-ever ground track across the central and eastern United States. After firing the orbiter's maneuvering engines and dipping into the atmosphere, Crippen and McBride guided the ship on its first "roll reversal" to bleed off speed at 174,000 feet over Knoxville, Tennessee, still going eleven times the speed of sound.

Minutes later, they rolled again, cutting through the air in a steep-banked turn over the Georgia-Florida state line. "When I came over Jacksonville, Florida, doing Mach 4, I could see the runway, and I was still about one hundred miles away," recalled Crippen. At twenty-nine thousand feet, as *Challenger* turned to line up for only the second landing on the KSC runway, its signature double-thunderclap sonic boom rippled across the Florida marshland.

Crippen, who had twice been denied a KSC landing due to the launch site's unpredictable weather, finally touched down on the fifteen-thousand-foot cape runway. Calling "Wheels stop" when the orbiter came to rest on the centerline, he immediately took some ribbing from CAPCOM Dick Richards: "*Challenger* Houston, we copy that Crip and you outfoxed us again—you landed at KSC, but the beer has been sent to Edwards!"

In his typical understated manner, Scully-Power explained that the entry was "far more benign than I expected." As a veteran of so many sea voyages, he found the process of readapting to Earth's gravity similar to returning to port after weeks or months of the human body being on a rolling, unstable surface. "You step ashore and the dock seems to be oscillating a little bit. It wasn't unpleasant," he later reported. "I've been through that set of experiences before, and after half an hour, it was fine."

For Australia's first claimed space explorer, the little more than eight days spent aboard *Challenger* studying the oceans of the planet as never before would be his only trip to orbit. Canada's Garneau, however, had even bigger spacefaring plans ahead.

Canada's Steve MacLean was slated to be his country's second man in space when he launched aboard STS-71F in 1987. This flight too was canceled in the wake of the *Challenger* accident, and he did not get his first opportunity to fly until 1992, as a payload specialist aboard STS-52. Roberta Bondar would fly aboard the Spacelab-based International Microgravity Laboratory–1 mission in January of that year.

With the exception of Ken Money, all of the original Canadian astronaut group would go on to fly one or more spaceflights. MacLean was assigned to NASA for mission specialist training in 1996, as was Thirsk in 1998. Both would fly missions to the International Space Station (ISS), and Thirsk would spend 188 days aboard the orbiting complex as a member of the Expedition 20–21 crew.

The Canadian Space Agency (csa) was created through an act of Parliament in March 1989, and Garneau retired from the navy that same year. He would join the ranks of nasa's mission specialist corps in August 1992, and given his country's contribution to the space shuttle program, he was assigned to the Robotics Integration Team for the Astronaut Office, flying in space two more times. Aboard sts-77 in 1996, Garneau took great pride in operating the Canadarm to deploy and later retrieve an experimental satellite. Four years later aboard sts-97, his crew would pay a visit to the first iss long-duration residents, and Garneau would again fly the arm to remove a huge station truss segment from *Endeavour*'s payload bay and attach it to the growing space complex.

After logging over 677 hours in space, Garneau was appointed as executive vice president of the csa in February 2001 and became its president later that November. After leading his country's space agency for four years, he left behind his spaceflight career, which had lasted over two decades, to enter national politics. Following an unsuccessful bid in 2006, he was elected as a member of Parliament for Westmount-Ville-Marie in October 2008 and was reelected in 2011 and 2015. In November 2015 Garneau was appointed as the minister of transport, where he continues to serve today, overseeing the safety of Canada's aviation, rail, shipping, and road transportation infrastructures. Among his many awards, honorary degrees, and military decorations, Garneau was given Canada's highest civilian honor, the Companion of the Order of Canada, in 2003.

All throughout his leadership of the csa and in public service, Garneau has never forgotten his days spent seeing the fragility of Planet Earth from space and the impact it had on his global perspective. "The change is profound," he told Canadian journalist Marie-Eve Larivee. "I see life and our planet differently." As a result, he acknowledges the potential impact humanity has on its only home and has always kept the environment at the forefront of his political goals.

Scully-Power held strong opinions about his role as a dedicated observer aboard a space shuttle mission. He found that the nasa crews were so busy over the course of weeklong flights that Earth observations and photography could only be accomplished as time allowed. In his mind, having someone present who specialized in a particular field produced far greater scientific return. "The advantages gained by having someone who has the time to focus on a particular aspect (in this case oceanography) throughout the flight cannot be underestimated," he advised following the mission.

Yet with the lone exception of an army officer who would investigate tactical observations aboard STS-44 in 1991, NASA never again flew a payload specialist with the sole purpose of observing the planet in any specific scientific field. Following the loss of the orbiter Scully-Power flew on, Bob Stevenson would never get his chance to pursue for himself the studies he had trained so many others to perform.

During the course of his mission, nearly 1,700 Earth-observation photographs were taken by the crew, and Scully-Power later reported that of those, "approximately 25 percent showed significant ocean dynamics." Adding to these unprecedented observations was a treasure trove of visible and infrared large-format-camera photos; SIR-B imagery; and coordinated Landsat, ship, and aircraft observations from the immediate areas studied. For the seasoned oceanographer and veteran of many surface research voyages, STS-41G was the opportunity of a lifetime to see the big picture he had always been denied.

"Far and away the most impressive discovery resulting from this flight is the realization that the submesoscale ocean (length scales less than one hundred kilometers) is far more complex dynamically than ever imagined in even the least conservative estimates," he concluded. Directly observing the small spiral eddies of the oceans connected for hundreds of miles, he was able to confirm something that "all the oceanographic research ships in the world" couldn't piece together. And in the years following his observations, the scientific community would at last begin to accept the complex interaction of the oceans' currents with the ocean of air above.

After his single trip to space, Scully-Power never ended his quest to learn more and to advance subjects that fired his imagination. In 1987 he was awarded the International Laureate of the Albatross, which is widely known as the "Nobel Prize" of oceanography, and earned his doctorate from Sydney University in 1990 for his thesis, "Remote Sensing of the Ocean."

Today his trademark red beard has faded to gray, but his eyes still twinkle in anticipation of what might be over the next horizon. Dr. Scully-Power, considered an unequaled expert in remote sensing in all its various forms, has traveled the world pursuing an eclectic career in marine science, aerospace, defense and national security, and education. He has headed numerous public and private advisory boards across the globe.

After twenty years in America, he returned to his home country, serving as chairman of the Australian Civil Aviation Safety Authority and later as the chancellor of Bond University in Queensland. His awards and accolades are too numerous to count, and he continues to be a very public figure in Australia. Among his many projects, he has been involved in designing an innovative lifesaving system utilizing Unmanned Aerial Vehicles (UAV) carrying a pod that contains a life buoy and shark shield that can be dropped into the ocean to assist swimmers. "If a lifeguard sees someone in an emergency, we can fly one of these drones out there, we can talk to them, drop them a life-support package," he said. The UAV could also be used to spot sharks swimming dangerously close to swimmers at surf beaches.

He has also traveled to Africa, where he led a team in developing an extremely efficient water-filtering system utilizing nanotechnology, in an effort to end water-borne diseases in Africa's underdeveloped countries. For his accomplishments in this field, he was conferred into knighthood in early 2014, adding one more to his impressive list of titles, although he downplays that a bit when asked. In fact, he has retained the old nickname given to him while training with NASA's astronauts and most often signs his correspondence simply "PSP."

He also follows his own personal mission to "give something back" to the youth of Australia, speaking to schoolchildren and inspiring them to fulfill their dreams. He regularly shares with both young and old his outlook on life: "When you come to a fork in the road, take it." And for Dr. Paul Scully-Power another fork may come if he secures enough funds to undertake his next great adventure—locating the lost city of Atlantis. Given his motivation, drive, and wealth of experience on, under, and far above Earth's oceans as the first oceanographer in space, if anyone could find it, it might be he.

5. Time to Specialize

Rather than containing experiments covering a broad range of
disciplines as in Spacelab 1, the Spacelab 3 payload
would focus on microgravity.

Douglas Lord, *Spacelab*

The Spacelab module flown on STS-9 had been gutted of its experimentation hardware and reconfigured for a whole new set of specialized experiments to be flown on the second Spacelab venture—Spacelab 3. As it happened, Spacelab 3 flew before the Spacelab 2 mission, due to delays in a critical piece of hardware required for the Spacelab 2 flight—the Instrument Pointing System.

Spacelab 1 had verified the pressurized module's capability as a research platform, and it was now deemed operational. The specialized investigations in materials science and fluid dynamics carried aboard Spacelab 3 on shuttle mission STS-51B required a stable microgravity environment, which would command the pilots to coax the orbiter into an orientation, relative to Earth, entirely different from that of previous shuttle flights. The purpose of materials science is to investigate the properties and characteristics of various materials, including plastics, metals, and ceramics. The science of fluid dynamics addresses the movement of liquids and gases. Improved materials and a better understanding of how fluids and gases interact held tremendous opportunity for a wide range of potential engineering advancements in technology.

Fifteen experiments in five scientific disciplines—materials science, fluid dynamics, life sciences, astrophysics, and atmospheric science—were the backbone of the Spacelab 3 mission to be carried out in the long Spacelab module and a multipurpose experiment support structure (MPESS), a lightweight carrier replacing the pallets developed for experiments employed on Spacelab 1 that required direct exposure to space. The MPESS cradled two atmospheric and astronomical observations experiments and two small, self-contained scientific experiments known in NASA parlance as "getaway specials," also called "tagalongs" by a retired NASA engineer.

Spacelab 3 was designed to specialize in far fewer experiments than those conducted on Spacelab 1, which covered a wide variety of scientific disciplines. Although this mission focused on five primary areas of investigation, the big hitters were in fluid dynamics and materials science. An MSFC paper, "Spacelab 3: Research in Microgravity" by George Fichtl et al., reported that NASA petitioned research ideas through several channels, including "NASA Announcements of Opportunity that solicited research ideas from the worldwide scientific communities and agreements with foreign governments." Twelve of the fifteen investigations came from the United States; two, from France; and one, from India. Once the experiments had been selected, the IWG—all the principal investigators—ensured that adequate resources were allocated for each experiment and that payload specialists were selected.

The STS-51B flight crew was made up of commander Bob Overmyer (the pilot on STS-5) and pilot Fred Gregory, who was making the first of his three eventual flights, while the payload specialist crew consisted of Dr. Taylor Gun-Jin Wang and Dr. Lodewijk van den Berg. Mission specialists Don Lind, Norm Thagard, and William Thornton made up the rest of the seven-person crew. Lind held a PhD in high-energy nuclear physics, while Thagard and Thornton were both physicians. Both Thornton and Thagard had flown once, but Lind was making his only foray into space. Overmyer, Lind, Thornton, and Wang made up the gold team, while Gregory, Thagard, and van den Berg comprised the silver team.

Burton I. Edelson, NASA associate administrator for space science and applications, complimented the IWG in a 9 June 1983 memorandum to Spacelab 3 mission scientist Dr. George Fichtl from MSFC for "soliciting and selecting Payload Specialists for Spacelab 3." Fichtl had recommended Wang and van den Berg along with Mary Helen Johnston and Eugene Trinh as the four final candidates three days earlier. Edelson advised that the designation of prime and backup crew members not be made until after at least six months of training so that all mission aspects could be considered when the final recommendation was made to him.

The payload specialists for Spacelab 3 were chosen for their specialized knowledge in materials science and fluid mechanics—the primary scientific objectives of this mission. Wang was an expert in fluid mechanics, whereas van den Berg was an authority in materials science. Born 16 June 1940 in Shanghai, China, Wang was the first person of Chinese ethnicity to fly into space. His family moved to Taiwan in 1952 but later moved to Hong Kong and eventually to the United States, where he received his bachelor of science and master of science degrees from the University of California, Los Angeles, in 1967 and 1968. He was awarded his PhD in 1971 from the same institute, in low-temperature superfluid physics and solid-state physics, and subsequently joined NASA's Jet Propulsion Laboratory (JPL) in 1972 as a senior scientist. He became an American citizen in 1975. Because of his academic background, JPL assigned Wang the task of researching containerless processing science and technology. He attracted NASA's attention after publishing a paper on the dynamic behavior of rotating spheroids in zero gravity. He continued his research in ground-based laboratories and in JSC's KC-135 zero-g flights, as well as with experiments loaded onto specialized rockets. It was this work that defined the parameters and procedures of the Drop Dynamics Module (DDM), a key investigation on Spacelab 3, which led to his selection as a payload specialist. Wang invented the DDM acoustic levitation and manipulation chamber, which allows an object or fluid to be suspended in air using intense sound waves. Unfortunately, in Earth's gravity the intense acoustic energy required to levitate the fluid perturbed the specimen, which compromised the experimental data obtained from Earth investigations. Wang was the principal investigator for the DDM, but during the time he was developing this innovative technology, he never considered that he would be the one to operate the DDM in space. Nonetheless, when NASA began to consider crew selection for Spacelab 3 in 1982, he decided to submit his name for consideration, although he wasn't very confident that he would be selected.

Dr. Eugene Huu Chau Trinh, Wang's alternate, was also a fluid mechanics specialist from JPL. Trinh was born 14 September 1950 in Saigon, Vietnam. He moved to Paris, France, at age two and then to the United States in 1968. He received a baccalaureate degree in 1968 from Lycée Michelet

School in Paris. Continuing his formal education in the United States, he earned a bachelor of science degree from Columbia University in 1972 in mechanical engineering and applied physics. Next, he moved to Yale where he earned a master of science degree in 1974, a master's of philosophy in 1975, and a doctorate of philosophy in applied physics in 1977. While at Yale he helped pioneer the use of acoustic levitation techniques to research the physics of liquids. Trinh was coinvestigator for the DDM investigation.

Trinh recalled his transition from pure academics to NASA's shuttle program once he arrived at JPL: "I came right out of graduate school as a postdoctoral fellow at the Jet Propulsion Laboratory. I had done my thesis work on acoustic levitation applications. I thought that was kind of esoteric and a little bit out of the ordinary, but little did I know that I was going to stray even further from the beaten path. It took me about four years to come from primarily laboratory research, into a full-fledged flight program."

Lodewijk van den Berg was the first person of Dutch descent to fly into space; however, he had already gained his American citizenship at the time of the STS-51B flight. Wubbo Ockels, who flew on the fourth Spacelab mission about six months later, became the first Dutch citizen to make it to space. Born in Sluiskil, Netherlands, on 24 March 1932, van den Berg earned his master of science degree in chemical engineering in 1961 from the Technical University at Delft in the Netherlands. He then moved to the United States, where he was awarded a second master of science degree by the University of Delaware in applied science and then a PhD in 1975, also in applied science. It was at this time that he became an American citizen.

Following completion of his PhD, van den Berg was employed by EG&G Corporation, a national defense contractor located in Goleta, California, where he was given the responsibility for operating a twenty-furnace crystal-growth facility. Van den Berg produced crystals with his equipment and racked up over twenty years of research and management experience in the growth of crystalline materials. This expertise was a perfect match for the scientific objectives on Spacelab 3 and played a large role in his being selected for this mission. Van den Berg became a coinvestigator of the Vapor Crystal Growth System (VCGS) experiment, one of the Spacelab 3 prime experiments.

Ben Evans, in "A Long Wait for Space: 30 Years since Mission 51B," cites that van den Berg was encouraged by EG&G to toss his name into the hat

10. Spacelab 3 payload crew preflight NASA portrait: Taylor Wang, Mary Helen Johnston, Lodewijk van den Berg, and Eugene Trinh. Courtesy NASA/Retro Space Images.

for a Spacelab 3 slot, rounding out the small group of potential materials science candidates. Van den Berg, in a 2011 TEDx lecture in Delft, which he called "How a Crystal Growth Scientist Became an Astronaut," joked that he figured his bad eyesight and advanced age—fifty-three when STS-51B launched—would eliminate him right off the bat.

Van den Berg's alternate was Mary Helen Johnston (later Mary Helen McCay). Dr. Johnston was born on 17 September 1945 in West Palm Beach, Florida. She earned a bachelor of science degree in 1966 and a master of science degree in 1969 from Florida State University. During this time, she was employed part-time at MSFC. Johnston was awarded her PhD in 1973 from the University of Florida in metallurgical engineering and became a full-time MSFC employee working on experiments and hardware for manned spaceflights. In 1980 she made an unsuccessful bid to become an astronaut in NASA's group 9.

Johnston, like van den Berg, was a materials scientist with expertise in crystal growth, but she worked on a variety of projects at MSFC during her career. In 1974 she and MSFC colleagues Dr. Ann Whitaker, Doris Chandler, and Carolyn Griner carried out a five-day, ground-based Spacelab simulation in MSFC's General Purpose Laboratory, a cylindrical proxy about the same size as the Spacelab module. Johnston also designed scientific payloads for Space Processing and Applications Rockets (SPAR), which were later used by Taylor Wang in his fluid mechanics research. The SPAR project provided an opportunity for a proof-of-concept verification of investigations in a microgravity environment. Additionally, Johnston participated in pressure suit training designed to better understand the difficulties of performing experiments in space.

Narrowed down to just four contenders, the prospective payload specialists for the materials science experiments were given tough mental and physical tests. Two failed this round, leaving van den Berg and Johnston as the final two contenders for one of the two materials science positions on Spacelab 3.

Mission manager Joseph Cremin wrote a special memorandum on 16 June 1983 congratulating MSFC on the selection of Mary Helen Johnston—one of their own—as one of the final four candidates. Cremin, obviously quite proud of MSFC's and Johnston's fortune, ended the memorandum on an upbeat note: "The job ahead is difficult and the time is short which makes this assignment a significant challenge that will require the utmost dedication and perseverance of Dr. Johnston. I have no doubt that she will accomplish this assignment in an exemplary fashion." Making the short list was no guarantee of flying into space as part of the Spacelab 3 crew; still, it was considered quite a feather in Johnston's cap.

Wang's knowledge and academic training weighed heavily in his favor to be selected as a prime crew member. Van den Berg's academic training and experience at EG&G Corporation also gave him an advantage. Wang wrote in "A Scientist in Space" that he and van den Berg were chosen as prime crew members in September 1984, a little over a year after Edelson had approved the final four candidates.

The mission-independent training for Wang and van den Berg was similar to that of the two previous payload specialists. Wang commented on his mission-independent training in "A Scientist in Space," an article speckled with wit and humor, that NASA had no way to tell if astronauts would get sick in space, so they made them sick on the ground to see if they could function, just in case they did succumb to SAS once in orbit. He also related that he had to become familiar with the entire spacecraft, jesting that he had to learn the function of every switch, just in case all the other astronauts died in space. If so, then he could bring the orbiter home. In the same article, he shared that during a training exercise, they practiced egressing from the orbiter and departing the pad to a safe location in the event of an emergency situation. They were required to run about five hundred yards to a bunker, which might allow them to survive if they could do it in ten seconds, a staggering feat that Wang undoubtedly embellished. Amusingly he quipped that NASA told them not to worry; they would surely be able to run much faster under real emergency conditions! Fred Gregory shared with the authors in November 2016 that Wang was a great guy—and funny too.

Mission-dependent training for the payload crew was not as exhaustive as it had been for the first Spacelab mission, because there were far fewer experiments. Additionally, the payload crew were not trained to be experts in every experiment; instead, they were given primary and secondary assignments. Each experiment had a prime crew member and a backup. However, each scientist was trained 100 percent in experiments of their own expertise. The payload crew also trained in the Payload Crew Training Complex located at MSFC, in a high-fidelity mockup of the Spacelab module. They were schooled on flight hardware at KSC during integration tests.

The first eighteen hours of the mission were to be devoted to astronomical observations using a wide field camera, also flown on Spacelab 1, to be located in the Spacelab air lock, which would provide direct exposure to the vacuum of space. Fichtl et al. described that most of the remainder of the experiments on this mission required the "best low-gravity environment that could be achieved within the capabilities of Space Shuttle and Spacelab systems," and this was to be achieved by assuming a gravity-gradient attitude—the orbiter tail pointed toward Earth with the right wing pointed in the direction of travel. This alignment promised to minimize the use of the orbiter thrusters, which would create forces that could hamper the sensitive experiments on this mission.

Wang's baby was the Drop Dynamics Module. During the mission, liquid drops could be formed within the DDM, which would float in mid-air, and then rotated and oscillated using acoustic energy, with the results observed and compared to theory. The beauty of containerless materials processing is that the material does not touch anything except air, eliminating possible contamination from the container.

A Spacelab 3 MSFC brochure described van den Berg as "an authority on the vapor growth technique for producing mercuric iodide crystal," and as coinvestigator, he planned to use the VCGS to grow better mercuric iodide crystals by taking advantage of the low-gravity environment provided in the Spacelab module. On Earth the weight of the crystal created strain dislocations within the crystals.

Crystals are extremely valuable as electrical materials, and scientists have learned how to improve what Mother Nature makes. However, scientists needed to better understand what causes defects in crystals to further improve their electrical capabilities. Unfortunately, gravitational forces stymie materials science research on the ground, so the microgravity environment promised to provide the opportunity to learn more. Van den Berg planned to use the VCGS to grow a mercury iodide crystal, a soft crystal with potential as a nuclear radiation detector. The concept was to vary experimental parameters and observe the results to better understand how to reduce defects in the crystal lattice, hopefully yielding a crystal as good as or better than the best crystals grown on Earth.

Van den Berg also made significant contributions to the design and science reviews for the Fluid Experiment System, another materials science experiment on Spacelab 3. The payload crew planned to use this hardware to grow a triglycine sulfate crystal, which might also provide scientists data about the formation of defects in crystals and how convection currents can cause such defects.

There was a variety of other experiments, including a handful of life sciences experiments. Two squirrel monkeys and twenty-four rats were safely tucked away in Spacelab; their primary purpose would be to verify the design of the Research Animal Holding Facility (RAHF)—NASA language for cages. The RAHF could accommodate animals varying in size from rodents to small primates. Thornton and Lind, working on alternate shifts, were responsible for caring for the animals, testing the facility, and collecting lessons learned so that NASA could offer investigators a first-rate system for experimentation on commonly used laboratory animals.

Don Lind was a coinvestigator for one of the two atmospheric sciences experiments, the auroral observations. Lind intended to take advantage of the orbiter's unique vantage point in orbit to make systematic observations of the Southern Hemisphere aurora, the Aurora Australis. Chris Kraft's insistence that most of his mission specialists were qualified to do many of the jobs assigned to the payload specialists was proving to be accurate. While mission specialist Lind was trained on orbiter systems, his scientific inclinations led him to carry out investigations that might have otherwise been assigned to a payload specialist. Prior to being selected in astronaut group 5 in 1966, Lind investigated low-energy particles within Earth's magnetosphere and interplanetary space at NASA's Goddard Space Flight Center. Lind had been trained to be a NASA astronaut and waited nineteen years to get into space, but because of his scientific background, he fit the bill for both payload and mission specialist.

A second investigation in the atmospheric sciences, atmospheric trace molecule spectroscopy (ATMOS), was designed to gather much-needed data on the chemistry and physics of Earth's poorly understood upper atmosphere using a laser spectrometer. Scientists wanted to better grasp the compositional structure of the upper atmosphere and how it varies spatially.

Like Spacelab 1, the science operations were to be handled by MSFC personnel out of the POCC located in building 30 at JSC. During the mission, the POCC was home for Trinh and Johnston, as well as for the cadre of mission managers and science teams dedicated to ensure mission success. The POCC had two shifts of about seventy-five people supporting the mission. The support teams planned to operate in shifts of eight or twelve hours and monitor, control, and direct the experiments in real time as they were being carried out in space. In addition to the payload control room, there was a mission planning room and six user rooms. Spacelab 1 had proven the value of direct communication between the payload crew and the POCC; therefore, experts in the POCC during the Spacelab 3 flight would be able to communicate directly with the payload crew using voice, text, or graphic links and could control some of their experiments by sending automated commands to computers located inside Spacelab.

Challenger along with its crew of seven astronauts, two squirrel monkeys, and twenty-four rats roared into orbit on 29 April 1985 from KSC's launchpad 39A following a short delay of just over two minutes. Thornton, Wang, and van den Berg sat in the middeck, with Lind and Thagard joining Over-myer and Gregory on the flight deck. After reaching an altitude of almost 220 nautical miles at a fifty-seven-degree inclination to Earth's equator, the gold team began work while the silver team went to bed—they would work in shifts just like the Spacelab 1 crew. The crew's sleep patterns had been adjusted prior to the flight to ensure that the silver team could get to sleep shortly after orbit was achieved. Still, with the beauty of Earth pass-ing below them and the unique sensation of microgravity, climbing into a sleeping bag just hours after launch and falling asleep must have been as difficult as a child going to bed on Christmas Eve.

Once the module had been opened and brought to life, the crew expe-rienced a number of frustrating problems. Plumbing and communications glitches complicated life aboard the orbiter. One of the monkeys became sick, and of more concern, the crew noticed pieces of food and fecal mate-rial that had escaped from the RAHF floating around the module, some of which eventually made it all the way into the orbiter cabin. By day four the crew resorted to wearing surgical masks to protect themselves from the foul-smelling debris drifting around them, being pulled by air currents into the nearest air-cleansing filter.

Surprisingly, the crew could not open the scientific air lock in the mod-ule on their second attempt, which is where the wide field camera had to be placed to take photographs—hence, this investigation had to be aban-doned. On the plus side, by day 3 the crew had eleven of the fifteen exper-iments successfully up and running as planned.

Of more concern, when Wang tried to activate his precious DDM on the second day of the mission, it didn't work. He immediately began trouble-shooting procedures; however, NASA deemed the likelihood of a success-ful repair very low. Furthermore, Wang had other duties for many of the other onboard experiments, and NASA was concerned that Wang would overdose on the DDM repair attempt and ignore those responsibilities. Con-sequently, Wang was informed to forget the DDM.

At this time, a series of events played out that has caused much specu-lation about Wang's mental state once he discovered the DDM was inoper-ative. Wang admitted that when he was forbidden to attempt to repair the DDM, he became severely depressed. Following the mission, Wang recalled, "The Drop Dynamics Module (DDM) did not work when we first turned

11. Payload specialist Taylor Wang floats in the transfer tunnel leading from the middeck of *Challenger* into the Spacelab module. Courtesy NASA/Retro Space Images.

[it] on, for some reason we still don't know yet. It was a big disappointment to me at the time. Fortunately, there was no exit; I might not even come back." Wang's comment about not coming back gave Overmyer grave concern about his mental health, although Gregory believes that the event was blown out of proportion. In 2016 Gregory shared with the authors that Wang was undoubtedly severely depressed and that to make matters worse, Wang had trouble using the toilet. The crew had been trained to work as a team, and they did everything they could to help and comfort Wang during his bout with depression. The ground even pitched in to help out; at mission elapsed time (MET) of three days, four hours, and forty-six seconds (3:04:46), an entry into the mission transcript profiles called for "Prayers for Wang" and "Anyone religious?—please go to church and pray." Wang needed all the support he could get to endure the setback; fortunately, he had a strong support team to get him through the ordeal. Wang persevered.

Against NASA's initial position, Wang was eventually allowed to attempt to repair the device and lived inside the DDM for over a day, his legs dangling out of the contraption while he toiled at breathing life back into the beast. Mary Helen Johnston, van den Berg's backup working out of the POCC in Houston, took advantage of Wang's predicament to compliment him on his "good looking legs," adding, "love that outfit," providing a bit of levity to the dour situation. The probability of fixing the DDM given the circumstances was low, but with strong crew and ground support, Wang determined that the conundrum was an electrical short and miraculously corrected the malfunction, calling it "bypass surgery." Wang explained that it was very difficult to troubleshoot and repair things in space—all he had was a voltmeter and a couple of screwdrivers. Mission scientist George Fichtl explained at the 3 May change-of-shift briefing that Wang "went through the entire DDM system, and he eventually got it down to a power supply that was problematic, and what he did there was isolate that power supply electrically, and the DDM is operating off of two remaining power supplies."

Once back on Earth, Wang recalled the tribulation: "I settled down, start[ed] . . . troubleshooting the system, and with the help of the ground crew and also the support of the flight crew, I was able to get that same system back on track, and we start[ed] to operate that system again. I have to apologize to the rest of the flight crew; when I first turned it on after the repair, I let out such a yell I woke up everybody and startled the people on the flight deck."

Gregory told the authors, with a chuckle, that over thirty years later he still remembers the bloodcurdling "Yeow!" that Wang screamed out when he finally revived the DDM. The mission transcript profiles captured that magical moment at MET 3:05:26: "We've got DDM working now. Great." The crew celebrated the awakening of the DDM and continued to share their elation with the ground. The shuttle crew reported, "DDM is working. You did a great job—you've never seen so much joy as was in Taylor's face. Taylor is glowing. We're celebrating DDM up here," which was acknowledged by the ground with, "Copy sounds like a party going on. Taylor are you going to be able to sleep tonight? I don't know, champagne and dancing girls." Once again, Wang proved the value of humans accompanying their scientific paraphernalia into space. Overmyer complimented Wang following the mission: "He is a superb mechanic, and he proved it . . . and proved the worthwhileness of having man in space to salvage an experiment."

Wang explained the situation years later in *Space Shuttle: The First 20 Years*, edited by Tony Reichhardt. The comment about not coming back worried a lot of people at the time, especially NASA management. Wang had spent five years of his life planning the DDM experiment, and the thought of abandoning it without an attempt to repair it depressed him. NASA was concerned enough with Wang's comments that they enlisted a psychologist to talk to the other crew members. Afterward, Overmyer assured his crew that Wang was fine. Gregory agreed that this event is likely what caused some commanders of later missions carrying payload specialists to add a lock to the side hatch of the orbiter, but he stressed several times that he felt Overmyer overreacted to Wang's depressed condition.

Wang was very complimentary of the ground support—especially his alternate Eugene Trinh and Arvid Croonquist, project scientist from the Jet Propulsion Laboratory—claiming that they slept very little during the mission. Mission scientist George Fichtl confirmed at the change-of-shift briefing on 3 May that "Taylor can stay up as long as he feels that he can and can turn in when he's ready." He had to be coaxed into bed. Wang rotated and oscillated his drops using a weak acoustic field until they transformed into an axisymmetric shape, which means symmetric with respect to an axis, or a little bit flattened at both poles of the axis—having an appearance something akin to a dog bone. With time, the axisymmetric shape becomes unstable, which is called the bifurcation point, and Wang was attempting to determine when the bifurcation point occurred. It had been calculated mathematically, but once that time was reached in his experimental work in space, the theory fell apart. Parts of the theory held, but Wang loved the theoretical mystery, partly because once back on Earth it allowed him to needle his theoretician friends—their theoretical thinking was not as good as they thought.

Wang remembered that by the end of the sixth day, the crew had completed all the experiments (at least the ones that worked) and began closing up Spacelab, which to their delight gave them about six hours—four orbits—to enjoy the majestic views passing silently below them. *Challenger* and its crew of seven astronauts and twenty-six animals left the confines of microgravity on 6 May 1985, landing at Edwards Air Force Base, culminating another highly successful Spacelab mission. They had traveled 2.9 million miles during their eight days in orbit.

12. Payload specialist Lodewijk van den Berg enters the Spacelab module from the transfer tunnel during his Spacelab 3 mission. Courtesy NASA/Retro Space Images.

NASA's mission manager Joseph Cremin gave the crew an A grade for their work on Spacelab 3. Fichtl echoed this view: "The Spacelab 3 mission, by any measure, was an outstanding success. We have learned how to utilize the Shuttle/Spacelab system to provide the best low-gravity environment achievable from this system. Much of the research begun on Spacelab 3 will continue on future Spacelab missions and will help set the stage for research aboard Space Station."

Dr. C. B. Farmer (known to everyone as Barney) was the principal investigator for the laser spectrometer experiment. He reported that nineteen observations of the ozone layer were made—more data than from ten years of balloon flights. Wang achieved almost 90 percent of his drop dynamics objectives, and Fichtl explained that these experiments "provided the first experimental data on free rotating and oscillating drops." Van den Berg also achieved impressive results; the downside was that even in space his crystals grew very slowly. He grew only one crystal in his VCGS, requiring about 120 hours and a lot of the payload crew's time.

Like the payload specialists, the monkeys and rats went to space for scientific research with the intent of flying on only one flight. They even received mission-independent training. According to Lind, "They had been on centrifuges. They had been on vibration tables. So they knew what the roar and the feeling of space was going to be like." The animals were tested and prodded once they were back on Earth to assess how their bodies were affected by the eight days of microgravity. Unfortunately for the rats, that research included being dissected so that their tissues, organs, and bones could be evaluated to determine the effect that space travel had on their bodies.

During the investigation into the cause of the loss of *Challenger* and its crew in January 1986 on the STS-51L mission, Overmyer learned that the O-rings on one of *Challenger*'s SRB joints had come perilously close to failing on 51B—portending the upcoming catastrophic breakup of *Challenger* and loss of its 51L crew. A mere three-tenths of a second made the difference between a highly successful science mission and the death of the crew of 51B.

Wang left JPL in 1988 and moved to Vanderbilt University, where he became the Centennial Professor of Mechanical Engineering, director of the applied physics program, and director of the Center for Microgravity Research, where he continued his research in microgravity science and applications, drop physics, physical acoustics, and biotechnology. He is now retired from Vanderbilt.

Van den Berg continued his career at EG&G after his flight and then went to work for the Constellation Technology Corporation located in Largo, Florida. As of 18 September 2015, he was Principal Scientist Emeritus at Constellation, continuing to grow his mercuric iodide crystals. Neither van den Berg nor Wang flew in space again.

Trinh would go on to fly as a payload specialist on STS-50 in 1992. Following the termination of the Spacelab program, Trinh reflected on the benefits that Spacelab contributed: "I would like to say that I regret that the Spacelab era is over. It has given me the unique opportunity to participate in one of the most exciting scientific adventures of recent times. I am really grateful to have been able to do that, and to have met so many dedicated scientists and engineers both at NASA in the United States, in academia, in Europe, and in Japan. I hope that I will be able to keep the same working relationship as we transition to the space station era."

Mary Helen Johnston, now Mary McCay, was one of the first women to break into the ranks of the male-dominated MSFC in the 1970s. In 1986 she left MSFC and became a professor at the University of Tennessee Space Institute. She was appointed director of the National Center for Hydrogen Research at the Florida Institute of Technology in 2003, where she researched the use of hydrogen as a renewable energy source.

Building on the concept that Lind was more akin to the payload specialists, Gregory recalled that "he flew, he was satisfied, and then went back to the academic world." It was exactly what NASA expected of payload specialists. Mission specialist Lind resigned from NASA shortly after his only foray into space to become a professor of physics and astronomy at Utah State University.

Wang summed up the crew dynamics in "A Scientist in Space." In spite of their idiosyncrasies and seeing each other more than they saw their own families during their months of training, they got along quite well. With his typical sense of humor, he wrote facetiously—the authors believe—that at least there were no open fights between crew members. More importantly, NASA had executed its second successful Spacelab mission with high hopes of flying two more science missions before the end of 1985. Spacelab had come into its own!

6. The Supermission

Its experiments call for the largest and heaviest astronomy
instruments ever taken into space.

Walter Froehlich, *Spacelab*

Payload specialist John-David Francis Bartoe paced back and forth across
the floor of the Debus Center at the Kennedy Space Center Visitor Complex
on 6 November 2014, orbiting around the room with both hands tightly
clasped around a microphone as he regaled the crowd with stories of flying into space. He lectured briefly about his 1985 STS-51F mission, joked
about his 1970s hairstyle that he sported on that flight, and then spoke
passionately for the next ten minutes about the International Space Station, a project that he championed following his flight. Earlier that day he
had spoken to another crowded room of visitors, sharing his impressions
of what it was like to fly into outer space. "Zero-g is an absolute blast!" he
said with a wide smile.

An entertaining and passionate speaker, Bartoe explained that swimming in space is not an effective way to move around, although many rookies cannot resist flailing their arms on their initial albeit brief experience
of weightlessness in the KC-135 Vomit Comet. His fondest memory of his
first (and only) spaceflight, as with many astronauts, was "looking out the
window. . . . It is an awesome experience to look at Earth." He told the
crowd that when he first peered out of *Challenger*'s window, he was completely lost, because there were no colors or lines like maps have, which
delineate Earth's geopolitical boundaries. It was another common reaction
from astronauts, especially first-time fliers.

Bartoe, a solar physicist, was born on 17 November 1944 in historic

Abington, Pennsylvania. He received a bachelor of science degree in physics from Lehigh University in 1966. Over the next twenty-two years, he worked as an astrophysicist at the Naval Research Laboratory in Washington DC, with a focus on solar physics observations and instrumentation. During this period, he advanced his education, earning his master of science and PhD degrees in physics from Georgetown University in 1974 and 1976. Selected as a NASA payload specialist in 1978 while working as a civilian employee for the U.S. Navy, he was coinvestigator on two solar physics investigations that flew on STS-51F for Spacelab 2—exciting and groundbreaking work that helped him collect his seat on that mission.

Unlike many of the NASA astronauts, Bartoe never had dreams of being an astronaut as a youngster. His education in solar physics and subsequent employment at the Naval Research Laboratory led him to build solar telescopes, which, along with a bit of luck, earned him a slot on the shuttle. These telescopes were designed to allow astronomers on the ground to view the sun with greater accuracy than ever before. NASA decided to fly Bartoe's telescopes into space on Spacelab and asked if any of the laboratory experts wanted to fly with them. Bartoe jumped at the serendipitous opportunity and volunteered for the journey of a lifetime.

Loren Wilber Acton, Bartoe's fellow payload specialist on Spacelab 2, enthusiastically answered questions on 24 September 2015 during an interview with the authors about his flight into space, with the same fervor and pride exhibited by Bartoe on 6 November 2014 at the Debus Center. When it was suggested that he must have had a great time during the mission, his response was quite surprising. "Well," he said after a pause, "you know I didn't." It turns out that Acton was so focused on doing his job, and also fighting space sickness, that he forgot to enjoy the fact that he was floating around Earth in the most complex machine ever built. "I did [have fun] in retrospect. But sometimes we learn about ourselves things that we didn't know. I expected this to be sort of a fun camping trip in space with my friends, and when I got up there, I found that I overdosed on responsibility, to a degree which really impacted the joy of spaceflight. By the time we got well into the mission, I did force myself to look out the window and enjoy the view. But I really blindsided myself in terms of what my reaction to being up there was. . . . It wasn't the experience I expected it to be, although in retrospect it was really great."

Acton was born the son of a cattle rancher in Lewistown, Montana, on 7 March 1936. He took his education in a one-room country school until the seventh grade, when his father sold their ranch and the family moved to Billings, some one hundred miles away, where he attended junior high and high school and was active in the youth group of the Church of the Air. Following his high school days, he entered the Multnomah School of the Bible in Portland, Oregon, for a year and then enrolled at Montana State College in Bozeman. Acton received his bachelor of science degree with honors in engineering physics in 1959 from Montana State University and his PhD in astrogeophysics in 1965 from the University of Colorado.

Lockheed hired Acton in 1964 to work at its Palo Alto Research Laboratory as a senior consulting scientist doing research in solar and cosmic astronomy utilizing space instrumentation. Acton was working for Lockheed when he was selected to become a payload specialist.

Bartoe and Acton's backgrounds and knowledge of the sun gave them a huge advantage in being selected as payload specialists for the Spacelab 2 mission. Although the selection of the Spacelab 1 payload specialists was announced before those for the Spacelab 2 crew, Acton remembers that he and Bartoe were the first payload specialists selected and that they were not selected in the same manner as the Spacelab 1 payload specialists. He explained that when they were chosen, "there weren't any rules, and so the IWG discussed how to select the payload specialists, and it was realized that for our particular mission, the solar experiments were the ones that could profit the most from experiments in the field." Spacelab 2 carried three solar experiments, and the solar investigators were encouraged to submit the names of ten individuals. If they passed the medical examinations, their names and qualifications would be passed on to the IWG for consideration, which would then vote on two prime and two backup candidates. Acton volunteered to write the requirements document, and once approved by the IWG, it used that document to make the final selections. One of the ten did not pass the physical, and another decided to withdraw from consideration, leaving eight contenders. Acton recalled, "There were actually only eight of us that gave our ten-minute talks. Of the eight, John Bartoe and I were selected as prime, and George Simon and Dianne Prinz were selected as backups." Acton fondly recalled with a bit of pride, "That was a good day!"

Spacelab 1 mission scientist Rick Chappell does not agree with his good friend Loren Acton that the Spacelab 2 payload specialists were the first to be selected. He contends that the same process used to select the Spacelab 1 crew was used to select the Spacelab 2 payload specialists, and that was the process developed for Spacelab 1. Both Chappell and Acton volunteered that it is nearly impossible to remember all the details some thirty years later; it's safe to say that all eight payload specialists, including backups, were selected within a tight time frame during an exciting and busy time at NASA.

Dr. George Simon, with a PhD in physics from the California Institute of Technology, was Bartoe's backup. Simon was a senior scientist in the solar research branch of the Air Force Geophysics Laboratory at the National Solar Observatory in Sunspot, New Mexico. According to a 1985 Marshall Space Flight Center publication titled *Spacelab 2*, Simon was working on several NASA experiments, which placed him at the right place at the right time to be selected as part of the Spacelab 2 crew. Like his predecessors on the Spacelab 1 mission, Simon would play an important role in the POCC during the mission.

Mission scientist Dr. Eugene W. Urban of MSFC was responsible for coordination between the scientists and management teams. Dr. Dianne Prinz, who held a PhD in physics from Johns Hopkins University, backed up Loren Acton. She was heading up the Atmospheric Spectroscopy Section at the United States Naval Research Laboratory's Space Science Division when she was selected as a candidate for the Spacelab 2 mission. She was a coinvestigator for one of the Spacelab 2 experiments, giving her a clear advantage for one of the payload specialist slots on the third Spacelab mission. She also worked diligently in the POCC during the mission in support of the scientific planning.

Gordon Fullerton, making his second shuttle flight, was the mission commander, with Roy Bridges as his pilot. Fullerton would work both the red and blue shifts as required. This would be Bridges's first flight into space. Dr. F. Story Musgrave, the third mission specialist, was also part of the flight crew. His job was to assist the commander and pilot in support of the specialized flying requirements on this Spacelab mission.

Mission specialists Tony England and Karl Henize rounded out the payload crew. England held a PhD in geophysics from MIT and would work

13. Spacelab 2 backup payload specialists George Simon and Dianne Prinz (*rear*) and prime crew members John-David Bartoe and Loren Acton (*front*). Courtesy NASA/Retro Space Images.

on the blue shift alongside Bartoe and Musgrave. Henize, assigned to the red shift along with Acton and Bridges, was an astronomer with a PhD from the University of Michigan.

Spacelab 2 did not carry a pressurized module like previous Spacelab missions. Instead, the instruments that the payload crew would use to carry out their scientific research were located on three pallets stacked inside the payload bay, operated from inside the orbiter on the flight deck, just behind the cockpit. The payload crew would carry out their duties in close proximity to the flight crew—a much cozier working environment than on the first two Spacelab missions.

Spacelab 2 was a verification test flight to confirm the operability of the pallet systems and interface capability of the pallets and the orbiter. But meaningful research was just as important an objective. Spacelab 2 carried thirteen scientific investigations in seven disciplines: solar physics, atmospheric physics, plasma physics, high-energy astrophysics, infrared astronomy, technology research, and life sciences. However, solar physics was the five-hundred-pound gorilla on this mission.

Bartoe and Acton were coinvestigators on three of the thirteen experiments, which made the mission-dependent training much easier for them; they were already experts in these areas. Acton and his backup, George Simon, were both coinvestigators on the solar magnetic and velocity field measurement system experiment—the Solar Optical Universal Polarimeter (SOUP). According to the *Spacelab 2* publication, the objective of SOUP was to "observe the strength, structure, and evolution of magnetic fields in the solar atmosphere and to determine the relationship between these magnetic elements and other solar features." Bartoe was coinvestigator on the solar ultraviolet high-resolution telescope and spectrograph (HRTS, pronounced "Hurts"), another solar physics investigation designed to study "features in the sun's outer layers: the chromosphere, the corona, and the transition zone between them." Simply put, the idea was to ascertain how the sun creates the solar wind. Bartoe and backup Prinz were coinvestigators on the Solar Ultraviolet Spectral Irradiance Monitor (SUSIM), which would assess variations of the total ultraviolet flux emitted by the sun—both short and long term. The only atmospheric experiment on board, SUSIM would measure variations in a range of wavelengths through solar cycles, which might influence Earth's climate. The third solar physics investigation, Coronal Helium Abundance Spacelab Experiment (CHASE), was to accurately measure the helium abundance of the sun. That left only ten experiments that the payload crew needed to become proficient in prior to launch.

The mission-independent training for Spacelab 2 was very similar to the two previous Spacelab endeavors. But Acton recalled that the payload crew

for Spacelab 2 had more control over how the mission-dependent training was carried out. Bartoe, Acton, Tony England, and Karl Henize were
assigned the task of writing the operations manuals and checklists for all
the experiments. This required them to spend a lot of time with the people building the experiments. Acton explained, "So we visited every exper-
imenter, and because we worked with them to write the books, we knew a
lot. And that was such a much better system than having some contractor
write the operations and then we have to learn them. By the time we flew,
we were very well knowledgeable about every experiment. It was great; it
was a lot of fun!" He said that in addition to learning the scientific basis
of the experiments and how to operate them, they also learned the intricacies of the hardware, which might come in handy once on orbit if they
encountered operational problems.

Acton was impressed with the mission-independent training program
and relished doing "the same sort of things that our real astronaut colleagues did, and I just enjoyed every moment of it." They rode shotgun
on the STA flights with the pilot and commander when they were practicing landings. T-38 familiarization and zero-g flights were also part of the
training regimen.

Challenger, with the Spacelab 2 pallets and telescopes nestled snugly inside
its cavernous payload bay, blazed a fiery trail into space on 29 July 1985.
Although one engine failed shortly after launch, the remaining two engines
performed well enough to push the orbiter to an altitude of 173 nautical
miles at an inclination of 49.5 degrees to Earth's equator. The orbit was
not ideal for pointing their cadre of specialized telescopes at their intended
targets, but the scientists and engineers on the ground were able to make
adjustments that allowed the payload crew to successfully accomplish all
the mission objectives. Acton recently shared, "The lower orbit had very
little impact on the science."

Once in orbit the payload crew quickly began their busy schedule for the
next week. The blue shift began to work while the red crew settled down for
a rest. Acton recalled that as the pilot, Bridges was responsible for ensuring
that spacecraft maneuvers were performed on time, which kept him quite
busy. Spacelab 2 carried a plethora of telescopes on the pallets and other
experiments that required the commander and pilot to perform numerous

14. Payload specialists Loren Acton and John-David Bartoe floating in their workstation located on the flight deck during their Spacelab 2 mission. Courtesy NASA/Retro Space Images.

changes in *Challenger*'s attitude; therefore, they stayed busy throughout the mission. Acton described how the astronauts worked on the flight deck. "We were close together so we could communicate readily," he explained. "The team that was off shift was down below sleeping and eating or doing whatever they were doing. So the layout of the orbiter for our particular function worked just fine." The flight deck was considerably smaller than the Spacelab module, but Acton remembered that it "was quite a convenient work environment. Karl Henize, who was the red team mission specialist worked on one side of the flight deck. He was responsible for Spacelab systems. I worked on the other side of the flight deck. I was responsible for experiment operations."

The principal investigators, along with Simon and Prinz, worked closely with the management team in the POCC during the flight to ensure maximum return on their investment from the battery of scientific investigations. Bartoe described the job of the alternate payload specialist as being much more difficult than actually flying the mission. He viewed Prinz's and Simon's positions as the "top of the pyramid," controlling all the scientists trying to get their own most important experiment particulars up to the astronauts. They had to manage a half dozen or so telephone discussions concurrently, stay in touch with the crew, and then make efficient decisions on the fly to maximize productivity. Prinz remembered that the scientists were naturally focused on their own experiment, forcing her to prioritize so as not to overburden the crew. Often she was called on to referee problems in the back rooms. She agreed with Bartoe; it was a demanding and tiresome job.

The primary objective of Spacelab 2 may have been equipment verification and scientific research, but the crew had one additional task to carry out that captured the attention of the media and public—the cola war. Bartoe explained that Coca-Cola had approached NASA for approval to test a new can that would allow soda to be consumed in space. Later, Pepsi found out about the deal and petitioned NASA to place Pepsi on board. NASA finally relented, but the executives at Coke were not pleased when they learned of the decision. U.S. senator Sam Nunn, who in 1997 became Coca-Cola's chief executive officer, wrote a blistering letter to NASA administrator James Beggs on 27 June 1985, demanding that Pepsi adhere to the same arduous development process they had been asked to follow.

According to Nunn, the initial agreement stipulated that only Coke would be allowed to fly their product on 51F in recognition of their initiative to develop a drink container technology. Other companies, they said, would be able to fly their product on future flights, but Coke demanded to be first. They had worked for over a year, spending over a quarter-million dollars, and Nunn expected NASA to require Pepsi to adhere to the same requirements. NASA held tight; Pepsi would fly along with Coke. However, NASA was not prepared to become a marketing tool for either company; they banned the astronauts from conducting or commenting on any taste test of the rival products over TV or radio while aloft.

Meanwhile, the astronauts were expressing annoyance over the overt preflight publicity being given to the so-called cola wars in the media. As astronaut Mike Mullane revealed in his memoir, *Riding Rockets*, a disgusted John Young had returned from a management meeting at which the cola rivalry had occupied valuable hours of the committee's time. One astronaut was heard to growl, "Sure hope they're spending as much time working on the things that can kill us."

Bartoe humorously shared that much to the company's satisfaction, Coca-Cola did score one major marketing coup when—under orders to the crew from NASA—it became the first soda to be consumed in space. The specially adapted zero-g containers resembled shaving cream aerosol cans and were designed to retain carbonation in the weightlessness of space without spewing its contents. Pepsi, Bartoe said, had less time to develop their can, and it was not as effective as the Coke can. Despite this, Bartoe claimed that the Pepsi can created wonderful Pepsi balls when the carbonated beverage escaped from the can, which were fun to investigate and manipulate as the gas separated from the fluid inside the ball. Coke and Pepsi created quite an advertising coup at the time, but neither drink has permanently returned to space. Acton lamented the fact that many of the questions he gets about his mission focus on the beverage of choice instead of the science.

Spacelab 2 carried several new major components, including an igloo and the Instrument Pointing System (IPS). The igloo, located on the pallet outside *Challenger*'s cabin, carried subsystems necessary for Spacelab to operate, including equipment for computer operations, data transmission, and thermal control. This equipment was located inside the pressurized habitable module, when it was flown. The IPS, tested in flight for the first time on Spacelab 2, was developed by ESA to accurately point instruments toward celestial objects.

The IPS was capable of accurately zeroing in on coin-sized objects almost three thousand feet away. Some of the solar telescopes that Bartoe had helped to develop, which he controlled from inside *Challenger*, were capable of focusing on tiny features of the sun, and accurate, unwavering pointing of his telescopes was vital to successful observations. Unfortunately, the IPS behaved erratically throughout most of the mission. The ground discovered a variety of problems, including software errors; but working together, the ground and payload crew made corrections and work-arounds, allowing the crew to eventually make the planned observations. Douglas Lord reported that the plan was to operate the SOUP telescope for fifty hours. Although it only attained sixteen hours of operation near the end of the mission, it took all 12,800 frames in its magazine.

In addition to the faulty software, the crew encountered another snag when operating the IPS; it operated in the same volume as the x-ray telescope (XRT), potentially allowing two expensive and delicate telescopes to collide. NASA had developed collision-avoidance software to prevent a potentially embarrassing situation. According to Fullerton, the software had to be activated six times during the flight, each time requiring ten to thirty minutes to recover. "During recovery the IPS had to be pointed forward so that solar observing was unlikely," he recalled. "We lost more than three solar passes performing collision-avoidance recoveries."

A smaller but significant problem was realized once the crew began their scientific investigations on the flight deck. Foot loops! With all the experience that NASA had gained over the years of flying to the moon and doing EVAs, it seems incomprehensible that inadequate foot loops on the aft flight deck became a problem on 51F. After all, foot restraints helped Buzz Aldrin carry out a successful EVA on the *Gemini 12* mission, following frustrating attempts on three previous Gemini flights. Although the payload crew were not working outside *Challenger*, the same problem of maintaining a steady base applied to them while working *inside* the orbiter. Fullerton noted that adequate foot loops were "indispensable for maintaining correct body position to carry out various tasks on the aft flight deck . . . crew members frequently found themselves sharing a foot loop with someone else's foot." There just weren't enough loops to pass muster while operating the computer keyboards or stretching to look out the payload bay windows for visual contact of external equipment.

In June 2016, NASA engineer Ed Rezac described the foot restraints as approximately twelve-inch square pieces of duct tape material that incorporated a cloth web strap loop in the center. "Prior to launch the backing was peeled away and the foot restraints were placed on the floor per crew preference based on their training on the ground," he explained. "Crew preference placement did not always take differences in 1 g and microgravity into account." Rezac recalled that additional restraints were usually flown, but removing the backing and placing the restraint accurately in a weightless environment would have likely been more work than it was worth. Bo Bobko had documented the need for adequate foot loops and restraints in the flight crew report for STS-51D—flown only three months earlier.

Acton assessed the ability of payload specialists on board to help troubleshoot and repair faulty equipment:

I think it was probably helpful. I don't think that we contributed anything that a mission specialist properly trained could not have contributed. The place where we were at an advantage was in the actual operations and choice of choosing targets and being able to communicate seamlessly with the solar astronomers on the ground about targeting and procedures. So I think that we were useful, but I don't know that we were particularly helpful in terms of instrument anomalies more than a well-trained mission specialist would have been. I think it was the scientific expertise that was an advantage to fly in our case.

Speaking frankly, Acton recalled the integration of the payload specialists into the crew alongside the NASA astronauts. Management and staff at MSFC welcomed the Spacelab payload specialists with open arms. They were provided offices in the hope that they were going to become MSFC's astronauts. Unfortunately, as he reflected, "the JSC people were not really excited about that, so there were some kinks to work out between the two." However, Acton made it crystal clear that he and Bartoe were made to feel like an integral part of the STS-51F crew and were never treated as outsiders.

Acton further commented on the ability of the payload specialists to assess the data they were capturing in real time and to make interpretations from those data. Most of the data were transmitted to the ground, never to be seen by the payload crew on orbit. However, they did have access to the telescope images from the SOUP instruments, from Bartoe's HRTS instrument, and some pointing information from the British instrument (a Hard X-ray Imager). Thus, they were able to provide some feedback and suggestions on where to point these instruments, allowing the ground to make the necessary adjustments. But for the most part the data from these experiments were analyzed by experts on the ground following completion of the mission, and the results were published in numerous scientific papers over the years, some coauthored by Acton and Bartoe. Their primary job, Acton related, was to capture the data accurately.

Acton admitted making a mistake during the mission while operating the HRTS experiment. "In fact, I made a really stupid blunder," he said laughing. "One of the HRTS sequences involved stepping the slit in the spectrograph across an active region [of the sun]. Well . . . for some reason I got my experiments mixed up, and I saw that slit moving and thought it was the IPS drifting, and very carefully zeroed all that out. [I] kept the slit in one place instead of letting it stand, which was a really awful mistake to make because that particular experiment was then compromised to some degree by me." Given the long hours the astronauts were working on each shift, along with the complexity of the instruments, it's no surprise that Acton made an error. Surely, he was not the first astronaut to have a slipup in orbit? Like a good scientist, he didn't dwell on the mistake; instead, reflecting back on his training, he analyzed what had happened and how to correct it.

> *I just mentioned one blunder, and I made some others on the flight, and my feeling is that my training in terms of following checklists was inadequate. A pilot learns to always follow the checklist, even though you know everything about everything, you go through the checklist. That in my case was not impressed upon me strongly enough, and I never really learned to do it. People sort of assumed that we knew what we were doing. I had always operated from experience of following the seat of my pants instead of rigorously using the checklists. And as a result of this I made some blunders. I really wish in retrospect that I had somebody beat me over the head and say, "Always follow the checklist rather than doing experiments from memory."*

The fuel cells performed better than expected; therefore, the mission was extended an extra day, allowing the crew to make up time lost by the erratic IPS. Approximately 80–85 percent of the mission's science objectives were realized. The telescopes on Spacelab 2 allowed the scientists undisturbed views of the sun, far superior to those provided by the solar telescopes flown on the *Skylab* space station over a decade earlier. The pallet-only configuration proved to be a highly effective platform for scientific investigations. Not surprisingly, the differences between the mission and payload specialists continued to be blurred, often out of necessity. For STS-51F, Fullerton made it clear that due to operational efficiency it was mandatory for Acton and Bartoe to operate certain pieces of equipment that would normally be controlled by the mission specialists. Special permission had to be given in order for them to operate the IPS manual pointing controller and flight camera, but with the appropriate training, Bartoe and Acton carried out these procedures safely and efficiently.

After 127 orbits and almost eight days in space, it was time for *Challenger* to come home. On 6 August 1985, having successfully completed its eighth space mission, the heat-scarred orbiter touched down and rolled to a halt on runway 23 at Edwards Air Force Base, California. Unfortunately, due to the heavy workload, the crew had been thoroughly occupied throughout the eight days and never found time to consume a meal together. Nor was there any time to exercise on the treadmill. Bartoe recalled that after landing he undid his harness but found he could not stand up. His body had easily adapted to microgravity in orbit, but now back home under the influence of the 5.9 sextillion tons of Earth's mass, he was paying the price for not exercising while in orbit. Fortunately, he recovered in about five minutes.

Mission commander Gordon Fullerton labeled the flight a "mission of challenge." Gratified with the outcome, he boasted, "The crew is proud to have been part of the great team that was able to meet the challenge to produce a very significant scientific success." Fullerton was a pilot from the old days but was exceptionally proud of his scientific experts. "Worthy of special note," he declared, "was the exemplary performance of the payload specialists, Drs. Loren Acton and John-David Bartoe."

Acton reflected on the legacy of Spacelab 2 in September 2015, very proud of the week that he spent off Earth.

> *My postmission information is pretty largely constrained to the solar experiments. I did follow a little bit the other experiments, but in solar it really changed and advanced a great deal the understanding of how gas flows in the solar atmosphere push around and concentrate magnetic fields. The prime objective of the experiments was to study solar magnetism and why it behaves the way we observe. Up to that time, active optics had not been invented, so the ground-based images in movie mode were always compromised by atmospheric affects. With the SOUP instrument, we had to believe every image, because every image was perfect optically. It was learned from that a lot about the motions of the weaker magnetic fields on the surface of the sun, so that was a real step forward. I think there were some comparable advances from the HRTS instrument. I know the helium-abundancy experiment, although they had considerable challenges in the data analysis, ended up producing a number for the abundance of helium in the sun's atmosphere. All in all, the solar experiments*

were a great success, and we won the Space Flight Achievement [Award]
for 1985 because of the good scientific results from the mission.

For his part, John-David Bartoe reflected on the social nuances of flying
a complicated science mission with a mixed crew of pilots and scientists.
He stressed that there was a lot of training overlap but that no one could
do everything: "I knew nothing about flying the front seat." In spite of all
the education and specialized training of the crew members, Bartoe believes
that being a team player is one of the most important skills required to be
an effective astronaut. He stressed that spaceflight looks easy, but it is not
routine: "We are pushing ourselves; this is what exploration is all about."
He called his crew a space family; they all became good friends.

Acton shares the same sentiments about the Spacelab 2 crew.

I think our crew was one of the most collegial and effective crews of the
Spacelab series because of the career astronauts that we flew with. Gor-
don Fullerton, Roy Bridges, Story Musgrave, although they—particularly
Gordo and Roy—didn't have a science background, they really appreci-
ated the importance of the science to the mission. Although they were test
pilots, they did not have a test pilot mentality. Our crew worked together
very well; there was never a harsh word in the years we worked together.
We had a lot of confidence in each other, and we have gotten together
from time to time postmission.

Following a short conversation with the authors about the skills and abilities of Story Musgrave, he added with a chuckle, "Story is a kick!" He then
teasingly tossed in a zinger: "I guess there were some missions in which
there were some [crew] issues." He would not elaborate!

Following his flight, John-David Bartoe went to work for NASA Headquarters, where he became the chief scientist for the space station from 1987
to 1990 and then director of operations and utilization in the Space Station
Office of NASA Headquarters from 1990 to 1994. He was then appointed
research manager for the International Space Station at NASA's Johnson
Space Center. He holds the distinction of flying into space before being
hired by NASA.

Loren Acton left Lockheed in 1994 after a long and distinguished career.
He then returned to his native state and went into academics as a research

professor of physics at Montana State University in the city of Bozeman, where he is still active.

David Simon and Dianne Prinz were subsequently assigned to a later solar physics mission, but it was cancelled following the loss of *Challenger* on 28 January 1986. Simon returned to the U.S. Air Force Geophysics Laboratory, while Prinz went back to the Naval Research Laboratory, where she continued her research with the SUSIM experiment. On 12 October 2002, aged sixty-four, Dr. Dianne Kasnic Prinz died at the Hospice of Northern Virginia after a long struggle with lymphatic cancer.

Spacelab 2 was another overwhelming success, providing further proof that scientists—payload specialists—could be recruited to fly on the shuttle and trained to carry out specialized scientific research in space to increase our collective knowledge of the universe and its many mysteries. The Spacelab 2 mission aboard STS-51F also provided further verification that career scientists could volunteer to discharge their scientific specialty in space and then return to their previous work without becoming career astronauts. The training provided by NASA gave these scientists the basic knowledge necessary to travel safely on the shuttle. They did not need to know how fly the spacecraft, nor did they need to understand the innards of the shuttle or be prepared to react to any of the hundreds of emergency situations that might occur. However, Bartoe—a noncareer astronaut—admitted, perhaps with a hint of jealously, that he would have loved to perform an EVA. "It was the thing to do," he mused.

7. Europe's Coming Out Party

DI is an ambitious and exciting mission and will require each of
us to perform at our best in order to achieve the
highest possible degree of success.

Hank Hartsfield

Famed German physicist and rocket visionary Hermann Oberth must have
felt a deep sense of national pride as he proudly witnessed firsthand space
shuttle *Challenger*, about three miles distant, majestically rise through scattered clouds into the blue Florida sky on 30 October 1985. Along with rocket
pioneers Russian Konstantin Tsiolkovsky and American Robert Goddard,
Oberth is considered to be one of the three great fathers of rocketry. Inside
Challenger rode two of Oberth's fellow citizens, German payload specialists Reinhard Furrer and Ernst Messerschmid, embarking on an ambitious
seven-day Spacelab mission planned and mostly financed by the German
Research and Development Institute for Air and Space Travel (DFVLR—
the forerunner of the German Aerospace Center, abbreviated DLR).

Representing the Netherlands, Wubbo Ockels accompanied Furrer and
Messerschmid on the STS-61A mission carrying the DI Spacelab module,
marking the only time in history that three payload specialists flew on a
single shuttle mission.

Oberth was one of the masterminds of the horrific and deadly German
V-2 rockets that inflicted fear and suffering on the citizens of London and
other Allied capitals in Europe during World War II. Following the war,
he made his way to the United States, where he worked with the legendary Wernher von Braun—another V-2 pioneer—on developing rockets for
the peaceful exploration of space. That day as he watched his fellow Ger-

mans ascend into low Earth orbit, the ninety-one-year-old Oberth believed that earthlings should set their sights on building an outpost on the moon. *Challenger*, circling Earth barely higher than two hundred miles, would not come close to meeting Oberth's lofty expectations, but it carried a bevy of promising scientific experiments, many designed and built by his fellow Germans.

The European Space Agency (ESA) held true to their commitment to assign Ockels to a later Spacelab flight following his bridesmaid role on the first Spacelab mission, STS-9, where he had served as backup payload specialist to Ulf Merbold. Along with Ockels, Germans Messerschmid and Furrer had also been in the running to be selected for the first Spacelab flight, but they lost out to Merbold. DFVLR was financing the Spacelab DI mission, so naturally they wished to choose German citizens for their scientific expedition into space. Initially, the payload crew was planned to consist of three mission specialists and two payload specialists. However, it was eventually realized that due to the heavy workload planned for the DI mission, three payload specialists were required to ensure that the payload objectives could be accomplished. Hence, a third payload specialist was eventually assigned to the DI flight. The sole backup payload specialist for DI, Merbold, would be responsible for supporting the payload crew on the ground once they were in orbit. Veteran astronaut Hank Hartsfield commanded STS-61A, with Steve Nagel as his pilot. Nagel would also support the payload crew. The remainder of the payload crew was comprised of mission specialists Bonnie Dunbar, James Buchli, and Guion Bluford. *Challenger* was the first and last spacecraft to date to carry eight humans into space and then return them home.

The science activities on this mission would be controlled out of the German Space Operations Center (GSOC) located in Oberpfaffenhofen, Germany, instead of the Houston-based POCC used on previous Spacelab missions. The mission manager and mission scientist, Hans-Ulrich Steimle and Peter R. Sahm, respectively, were both from DFVLR.

The Europeans called Merbold, Messerschmid, Furrer, and Ockels science astronauts, instead of payload specialists, fueled by their belief that they were career astronauts and not someone slated to fly only once and then return to their established career aspirations. Merbold explained that their management wanted to ensure the distinction was made between their

15. Spacelab D1 payload specialists Wubbo Ockels, Reinhard Furrer, Ulf Merbold (backup), and Ersnt Messerschmid. Courtesy NASA/Retro Space Images.

scientists and other hitchhikers on the shuttle, such as a senator or Arab prince—referring to the STS-51D and STS-51G missions, which had flown earlier in 1985. U.S. senator Jake Garn and Saudi Arabian prince Sultan Salman Abdulaziz Al-Saud had flown as payload specialists on these two missions and were often referred to as "passengers" instead of full-fledged astronauts. As quoted in the *Aviation Week* magazine from 11 November 1985, Steimle accused NASA of "running a travel office for visiting dignitaries" and felt this slight was counterproductive to doing serious science.

DFVLR hoped that the Spacelab D1 mission would progress their ability to carry out scientific research in space. Valuable management skills should result from this endeavor, as they would be in control of a fully outfitted and operational research laboratory—the second Spacelab module. Two Spacelab modules—LM1 and LM2—had been built. LM1 flew on STS-9 and STS-51B. The second Spacelab module—LM2—was flown for the first time on STS-61A.

The Germans referred to D1 as "Deutschland Eins." West Germany paid NASA $65 million for the right to devote the mission to their Spacelab exper-

iments. Years later when NASA invited Germany to participate in building the ISS, the Spacelab module was the template for what became ESA's
Columbus module, an integral part of the ISS. Columbus utilizes standard-
ized science racks just like those on Spacelab, is about the same size, and
very much resembles Spacelab in outward appearance.

According to mission commander Hartsfield, NASA's primary flight objective was to "successfully launch, operate, and return the German Spacelab
DI payload," as well as to deploy a NASA scientific satellite. There was also
a NASA materials-processing experiment on board.

This fourth Spacelab flight would host experiments in the fields of materials science, physics, chemistry, biology, and related fields that required a
microgravity environment. Spacelab DI was not that dissimilar to Spacelab
I in terms of the scientific payload, but the experiments on DI would be
managed by the Germans.

Ernst Willi Messerschmid was born in Reutlingen, Germany, on 21
May 1945. He had no dreams as a child to ride rockets into space, but the
American lunar landings and his work at university aroused his interest
in international science. He earned a degree in physics from the University of Tübingen and Bonn in 1972, followed by experimental work from
1972 to 1975 focused on proton beams and plasmas at CERN, or the European Organization for Nuclear Research, in Geneva. He continued his
higher education as a research assistant at the University of Freiburg–
Breisgau in Germany and at Brookhaven National Laboratory in New
York, from 1975 to 1976, earning his doctorate in 1976 from the University of Freiburg–Breisgau.

After completing his doctorate, Messerschmid learned from public adver-
tisements that Europeans were preparing in early 1977 to select astronauts
for Spacelab missions aboard the American space shuttle. After reading
what they were looking for in a European astronaut, he immediately concluded that he was more than qualified. He was healthy and physically fit,
of sound mind, fluent in English, had the required scientific background,
and was experienced in the international environment. He applied once
Germany announced the selection process and was one of the finalists
for the European payload specialist position on Spacelab 1. He eventually
accepted a position as a researcher in 1977 at the German Electron Syn-
chrotron (DESY) located in Hamburg, where he developed an interest in

space technology and utilization. DESY is known for its particle accelerators, which scientists use to study the curious structure of matter. From 1978 to 1982 he was employed by DFVLR, where he worked on space-borne communication and navigation systems.

Reinhard Alfred Furrer was born 25 November 1940, in what is now Worgl, Austria, in the state of Tyrol. At the time of Furrer's birth, early in World War II, Worgl was part of Germany, making him a German citizen. Following the war, the family moved to Bavaria, Germany. Furrer attended the University of Kiel and then transferred to the Free University of Berlin, where he received his degree in physics in 1969, eventually earning his PhD in 1972 in physics. He became an assistant professor in Stuttgart, earning full professorship in 1979. Furrer migrated to the University of Chicago in 1980 and then to the Argonne National Laboratory in Chicago in 1981. He netted his private pilot's license in 1974; flying would be a large part of his life.

Like Michael Lampton, Furrer was involved in an activity as a student that gained him some measure of notoriety. Furrer helped fifty-seven of his fellow Germans escape from communist East to free West Berlin in a tunnel beneath the Berlin Wall. Known as Tunnel 57, it measured almost five hundred feet in length and required moving tons of dirt, as well as careful measures to ensure secrecy from the deadly East German police.

The tunnel was begun in West Berlin in an old disused bakery located along the contested border and fortuitously emerged into an old outhouse located near an apartment building. The escape to freedom occurred on the nights of 3 and 4 October 1964. Furrer's job was to help direct East Berlin fugitives into the tunnel opening from the East Berlin side. Unfortunately, East German officers had become aware of the escape plot and were on hand with soldiers to thwart the operation on the second night. Furrer suddenly recognized a threatening gun pointed in his direction and, in the darkness, made a mad dash for the tunnel to warn his fellow accomplices. Gunfire erupted in the melee, killing one of the East German border guards. Furrer managed to escape harm that night, and scores of persecuted East Germans made it safely to freedom.

Like Messerschmid, Furrer applied for the European Spacelab astronaut program in 1977 and likewise made the final cut for the first Spacelab mission. Furrer was braggingly confident of his chances for being selected; on the ESA website, Lena Fuhrmann quoted Furrer as proclaiming in 1978, "I'll be flying on that [Spacelab]."

Ockels recalled his first dreams of flying into space in 1977 after noticing a bulletin calling for European astronaut candidates posted in the hall while completing his PhD at Groningen (Netherlands). Some of Ockels's classmates had written jokes on the notice, but after a bit of serious soul-searching, Ockels decided to write for more information. Soon he realized that he had found the perfect job opportunity and promptly applied. He was one of a handful of finalists who included Merbold, Messerschmid, and Furrer.

Merbold's expertise in materials science was a better fit with the specialized experiments planned for the first Spacelab mission; consequently, he was selected for that flight, although Furrer, Messerschmid, and Ockels were strong contenders for the mission. Disappointed at not being chosen for Spacelab 1, Messerschmid remembers being told at the time that a German Spacelab mission was in the making and that the powers that be wanted him on that flight. Messerschmid shared in a 2010 ESA interview that both Ockels and Nicollier were in consideration to fly as an ESA science astronaut on the D1 flight because there were new ESA payloads on board and ESA was providing financial backing. Ockels was a logical choice to be selected as the payload specialist on the D1 mission; he had served as Merbold's backup on the Spacelab 1 mission, was trained, and was available. Nicollier had remained at JSC following his training as a mission specialist.

Ockels, Messerschmid, and Furrer began their training for the D1 mission in 1983. At this time, the decision to include three payload specialists on the flight had not been made. Ockels, representing ESA, had already been assigned to the flight, leaving only one payload specialist slot open on the crew that had been planned for seven people. Therefore, Messerschmid and Furrer were in competition for a single opportunity to fly on D1. Messerschmid claims that whereas Furrer was extroverted, he was introverted, making the fight a bit more difficult for him. On the other hand, Furrer felt he was at a disadvantage because he was a bachelor, believing that the Americans favored candidates who were married.

As the mission planning progressed, both Messerschmid and Furrer came to realize that three payload specialists were going to be required to carry out the heavy scientific workload planned in orbit. They eventually convinced NASA of the need, and about one year before the flight, NASA developed a plan to add an eighth seat to the orbiter, which meant that both men would fly. ESA pressed NASA to add Claude Nicollier to the flight as one of the mission specialists. Nicollier had hinted at this possibility in his 25 September 1981 memo to the Spacelab investigators informing them that Ockels was going to leave the mission specialist training program to provide much needed support to the Spacelab 1 mission. Reflecting on Ockels departing mission specialist training, Nicollier wrote,

> ESA *decided that it would be best for one of us to fully concentrate on the Mission Specialist training and activities, with view for possible assignment as such on the DI mission. [O]n personal grounds, I regret that such a decision had to be taken, but this action is, without any doubt, for the benefit of Europe's future involvement in manned space flight, as it permits to keep open the European Mission Specialist's option, targeted towards the DI mission, and without affecting the first Spacelab mission in a significant manner. Be sure that I will be following very closely the mission preparation and the mission itself, and I look very much forward to seeing a number of you aboard DI or any future Spacelab mission.*

The popular German-based website Spacefacts claims that there were discussions between NASA and ESA, but NASA eventually rejected ESA's proposal to include Nicollier on the flight. Besides, he had already been assigned to a later flight.

By virtue of moving back to the payload specialist program, Ockels forfeited a similar opportunity to Nicollier to become a NASA mission specialist. Meanwhile, Nicollier stuck with the mission specialist program and eventually flew on four shuttle flights as a mission specialist, including an eight-hour EVA and two Hubble-servicing flights.

The training for the DI mission followed a similar routine to previous Spacelab flights—long hours of mission-dependent training and an abbreviated mission-independent training regimen just prior to launch. Furrer told Lena Fuhrmann in an 11 February 2011 DLR interview that the mission-dependent training took approximately two years to complete and included learning procedures not part of his advanced educational studies, such as how to insert needles into human test subjects and take blood pressure measurements.

Once Hartsfield was assigned as mission commander, he meticulously took control of the payload preparations to ensure that all experiment training objectives could be accomplished on schedule. Hartsfield was a man of few words, with a soft voice. But he was a natural leader; failure, for him, was not an option. NASA was deeply concerned with the science portion of the mission being run out of the facility at Oberpfaffenhofen. According to Hartsfield, the control team there had not previously planned or run a science mission, and it was uncertain if their training had prepared the Germans to run a complicated mission like D1. Therefore, members of the Houston MCC made a trip to Oberpfaffenhofen to run an early simulation and share their experiences with the German control team.

DFVLR ran the simulated flight along with a JSC training representative, but NASA wasn't very impressed with the initial efforts. Hartsfield explained, "They lacked a comprehensive training plan and syllabus, and they had very few experiment flight procedures to train with. They were unaware of the operational flight constraints and responsibilities of the crew, and they did not recognize the difference in training requirements between the MSS and PSS. Initially, the MSS had to spend a large amount of time educating the user [DFVLR and the PIs] in flight training techniques and FDF [flight data files] procedures." Hartsfield believed there was a "dramatic learning curve" that came out of this exercise, which was crucial to the success of the mission.

The payload training played second fiddle once the final mission-independent training was in progress. Hartsfield was comfortable with the experienced backup Merbold sliding onto the crew as little as one month prior to launch, if it became necessary. But Messerschmid, Furrer, and Ockels were eager, healthy, and fully trained come launch day, so Merbold would have to wait awhile for his second trip into space.

The racks nestled inside the Spacelab module carried an extensive array of over seventy-five experiments, including materials science and life sciences experiments. Some of the investigations were repeats from Spacelab 1, such as the hop-and-drop experiment; others were brand new, while many were similar to previously flown devices. Many were conceived to take advantage of the microgravity environment. Hartsfield and Nagel would be required to maneuver *Challenger* into a gravity-gradient attitude—nose pointed toward Earth—for approximately fourteen hours in support of the materials-processing experiments.

Perhaps the most interesting investigation was one conducted using a vestibular galvanic stimulation, or VGS, device, which in less imposing terms was simply called the vestibular sled. Designed to investigate the effects of SAS, it was attached to the floor of the module on rails and looked more like a torture device from the Middle Ages than a state-of-the-art scientific apparatus designed for research in outer space. It was conceived to test the human vestibular and orientation systems under microgravity conditions. The astronauts would be buckled to a seat that sat on fixed rails, sitting in an almost half-lotus yoga pose and wearing a large boxlike apparatus on their heads. An astronaut secured to the seat could be moved along the rails back and forth and accelerated up to 0.2 gravity forward or backward while thermally stimulating the inner ear and following movements of the eyes.

In the few months prior to launch Hartsfield assessed that STS-61A training was significantly behind schedule. Six weeks before launch Hartsfield became extremely worried that the entire crew would be spent before they ever launched. The amount of training time required in the European locations and complications from the Spacelab portion of the mission being controlled by the Germans, all added to the hectic schedule. The mission and payload specialists had to participate in three days of baseline data collection (BDC) for the life sciences experiments. One day was eventually canceled due to the tight schedule. Even so, these ever-so-important sessions had to be undertaken on the weekends in order to minimize the impact on the remaining last-minute shuttle training exercises. The commander and pilot also had weekend STA flights. Late-arriving software and concerns with software compatibility added to the problem. The crew had difficulty finding time for important orbiter planned training—just about to the point to where it was very nearly a bare bones training effort that would provide only the minimum level of proficiency before it was time to launch. This rushed and hectic arrangement gravely concerned Hartsfield, as the crew had very few days of free time during this period. Hartsfield lamented, "The crew was tired and needed the relaxation enforced during the L-3 day prelaunch period at KSC."

On 30 October 1985, *Challenger* inched upward from launchpad 39A, slowly winning its bout with the law of gravity, soon to deliver the largest crew ever into an orbit of 207 miles above Earth's surface. Following a routine climb to orbit with a fifty-seven-degree inclination to the equator, the crew began preparing for the upcoming scientific marathon they had been entrusted to execute. Ockels described the launch as being very intense, but once orbit had been achieved, that reaction slowly transformed into one of emotion, overwhelming Ockels when he took his first look at the beautiful blue planet rotating slowly and majestically below him. He claimed that he felt extraterrestrial!

Led by Buchli, the red team of Bluford and Messerschmid began to methodically carry out the planned experiments, whereas the blue team—Nagel, Dunbar, and Furrer—settled down for their sleep period. Hartsfield explained that Ockels was not assigned to either of the two shifts; instead, he "sort of floated between the two teams; we kind of called him purple." Both Hartsfield and Ockels worked on both shifts as needed, but they usually worked with the blue shift.

Messerschmid succumbed to SAS symptoms and vomited soon after he reached orbit. It took him several hours just to learn how to remain still; he soon learned that the trick was to locate a solid anchor point and hold to it tightly. Shortly, he was going to have to carry out sickness-inducing experiments as part of the life sciences investigations, and the schedule was jam-packed with a variety of experiments to be executed or monitored. The discomfort from SAS was not likely to dissipate anytime soon. Still he had a job to do, and he worked through the discomfort. To make matters worse, Messerschmid had trouble sleeping the first night; it was cold and he kept seeing bright flashes in his eyes. This phenomenon commonly occurs when spacecraft fly through the South Atlantic Anomaly, where the Van Allen radiation belts gently kiss the upper portions of Earth's atmosphere, briefly exposing the astronauts to the bombardment of high-energy protons, which induces bright flashes in the eyes.

Messerschmid felt a huge weight on his shoulders to operate all the experiments exactly as he had been trained. Although many of the experiments ran autonomously, they had to be checked, serviced, or reconfigured regularly. A lot of taxpayer money had been spent to finance the payload experiments, and the scientists on the ground had sacrificed significant portions of their careers preparing the experiments—and they expected good results.

16. European payload specialist Ernst Messerschmid experiences the sensation of zero gravity in the NASA KC-135 Vomit Comet. Courtesy NASA/Retro Space Images.

Thus, the payload crew was more than willing to give up their leisure time to work longer hours on the experiments to ensure they came off as planned. Messerschmid felt that the pressure to do the experiments correctly was far greater than the worry of a life-ending accident occurring. *Challenger* might be struck by a stray meteroid or errant piece of space junk, causing it to depressurize, inviting the vacuum of space into the bodies of the crew, and sending them into paralysis and convulsions within seconds. Their bodies would swell, and their hearts would stop beating shortly thereafter. Their blood pressure would drop to zero, blood would cease to flow, gases and water vapor would spurt out of their mouths and noses, and their bodies would cool slowly. Likely the crew would expire within ninety seconds. Messerschmid was more concerned about returning to Earth and having to tell a brilliant scientist that the experiment had failed.

Just like on Spacelab 2, there were some equipment failures right away that threatened to compromise the mission, possibly even end it. Once Messerschmid entered the Spacelab module, he saw red and yellow lights galore, signaling that there were hardware problems—ostensibly suffering their own form of SAS. One of the experiments required a vacuum, which was obtained by taking advantage of the uncomfortably nearby deadly emptiness of space surrounding the orbiter. However, there was a slow leak somewhere in the connection to outside the spacecraft. The crew was told the mission would be cut to two days if the leak could not be stopped, as they were losing life-sustaining air. Fortunately, a fix was soon discovered, and the mission proceeded as planned.

Two days into the flight, the medical and biological experiments were progressing well, but the materials science investigations were encountering some problems. The MEDEA, a very expensive materials science experiment, failed to come to life. The fix was to cut a cable in one of the furnaces, just one of a spaghetti mess of wires. The problem was that the payload crew had to figure out the correct wire to cut. Fortunately, Ockels came to the rescue; through consultation with the experts in the GSOC, he severed the appropriate wire, curing the malady. The crew also had to replace a lamp in the MEDEA's furnace. Not a big deal for an expertly trained crew, but valuable time and data were lost. NASA considered extending the mission an extra day, but inadequate power levels would not permit it.

Guy Bluford recalled performing runs on the vestibular sled. With a contraption and accompanying instrumentation that engulfed the entire head of the subject, the sled promised to upset the vestibular system of even the hardiest astronaut. In spite of its foreboding appearance, Bluford claimed that it was relatively easygoing: "It looked rather provocative from the spectator point of view, but it proved to be very benign from the rider point of view."

The ESA-sponsored Biorack carried a hermetically sealed glove box and a variety of organisms, including bacteria, fruit flies, and frog embryos. In orbit, the embryos hatched into tadpoles, which, to the surprise of the scientists, exhibited aberrations in their swimming patterns once back in

Earth's gravity. The fruit flies were studied to assess the development of life from embryo to adult. Ockels explained what they learned from their observations: "This was the first flight which showed such a systematic large biology research. And already there we found an absolutely new phenomenon that flies in space do not know where to put their eggs." The flies were also apparently quite clever. Although the crew was assured that the flies could not escape their containment filter system, some did, and one wily fly bonded with the crew, earning its own name. As Hartsfield jested, "In fact, more than one [fly] did [escape], although Willie garnered the honors as the sole survivor."

Playing with—rather, making scientific observations of—fluids in the microgravity environment seemed to be a favorite pastime of just about every shuttle crew, but it tickled the scientist-astronauts right down to the tips of their floating toes. On D1, orange juice was a favorite, and with a few tools to stimulate the droplets, Ockels was a child again, as he explained once back on Earth.

As a nuclear physicist I'm always interested in seeing liquid drops being excited with different modes of vibration . . . and you sometimes see that the droplet really moves and sometimes gets even into a square shape. It's really impressive; zero gravity floating is something which you fall in love with very quickly. Actually, it's very difficult as you come back to get used to this sticky Earth which pulls you down all the time. You can very gently try to move a big blob of liquid around and try to get it in different modes of oscillation. The only thing you have to make sure is that it's not that big that eventually if you need to do it you can still swallow it.

At one point during the mission, Ockels spun a blindfolded Furrer, like a child's toy, to see if he could tell which direction was up—relative to his surroundings—once Ockels stopped him spinning. "Wubbo stops me someplace, and then he asks me, 'Where is your up?' And at this moment I just say I cannot tell anymore. Because we proved with this experiment that there is no integrated mechanism that can tell you as a subject what happened to [you] motionwise."

The silver-haired Hartsfield was a stickler for safety, perhaps no more than any other astronaut, but he was often quick to pontificate on potential safety issues. As commander, he needed to know everything that was

17. Holland's first astronaut to fly in space, Wubbo Ockels, along with German Reinhard Furrer float in the middeck of *Challenger* on the STS-61A mission. Courtesy NASA/Retro Space Images.

happening during the flight and whether it was potentially a problem, and he didn't speak German or Dutch. Consequently, all crew members were required to speak the agreed-on language, English. "The orbiter is a complex machine," Hartsfield stated, "and space operations are not in any way as routine as airline operations. . . . In the much more hazardous arena of Space Shuttle operations, a common operational language is unquestionably mandatory."

Dunbar explained that there were exceptions. If an investigator from a country where English was not their first language needed to talk to the crew, they were allowed to use their native language, as long as it was pre-coordinated from the ground, which included using a translator. Bluford confided that there were times, although infrequently, when the European science astronauts would inadvertently switch to German during the flight. Bluford recalled that he and Dunbar took Berlitz language lessons in German during their training, which made it much easier to converse and work with their European crewmates.

The failure of equipment hardware and language issues could bring a mission to its knees if not dealt with adequately. But little things—such as clothing—could also adversely impact the success of the mission. The crew was not overly thrilled with the elastic waistband in the specially designed trousers they had been given to wear during the flight. The waistband was simply too tight and uncomfortable for some of the crew. There was no need for such a hefty system to keep their trousers on, for as Hartsfield rightly pointed out, "Pants will not fall off in zero-g." The accompanying jacket was "almost useless" according to the commander—he had to use his "right hand to get into the left pocket; it reminds one of a straitjacket." Bo Bobko noted similar concerns with the elastic in their trousers on STS-51D, flown in April 1985. The pants fit well enough during training, but once in space they were extremely uncomfortable, likely due to shifting body fluids once in orbit. Their solution was to simply cut the elastic band.

Just like the POCC, the German control center also harbored a glut of personnel to ensure that the scientists in space had everything they needed to do their jobs as planned. Mission scientist Peter Sahm recalled that up to 250 scientists and managers vigilantly followed the flight at Oberpfaffenhofen, checking and double-checking the schedule, following every mission detail. It was Sahm's job to decide if an experiment justified additional time and how to adjust the schedule and to ensure that every scientist on the ground got a fair shake. Bluford recalled that there was a lot of valuable discussion "between the payload crew and the PIs and CICs [crew interface coordinators] on each shift," which made a significant contribution to the mission's success.

As the mission crept to an end, it was clear to the crew and those in the GSOC that the long hours and hard work had paid off; the Germans had carried out an exceptionally successful science mission. Unfortunately, the payload crew had little time to enjoy the wonders of space travel. Bluford recalled giving some well-deserved time off to Messerschmid to head to the flight deck on the last day so he could appreciate his celestial surroundings.

Another defining moment for Ockels came as the mission eased to an end. He recalled that he and Messerschmid were watching the payload bay doors slowly close from the rear windows of *Challenger*'s flight deck. Ockels considered grabbing his camera for a photo opportunity but, at Messerschmid's suggestion, changed his mind. Instead, he savored the moment—one that he would remember for the rest of his life.

Challenger landed at Edwards Air Force Base on 6 November 1985. After *Challenger* had come to a safe rest, Ockels unstrapped himself from his safety harness, stood up, and immediately sensed the biting grip of Earth's gravity, which at that moment made him feel as if he were accelerating upward at a high rate of speed. Spaceflight had a life-changing impact on Ockels, and this experience was one of several that overwhelmed him during the flight. These were glorious epiphanies that affected his view of Earth and the cosmos for the remainder of his days.

Twelve of the seventy-plus experiments required some degree of repair on orbit, but the mission was nevertheless considered 95 percent successful. Messerschmid counted many positives from the mission, including better production techniques of crystal growth and solidification and community support for future space research, which eventually led to the ISS. He proclaimed in a 26 October 2010 interview on the ESA website that the DI mission had "changed the textbooks."

Hartsfield was ecstatic over the performance of the payload crew and proudly exclaimed, "They were an exceptional crew. I've never seen five people work in a Spacelab as hard as they did. We planned twelve-hour days in the lab . . . they came closer to fifteen-hour days, but the results speak for themselves."

Hartsfield noted several faux pas that occurred on the flight without identifying the names of the guilty parties. There were times when payload specialists operated Spacelab subsystems without proper authorization. In-flight maintenance was also performed with no onboard coordination or approval from the MCC. In addition to potential safety concerns, without knowledge of unplanned and poorly communicated procedures, the vast flight experience that NASA had accumulated over the years was rendered useless. Given the rigorous and thorough training that NASA provided for their mission specialists, it seems likely that Hartsfield was referring to the less well-trained science astronauts from Europe.

The commander also hinted at some additional sore points after the flight in his flight crew report but was short on details. He made it abundantly clear that they—the Germans—"should be informed of the pre-flight requisite to sign a PS agreement relating to not realizing personal gain from the flight." Additionally, "No unapproved items will be stowed on the spacecraft or carried on board in flight suits." Nor should any personal articles—including those in each crew member's PPK (or personal preference kit)—be taken from the spacecraft after landing unless authorized prior to the flight. "Any such items discovered may be confiscated." Hartsfield was an easygoing leader, but clearly, he didn't appreciate rules not being followed.

Hartsfield also felt the sleeping conditions were far too difficult with the eighth crewperson on board, especially with the two-shift operations typical of Spacelab missions. Ockels slept in the air lock, and his sleep was constantly disturbed by the working crew members. Hartsfield stressed that "unless an acceptable fifth sleep station can be provided, a crew size limit of seven must be observed." Ockels readily agreed.

ESA participated in Spacelab 1 back in late 1983, but NASA still pulled all the strings, even with the scientific investigations. Messerschmid saw it a bit differently for D1; in a September 2010 DLR (DFVLR) interview, Manuela Braun quoted Messerschmid as saying that for D1 "DLR was in the driver's seat." Messerschmid considered the shuttle to be a taxi to carry the European experiments and the precious Spacelab module into space, even boldly proclaiming in the same article that the mission specialists were the "helpers" and "helped us prepare our meals." Chris Kraft may not have appreciated Messerschmid's perspective.

The Germans were proud of their mission, and Oberpfaffenhofen became known as the Bavarian Houston to many people. The training simulations held in the GSOC prior to the mission paid huge dividends. Hartsfield crowed, "Actual flight operations interfaces with the GSOC were excellent." Bluford complimented Ulf Merbold on his role as the crew interface coordinator in Oberpfaffenhofen; he provided excellent support of the payload crew in orbit and worked seamlessly with the principal investigators in the GSOC.

As with previous shuttle missions, the scientific research still had to be completed after the payload crew was back on Earth. They remained at Dryden Flight Research Center (now the Armstrong Flight Research Center) for several days of additional tests to determine how their bodies and physiological reactions readapted to Earth's gravity.

None of the D1 European science astronauts would fly into space again. Ockels worked on human spaceflight projects from 1986 to 1996 at the European Space Research and Technology Center located in Noordwijk, Netherlands. It was here that he contributed to the planning of the Columbus module, which became an integral part of the ISS. In 1992 he officially retired from the European astronaut corps, and soon after, he accepted a position at the Delft University of Technology in the Netherlands, as a full professor of aerospace for sustainable engineering and technology. Ockels became a champion of sustainable energy, which he believed was a must in order to preserve the beautiful planet that he orbited 112 times.

Wubbo Ockels passed away on 29 May 2013 from kidney cancer—a disease that he had conquered in 2008, only to discover it had returned in 2013. Sadly, he could not defeat the disease a second time. At the time of his death, he was still active at the Delft University of Technology.

Ernst Messerschmid went on to hold a variety of important positions at the University of Stuttgart. He became professor and director of the Space Systems Institute (IRS) in 1986 and then served as the chairman of a collaborative research center involved with numerous projects at university institutes, industry, and DLR laboratories. Beginning in 2005 he took leave from the University of Stuttgart to head up the European Astronaut Centre (EAC), returning to the University of Stuttgart in 2007 as a full professor.

Reinhard Furrer became a professor and director of the Institute of Space Sciences at the Free University of Berlin in 1987, where he was employed until 1995. Flying remained his passion, and he made some very daring long-distance flights in single-engine aircraft including a 1981 solo crossing of the Atlantic Ocean from Germany to Quito, Ecuador. Furrer was killed on 9 September 1995 when the Messerschmitt Bf 108 World War II–era lightplane he was riding in encountered problems immediately after takeoff and crashed into a nearby field during an air show at Berlin's Johannisthal Airfield.

Sadly, two other members of the STS-61A crew are also deceased. Steve Nagel died on 7 September 2011 from advanced melanoma. Mission commander Hank Hartsfield succumbed to complications from back surgery on 17 July 2014.

Spacelab flights would take a hiatus following the loss of *Challenger* in January 1986 on the STS-51L mission. But both Spacelab modules flew again, and payload specialists continued to play an integral role on these missions. The next Spacelab mission (ASTRO-1) following STS-51L was dedicated to astrophysics and flew in December 1990 aboard shuttle *Columbia* on STS-35. The Germans flew a second highly successful Spacelab mission

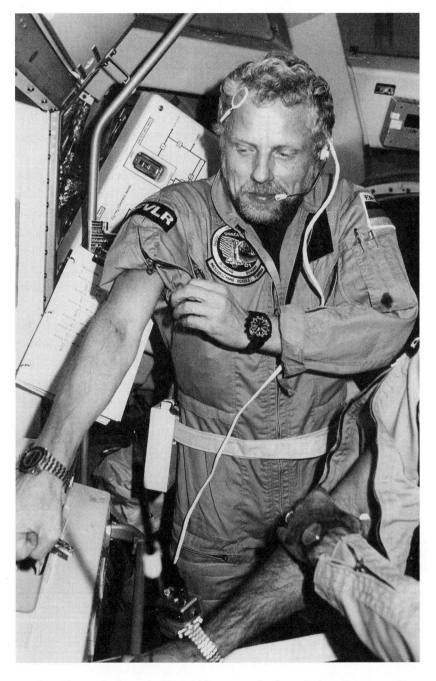

18. Spacelab D1 payload specialist Reinhard Furrer preparing for medical experiments on orbit.
Courtesy NASA/Retro Space Images.

on STS-55 in April and May of 1993. The final Spacelab mission flew aboard *Columbia* on the STS-90 flight in 1998.

The four Spacelab missions flown from 1983 to 1985 laid the groundwork for the success of the next thirty-two missions. The Spacelab module flown on the D1 mission is now appropriately displayed in Germany at the Bremen Airport, whereas the first Spacelab module to fly resides at the Smithsonian Udvar-Hazy Museum in Washington DC.

Spacelab was truly an impressive and tremendously prosperous program. Thirty-six Spacelab missions (sixteen with the pressurized module) were flown over a period of seventeen years—totaling 375 flight days. According to Dr. Arnauld Nicogossian, NASA chief medical officer and acting associate administrator for life and microgravity sciences and applications, over eight hundred individual investigations were completed, leading to more than one thousand papers being published in technical journals. Well over 250 master of science and PhD degrees were awarded based on the research carried out on Spacelab. He cited many advances and discoveries that came from the research and investigations performed on Spacelab, including advances in protein crystal growth techniques, new insights into metal formation and structure, astronomical observations of distant galaxies, and many more. At a Spacelab forum held 10–11 March 1999 in Washington DC, Nicogossian shared an unexpected discovery: "One of the most fascinating stories about Spacelab is the discovery of the ancient caravan routes, which led us to the finding of lost water wells along roads which were covered by sand long ago. When those wells were opened up, they were able to improve irrigation in some areas." Spacelab was living up to the grand expectations envisioned in the early 1970s.

8. Supersonic in a Paper Airplane

Air power alone does not guarantee America's security, but I believe
it best exploits the nation's greatest asset—our technical skill.

Hoyt S. Vandenberg

As with many astronauts, Gary Payton had been awestruck by spaceflight
from an early age. He graduated from high school in 1966 at the height of
the Gemini program, but unlike many youngsters of the day, he did not initially aspire to fly in space himself. There was a nationwide military draft in
effect at the time, so with "that rude reality staring you in the face," as Payton related to the authors, he made one of the most important decisions of
his life: "[I] was at that age, very impressionable about airplanes and rockets, so I was drawn to the air force. This thing called the Air Force Academy was brand new, and I was drawn to it for that reason. My real intent
was to be in the rocket side of the air force, either in launch vehicles or ballistic missiles. The idea of the advance of flying people in space didn't grab
my attention as much as the rockets and missiles of the air force."

Nestled up against the front range of the Rocky Mountains in Colorado
Springs, the academy offered Payton his first experience with flying an aircraft. The school provided cadets with several opportunities to take rides
in air force planes for orientation purposes, and Payton was immediately
captured by the thrill of flight. His first reaction, as he recalled decades
later, was "Wow! Flying airplanes is a lot of fun, so if the air force is going
to pay me to fly airplanes, I'll go do that!" But even with that new enthusiasm, he was still committed to learning all he could about the engineering of rockets and the complex dynamics of orbital mechanics.

Honored as a distinguished graduate in the class of 1971, Payton immediately set off for Purdue University following his commissioning in the air force. "I majored in astronautical engineering and then got a master's degree at Purdue right after graduation from the academy," he shared. Upon completion of his graduate studies, Payton was assigned to Craig Air Force Base in Alabama, where he would pursue his newly discovered passion for aviation. Again, the young air force officer exceled, graduating in 1973 with such high marks that he was offered the opportunity to return to the school as an instructor pilot. Payton remained at Craig until 1976, flying and teaching in several high-performance jet aircraft, including the Cessna T-37 Tweet and the Northrup T-38 Talon.

But the air force had other plans for Payton. For his part, he still had a desire to be involved with rockets and to put all his hard-earned education to work in the branch's space programs. At the completion of his tour as an instructor pilot, he was assigned to the Cape Canaveral Air Force Station as a spacecraft test controller, where he would spend the following four years. "My first nonflying job was at Cape Canaveral launching military satellites on expendable rockets: Atlases and Deltas and Titans," Payton remembers. "This was just before the shuttle got started. That wasn't flying, but that was the greatest nonflying job."

It was during Payton's time at Cape Canaveral that the space shuttle began to take shape, and like most of his peers, he kept his eye on the development of the orbiter as its military uses were still being pondered. While he could not know it at the time, some of the high-level decisions being made by NASA and the Department of Defense would have a profound impact on his future.

"I've always loved space. I mean from when I was a little kid, my goal was to fly in space, and everything I did was to prepare me for that," remembers Frank Casserino. Growing up in the Bronx, New York City, these high aspirations guided many of his decisions as he prepared to select an appropriate school to attend. A man of deep faith, a gifted student, and an avid lacrosse player, Casserino was offered scholarships to several Ivy League schools, but none fit his plan better than the Air Force Academy. He never regretted his decision.

While attending the academy, Casserino was assigned an academic advisor who had previously worked at the Satellite Test Center at the Sunnyvale

19. U.S. Air Force major Gary Payton was a spacecraft test controller at the Cape Canaveral Air Force Station before his selection as a manned spaceflight engineer. Courtesy U.S. Air Force/Retro Space Images.

Air Force Station in California. That advisor came along at an opportune time for the young Lieutenant Casserino, as he was trying to break the conventional thinking that new graduates should go directly into what were considered to be operational assignments. The Air Force Academy had a mindset that flying satellites at Sunnyvale was more a research and development assignment and did not believe that new air force officers stationed there would get the kind of experience valued by the military.

But Casserino was undeterred and jumped at the chance to get a space assignment right after graduation in the spring of 1977. "Well, the academy just didn't realize that if you're talking operations, going to Sunnyvale and operating satellites was probably as operational as you're gonna get unless you're gonna fly aircraft," he recalls. "So it was an awesome first assignment."

It was indeed a dream job for the newly minted second lieutenant, who found himself working deep inside the iconic Blue Cube at Sunnyvale. Known officially as building 1003, the windowless, pale-blue facility was complemented with three large, swiveling, parabolic satellite dishes. These arrays, linked to seven far-flung tracking stations around the globe comprising the Satellite Control Facility, were used to command and control covert military assets orbiting high above the earth.

Casserino had just been promoted to first lieutenant on 1 June 1979 when his mentor at Sunnyvale came to him and asked a question that set him back on his heels. "Hey, did you hear about the application that came across the wire?" he asked. Casserino had no idea what he was talking about. He was then told that the air force was secretly recruiting suitable candidates to become manned spaceflight engineers—*astronauts*! "The applications have to be in tomorrow," he added.

"You've got to be kidding me!" gasped Casserino. He was overwhelmed with excitement but, at the same time, filled with dread that he had missed out on the opportunity of a lifetime. As fate would have it, one of the officers who was in charge of the recruitment had previously worked as a mission director with Casserino's mentor, and they knew each other well. "Let me give him a call and tell him that you're really interested, and I think he will wait until you can get your application in," he reassured him.

Casserino spent the following days filling out all the necessary paperwork, but the exercise only highlighted in his own mind how slim his chances were.

I was only a first lieutenant—I didn't have that much information to give! I thought this is gonna be [a] long shot. They're looking for people that have so much more experience than me, and so I told my buddy, Jeff [Detroye], who was a classmate of mine, about the application, and he either had his application in or he did the same thing I did and hustled to get it in. I guess they sifted through the applications, and somehow they saw something in the words that we put down and thought that we were at least worthy to be interviewed.

John Brett Watterson, of Garden City, New York, came to the U.S. Air Force with a degree in physics after graduation from the exclusive Virginia Military Institute in 1971. Known as jovial, salty tongued, and exceptionally smart, he was initially assigned as an intelligence officer, deployed to the Royal Korat Air Force Base in Thailand from 1972 through the following year. Upon returning to the United States, he would earn a master's degree in engineering physics from the Air Force Institute of Technology at Wright-Patterson Air Force Base in Dayton, Ohio.

Assigned to the Foreign Technology Division at Wright-Patterson, he advanced the country's knowledge of its Cold War adversary's military capabilities. "I was assessing and reporting on the Soviet ballistic missiles," he explained. "At the time, the SS-17, 18, and 19 were being developed by the Soviets as a new generation and even, perhaps, first-strike capability against the United States. So we were doing assessments against that."

The U.S. Air Force's Special Projects Office—or in military parlance, Secretary of the Air Force Special Projects (SAFSP)—at Los Angeles Air Force Base in El Segundo, California, was one of four major organizations comprising the supersecret NRO. With his extensive experience in the complex world of aerospace delivery vehicles carrying nuclear payloads, Watterson was recruited into this organization after just two years at the Foreign Technology Division. There, in the payload office responsible for the largest and most complicated spy satellite in the nation's inventory, the KH-9 Hexagon, he would become intimately familiar with the very payload that had defined the size and shape of NASA's space shuttle.

At the time, surveillance satellites did not have the ability to transmit electronic images to the ground and were therefore launched with multiple reentry pods containing film reels that were exposed over denied areas of interest. The KH-9, the latest in the series of Keyhole spy satellites, would eject these acorn-shaped capsules to drop into the atmosphere and be snagged in midair by retrieval aircraft using long loops of cable trailing behind them.

When the top secret announcement for MSE candidates found its way to Brett Watterson in June 1979, he happened to be in a uniquely qualified position to capitalize on the new relationship between NASA and the Department of Defense. "I was very interested in manned spaceflight, had been all of my life," he shared. As it was presented to him, the MSEs were the embodiment of various political contingents, ensuring that "interests of the DOD, interests of the program offices, and interests of the satellite builders and intelligence community were not forgotten, [and] had a role."

Tonopah, Nevada, was home to Eric Sundberg when he was born at the end of World War II. His father was a gunner on B-17s and B-24s, and while they didn't have much, his parents would always remember their days living in a lean-to in the dusty town as some of their happiest. After several moves around the western states, his family settled in the Black Hills of South Dakota, where Sundberg began dreaming of spaceflight. "I still have some of my scrapbooks from that time where I had been drawing rockets and putting astronauts on them," he recalled to the authors. "[I] tried to figure out how I could launch my little toy soldiers, how high I could get them, and that lasted most of the rest of my life—trying to figure out how to launch."

He entered the U.S. Air Force in 1968 with a degree in physics and almost immediately the service recognized where they could best put the new lieutenant to use—in Vietnam. "It turned out I came in right during [the Tet Offensive], and they didn't need physicists. They needed meteorologists, because they were all getting killed. They said, 'Physics—does that have anything to do with weather?' And I said, 'Well, weather is the art of physics,' and they said, 'Good,' and they sent me immediately back to school."

The high mortality rate among the combat meteorologists in the Vietnam War was the result of the air force's failure to train them properly for combat. "They would go out with army units," explains Sundberg, "and when everybody else would duck, they would look up to find out what the weather was." Fortunately for him, the leadership changed the policy before he was deployed, and he would serve in the relative safety of the Tan Son

Nhut Air Base, near the city of Saigon in southern Vietnam. When the war ended, Sundberg filed forms to separate from the air force, telling the colonel he worked for that he wanted to pursue a career in the aerospace industry. Immediately, the senior officer advised him, "Pull your papers. I can't tell you anything, but I'll get you in the space business!"

Sundberg was transferred to SAFSP and assigned as a staff meteorologist at Sunnyvale. It was an opportune time to come into the organization, as a large number of personnel were rotating out of their assignments and needed to be replaced. In short order, Sundberg earned a slot as a payload controller, working alongside the crewmen who "flew the bus"—the imaging satellites high above the planet. In 1975 he would begin his studies in laser optics at the Air Force Institute of Technology, earning a master's degree in physics a year later. Returning to SAFSP's launch office, he learned of the MSE announcement. "They said, 'The shuttle's coming. We're gonna have a need for some astronauts,'" Sundberg recalls. "Immediately, my head poked up. It was no question, once I found out about it, to volunteer."

Payton, Casserino, Watterson, Sundberg, and Detroye reported to the interviews along with many other promising candidates in July 1979. They met with and were interviewed by a panel of representatives from the air force, NASA management, and the Astronaut Office. "I remember sitting in this wood chair in the center of a small circle of people," remembers Sundberg. "You had no idea where the question was coming from."

"I was kind of starry-eyed about the whole thing," Casserino shared, as he found himself in contention for a position he never dreamed would come so early in his career. But at the same time, he was surrounded by an intimidating group of officers with many more years in the service. Being such a junior officer, he formulated a strategy to set himself apart from the rest of the group. He suggested to the panel that while the higher-ranking candidates might spend a short time in the program before moving on, he would be in for the long haul: "Basically my approach to the interview was, 'We need some young people to start out in a program that can grow up in a program and that can basically be the gophers to start but also learn and then be the history, be the experience throughout the program. I believe that I have the enthusiasm and the talent and the energy to be able to contribute to the program and learn and be an essential part of it.'"

Following the interview process, the candidates were sent to Brooks Air Force Base in San Antonio, Texas, for thorough medical evaluations. While some of the tests were fairly routine, others would leave curious impressions on the astronaut hopefuls. For Casserino, the entire secretive process would seem strangely familiar when several years later he saw a famous motion picture about the Mercury astronauts. "We went through six days of medical tests, psychological tests," he recalled. "You remember the guys doing all the tests and all that they had to do, running around with robes on—*The Right Stuff*—it was the same exact thing. It was kind of hilarious, when you think about it!"

Sundberg remembers one test in particular—it involved several needles being poked into his head. "[It was a] helmet, with all of these little needles and they'd have you sit down and try to map out what your thought processes were. That was a little weird." But far more interesting to him were the psychological exams. Over the course of several different tests, the analytical, calculating mind of Sundberg was revealed. "They had a psychiatrist, and the thing I remember from that was at the end of that interview, when he wrote it up, he used the term 'euthnic' when he was trying to describe me," he relates. "[I] accept things as they are. [I] don't get excited and don't make any decisions based on how I feel. I run numbers."

When considering the role the new corps of MSEs would perform, Payton uses the term "analytical integration" to describe the wide variety of engineering and operational responsibilities they would have. The group would have significant input on issues such as the evaluation of vibrational environments the payload would be exposed to and loads it would encounter during the ride to orbit. They would also develop operational procedures, such as what attitude to put the orbiter in and at what time during the flight in order to do the military mission. MSEs were expected to study how to design the military spacecraft so as to allow deployment, servicing, and repair by a spacewalking astronaut, should the need arise. So in Payton's understanding, the MSE assignment was "mostly an engineering and integration responsibility, over and above the opportunity to fly with the payload."

With the interviews and medical screenings completed, the candidates returned to their respective assignments and tried to concentrate on their current jobs. Frank Casserino, for one, had big plans in the works even if he didn't make the long shot of becoming an air force astronaut. He was married in August 1979 and, even before the interview, had been pursuing his master's degree. He and the others would not have to wait long to hear the news.

Eric Sundberg was working in his office when his boss, Col. Larry Gooch, rapped on the doorframe and stepped in. "You got selected," he said with a smile. "Oh, that's cool," Sundberg replied unemotionally. He asked if he was allowed to tell his wife, which Gooch allowed. "So I went home, told my wife, and that was about it," he recalled. "I mean it was a dream come true, but the challenge was now . . . now what do you do with it? Not get too excited about being chosen."

Casserino got the call too but received it with a bit more excitement. "I was just floored. I mean, first of all, to be selected as a young person and then to be selected in this first group. I just couldn't believe it!" he remembers fondly. In his own mind, his success in being selected was an obvious path: "I believed that this was God's plan for me. This is the only way to say it. He knew that this was the desire of my heart, and he blessed me with this opportunity. That's the only way I looked at it."

Payton, Casserino, Watterson, Sundberg, and Detroye were joined by eight others in the first class of manned spaceflight engineers. The remainder of the group was comprised of air force officers Michael A. Hamel, Terry A. Higbee, Daryl J. Joseph, Malcolm W. Lydon, Jerry J. Rij, Paul A. Sefchek, and Keith C. Wright. The cadre was rounded out by David M. Vidrine of the U.S. Navy. "The first group was an interesting bunch of characters, to say the least," Casserino jokes today.

The thirteen were all selected for their advanced engineering degrees and extensive experience in the aerospace field. However, one qualification set Gary Payton apart from the rest of the group—he was the only pilot. Quite surprisingly, this was seen as a potential problem for the fledgling astronaut: "I was the 'alternate.' For some strange reason, they chose that term. They selected twelve guys, and I was the alternate, because I had to go fly air force airplanes while I was doing the engineering job also. None of the other folks had to do that. I had to do that in order to retain my flying status. I guess that's why they called you an alternate, because they didn't know if that would work—that overlap of flying and engineering."

One of the most difficult aspects of being selected for the MSE program was the tight lid of secrecy. The nation's newest group of potential astronauts was not allowed to discuss the program or their involvement in it with practically anyone without a need to know. While their wives and families may have known of their selection, Brett Watterson recalls of the time, "this whole thing was embedded in a world of top secret code word stuff. And oftentimes we couldn't tell our wives, when we were on a business trip, where we were going. And we always traveled in civilian clothes. Again, it was a covert organization at that time. Later, when I became a payload specialist, my presence was classified for a while, which was really awkward as hell."

The group's predecessors of the X-20 Dyna-Soar and the Manned Orbiting Laboratory programs were introduced to the public with an attempt at fanfare similar to that of NASA's astronauts, but for this new team of Cold War warriors, none of their names would be released until just a few weeks before their assigned military shuttle missions. The flights of Dyna-Soar and the Manned Orbiting Laboratory were to be primarily tasked with manned space-based reconnaissance. Now, even though this new group would not be directly involved in observations of denied areas, the payloads they were responsible for were so secretive that the air force went to great lengths to conceal the cadre's presence at NASA.

Several of the MSEs were already assigned to SAFSP, and the rest reported there in January 1980 with the exception of Frank Casserino, as the air force allowed him to remain in Sunnyvale to complete his graduate studies. Their training began immediately with an intense course of study that would take them deeper into the space shuttle program than any other payload specialists would ever be afforded. For Brett Watterson, it was a real "nuts and bolts" education on their new spacecraft. "It started with going to Downey, to the Rockwell folks, who were the builders of the space shuttle, and having them brief us on the Space Transportation System," he recalls. "The space shuttle itself, critical interfaces, whether they be electrical, mechanical, and that lasted about a year."

The team would travel extensively not only to the prime shuttle manufacturer but to various NASA centers and payload contractors as well. "It was like a master's degree in shuttle," is how Sundberg characterizes the blizzard of information being presented to them. Each was assigned to a system program office (SPO) where they would become specialized in and be the group's expert on that classified payload. Frank Casserino would join the rest of the MSEs as they attended various briefings at the air force contractors and orbiter training at the Johnson Space Center. For the young lieutenant, it was an exciting time. "These guys rolled out the red carpet when we were there," he recalled.

At JSC they were integrated into the shuttle simulators not just to learn how to operate the shuttle's systems but to provide engineering feedback on how to better design the controls and payload interfaces that they expected to be using on their spaceflights. The air force saw their new cadre of astronauts as equals among the civilian counterparts, and with the large number of DOD flights then planned, they were assumed to have significant influence within the program. But unbeknownst to the generals of Special Projects, some within the NASA organization would see things differently.

The Consolidated Space Operations Center at what would become Falcon Air Force Station in Colorado Springs had been approved in 1979 and would consist of a satellite-operating center and a separate Shuttle Operations and Planning Center (SOPC). This section would provide on-orbit flight control of classified space shuttle missions and complete training and simulation facilities for controllers and astronauts. Until this top secret facility could be completed, the Defense Department would operate from a sealed-off level of the MCC in Houston, with both air force and civilian NASA controllers working side by side. Additional support during DOD missions would come from within the Blue Cube at Sunnyvale, where several of the MSEs had served previously. A new Manned Spaceflight Control Squadron would later be formed to support the missions, with the intent of providing valuable experience to the military personnel who would eventually staff the SOPC.

As the MSE group was beginning to integrate itself into the shuttle program throughout 1980, the embryonic relationship between the Defense Department and NASA began to display its first cracks. Casserino, in retrospect, takes a high-level view of these early teething pains: "Both the air force and NASA were very proud organizations that basically controlled their destiny from womb to tomb, from building, testing, launching, and operating things and then killing the satellites or the operations. They had total control of their destinies separately from each other. It's like taking the navy and the army and saying we're going to put you two services together and you're gonna be one service. NASA and the air force [were] like oil and water. They just didn't mix."

These were the complex operational reasons that caused the clash of cultures between the civilian world of NASA and the covert environment of SAFSP. The most obvious was an issue of concern ever since the partnership was first envisioned—NASA had always operated in the open and had never had to deal with classified operations. "I don't think they owned any safes!" suggested Casserino. The additional cost of initiating a system of securing classified material, developing secure communication protocols, and limiting access of personnel to facilities and hardware was enormous. "It was a nightmare for them! An absolute nightmare!" he concluded.

From the air force's perspective, the payloads they launched had always been lofted to space on unmanned rockets and now had to be "man rated" to fly aboard the space shuttle. This meant a costly process of looking at every component of every system to assure that it would not pose a risk to the human crew when integrated with the space shuttle. In addition, the agreement between the DOD and NASA for launching national security payloads had an unanticipated effect on the design requirements of current and future spacecraft. Once shuttle pricing strategies began to be laid out, the military was forced to adapt. Edward (Pete) Aldridge, undersecretary of the air force and director of the NRO for much of the 1980s, explained to NASA's Rebecca Wright how it affected "all the satellites that we had that were flying on the expendable launch vehicles, because the Shuttle bay was different and the loads on the Shuttle and the acoustics were so much different that we had to redesign all the national security payloads to fit in the Shuttle bay and to take the Shuttle environment. Since we were paying by the linear foot rather than the diameter, all the national security payloads got short and fat, because that's how they charged us."

The much-anticipated cost savings expected to be achieved by consolidating the launch operations of the air force and NASA rapidly evaporated. The financial burden that both of the organizations had to bear as a direct result of the policy decision was incredible. "I don't know that there were any savings," wonders Casserino. "But there definitely was more aggravation than you would ever want." It was in this environment that the new corps of MSEs began struggling to find their place within this new partnership. Being essentially a payload-oriented group without an operational launch vehicle, it seemed that NASA had little use for the air force's payload specialists.

Gary Payton and his fellow MSEs were busily immersed in the operational world of learning all they could about the orbiter and their payloads. From his position in the program, they were somewhat isolated from the bureaucratic infighting that was going on among the agencies. In fact, his experiences in the space shuttle program seemed to be an improvement over his earlier days working with the space agency. "I was really surprised," he recalls. "I'd worked with NASA at KSC when I was at the cape, and they were a little aloof, and they were a little separate. And they thought they were pretty good. Well they were . . . they had just finished Apollo when I was there at Cape Canaveral, and the operational side of [JSC] wasn't like that at all."

While they had little influence on the broader interagency issues borne out of the new relationship between NASA and the DOD, the thirteen had their own more pressing battles to be fought within the halls of Houston's building 4. The Astronaut Office included a handful of experienced space flyers remaining from the Apollo and Skylab programs, as well as a new class of thirty-five eager young pilots and mission specialists who would all be vying for their first trips into orbit. May 1980 would bring another group of twenty-one astronaut candidates into the mix. In the hypercompetitive and mysterious selection process for flight assignments, the civilian corps cast a wary eye on their military counterparts. "To be honest, I believe that initially at least, there was a feeling that neither PSs nor MSEs were required for flying the missions they were flown on," admits astronaut Loren Shriver. "A possible exception is if the PS had a direct hand in the design and construction of the experiment and therefore could operate and troubleshoot the experiment equipment with intimate knowledge."

The question to some in the Astronaut Office was just how large the MSE's role would become. Were they going to be flying one or two at a time, as the other science-oriented payload specialists were envisioned to do, or would they fill up every available seat for the DOD missions? Early on, there was still talk of a fifth orbiter being built that would be dedicated to classified missions from Vandenberg Air Force Base in California.

"In my mind, there was already a little bit of animosity between the professional astronauts down in Houston and the people they relegated as passengers," recalls Brett Watterson, "and that's not how I think we saw ourselves. We saw ourselves more as being a crew member." This impression on the part of the MSEs was due largely in part to the extensive training that they received when they were brought into the program. As Frank Casserino explained, "We were a lot more trained and experienced than were normal payload specialists. The extensive interface that we had with all of the different contractors and the systems on the shuttle went way beyond what a normal payload specialist would get. We had some things to offer, but we had to approach it and communicate it in a sort of a humble kind of a way and gain their trust."

If one aspect of their training set the MSEs apart from any other payload specialists, it was extravehicular activity, more commonly known as spacewalking. From the very beginning, the air force had been interested in studying what kinds of tasks a military man in space could perform outside the spacecraft to assist in deployment of satellites and assembling large structures. Of interest to military planners was the on-orbit deployment or even construction of very large dish antennas that might be required for electronic eavesdropping spacecraft.

No other payload specialists were ever expected to perform EVA work, as it was an extremely dangerous activity that required many months of practice and strict adherence to procedures that could mean life or death. NASA thought it best to leave this type of hazardous effort to the professional astronauts so as not to add additional risk to the spacewalking crew members or even the orbiter itself. But as was often the case throughout the early days of the DOD-NASA relationship, one party would have a different vision than the other.

While the air force didn't know exactly what their crews might be doing on future clandestine space walks, they were most interested in learning what they *could* do. So they sent their cadre of spacemen to MSFC in Huntsville, Alabama, to first learn how to become frogmen. "We went down there, and we trained under the water for hours and hours and hours," recalls Casserino. "First of all, we got SCUBA certified, to be able to operate under the water, and then after getting SCUBA certified, we went down and spent hours under the water training in the Apollo astronaut suits, which was pretty cool!"

Inside the seventy-five-foot-wide, forty-foot-deep Neutral Buoyancy

20. Brett Watterson (*left*) and Eric Sundberg, wearing Apollo-era training spacesuits, at the Marshall Space Flight Center's Neutral Buoyancy Simulator in Huntsville, Alabama. MSEs spent countless hours underwater evaluating what tasks spacewalking military men were capable of. Courtesy Eric Sundberg.

Simulator (NBS), the astronauts would develop and test hardware and procedures that would not only have military applications but help in verifying tasks for civilian missions as well. As Casserino explained, "We didn't just kind of float around in the water. We were actually involved in some interesting studies under the water and also construction applications to see the kind of things we could build—antennas and replacing boxes like they do on the Hubble Telescope. It was very, very fun stuff."

Working for up to three hours or more at a time in the 1.3 million–gallon water tank, Casserino and the others were getting the first taste of what it was like to be real astronauts. At one point while getting zipped up for another grueling session of EVA training, one of the MSEs happened to look down at the frayed name tag on the old class 3 Apollo training suit. "Hey man! I'm in Buzz Aldrin's old suit! Wow!" he blurted out, as the history of what they were involved in suddenly hit him.

The NBS at MSFC would also become the scene of one of the more contentious flare-ups in the air force program's rocky relationship with NASA management. The facility could nominally accommodate two test subjects, typically astronauts or engineers, and each activity would require six safety divers to look after the space-suited crew and assist them with tools and umbilical hoses. It could easily become a crowded space. On this occasion, as the tank was being used by NASA personnel, some "young, aggressive, alpha-type officers took it upon themselves to jump into the pool in an 'unauthorized fashion,'" remembered Brett Watterson. "Of course, they got noticed; they got reported. That embarrassed the generals and had the center director of Johnson Space Center [Kraft] calling up three-star generals, saying, 'Keep your people under control!' The whole group got castigated because of those actions. And while the program progressed on, it got pretty silly."

Characterizing some of his MSE teammates in aeronautical terms, Watterson added, "A lot of these guys had a lot of airspeed but not a lot of vector."

Columbia's June 1982 mission was the program's fourth and final orbital flight test. Commanded by Ken Mattingly and piloted by Hank Hartsfield, it carried an experimental DOD payload and tested secure communications with its air force controllers. Casserino, Payton, Jeff Detroye, and Mike Hamel were assigned to support the mission from the military command facility in a new role that had been envisioned by the DOD, as Casserino relates: "They created a position called paycom, which was a payload communicator, and we were located at Sunnyvale, and we were assigned to speak with the crew when they were going to start working the DOD experiments on orbit. And we would also be there if there were any problems and the crew had any questions."

This new role would be critical in future classified missions on which security would be paramount, and the four worked closely with the astronauts and mission control personnel to develop a method of communications that would not transmit any classified information over the unencrypted voice link. The group also assisted with the preparation of procedures and manuals prior to the mission, so they were intimately familiar with the experimental payload. "We were the payload experts, and we developed the payload procedures in conjunction with the crew, payload communication methods with the crew, and we were future payload specialists, so who else better to be the paycoms than us?" Casserino surmised.

The payload itself was known as DOD 82-1, and while the system itself was not classified, it was treated as such by those involved in order to shake the bugs out of working in a classified mode. Brett Watterson would monitor the STS-4 mission from JSC in Houston, where he too was in awe watching the legends of the Mission Control Center in action: "I was in the MCC, and it was really fascinating to see the MCC work, and Gene Kranz work. I really didn't have much of an active role, until it broke."

"Fortunately, or unfortunately, however you want to look at it, during the mission we had an anomaly," recalled Casserino, "and the anomaly was serious enough that it required extensive communication with the crew on orbit. And we had to develop some real-time procedures and send them up to the crew." Suddenly, rather than being in a monitoring role, the MSE paycoms in Sunnyvale found themselves in the middle of the action. And as they transmitted instructions up to Mattingly and Hartsfield in well-rehearsed coded language, the eager press monitored the unencrypted frequencies in an effort to uncover any shred of information they could learn about the "secret" payload.

Casserino found great satisfaction as the entire team pulled together to work a real-world problem. The exercise proved out some of the procedures and revealed issues that would have to be corrected before the first truly classified DOD space shuttle mission. Operational flights would begin with the next mission, STS-5, in November 1982, and soon thereafter the critical national security payloads the MSEs would be responsible for would begin flying.

Gary Payton remembers this as a very exciting time for the cadre of MSE trainees: "So then somewhere around '82, '83, it looks like we were going to actually fly a large number of military missions on the space shuttle. It was looking like maybe a third of the annual manifest on the space shuttle was going to be military flights. That was a big impact on NASA to fly that much military hardware, and so once we started marching down that path, it was [a] serious amount of assigning MSEs to the various launches that were on the schedule."

As the events of 1982 unfolded, the air force took a different approach with the second MSE selection as the pace of training and operations rapidly picked up. Rather than continuing with the often-awkward lid of secrecy on the team's identities, the twelve new officers selected were announced publicly by the DOD. "All of that stuff sort of happened together," remembers Casserino. "The second group came out, the shuttle test flight was complete, and we came out of the shadows and were integrated with the second group." Along with the public announcement of the new MSEs, a cover story was put forth by the air force for reasons unknown to the team's original members. "They put out a story that said, 'We've had a test group running, and now we're going to integrate this test group into this second group that we've announced.'"

In October 1982, still fresh from a postflight tour of the country following STS-4, Ken Mattingly was approached by Deke Slayton with an offer to command the first classified space shuttle mission. The time had also come for the air force to decide which of their MSEs would lead the way into the new era of military operations on the space shuttle. Those responsible for the selection had their own ideas on the issue but also sought the input of their partner agency. According to Gary Payton, "In fact, I remember, before the air force selected me, the colonels called down to Johnson Space Center and asked if they had any preference about who the air force flew on that flight. NASA was very adamant and said, 'No, that was your decision; you can pick anybody you want, and we'll work with them just fine,' so NASA was very open about that."

The payload to be launched aboard the orbiter was not Payton's prime responsibility during his assignment to the MSE group. "He wasn't the MSE working his payload," says Brett Watterson. "He was in the launch and integration office, but he wasn't specifically assigned to his satellite." Although he would have very limited exposure to working with the crew, Keith Wright was selected to work with Payton on preparation of the payload. "NASA, unlike Apollo, abandoned the notion of one-for-one backups," Payton relates. "They realized that if they're going to fly eighteen or so a year and your flights got anywhere between five and seven people on board, it's just too much workload to have a one-for-one backup for every person on the crew." Still, the military opted to assign pairs or teams to each of their payloads, with the assumption that each crew member would fly with that type of payload at least once.

Along with the Payton and Wright assignment, an air force selection board named Detroye, Sundberg, and Watterson to the payload targeted for STS-15, and responsibility for the STS-16 payload to Casserino and Joseph. These assignments, however, were still classified in nature and known only to the MSE group and their military superiors. On 20 October 1982 NASA released a statement announcing the first astronaut crew in its history assigned to a classified manned spaceflight: Mattingly, Lt. Col. Loren Shriver of the U.S. Air Force, and mission specialists Lt. Col. James Buchli of the Marine Corps and Maj. Ellison Onizuka of the U.S. Air Force. Aside from the commander, who had not only test-flown the space shuttle but had traveled to the moon on Apollo 16, they were all space rookies. Near the end of the press release was the cryptic statement, "The fifth crew member, an Air Force manned spaceflight engineer, will be named at a later date."

Even though the air force had revealed the MSE groups' existence, the military astronauts would remain out of the public eye until such time that their activities leading up to launch would expose them to the press. The mission, known as STS-10, would launch from KSC in the last quarter of 1983. It was planned to be the fourth flight of the orbiter *Challenger* and the tenth mission of the space shuttle program.

The secrecy surrounding the identity of the military payload specialist for the mission may have seemed unnecessary to some, but the policy was an attempt to keep the media from putting too many pieces of information together. "If you had a press guy that was parked outside of JSC and they saw this person interfacing with the crew, they could make an assumption that maybe this guy is the payload specialist," explains Casserino. "We knew that right away the press was going to try and get some information about the flight and put that person in a difficult position."

The military took a firm stance on the issue of security, setting a precedent that would require a major shift in NASA's culture of openness with the public. "Because of that collision of those covert worlds of the NRO and the publicity-seeking, acclimation world of NASA manned-spaceflight activities," recalls Watterson, "the DOD came up with what they called the umbrella policy." This policy required that not only would the classified payload remain a closely guarded secret but everything associated with the mission would be contained within the protective envelope of nondisclosure.

The DOD-imposed policy placed restrictions on discussing the number of payloads on board, their weight, and the delivery method, be it by an upper-stage rocket or by the orbiter's remote manipulator arm. In addition, the launch window, launch time, mission duration, and landing time were all classified. These requirements were demanded in order to deny the Soviets or other enemies observing the flight, which might lead to the nature and purpose of the payload being discovered. However, the highly compartmentalized, classified world of the military would have a great impact not only with NASA's press relations but on the ability of the organization to effectively plan, train for, and fly an operational space shuttle mission.

Gary Payton took a particularly keen interest in the maiden flight of the orbiter *Challenger* in April 1983. Only the sixth flight in the space shuttle program, the four-man crew's primary mission was to deploy NASA's first TDRS, which would be the first of several boosted to geosynchronous orbit by the air force's interim upper stage (IUS). This two-stage, solid-propellant rocket motor was designed by the Boeing Company to serve as an upper booster stage for both the Titan 34D generation of rockets and the space shuttle. It could loft a five-thousand-pound payload into geosynchronous orbit or even propel NASA's interplanetary probes out of the gravity well of Earth. The booster delivering the TDRS to its high perch above Earth would be the same type to be used by the top secret satellite Payton was preparing to fly into orbit with.

The satellite was deployed flawlessly from *Challenger*'s payload bay while orbiting in the darkness of Earth's shadow half a world away from Houston. It was not long afterward, though, when the IUS began rocketing the satellite away from the shuttle, that telemetry showed something going very wrong. The second stage of the booster tumbled violently after ignition, leaving the TDRS in a low, lopsided orbit that appeared to render it all but useless. Without TDRS, shuttle missions were forced to continue reliance on ground communications stations, and Spacelab 1 in particular was severely impacted by the anomaly.

"It was a significant failure, truthfully," recalls Payton. "So the IUS had to stand down for redesigns. It stood down for about a year, I think. That impacted the schedule for my flight and a whole bunch of other folks who were using the IUS, too." And indeed, the failure did throw the entire space shuttle manifest into disarray. There were several more TDRSS on the schedule to be launched by the shuttle-IUS system, as well as the payload for STS-10 and several other classified DOD missions. All the preparations for these flights came to a halt, awaiting the outcome of the formal investigation into the failure on STS-6, and the previously named MSE assignments were now clouded in uncertainty.

Watterson had earned himself a reputation in the MSE corps as a dependable officer who did things by the book and followed orders without complaint. Immediately following the IUS incident, he was summoned by the leadership for a new assignment, one that would seemingly put him on a path away from flying in space. "The general called me and another guy up, had me meet him at seven o'clock in the morning," he recalls. When the two officers reported to the Space Division of SAFSP as ordered, they were introduced to the program manager for the IUS. "And the general pointed a long, boney finger at both of us and said, 'You guys belong to him. Don't come back until it's fixed.'" With that, Watterson resigned himself to the fact that he would have nothing else to concentrate on for the next year, other than finding the root cause of the IUS failure and fixing it. Until that happened, the crew of STS-10 were told they had no mission to fly.

Mission commander Ken Mattingly took advantage of the delay to help bring Payton, his payload specialist, fully up to speed on how to operate effectively as a crew member on what would become STS-51C under NASA's new designation. "The 51C experience demonstrated that the majority of

PS training resulted from his association with the NASA crew rather than from any formal program," Mattingly would report postflight. "51C had the luxury of spending an unusual amount of time in the mission-preparation phase, which allowed developing a particularly close relationship between the PS and his NASA crew members."

Mattingly also found that Payton's flight experience in high-performance jets was a critical asset in his successful integration into the world of space-flight. The one qualification that had cast doubt in the minds of the generals at Special Projects—that Payton could handle multiple responsibilities of engineering and flying—now set him apart. Mattingly adamantly reported following the mission,

> *Space operations and the Shuttle working environment are such that close crew integration is absolutely imperative. 51C was assigned a DOD PS who was already a rated pilot and therefore easily adjusted to the necessary crew discipline. The ease with which non-rated PS's will adjust is a very individual matter and cannot be specified. One of the most powerful tools the commander has to assess the PS adjustment is the one T-38 flight which was accomplished early in the training cycle. This flight not only allows the commander to form an operational suitability assessment, but it also allows the PS to develop the personal confidence in his commander which is necessary for him to function effectively.*

Fortunately for Mattingly, he also found that his resident MSE could be a critical asset to the crew in navigating the maze of the military bureaucracy. "The PS is familiar with the USAF internal organization and can be extremely useful in breaking the ice," he reported. "He has access to the critical information and communications channels that all organizations depend on, which becomes particularly important during the final months of mission preparation."

The crew would have to concern itself with keeping its own training documents, such as checklists and procedural manuals, under lock and key in an austere conference room featuring a single telephone. Mattingly remembers being told, "If certain people need to get hold of you, they'll call this number," as he related for NASA's Oral History Project. "You've got to keep this out of sight, don't let anybody know you've got it, and this is how we'll talk to you on very sensitive things." As far as anyone remembers, the phone rang only once in the many months the crew trained together, and the caller was looking to offer a long-distance service to the phone's owner!

Training and simulator sessions were complicated by having to restrict personnel who did not have security clearances to take part, and the crew encountered problems with their schedules due to the hypersensitivity over secrecy. Simply being informed about meetings became burdensome, as their names were left off distribution lists so as not to reveal their association with anything even remotely related to the mission. Added measures were taken when the crew had to travel to various contractors and facilities in the course of their mission preparations. The crew would spend several periods at the Boeing plant in Kent, Washington, for hands-on inspection and familiarization of the IUS and its associated flight support hardware, and seminars were held at the Sunnyvale Satellite Control Facility for the astronauts and flight controllers.

Each of these trips required special precautions on the part of the crew. "Whenever we went to a contractor that was associated with the payload or with the people we were working with, they didn't want us to get in our airplane and fly to that location," Mattingly recalled. "They wanted us to file [flight plans] to go to Denver and then refile inflight and divert to a new place so that somebody who was tracking our flight plans wouldn't know." The crew would then check into hotels under prearranged pseudonyms in an attempt to keep a low profile.

The cloak-and-dagger nature of their training even led to some vampire-like hours on the part of the crew and support personnel. "To keep the launch time classified, they wanted us to make all our training as much training in the daytime as at night, so that someone observing us wouldn't be able to figure this out," Mattingly added. "They never convinced me that anyone cared, but they did convince me that if you watch these signatures you could figure it out, and it is secret because [they] said it was."

Once the IUS was cleared for flight, bonding problems with *Challenger*'s heat-resistant tiles forced a switch to the orbiter *Discovery*. But with these technical challenges now behind NASA and the air force, everything finally seemed to be coming together for the new era of military space shuttle operations to get underway.

Payton had been in the glare of the media spotlight, along with the rest of his crew, for the several weeks since the countdown demonstration test at launch complex 39A. Reporters and photographers clamored for any detail they could squeeze out of the crew, but they were stymied by the group of professional military officers. Shriver remembers that while they were not overtly isolated from the press corps, the encounters were usually kept quite brief by NASA Public Affairs in an effort to minimize the pressure being applied.

Payton was allowed the luxury of watching his crewmates, much more adept than he was at handling the press, deflect most of the attention away from him. Onizuka in particular made an impression on the astronaut who had only recently come out from the shadows. "My military space experience was in the classified side of the house. I wasn't too much into these things like press conferences," Payton would state. "He [Onizuka] was more comfortable in things like press conferences and giving speeches to forty thousand and stuff like that. My background had never put me in that position."

As the STS-51C launch date drew closer, the public debate over the secrecy of the upcoming space shuttle mission grew in volume. In the age of President Ronald Reagan's Strategic Defense Initiative, speculation ran wild in the nation's press about the space shuttle eventually taking weapons systems into orbit. One political cartoon depicted an orbiter piloted by Darth Vader carrying the president as a passenger. On the side of the ship were the words "Reagan Space Militarization Program."

While the press criticized and the public reacted, the crew remained largely isolated from it all as they made their final preparations for launch. Payton, with almost all the training behind him and little else to do but anticipate his first experience in space, sought out the counsel of a trusted friend and fellow payload specialist: "The smartest thing I did was sit down with Charlie Walker, a McDonnell Douglas payload specialist who flew a couple flights before me. And after his flight I sat him down and bought him a beer and had him talk to me about the flight. He did a good job of describing [being there for] launch, on orbit, landing, everything. So that was good. I'm still dear friends with Charlie."

23 January 1985 was the planned launch date for *Discovery*, but as the weather forecasts firmed up, unusually frigid temperatures would cause enough concern to postpone for one day. After the twenty-four-hour stand-down, the crew was up early for the typical launch day rituals, although all these

21. Ken Mattingly, commander of STS-51C, salutes photographers as he leads his crew from the Operations and Checkout Building on 24 January 1985. Gary Payton is third in line, behind pilot Loren Shriver. This and all other activities leading up to launch were kept secret so as not to reveal the actual liftoff time. Courtesy NASA/Retro Space Images.

activities occurred out of the public eye so as not to allow any estimates on the launch window. After breakfast and a final weather briefing, the five-man crew—all wearing sky-blue one-piece flight suits and baseball caps, each adorned with a full-size mission patch—were led out by Mattingly to the waiting Astrovan.

The commander snapped a sharp military salute to the few cameras that were there to record it. Payton emerged from the crew quarters third in the line of astronauts behind the commander and pilot, with a unique rectangular white patch on his right sleeve with blue letters "USAF" being the only item differentiating him as someone from outside NASA.

With the chill of the previous few days still in the air, *Discovery* stood poised toward a crystal-blue sky as the iconic countdown clock at the press viewing site stood frozen at 00:00. It had displayed the large yellow zeros all morning long while launch controllers worked through a handful of technical issues that would need to be cleared before the orbiter could begin its third mission. It seemed surreal that with the spectacular display of smoke, fire, and noise that was about to unfold, nothing more than a small group of reporters, family members, and officials were on hand to witness the event. It was reported in the press, although never confirmed by the Department of Defense, that a "small fleet" of Soviet fishing trawlers and submarines lingered offshore from Cape Canaveral in an effort to monitor and report on the shuttle's ascent from Florida's east coast.

Seated alone on his back in the middeck of *Discovery*, Payton patiently stared at the wall of lockers directly in front of him and occasionally glanced through the small, round hatch porthole to his left at the now empty White Room. As he listened to the prelaunch chatter inside his tight, double-visor helmet, he was intently focused on the mission ahead and the clandestine national asset in the cavernous payload bay beneath him, which he was charged with looking after. The remainder of the five-man crew were seated on the flight deck, working through their procedures in preparation for launch.

It had been a long morning for the crew lying on their backs in the crew module. They were already an hour and a half into the three-hour launch window, holding while launch controllers fussed over a high helium concentration reading in the midbody of the orbiter. Then, at 2:41 p.m., without notice or fanfare, Hugh Harris, the voice of launch control, keyed his microphone for the first time, announcing the commencement of the countdown. As he spoke, the huge clock at the press site three miles from the launchpad finally started ticking off the seconds. Up to that point, Payton was not completely convinced that they would fly that day. "Many countdowns got started and then had to abort for technical reasons," he explained. "We got down to about T minus two and a half minutes—when you started to turn on [the] auxiliary power units—and T. K. [Mattingly] said, 'Yeah, looks like we're gonna fly today!' We were all surprised!"

No communications between *Discovery* and the launch controllers would be broadcast to the world, as had been the norm for NASA missions over the decades. For those watching on television, the silence was filled with a monologue of speculation from seasoned space reporters not accustomed to the secrecy and a lack of any real information to report regarding the flight.

With just seconds remaining in the count, Payton could feel the vehicle rumble and strain against the pad's hold-down bolts as the three main engines sent sharp ripples of vibration up through its spine. The entire stack of the orbiter, external tank, and SRBS flexed and tipped forward from the off-center torrent of thrust roaring out of the three engine bells. As the enormous booster rockets reached the limit of how far they could bend and snapped back to the vertical, they simultaneously ignited in a blinding burst of orange fire.

"That's a stupendous slap in the back," recalled Payton. "It's just a shock that runs up through the whole vehicle. The engineers use the term 'vibroacoustic environment,' where the noise from the solid rocket boosters is so loud, the *noise* shakes the vehicle. So you're riding, well it's kind of like riding the front of a steam locomotive, I would guess. All the vibration and noise and shaking and rattling." Pilot Shriver, seated in the front right-hand seat of the flight deck on his first spaceflight, was shocked by the intensity of the ascent. Even with his years of flying experience in high-performance jet fighter aircraft, his first shuttle launch was surprising in every aspect. "The entire ascent phase is intense in so many ways; there is no way to prepare yourself just by listening to debriefings," Shriver recalled.

The vehicle rolled around in a slow spiral to point itself downrange as it ripped through the air, gaining speed at an incredible rate. Shortly thereafter, Payton had an unusual impression of the ship he was riding into space. "As we were going uphill, somewhere around T plus thirty-seven seconds, you go supersonic," he recalled. "And the thought that went through my mind was that it felt like we were breaking the sound barrier *inside a paper airplane.*"

The SRBS continued to push *Discovery* higher and faster until they depleted their fuel and then jettisoned from the brown external tank with a momentary flash across the orbiter's front windows. From that point, the main engines would provide the crew a "comparatively luxurious ride" the rest of the way to space. For the hundredth time in spaceflight history, a crew of astronauts disappeared over the horizon riding a bright-blue dot of flame into orbit.

In the skies over KSC, the twisted white column of smoke began to dissipate as recovery ships raced to the predetermined point in the Atlantic Ocean to retrieve the twin rocket boosters floating down under their parachutes east of the launch site. These boosters, once returned to the engineers for postflight evaluation, would reveal significant erosion of the O-ring seals that joined the segmented cases of the rockets. This failure allowed hot rocket gases to breach the primary ring and damage the backup seal. It would be the most significant burn-through to date, but the link between the severity of the damage and the cold temperatures at launch would not be fully acknowledged until a tragic event a year later.

The orbiter continued to accelerate toward space under the power of its three main engines. As the huge orange-brown tank was drained of liquid hydrogen and liquid oxygen, its weight steadily decreased while the engines continued to produce the same thrust, resulting in an increase in the g-load on the vehicle and crew.

As the massive force pressing on their chests increased above 2 g's, several crew members had the sensation that they were sliding up in their seats. Left with nothing but a black sky in his small porthole for the remainder of the ride to orbit, Payton felt the vehicle's computer-controlled powerplants gradually reduce their thrust. "Almost the last full minute of powered flight, the main engines start to throttle back, so you don't exceed 3 g's on the vehicle," he explained. "And then we went up, completely nominal ascent, had no problems at all, got on orbit, got up above the atmosphere, [and] got the main engines shut off."

At mission control in Houston, the large map of *Discovery*'s orbit around the globe turned to a red background, and the arcs crisscrossing the continents disappeared. The NASA public affairs officer fell silent. STS-51C, so far as the public was concerned, was now completely hidden behind the Pentagon's black curtain of secrecy.

As *Discovery* slipped into orbit and prepared for its second orbital maneuvering system (OMS) burn, the crew caught sight of something quite unexpected. "Because we launched into night, we were able to view the external tank reentering the atmosphere just prior to the OMS 2 TIG [time of ignition]," Mattingly reported later. "It could be seen until about one minute after OMS 2 TIG." This was the first time the entry had been observed by a shuttle crew, and in one of the rare status reports released during the mission, Shriver was quoted as saying it was "a beautiful display of fireworks."

Down below on the middeck of *Discovery*, Gary Payton wasn't feeling too well. After thousands of hours flying in combat aircraft, he never expected to have an issue with the dreaded space sickness, yet here it was.

As his white helmet bobbed weightlessly in front of him, he unstrapped and began moving around slowly to accomplish his stowage tasks. Postmission, Mattingly would report wryly that in attempting to become accustomed to zero gravity, "KC-135 [familiarization] flights, on a not-to-interfere basis, were accomplished, but the PS did not believe that they helped in his adaptation to the zero-g environment."

As the shuttle continued its first orbit around the dark side of Earth, mission specialist Buchli began the process of opening the two payload bay doors. "The payload bay doors on the orbiter have to get open early in the flight, because on the inside of the payload bay doors is where the radiators are," said Payton. "So you've got to open the doors and get the radiators exposed to space so they can get rid of the heat generated during launch." The sun burst into the flight deck of *Discovery* as it sped high above the Pacific Ocean, and Payton gingerly floated up through the interdeck access hatch with just a light push off from the now-useless ladder, getting his first glimpse out of the large overhead windows: "T plus fifty-three minutes, I still remember it. We launched out of Florida, going east in the afternoon, so it's nighttime over the Indian Ocean and Indonesia and that area. But at T plus fifty-three minutes we were in between Hawaii and Baja, California, and Jim Buchli opens the payload bay doors, and you look down on this gorgeous, dark-blue Pacific Ocean with these cumulus clouds—white puffy cumulus clouds—scattered around the top of the Pacific Ocean. [It] looked like popcorn on top of the ocean."

Setting aside his queasiness for a moment, the newly minted astronaut relished the fact that he had finally made it safely into space, but he was equally eager to see that his payload had not suffered any damage on the violent ride up. "Having gone through all the shake, rattle, and roll of launch, I was really pleased to see the spacecraft had survived it too!" he reflected. "That's why I was on the flight; the tender care and feeding of the spacecraft. So, I survived launch. The spacecraft survived launch. It was great!"

The crew had a long day ahead preparing the clandestine DOD payload for deployment from the orbiter's payload bay. Over the course of four orbits of the planet, Buchli and Onizuka checked out the satellite for any abnormalities. It was during this electronic inspection of the spacecraft's systems that significant differences between the shuttle mission simulator and the actual flight hardware revealed themselves to the crew. "Many of the actual signatures seen on-orbit could not be properly simulated due to software or hardware problems," the commander would report postflight. "A significant deficiency was seen on the payload communication training due to inadequacies in the hardware/software integration of the encryption/decryption equipment." As a result of the inability to accurately simulate the complex, coded, digital vocabulary of the spacecraft during training, Buchli, Onizuka, and Payton were seeing characteristics of its electronic nerve system for the first time in space.

The crew focused the aft cameras of the payload bay on the rocket nozzle of the redesigned IUS and ran the cone through a test, wiggling it in all axes to ensure it would properly steer its precious cargo into its intended orbit. Then the ringed tilt table, which wrapped around the cylindrical IUS booster, was commanded to raise the combined stack up in steps to its launch position above the payload bay. Finally, on the seventh orbit of the mission, it was time for the space shuttle and the top secret electronic spy in the sky to part ways.

The orbiter's onboard computers counted down to the deploy time and sent the electronic command to the raised tilt ring to silently spring the massive stack gently upward out of the payload bay. "During the deploy of the IUS, we did not notice any pitching effect of the Orbiter nor did we hear any sounds or noise," Mattingly reported. "The payload proceeded straight out of the tilt table without any pitching or yawing motions."

"We separated the payload from the orbiter at the right time on orbit," said Payton. "The spacecraft [was] *just gorgeous* as it separated from the orbiter." The crew snapped countless photos of the satellite as it left the bay; photos that even more than three decades later have never been seen publicly. In its first critical test since the failure on STS-6, the IUS performed flawlessly as it propelled the electronic sentinel, now known simply as USA-8, up to its perch high above the planet. Although it has likely exhausted its supply of maneuvering fuel by today, Payton said, "The last time I checked, it was still working on orbit . . . probably working better than me now! I'm thirty years older!"

Back on Earth, NASA spokesman Dick Young was asked bluntly by a member of the press if a satellite had indeed been deployed by *Discovery's* crew. He simply shrugged his shoulders and replied with all the brevity he could muster: "Beats me."

MISSION ELAPSED TIME (MET) 00:10:10

This is Mission Control Houston at 12 o'clock midnight Central Standard Time with the status report on space shuttle mission 51C. At mission elapsed time 10 hours 10 minutes, the Orbiter Discovery, *its crew and elements of the Space Transportation System are performing satisfactorily. Earlier the crew reported breakup and entry of the external tank. The right combination of darkness and vehicle attitude enabled them to be the first Shuttle crew to do so. Capcom Robert Springer on behalf of the Mission Control team, voiced up thanks to mission specialist Ellison Onizuka. Onizuka, who is a native of Kona, Hawaii, furnished the Mission Control team with a supply of Kona coffee and macadamia nuts. The next mission 51C status report will occur in approximately eight hours, or earlier if conditions warrant. This is Mission Control Houston.*

That was it. That was all NASA and the DOD had to say about the fifteenth mission of the space shuttle program. The boilerplate statement would be read by the NASA public affairs commentator again exactly eight hours later, leaving a frustrated media corps wondering why flight controllers eating macadamia nuts was worthy of reporting twice. There would be no real information released regarding the mission until sixteen hours prior to the intended landing time, and even that report would be minimal.

For the crew and the entire team of NASA, DOD, and contractor personnel, the primary mission of *Discovery* was complete with the end of the first day on orbit. After more than a decade of planning, developing, testing, and training, the first national security payload had been deployed into service by a shuttle with no major technical issues, and the much maligned IUS had performed magnificently.

As the rest of the crew prepared for their sleep period, Payton drifted up to the large double window of the flight deck and once again took in the breathtaking panorama of the planet below. "I use the term nowadays that Disney and Pixar couldn't come close to equaling that view," he says today. "The English language just doesn't have the words to describe it, truthfully."

The specially built zero-g treadmill bounced up and down noisily as Loren Shriver, strapped down by bungee cord straps over his shoulders, jogged along in blue shorts and socks. The floor panel it was anchored to covered the replacement lithium hydroxide canisters in the lower deck, but the compartment cover's latches weren't tight enough to take the beating punishment of the exercise device. The racket was tremendous throughout the cabin of the orbiting space plane, but despite the noise, Mattingly reported postflight that the machine worked quite well: "The treadmill was useful for exercise and also was useful for exerting some pressure on the shoulders and lower back, which was helpful for some crew members during the first two days."

Onizuka anchored himself with a toe through a fabric loop on the floor, pointing a fish-eye lensed Arriflex camera at the sweaty space shuttle pilot for the traditional mission film that would be put together after the flight. The treadmill would serve another purpose during the flight, with the evaluation of the reduced-tension tether reel. "51C carried a modified EVA tether reel which provided one-half of the tension of the standard reel," Mattingly described. "It was evaluated on the middeck to determine that it would indeed retract with the reduced tension and to qualitatively determine the effect on simulated EVA tasks."

The astronauts were tasked with several medical experiments while on orbit, and as usual these "supplementary objectives" were looked on by the crew as something to be avoided if at all possible. "We treated these experiments as shopping list items to be performed as time permitted," Mattingly said. "A considerable amount of time was required to perform a set of these experiments, and therefore, interruptions or other interferences were common." The commander went on to recommend formally that medical experiments be limited in number on future missions and that "investigators be encouraged to design 'user friendly' experiments."

The crew also operated a Martin Marietta–sponsored middeck experiment called the stored-fluid management demonstration. NASA was interested, as were military satellite designers, in how rocket fuels behaved within the complex propulsion systems of spacecraft in zero gravity, particularly when being transferred from tank to tank. The demonstration used a test fluid from a receiver tank and moved it under slight pressure into various supply tanks of different designs. The entire apparatus, including external floodlights, television, and still photography took up a considerable amount of middeck space and required nearly ten hours of crew time to complete, but it provided good results for later analysis by engineers on the ground.

22. Manned spaceflight engineer Gary Payton on the flight deck of *Discovery* during the first classified mission of the space shuttle program. In the more than three decades that have passed since the flight, no photographs of the payload have been made public.
Courtesy NASA/Retro Space Images.

The teleprinter on the middeck of *Discovery* chattered away furiously. Mattingly knew what the message said even before he tore the paper off to read it. He had it all planned out. As his ship sailed high above the United States, the crew was going to play down to the ground controllers patriotic recordings of the U.S. Navy, U.S. Army, and U.S. Air Force service songs as the television cameras offered a view of the country from coast to coast. But they had no way of knowing that a brief communication dropout would occur just after the army song had been played. An amused Mattingly released the curled page, drifting it across the cabin for Payton to read. "You've got thirty seconds, and if the Air Force song isn't on the air, don't bother to come home," the sheet read.

However, the program managers wanted nothing more than for *Discovery* to come home, and soon. Its primary mission as a payload launch vehicle complete, there was no reason to stay up any longer than absolutely necessary, and very shortly before launch, Mattingly became aware of another priority that had come down from the program managers. "In January it became apparent that the programmatic intent was to not only insure a KSC landing but also to do it as soon as feasible," he recalled. After replanning the entire mission to allow for this possibility, the commander assumed that he would be informed as soon as the decision was made by flight controllers.

The plan seemed sound, but Mattingly was taken by surprise when, on 26 January, mission control announced the decision to land at KSC the very next day. The crew would spend the evening of flight day 3 stowing all the gear away in the middeck lockers and preparing the vehicle for entry the following afternoon.

The first perceptible vibrations began to be felt throughout the orbiter as it made its transition to a hypersonic glider, sailing along at over 240,000 feet. "*Discovery* felt a little bit 'limber' during reentry," Mattingly later reported, "like a result of being in a big, flexible airplane." As the mission commander recalled for NASA's Oral History Project:

> *We were all bug-eyed about this entry and being able to see out the windows and see things that you couldn't see before. Sailing down over the coast is just—gosh, it's really, really beautiful. I remember as we crossed over Mexico and out into the Gulf, having come down from orbit, we were still at probably a hundred, maybe 150,000. [Loren] and I looked out the window, and [he] says, "Are you sure we're going to glide all the way to Florida from here?" Looked at that, said, "Well, the little light on the CRT says we are, but it sure doesn't look that way." And sure enough, the CRT was right. We did make it to Florida.*

As the orbiter slowed to Mach 4, a whistling wind noise became noticeable to the crew and became even more pronounced at forty thousand feet and 270 knots, as Mattingly took control from the computers and flew a sweeping arc around to the southeast, lining up with runway 15 at the Shuttle Landing Facility. Now he felt like he was right back in the Shuttle Training Aircraft. "The roll response of *Discovery* felt exactly like the STA," Mattingly later reported. In the final seconds of his third and last spaceflight, the test pilot turned astronaut smoothly pitched the nose of the shuttle up in the preflare maneuver and called for Shriver to deploy the landing gear.

As the heat-scarred ship settled over the fifteen-thousand-foot concrete runway, the enormous pressure wave of air beneath its delta wings kicked up white clouds of dust and swirled them in the wake left behind. Handling a slight crosswind, Mattingly gently touched down on the right main wheel and then the left. Each contact was marked by puffs of tire smoke and cheers from the handful of family members and recovery crew members.

As he slowed to a stop, the recovery convoy rushed to meet the vehicle on the runway. With just three days, one hour, and thirty-three minutes logged by *Discovery* and its five-man crew, the DOD's first space shuttle mission would go down as the shortest operational flight in the thirty-year span of the entire STS program.

The crew came down the stairs from *Discovery*'s open hatch with Loren Shriver leading the way. Payton disembarked wearing sunglasses and a huge smile. Mattingly was last and descended from his spacecraft without even holding onto the handrails. Even as they walked briefly around the shuttle to inspect it for damage, a small team of air force personnel was gathering up all the checklists, notebooks, and exposed film from aboard the ship to avoid any classified material becoming unaccounted for. It would take weeks for the air force to complete an assessment of what data, audio recordings, and still and motion photographs were classified and what were releasable, even to the crew that flew the mission.

Having guided the first classified space shuttle mission from conception to touchdown at KSC, Mattingly left NASA after accruing some 504 hours logged over three spaceflights. Just two days after landing, NASA named El Onizuka to the crew of 51L, commanded by Dick Scobee. Both Shriver and Buchli would soon be given new flight assignments as well. The air force had another assignment ready for Gary Payton as soon as the STS-51C postflight debriefings were completed. He would return to SAFSP and assist in the preparations for the first planned launch from Vandenberg.

He took the news in stride and undertook this new endeavor with some enthusiasm, but having just returned from such a brief voyage full of so many vividly intense experiences, he was ready to get right back in line for another spaceflight. Now that the DOD missions were underway, there was little doubt that there would be plenty of opportunities for him and the rest of the air force's corps of space engineers.

9. The Highest Ground

Once the command of the air is obtained by one of the contending
armies, the war must become a conflict between a seeing
host and one that is blind.

H. G. Wells, *Anticipations*

Eric Sundberg needed a rocket engine. Not to propel anything into space,
but rather to use its components to burn hydrazine. A joint team of NASA
and U.S. Air Force engineers were tasked with developing an on-orbit test to
transfer the highly toxic lifeblood of a spacecraft from one tank to another
after being connected by a spacewalking astronaut. One of the many problems they were faced with was the fact that a spacesuit glove acted as a wick
that would soak up stray hydrazine during the tests. "He'd be a very unpop-
ular person in the crew cabin," explains Sundberg, "because hydrazine is
about half as lethal as saran when you get close to it. When you can start
smelling hydrazine, you're in trouble."

Walking by an open office door at the Lockheed Missile and Space Company one afternoon in 1984, Sundberg happened to spot an old motor set off
to one side of the engineer's floor. "I'm taking this," he stated flatly. "This
works doesn't it?" The stunned worker's head nodded in the affirmative.
"Okay, good." With that, he picked up the old relic and marched out into
the hallway with his commandeered rocket engine. But the real fun began
when he arrived at the airport to take it back to Los Angeles with him, as
Sundberg recalled: "I packed it in a big suitcase and got on an airplane. It
was fun because they were just then starting to inspect luggage. And they
wanted to know what was in this fairly heavy package, and I said, 'A rocket
engine.' And the guy looks at me like, oooh, I don't know about this. And

I said, 'It's for the shuttle.' And all of the sudden it's like 'It's for the shuttle' became magic words because [he said], 'Oh, yes, let me help you!'"

Sundberg's caper was just one example of how the manned spaceflight engineer group had to improvise to accomplish their individual assignments within the NASA bureaucracy. From the very beginning of their involvement with the program, they had been coming to terms with just how little the air force knew about the orbiters and how their payloads would interface with them, and in many cases, it fell to the MSEs to make it all work. While the shuttle was physically sized to accommodate DOD payloads, the means to interact with those payloads electronically were never considered in the design.

"It's like all of the sudden, we don't know this," recalls Sundberg, "and then it came time to start looking at flying things in the shuttle, and you say, 'Well, where do I plug this in?' Uh, there's no place to plug it in. Now, physically, was the hole big enough? Yes, but the other parts were not." These problems became readily apparent when Col. Larry Gooch, then head of the SPO that managed the MSEs, came to Sundberg early in the program and assigned him to develop an instrumentation package to fly on the orbital test flights to measure the dynamic environment of the payload bay during flight.

So, in addition to his developmental tasks with his primary payload, Sundberg and his team also had to scrape together all the necessary parts to assemble the package and make it flightworthy. With time of the essence, Sundberg relates, "we had to go steal parts from everywhere. All the transducers we got—and everything else—we basically took off other programs, put them together, and got them running. Connectors turned out to be our long pole—the RF connectors and electrical connectors. We actually ended up taking used ones, electrostripping them, replating them, and using them because we couldn't manufacture fast enough."

The device would be fed data from instrumentation throughout the payload bay, including thermometers, acoustic sensors, and accelerometers. Even though they worked feverishly, it was too much to ask to have the package ready for STS-1, but the team had the equipment ready for the remainder of the test program. The air force needed this critical data in order to confirm that their payloads could safely ride aboard the shuttle, and from the time the requirement was identified, Sundberg's group had the gear ready to fly in just eight months. "It's fun to have a project where there's this tremendous urgency," he recalls, "because all of the BS and all the posturing goes by the wayside and it's, 'Let's get the job done.' But [we] got *tremendous* help out of the Kennedy [Space Center] people and the Johnson [Space Center] people in terms of putting that package together and getting it flown."

Special Projects (SAFSP) in and of itself was not classified, but virtually every program in which the office was involved fell into that category. The organization was tasked with some of the nation's most closely guarded secretive space programs, and since the first MSE group was assigned there, it too was kept under wraps. But at the Los Angeles Air Force Station, right across the intersection of Aviation and El Segundo Boulevards, another office building housed the Space Division (SD). This organization was responsible for the DOD's communications, weather, and soon-to-be-launched navigation satellites.

Since the space shuttle was to be carrying virtually all these military assets into orbit, SD leadership decided to have its own group of engineers selected to accompany its spacecraft into orbit. The group, recruited exclusively from air force personnel, was composed of James B. Armor Jr., Michael W. Booen, Livingston L. Holder Jr., Larry D. James, Charles E. (Chuck) Jones, Maureen C. LaComb, Michael R. Mantz, Randy T. Odle, William A. Pailes, Craig A. Puz, Katherine E. Sparks Roberts, Jess M. Sponable, William D. Thompson, and Glenn S. Yeakel.

LaComb and Roberts were the first women selected for the program; and Holder, the first African American. The group also differed in that they came from a wider range of backgrounds than the first MSE cadre. Some had scientific backgrounds, while several were computer specialists. Two of the new group, Armor and Puz, had held the keys of nuclear-tipped Titan II and Minuteman missiles deep inside their hardened silos, ready to launch them in an all-out strike against the Soviet Union. Only Pailes, a pilot with two degrees in computer science, had any flight experience.

Bill Pailes, born in 1952 in Hackensack, New Jersey, spent most of his formative years in the small bedroom community of Kinnelon. "I did well in school, and I really liked math and science," he told the authors. He earned an appointment to the U.S. Air Force Academy but was disqualified from pilot training when he failed a color-vision test during his entrance physical. "I wasn't pilot qualified when I chose my major as a sophomore at the academy, so I was focused on academics," Pailes recalled. "I really enjoyed my freshman computer-programming course and chose this as a major simply because I liked it."

Flying had never been a boyhood dream for Pailes, yet in his junior year, he took another color-vision test and unexpectedly passed. The opportunity to become a pilot was something he couldn't turn down, so he took an assignment to pilot training after graduating in 1974. Toward the end of that training he had to decide what type of flying he wanted to do: "Because flying had not been a long-time goal or aspiration, I gave a lot of thought to what kind of mission I wanted. One of the biggest motivations for me was to have a peacetime mission. I asked specifically for HC-130s because of the variety of missions HCs were used for in the Aerospace Rescue and Recovery Service—combat search and rescue (SAR) and rescue helicopter air-refueling, equipment drops, and pararescuemen (PJ) deployments, peacetime humanitarian SAR, helicopter deployments, fighter deployment escort, and, sometimes, recovery missions."

Pailes thoroughly enjoyed his training and assignment as an HC-130 Hercules pilot. Being a devoutly religious person, he found great satisfaction in helping those in need—be they combat troops requiring supplies or a lost civilian hiker seeking rescue from the mountains of Washington State. "I participated in a medivac mission in Iceland, to get a woman—who was pregnant, if I remember correctly—to a hospital," Pailes shared, and "escorted and air-refueled an AF helicopter out to an Islandic fishing vessel, so a PJ could help an injured fisherman."

While a copilot in his first operational flying assignment, in the Forty-First Aerospace Rescue and Recovery Service Squadron at McClellan Air Force Base near Sacramento, Pailes had the opportunity to fly several air-to-air recovery missions in Panama. Researchers using high-altitude balloons would package their instruments in a pod that was released to descend by parachute, and Pailes helped the aircraft commander snag them in mid-air. Much like the recovery technique used for the reentry film pods of the military's spy satellites, long poles extended from the open ramp of the HC-130 with cables strung between them were used to capture the descending parachute with a very close, precisely timed flyover by the pilots.

After a year and a half at McClellan, Pailes flew air rescue missions from Woodbridge, England, for almost three years before returning to earn his master's degree in computer science from Texas A&M University in 1981. Following graduation, Pailes was sent to a "rated-supplement assignment," a nonflying position in a computer services squadron at Scott Air Force Base, Illinois, where he could use his new advanced degree. That assignment would be the first in a string of events that would unexpectedly lead to Pailes flying in space:

> *Early in 1982—I'd just been at my assignment at the computer services squadron for about two months—my wife and I attended a church event, and the speaker encouraged us to just ask God for something . . . kind of personal, something that's important to us. And I had the thought of asking him for an assignment in the space program. I wasn't thinking about going up into space, I was just thinking about doing something that was a little more interesting than what I was doing right then. And it was about six weeks later that I read about the* MSE *program in the* Air Force Times. *My wife and I talked about it; we agreed that that was an answer to the prayer.*

Pailes honestly didn't think he had even a remote chance of getting selected for the program, given the fact that he hadn't done anything associated with space in his career to that point. In addition, the ad didn't even specify a need for rated pilots. "That was not only *not* a requirement; it's pretty obvious that that was not an important qualification," he recalled. Almost immediately, his flying experience caused an issue that could have disqualified him.

In order to be considered, the air force required a rated pilot to have met the first flying gate in their military career, which meant seventy-two months in the cockpit, but Pailes had only seventy-one. Fortunately for him, though, the flight management office took another look at his records and found that they had made a mistake, failing to credit him for his first month of pilot training. "All of the sudden, I went from not being eligible to being eligible," Pailes recalled. What followed was a comprehensive review of his military records and a thorough medical examination at Brooks Air Force Base, Texas.

The Space Division, however, did not conduct interviews for their group of MSEs. Pailes only needed to provide a recommendation from his unit commander. He'd only been in his current assignment for six months, but after talking to his commander about what he was applying for and because his air force record was good, his commander felt very comfortable recommending him.

The closest Pailes ever got to an interview for the MSE assignment was the psychological exam at Brooks. "Mine was pretty positive, and obviously he must have recommended me, because I guess nobody said no." When the selection announcement was made in December 1982, Pailes remembers being "a *little* bit surprised," yet he reflected on how many things had fallen into place to make it possible. He was able to get his flight records corrected, and given that the project he was assigned to was nearly over, his commander was able to let him go— something that may not have happened had he remained in a flying assignment.

The men and women of the second MSE group reported to SD at the LA Air Force Station in January 1983 and immediately got down to training. Much like the first group, they too were sent to various shuttle and payload contractors for training on various systems and NASA processes. In preparation for their EVA training, they were also sent to the U.S. Navy Dive School in Coronado for scuba training. By the time the second group arrived, however, much of the exploratory work had been accomplished by the first cadre, and the space walk training was more intended to simply familiarize them with the operational environment they were to be working in with NASA astronauts. "I never heard of any MSEs planning to do an EVA," recalled Pailes. "Beyond the turf and responsibility aspect, I'm sure NASA, for very good reasons, would have wanted to maintain complete control over training and certifying people for EVAs, which are difficult things to do."

Sundberg would often watch over the new cadre during the course of their training. As a practiced free diver, he could hold his breath longer than most men and would routinely jump into the pool without any breathing apparatus and drop right to the bottom. "They had the safety divers on scuba equipment and everything else, and I could get in the water and go down and sit with them without tanks on," he recalled. "Yeah, forty feet down—that usually gets people's attention."

Another unique opportunity for the second group came when the MSE support office arranged for them to go to the Martin Marietta Corporation to fly the Manned Maneuvering Unit (MMU) simulator. The MMU was to be test-flown on an upcoming mission before being utilized by a NASA astronaut to recover the failed Solar Max satellite later in 1984. "At the Martin simulator, they had this rotating Solar Max thing, and you flew the simulator with the MMU controls to see if you could latch on to it," recalled Pailes. "It gave us an appreciation for what the Solar Max mission entailed, but it also was a fun thing to do."

During that first year of training, each member of the second MSE cadre was assigned to a specific SPO—the DOD payload that they would become experts in and presumably fly with. Pailes, along with Mike Booen, was assigned to the Defense Satellite Communications System (DSCS, pronounced "dis-cuss"). Declassified some years later, these spacecraft operated multiple channels of super-high X-band frequencies and were extremely resistant to jamming by potential enemies.

When *Discovery* returned from the first classified mission in January, the space shuttle program was in high gear, and the DOD's part in it took on a much more visible and important role in terms of ensuring the nation's edge in the Cold War with the Soviet Union. But even with the momentum building up toward regular DOD shuttle operations, the air force and the NRO had begun to lament the continuously slipping schedule of what was supposed to become their sole launch vehicle. Proponents for a mixed-fleet strategy, most notably Undersecretary of the Air Force Edward Aldridge, pushed to ensure rapid, timely access to space for the intelligence-gathering fleet of spy satellites.

Within the Special Projects Office, the first signs of frustration had already become evident back in March 1983, when Gen. Ralph Jacobson convened a meeting of the first MSE group for what would come to be known as the Saturday Morning Massacre. The general wanted to make it perfectly clear to his aspiring astronauts that his command had one primary mission— launching critical national security payloads in defense of the United States. The delays in the shuttle schedule were interfering with that goal, and in his mind, it didn't matter how those secret satellites were launched or that his MSEs were involved. Their dreams of flying in space were of little importance compared to the national security interests of the country.

Things got worse for the team when Secretary of the Air Force Vernon Orr handed down a new directive that officers were not expected to spend any more than four years in a particular assignment before moving on and that any deviation could result in being held back for promotion. Many of the first MSEs had already been at SAFSP longer than that and were forced to begin considering other postings without ever flying in space. One of the first to leave was Eric Sundberg; as he told the authors, "It had become very clear to me that my chances of flying were essentially zero, and by that time, all of the military programs were getting off of the shuttle program itself. And so I had sat down with our director of Special Projects at that time, and he counseled me to move on and asked me where I'd like to go, and he said, 'I can set you up.' It had become clear to me that the MSE program had run its course."

"We were well aware that there were issues between NASA and the air force about military payload specialists being on shuttle flights," recalled Pailes, "but we MSEs (at least in the second group) did not have to fight those battles." Even as the DOD and NASA continued to work toward an improved working relationship and the future of the MSE program was not clearly defined, the air force decided to bring on board five new engineers in August 1985—Joseph J. Carretto, Robert B. Crombie, Frank M. DeArmond, David P. Staib Jr., and Theresa M. Stevens.

Paul Sefchek, of the first MSE group, had been attached to one of the air force payloads that was planned to fly aboard STS-62A, the program's first launch into a near polar orbit from Vandenberg Air Force Base in California. Like every officer who had signed up for the MSE program in the first place, Sefchek fully expected to get a mission to space. "There were those who wanted to fly because it's a neat thing to do, and there were those who wanted to fly because of the alpha male type of stuff," remembered Brett Watterson, who clearly considered Sefchek to be in the first category. But in late 1984, when the air force decided on crew assignments for two upcoming missions, Sefchek's name was not on the list. The top brass had instead selected Watterson for the historic, coveted position, along with Randy Odle from the second group. According to Watterson, Sefchek was "one of my erstwhile buddies," and the assignment would strain their relationship.

Fresh from his assignment to the investigation of the IUS failure, Watterson had been far removed from the highly competitive environment of

SAFSP for a year and a half. "I neither lobbied for nor said I wanted that job," he recalled. "I was just called up to the general's office one morning, and [he] said, 'We've made a decision, and you've been selected as a crew member.' I wasn't given a chance to turn it down." Much like the mysteriousness surrounding the astronaut assignments of George Abbey, JSC's director of Flight Crew Operations, the decisions being made by the air force generals left many of the other MSEs in the dark, and in some cases, animosity would be directed toward the selectees. "A lot of people I thought were friends were competitors," Watterson revealed." The angst over his assignment to STS-62A on the part of several of his fellow officers soon washed away his initial excitement from hearing the news.

More politics would soon intervene in the crew assignment for *Discovery*'s maiden flight from Vandenberg. Pete Aldridge had been representing the DOD in endless meetings with Congress and NASA over shuttle launch pricing, the mixed-fleet strategy, and the possibility of procuring a fifth orbiter. With a price tag of over $2 billion, Aldridge was very publicly opposed to the need for another shuttle. Senator Jake Garn and Congressman Bill Nelson, who would both garner rides aboard space shuttle missions, had been in favor of the fifth space plane, suggesting that as many as thirty-three flights per year would be required to support the space station and the Strategic Defense Initiative.

NASA administrator James Beggs, after accusations that the air force was looking to get out of the shuttle program entirely, secured a compromise with the DOD to purchase as many as one third of the shuttle flights per year. Beggs, in turn, would stop publicly arguing against the production of the expendable launch vehicles. Both NASA and the DOD would work together to design and fund the next-generation shuttle replacement. In attempting to reestablish a cooperative partnership between the two agencies, Beggs made an offer, as Aldridge related to NASA's Rebecca Wright:

Jim [Beggs] decided that it would be appropriate to have an Air Force official fly. Well, they asked the Air Force official according to the pecking order. The first person on that list is the Secretary of the Air Force. So Jim asked Verne Orr . . . would he be interested in doing that. Orr at the time says no, he would not, because one, he was older; I think he was in his 70s at that time, and the more appropriate person to do this would be me anyway. So Beggs offered for me to fly. Since the Air Force responsibility was to build Vandenberg Air Force Base, the SLC-6 [Space Launch Complex-6] there, it would be very appropriate for the first [Air Force] official to fly out of Vandenberg.

In August 1985 Orr made it official and announced that Aldridge would be a payload specialist aboard *Discovery* "to illustrate the Air Force's commitment to the [shuttle], enhance the cooperative spirit between NASA and the Air Force and DOD, and provide valuable insights to guide our future space transportation system developments."

Decades later Casserino finds it easier to laugh about the arrangement. "Well, the [under] secretary of the air force can kind of go wherever he wants to go," he surmised. But immediately upon getting involved in the planning for the Vandenberg mission, Watterson realized that the challenge ahead for him was no laughing matter. He found that the justifications for having MSEs on board at all were "less than optimum." There were two primary payloads on the mission. AFP-675 consisted of a cryogenically cooled experiment to observe auroral and airglow phenomenon, which would remain within the payload bay, and Teal Ruby was a free-flying, experimental sensor package that would be left in orbit.

Watterson had primary responsibility for the stationary AFP-675. "They designed this thing so it didn't have any telemetry," he explained, "nor did they route any telemetry through the shuttle, so it was all on tape recorders. In fact, they had built this thing such that it *required* a payload specialist." The on-orbit and malfunction procedures for these payloads were a jumbled mess, and the first thing *Discovery's* commander Bob Crippen charged Watterson with was to rewrite the "very abstract and obtuse mission plan," which only the air force personnel could interpret, into a checklist format. Thus, he enlisted the help of group 2 MSE Scott Yeakel and set about reorganizing the procedures into documents the entire crew could understand. "Scott, he was like a brother to me," remembered Watterson. "He was smart. In fact, there were times if I could say, 'This isn't for me,' I would have forwarded Scott Yeakel's name. He was a great guy."

Teal Ruby was a troubled program dating back to 1977. Notoriously over budget and fraught with technical problems, the system utilized charge-coupled device technology in a cryogenically cooled telescope to detect the infrared signatures of missile launches and jet aircraft exhaust in the atmosphere. The two-thousand-pound P-80-1 satellite on which it was mounted was originally intended to be deployed at an altitude of four hundred nautical miles, but shuttle performance from Vandenberg would make that impossible. The mission plan, as Watterson recalled, was for *Discovery* to take P-80-1 (later designated AFP-888) up to an altitude of 250 to 270 nautical miles, deploy it, and then drop down to 200 miles and spend the remainder of the seven-to-ten-day mission operating his payload.

By early 1985 Watterson had packed up everything he owned and was transferred to the air force detachment at JSC. There, he took up residence in building 4 and would soon become an officemate and friend of teacher-in-space selectee Christa McAuliffe and her backup, Barbara Morgan. "I couldn't tell anybody why I was down there," he explained. "And really why I was down there was, one, 62A was an important first-of-a-kind mission, but second, I think it was the way they had to get me out of Los Angeles, because I had too much time on station." With eight years tenure at Los Angeles, getting reassigned to detachment 2 in Houston allowed Watterson to avoid being sidelined by Secretary Orr's recent directive.

On 15 February 1985 the crews for two upcoming classified missions were named. Karol (Bo) Bobko's crew would eventually become STS-51J, and Bob Crippen's would undertake the inaugural Vandenberg flight. Just ten days later President Ronald Reagan signed the National Security Launch Strategy, directing the air force to purchase ten expendable launch vehicles and "launch them at a rate of approximately two per year during the period 1988–92." As had become the norm, no MSE payload specialists were publicly named with the NASA crew announcements. But at the program's headquarters at the Los Angeles Air Force Station, the word had come down—Odle was replaced on STS-62A by Aldridge, and the next DOD mission to fly in the fall of that year would include an MSE from the second group, Maj. William Pailes.

STS-51J would loft the first two DSCS III satellites, and as it turned out, these came from the SPO that Pailes was assigned to when he joined the MSE program. When the decision was made to fly an MSE on STS-51J, the air force decided to draw from that office. "Theoretically, every MSE in my group was a candidate," explained Pailes, "but SPO assignment, apparently, was a big factor."

Pailes would be joined by his backup Michael Booen, also of the second group, in training for the classified mission. The news came as Frank Casserino and Daryl Joseph, who had been left in limbo with their payload when the IUS failure occurred, still waited for their first spaceflights. Their payload had not yet been remanifested, and now they watched as two officers selected for the program after them were assigned to a mission just a few months away.

Casserino and Joseph had been targeted for STS-16 when the original assignments were made in the summer of 1983. "Daryl was seven years older than me," Casserino explained. "He graduated from the academy in 1970. I graduated from the academy in 1977." Yet it was Casserino who got the prime MSE spot for the mission.

> When the time came and I got a call from General [Ralph] Jacobson and he told me, "Frank, congratulations, you're identified as the primary payload specialist," I was just as blown away about that as I was when I got selected for the program back in 1979. So, it was great; it was humbling. Daryl, then, even though he was seven years my elder, basically was my protector. His attitude was, "I'm gonna protect you from NASA; I'm gonna protect you from everybody. You're gonna be the most successful payload specialist, and then I'm going to fly after you." Daryl ended up being a great friend and a great partner.

But for now, all the pair could do was watch as the first two DOD missions were flown in 1985 and as planning progressed for the high-profile Vandenberg flight.

Construction of the Vandenberg launch facility was nearly completed by the fall of 1985. The launchpad, service structures, and two new flame trenches had finally come together. Additional facilities to receive and service the SRBS and external tank were being prepared to accept hardware. The orbiter processing facility was constructed near the facility's newly extended fifteen-thousand-foot runway at the north base, requiring an arduous twenty-two-mile road journey for the shuttle on the way to SLC-6.

Many challenges still lay ahead before the facility would be ready for *Discovery* to begin operations from it, the most serious of which being the possibility of unburned hydrogen being trapped in the curved exhaust

23. Space shuttle *Enterprise* stacked for fit checks at Vandenberg Air Force Base's Space Launch Complex 6 in February 1985. Critical to the DOD's plans for polar-orbiting classified missions, the facility was plagued with technical problems, and no shuttle would ever launch from the West Coast launchpad. Courtesy U.S. Air Force/Retro Space Images.

duct and causing an uncontrolled fire or explosion. Acoustic overpressure reflecting off the launchpad and even the surrounding mountains threatened to damage the orbiter and the service structures during launch. Even the launch control center full of personnel was at risk, being located just 1,200 feet from the pad.

In addition to the issues surrounding the launch facilities themselves, operational risks for the shuttle's ascent were a top priority. "There were abort gaps, which violated flight rules," explained Watterson. "We were firing on 109 percent SSME [space shuttle main engine] thrust." To cut down on weight and meet the air force requirement to loft a thirty-two-thousand-pound payload into polar orbit, new filament-wound SRBS were to replace the typical steel-cased boosters, and their development was plagued with technical problems. Former flight director Glynn Lunney shared in his NASA Oral History interview that "Vandenberg was a tough place for us, because it's very windy and it tends to be kind of rainy and cloudy, so a difficult launch, but even more difficult landing site for the orbiter." As Watterson concluded to the authors, "There was a lot of der-ring-do on our mission."

A dramatic glimpse into the future occurred at SLC-6 in February 1985. With the planned maiden flight from Vandenberg still several months away, the prototype orbiter *Enterprise* was rolled from the processing facil-ity at the north base and driven on a purpose-designed transporter down to the base of the launchpad. There, inert SRBs and an external tank had been stacked awaiting the shuttle for fit checks and prelaunch-procedures testing. Unlike the process used for decades at KSC, the air force would erect the stack on the launchpad and enclose the shuttle inside the massive, movable Shuttle Assembly Building and mobile service tower. It was a sur-real sight, with the space shuttle pointing skyward in stark contrast to the backdrop of California coastal hills and the nearby Pacific Ocean shoreline.

Walking through Red Square in Moscow in early 1975, Karol (Bo) Bobko glanced over at Bob Overmyer: "I never doubted that I'd be here. I always thought it would be at two hundred feet and at full afterburner." The two former Manned Orbiting Laboratory astronauts had spent a major-ity of their military careers training to fight and later conduct espionage from space against the great juggernaut that was the Soviet Union. As Bobko shared with NASA's Summer Bergen in a 2002 interview, they now found themselves part of the American delegation working toward the Apollo-Soyuz Test Project, the first joint mission between the Cold War adversaries.

"I think we were the first people to be down at the launch site in Kazakh-stan and to know the Russians, to learn to speak Russian," he related. "So that was an interesting couple of years." A decade later, those days of détente were long past, and as the pendulum of history swung back toward chill-ier times between the two countries, Bobko found himself at long last in command of a military mission to space. Joining his STS-51J crew late in training from his April mission aboard *Discovery*, he would now command the first mission of *Atlantis*, with its twin DSCS III spacecraft stacked on a single IUS.

Now heading into his third training cycle, Bobko easily assimilated him-self into this crew of mixed experience. Pilot Ron Grabe, mission special-ist Dave Hilmers, and Pailes were all rookies, while Bob Stewart had one spaceflight under his belt, test-flying the Manned Maneuvering Unit on STS-41B in early 1984. For the two MSEs assigned to the flight, the transition to being crew members could not have gone smoother, as Pailes recalled: "After I was assigned to my mission, not only did I have absolutely no difficulties with the NASA crew members, but they accepted me completely. Maybe that was a function of the specific individuals, but [they] made me feel as though I was a full member of the crew. The NASA training and support personnel, at both JSC and KSC, treated me and Mike Booen as though we were NASA astronauts. I neither encountered nor sensed any ill feelings, let alone animosity, at all."

Many of the technical challenges experienced by the first DOD mission crew with their IUS payload were smoothed out in the intervening months, but classification still remained a stumbling block. Checklist books used by the crew for post–orbital insertion and deorbit preparations would have pages of classified changes added to them. "We found this system to be cumbersome, confusing, and possibly error producing," Bobko pointed out. In one example of the inefficiency of the flight documents, an entry in the deorbit checklist instructed the crew to "perform payload safing." This led the astronauts to another classified checklist for the payload, which in turn referred them to a third document, which incredulously read, "No action required."

Secondary payloads on the classified mission became a serious issue as well. "This process evolved as it was 'discovered' that our flight existed and that room might be found for additional experiments," Bobko said of the increasing burden on his crew. Even up to just one month prior to flight, more and more proposals kept coming forward to be stashed aboard *Atlantis*. The major problem for Bobko to contend with was that given the secrecy surrounding the flight, most of the procedures for these experiments had to be developed by the crew members themselves, due to the complications associated with getting clearances arranged for an increasing number of engineers.

Early on the morning of 3 October 1985 Bill Pailes stood on the launch tower platform 195 feet above pad 39A, waiting for his turn to board *Atlantis*. Admiring the beautiful, clear, peaceful Florida morning, he took a moment to consider what he was about to undertake:

I could hardly believe that I was where I was—just a couple of hours away from going into space. It wasn't that it didn't seem real, because everything about it was very real. It was that I was so fully aware of and so very appreciative of the fact that, not only was I participating in a space shuttle mission, which thousands of people had worked on, but I was in one of the most privileged of positions—the crew members—the people who get to see and experience the culmination and very purpose of all those people's efforts. I was so thankful.

As had been the case with STS-51C, the morning rituals of a departing space shuttle crew were kept from the view of the public, in order to foil any predictions of the exact launch time. The countdown clock held firmly at T minus nine minutes, leaving reporters and family members to wait impatiently for the first movement toward launch. *Atlantis*, being a factory-new orbiter, had only fired its engines once before, in a flight readiness firing test on the pad a few weeks before. Now poised to carry out a critical mission to help ensure the nation's security, the shuttle presented few problems for the crew and technicians to address.

Without warning, the clock suddenly started ticking down the final nine minutes. "It was at that point that the realization that I was about to go into space struck me, and I got really excited about what was about to happen," recalled Pailes. "The reason, I think, this didn't happen earlier is that up until those final [nine] minutes, there always was something else that had to be done before the mission. After the hold was done, there was nothing left to be done before the launch. It really was about to happen!"

Finally, at 11:15 a.m. *Atlantis* roared to life once again. The hold-down bolts were blown, and the shuttle took its first leap off the Florida pad into what would become a storied career. For the first-time payload specialist seated in the middeck, it was an unforgettable ride: "The launch itself was absolutely incredible! I could feel the main engines start, and when the SRBS lit, we were off the pad instantly. The shuttle accelerates faster than a T-38 on takeoff roll and reaches one hundred miles per hour by the time it clears the launch tower. The force of over 6.5 million pounds . . . is amazing. And it was thrilling—nothing unpleasant or the least bit frightening at all. A fantastic ride!"

Pailes would remember over three decades later that he felt absolutely no fear during the impressive ride to orbit. "It wasn't because I'm any more courageous than others," he said. "My definition of courage is doing something that is scary. This was not, to me." While launching into space was a big jump from flying military aircraft, he saw it as a reasonable progression both in performance and reliability. "Military pilots are success oriented. We expect the planes to work, so we don't dwell on the possibility of failure," he concluded.

As Bobko and pilot Grabe worked feverishly through their post–orbital insertion checklists, they wanted to snap a few photos of the slowly tumbling external tank as it drifted away from *Atlantis*. On the middeck, Pailes unstrapped and floated over to an equipment locker. "I'm downstairs in the middeck and Karol Bobko gave me permission to get out of my seat," he remembered. "I got a camera out and floated up to the flight deck and gave it to Ron Grabe, who could look out the front window and take a picture of the tank. [It was] fun right away," he said. "It took me just a few seconds to feel comfortable. I'm sure I got better at stabilizing myself over time, but it felt natural and easy immediately." Contrary to Payton's initial reaction to the alien environment, Pailes thought the experience of the Vomit Comet had indeed helped him in adjusting to space.

Shortly after the payload bay doors were opened, he floated to a window to see "the most impressive view" of the curved blue horizon of Earth filling the upper portion of the windows of the upside-down orbiter, and the top of one DSCS III satellite sparkling in the harsh, unfiltered sunlight. For Pailes, it was a very spiritual experience. "When I first looked at the entire scene outside the payload bay windows, with the spacecraft in the bay and the earth above, I couldn't help but marvel at God's creation, and I felt small and insignificant in comparison," he recalled. "But God didn't let me stay on that thought, because He conveyed to me that although I obviously am small in size, I'm more important to Him than His creation." It was a powerful moment.

Mission specialists Hilmers and Stewart got to work preparing for the deployment of the double-stacked communications satellites on their IUS booster. As the tilt ring was raised up to the proper position, Pailes carefully examined and photographed the two spacecraft and the cylindrical white booster rocket—the same type that had sent Payton's payload to orbit

24. *Atlantis*'s payload bay doors are opened to reveal two Defense Satellite Communication System (DSCS III) spacecraft stacked one atop another on their interim upper stage (IUS) booster rocket. Courtesy NASA/Retro Space Images.

nine months prior. Several orbits into the mission, at the precisely defined time that the launch had been keyed to, the IUS completed its automated countdown and was sprung from the grasp of its launch support.

Gliding ever so slowly up into the inky blackness of the dark side of *Atlantis*'s orbit, the twin spacecraft began their journey to a high perch above the planet from which they would route military communications for years to come. "Deployment of the satellites was a very straightforward process," Pailes related. "[Simply] releasing the stack and letting it drift away from the orbiter."

Bo Bobko made a mental note for his postflight report as he finished the complicated procedure of "taking care of business" without the beneficial effects of gravity. A "coffee can" with a plastic bag insert was used to dispose of wet tissues, which would then be tied closed and placed into a wet-trash container. "The entire operation was clean and efficient," the commander later wrote, but "the reason for clear plastic sides on the bag is not apparent as none of the 51-J crew members felt inclined to inspect the contents of the bag during its transport to the wet trash compartment."

Only two technical issues came about that required the crew to perform in-flight maintenance: one repair to an electrical box on one of their secondary experiments and the routine filter cleaning. The latter led to Bobko reporting a minor theft following the mission, in his typical, understated humor: "A large number of hardware items were encountered and collected mostly by hand. These articles consisted mainly of screws, nuts, bolts, and fasteners. The largest article encountered was a substantial coaxial cable connector assembly. One U.S. quarter dollar coin was also collected." But after landing, Bobko noted that these "space-flown" items, including the quarter, had been pilfered by ground personnel. "This deprived the 51-J crew of their hard earned flight bonus of 5 cents each!"

Over the course of the brief four-day mission, the crew performed several experiments and more medical tests. A black-hooded device designed by astronaut Jeff Hoffman was placed in the orbiter's windows to block cabin glare while photographing various celestial phenomena. Pailes reveled in the zero-g world of orbiting the planet as he undertook his assigned tasks. "The weightlessness was fine, I was comfortable with that," he said. "It just felt *right*. It felt the way it ought to be."

It wasn't until the second day of the flight that he had a true opportunity to look at Earth from a place he never imagined he would. The impression he was left with was somewhat different from many others. "Being in Earth orbit is different from being out in space returning from the moon, so you're not seeing a ball in the windscreen; you're seeing a big disk," he related. "I just found the whole thing to be thrilling, but I couldn't get away from the creation standpoint. I had a chance to look at Earth—this planet that God created—from 350 miles up, and it was just great!"

But in addition to the spiritual experience of it, one other feature of the planet immediately stood out to Pailes: "I didn't look at the earth as being

25. Manned spaceflight engineer Bill Pailes, camera in hand, in the middeck of *Atlantis* during its maiden flight, STS-51J. Courtesy NASA/Retro Space Images.

fragile. It didn't strike me as being fragile at all. I saw it as a remarkably *sturdy* planet. I thought to myself, 'God made a good planet. He made a really good planet that's serving the needs of the human race.' That's not to say I'm indifferent to environmental things, because I'm not. That simply was my reaction, but it doesn't mean anybody else's reaction, just because it was different, was any less legitimate. They're all legitimate."

The one surprise that came to Pailes during the mission was the nighttime view of the sky literally blanketed in pure-white, sharp, clear stars. "There were more stars than you can see below the atmosphere," he remembered. "I was really kind of surprised at how many." It reminded him of the view from high atop a Colorado mountain on a clear night, only "double that." On the morning they would return to Earth, Pailes awoke early and, like many of the other payload specialists who had flown, took one last opportunity to savor the wondrous beauty of the planet from space. "I'd have enjoyed a couple more days," he recalled. "It's almost like four days—you're just feeling really comfortable, you're enjoying yourself, and now you've got to go home. But I was and still am thankful for the time in space we had."

Atlantis arced across the Pacific Ocean on its first reentry enveloped in a neon-orange sheath of plasma. "The high heating phase of the entry was at night with the crew able to witness significant entry glow," Bobko wrote after the mission. "The orbiter was encased in [a] glow that became brighter as the RCS jets were fired. It appeared as if the Orbiter was flying through an orange-yellow cloud with an occasional lightning strike nearby." Pailes, seated back in his launch position next to the tiny hatch window, described it later as a very smooth flight, with a gentle buildup to not more than 1.5 g's. In observance of the protocol for every maiden flight of an orbiter, *Atlantis* would return to the wide-open expanse of Edwards Air Force Base. Having blown a tire on *Discovery* just a few months prior while landing at KSC, this suited Bobko just fine.

After slowing to subsonic speeds and taking over manual control, Bobko glided the orbiter to a perfect landing on the concrete runway at Edwards under a clear blue sky with a ghostly crescent moon above. As he slowed with the touchy wheel brakes, though, he felt the right brake pressure being released automatically to prevent yet another skid. "Since we had been briefed that at speeds below 130 knots, it was practically impossible for the anti-skid to release, the [commander] assumed it was a skid and backed off on the brakes," he reported.

With the call of "wheels stop," loudspeakers at the desert landing strip blared out the "Star-Spangled Banner" for the small number of spectators and reporters present to hear it. *Atlantis* still looked virtually brand-new after just four days in space, having travelled 1.7 million miles on its maiden voyage. Upon postflight inspection, though, a significant gash was found in the trailing edge of the left wing—likely caused by a loose gap filler that blowtorched hot plasma onto the spot during entry.

Bill Pailes immediately began readapting to the heaviness of living on Earth, having been off it for several days. "The entire experience was an incredible opportunity. There were no downsides. The NASA crew was great, and working with them was a real pleasure. The actual experience of going into space was absolutely incredible!" But as meaningful as it was to him that he had been part of a vital national security space shuttle mission, he firmly believed that the best part was that God had put him there. "Applying for the MSE program had been His [God's] idea, and He had gotten me past a couple of the hurdles in the application process. I believe He had orchestrated my selection as an MSE, had arranged my assignment to the DSCS SPO, and, finally, my selection to be the [payload specialist], and the final agreement to include me on the mission."

Bobko would continue to struggle with some of the awkward arrangements caused by classification following the mission, but for the most part, many of the issues that had pervaded the first DOD mission had been ironed out. "This entire operation was greatly improved over 51C and shows significant development of the system," he reported. "The smooth working relationship with DOD is also an indication of a mutually maturing relationship that allows complex missions to be effectively flown."

For Pailes, it seemed everything had fallen into place, and he was even looking forward to another opportunity to fly again as an MSE. "Right after my flight I was told that I might very well go on the next DSCS mission," he recalled. But the events of the next few months would change everything for the MSEs who remained as part of the air force's dedicated corps of astronauts.

On 25 August 1985, just weeks before the STS-51J mission, a Titan 34-D launched from Vandenberg Air Force Base failed during ascent and deposited its top secret payload into the depths of the Pacific Ocean. The workhorse expendable booster favored by Aldridge for its capability to launch on demand would now find itself under scrutiny. But no one in the intelligence community could have imagined what would happen over the coming months. *Challenger* and its crew of seven would perish on 28 January 1986. Barely four months later the unthinkable happened—on 18 April another Titan 34-D, carrying the last Hexagon satellite, exploded spectacularly as it left the launchpad at Vandenberg. A strap-on solid rocket motor had blown apart and destroyed the vehicle, leaving behind a cloud of flaming tentacles that engulfed the pad area like a gigantic smoky octopus. For the immediate future, the DOD had no means of replenishing its critical flotilla of reconnaissance satellites to protect the country.

With the loss of *Challenger*, the fate of the MSE program was sealed. No one knew at the time how long it would be before the shuttles were able to fly again, but when they eventually did, the air force would have no further interest in having their own personnel accompany classified payloads into orbit. For many of the officers that remained in the MSE program at the time, there was little left to do in the wake of the accident. The program was officially terminated in 1988, and by June of the following year the Manned Spaceflight Control Squadron in Houston was disbanded. After an estimated cost of $5 billion, the SLC-6 launch site at Vandenberg was mothballed and the air force's Consolidated Space Operations Center in Colorado Springs was, for a time, transferred to the Strategic Defense Initiative.

The MSEs would all move on to other assignments or out of active service altogether. It would be two and a half years before the shuttle once again rose from the Florida coastline, and the air force would have to ground several clandestine payloads that could only be launched on the orbiters until they were manifested onto a handful of early postaccident missions. "After the *Challenger* accident, you couldn't separate fast enough," Frank Casserino recalled. "The air force was happy to get back to controlling everything on their end, and NASA was happy to get back to controlling everything on their end."

Casserino and Daryl Joseph had been deeply involved with their top secret payload before the IUS failure occurred in 1983. Casserino was to have finally flown into space with that satellite aboard STS-6IN in September 1986. Following the loss of the shuttle, that payload had been placed aboard *Columbia*'s STS-28 mission, commanded by Brewster Shaw. By August of 1989, when their payload was finally launched, the MSE program was a distant memory, but Casserino and Joseph found themselves side by side at the Satellite Test Center in Sunnyvale supporting the mission— *their* mission. "I had left the air force shortly before the flight, and I was a civilian contractor with the air force to support shuttle missions," Casserino explained. Joseph was a lieutenant colonel still on active duty and had been assigned to Sunnyvale as well.

Casserino remembers today that, serving once again as paycoms, "[We were] watching the mission that we would have flown going on saying to ourselves, 'Boy, we should have been there.'" As they monitored their payload from consoles within the Blue Cube, their thoughts rarely strayed far from what could have been. "It was an interesting way to end that whole thing for us," he shared. Immediately following the *Challenger* accident, Casserino had been assigned to help reintegrate DOD payloads back onto the expendable launch vehicles, except for those that could only be accommodated on the shuttle. He would continue to work with the STS-28 crew closely, particularly mission specialist Mark Brown, in the months leading up to their flight.

When *Columbia* launched to deploy the DOD payload on the third post-*Challenger* mission, the crew took along a photo of Casserino and Velcroed it up in the aft flight deck. Today, framed on his office wall is that very flown photo, along with a photo of the crew with his image on the flight deck in orbit, as if he were part of the crew. Brown had inscribed on the photo, "I'm sorry you weren't there in person, but at least you had this picture. Hope to see you soon. Sincerely, Mark." It was a heartfelt tribute to Casserino's dedication to the mission but also a sad reminder of the loss of a dream.

Casserino would continue to serve in the U.S. Air Force Reserves for almost twenty-four years, retiring as a major general. One of his proudest accomplishments was the development of the first space-dedicated unit in the reserves, the Seventh Space Operations Squadron, in 1993. As he recalled, "[I] got blessed in my career on the reserve side from there, because of all the good people who made me look good and develop to the point that the program that I started with twenty people is now the first Air Force Reserve space wing with over a thousand people in it, which was pretty cool." Even after retirement, Casserino has on occasion returned to his old unit to reunite with the officers, airmen and airwomen who carry on the mission today. At an April 2017 awards ceremony, the current commander of the 310th Space Wing introduced the former MSE as the "founding father of space" in the U.S. Air Force Reserves.

Following the disbanding of the MSE team, Brett Watterson transferred to another classified assignment in Germany as a station commander for three years. Today, he admits that he "had some interesting feelings about being that close to flying and not flying." It was the most disappointing "professional regret" he had ever experienced, having put as much as any other air force officer into the program and its mission. But he was able to harness those feelings and experiences later when he was involved in space policy making at the Pentagon, before returning to southern California and retiring a full colonel in 1997.

He would join NASA at the Jet Propulsion Laboratory as the director of system safety, a career that he carried on to the Aerospace Corporation before retiring for good in 2010. At a 2005 reunion of the STS-62A crew hosted by Bob Crippen in Houston, Watterson was joined by all his old crewmates with the exception of Aldridge. In light of the many issues that conspired to delay that flight beyond the tragic loss of *Challenger*, he recalls that "even though it was a mission filled with risk, everybody—to a man—regretted not flying on that."

Watterson is today still very adamant about one point—"I'm not an astronaut," he insists. Even though he invested so much of his life to the space shuttle program, trained as an astronaut, and was assigned to a high-profile mission, he prefers to refer to himself simply as a crew member. "I think that's right," he rationalizes, "because I wasn't just watching; I was participating in the mission's success."

Eric Sundberg enjoyed a long career in the air force, government, and civilian sector after the MSE program. After several challenging assignments in the space command and as the space chair at the Air University at Maxwell Air Force Base, he was promoted early to colonel and landed a job at the NRO Headquarters in Washington DC. He would spend seven years there before retiring from the air force in 1997. Through an intergovernmental personnel assignment, he was hired by Georgia Tech and returned to the same NRO offices as a civilian.

Sundberg later left the NRO and joined the Aerospace Corporation just as Watterson had done. When asked if he holds any regrets over not fly-ing in space, he responds with an emphatic, "Well, yes! There is a voyeuris-tic part of that that says absolutely." But there was an important lesson, in Sundberg's notoriously analytical mind, that came out of his time in the MSE program. "I spent five years training for something that would last between three and seven days. That's not a good ratio."

As a senior colonel in the NRO organization, Sundberg was often asked to give motivational talks to contractors and air force personnel on the space activities of the military. During one such visit to the Air Force Academy, he had a chance meeting that would change his life: "I met a young cadet who I just related to perfectly. His name was Jack Fischer. It turned out that Jack had just lost his Dad. He was a little bit in the confusion of where he was going, and at the same time, I had just lost direct contact with my kids through a divorce. The two of us gravitated toward each other."

Sundberg brought Fischer and several other cadets out to Washington one summer to give them a glimpse into the NRO's activities and then arranged for them to spend some time working at the nearby Naval Research Lab-oratory. "Over the years, we became closer and closer until we effectively became family," Sundberg reflects. As their relationship grew and Fischer was commissioned and got married, he and his wife would ask Sundberg to become a surrogate grandfather to their children, an honor he happily accepted. "It's nice to be able to choose your family," he says.

"One of the reasons Jack and I got along so well is that I had this dream of flying on the shuttle and flying in space, and he had the dream of flying in space," shared Sundberg. Fischer would go on to become an F-15 fighter pilot, attend the U.S. Air Force Test Pilot School, and do test work on the F-22 program before being selected as a NASA astronaut in 2009. On 20 April 2017, after years of training and waiting, Fischer launched to the ISS from Kazakhstan aboard a Russian Soyuz spacecraft along with cosmonaut Fyodor Yurchikhin. Sundberg made the long trip to Russia to see him off and was able to greet him by radio later that day as the hatches between the Soyuz and the orbiting laboratory were opened. Beaming with pride, the former MSE told him simply, "Jack, you are living my dream." Fischer responded with a heartfelt, "Well, sir, I'll do the best to make all I can out of it and appreciate it for the both of us."

Gary Payton never flew in space again, but success continued to follow

26. NASA astronaut Jack Fischer (*left*) with MSE Eric Sundberg. The two met when Fischer was a cadet at the U.S. Air Force Academy, and they became lifelong friends. Fischer would launch on his first mission to the International Space Station in April of 2017, accumulating more than 135 days in space and nearly six hours of EVA time over two space walks. Courtesy Eric Sundberg.

him in the ensuing years. After nearly a decade at the Pentagon in Washington, he retired from the air force and went to work for NASA, involved in the development of various next-generation vehicles to replace the space shuttle. In addition to management of the X-33 and the X-34 technology demonstrators, Payton would cross paths with moonwalker Charles (Pete) Conrad from McDonnell Douglas while pursuing the DC-X vertical take-off and landing test vehicle. Single-stage-to-orbit concepts have been investigated vigorously, but to date, it remains an elusive goal.

One project from Payton's NASA days did prove successful, though—the X-37A would be transferred from NASA to the Defense Advanced Research Projects Agency in 2004 and would lead to orbital flight tests and the eventual X-37B Orbital Test Vehicle, the air force's own version that is still in use today. A smaller-scale unmanned space plane design, the winged vehicle has conducted several top secret missions in orbit, one of which notably lasted nearly 718 days before gliding to an automatic landing at Vandenberg Air Force Base in May 2017.

In 2005 Payton was named deputy undersecretary of the air force for space programs. Reporting directly to the secretary of the air force, he recalls these days as "Mr. Space" at the Pentagon as some of his most rewarding: "I got in on starting a whole bunch of things, some of which have been successful, some of which are not. The x-37's one of them. I started it the first time—I was at NASA Headquarters—but then worked on it again when it became an air force project. I also started something called Operational Responsive Space, which was another success. I pushed through the Pentagon bureaucracy on new technology demonstrations on orbit that will be the foundation for the next generation of our missile-warning satellites."

Today, Payton has returned to the Air Force Academy, where his journey to space began. As an endowed professor in the astronautics department, he teaches classes in human spaceflight, incorporating the lessons of the *Challenger* and *Columbia* accidents into a curriculum for a new generation of military aerospace leaders. Payton also mentors engineering cadets in the academy's FalconSAT Program, in which students design and build small experimental satellites for launch into space. Of his experiences passing the torch to the air force's newest officer corps, Payton relates that "the highlight of this job has been being asked four times to swear in cadets to their commission into the air force. Seeing these bright-eyed, bushy-tailed brand-new lieutenants march off into the sunset is great."

Bill Pailes returned to flying the HC-130 after leaving the MSE program in 1987. "The air force for good reason said, 'You need to go back to flying, you're a pilot,'" he recalled. "And I couldn't come up with a good enough reason to not do that." The rescue birds were being transformed into a Special Operations mission, "flying at very low level on night vision goggles. It was all more secretive," Pailes said of his new mission.

After a staff assignment to Twenty-Third Air Force headquarters—which became Air Force Special Operations Command during his tour there—and almost a year at the Industrial College of the Armed Forces, he spent the remainder of his military career at the Defense Information Systems Agency, retiring in 1996. Upon entering civilian life, Pailes answered a call to become an assistant pastor at his northern Virginia church, where he spent three years. In 1999 he entered the business world as a consultant for the Swedish company Mercuri-Urval, where he would serve until the post-9/11 recession. But that pivotal event was what led him to an opportunity he had always had a desire to pursue.

He had moved his family to his wife's home state of Texas in 2000, and with time to now contemplate his future, he learned of an opening as a Junior Reserve Officer Training Corps (JROTC) instructor at a local high school. "I had always wanted to get into teaching in some capacity but hadn't given it a lot of thought," he recalled. While he was simultaneously offered a position at Baylor University, "my wife and I prayed about it, and we felt God said he wanted me to teach Junior ROTC." With nine years at Corsicana High School and now six at Temple High, he has no current plans to quit.

People sometimes politely ask him, "What's a former astronaut doing teaching high school?" but Pailes doesn't look at it that way. "If God wants me to do something, I care what it is, but I don't really care what prestige is associated with it," he shared. He happily accepts the astronaut title, with one caveat—"I point out that I was an 'air force astronaut' and not a NASA astronaut," he said. "The distinction doesn't seem to be important to people, but I don't want to give the wrong impression." During the course of the JROTC program, his students hear firsthand about his experiences flying, his time as an MSE, and the history of the air force in space and its corps of Manned Orbiting Laboratory and shuttle astronauts.

In June 2011, for the first time since his only spaceflight a quarter century before, Bill Pailes went to KSC to witness a space shuttle launch. Having flown on its inaugural mission, he took the opportunity to witness *Atlantis*'s last, STS-135. After a brief, unplanned hold, his old ship and the four-person crew roared from the launchpad to be quickly swallowed up in a low deck of clouds. "And that was the only one I saw from outside the shuttle!" he says with a chuckle. "So I'm glad I had that opportunity to get down there for the last one."

Of the thirty-two MSEs selected, five would go on to become generals in either the active-duty air force or reserves. Michael Hamel and Frank Casserino of the first cadre and James Armor, Larry James, and Katherine Sparks Roberts of the second group would all attain one star or more in the years that followed. "You had a totally disproportionate number of MSEs made general officer," Sundberg remembers proudly, "and those who didn't make general officer, a very large portion of them, made colonel—beyond what would be normal air force statistics."

Many of them crossed paths later in the aerospace world and still stay in touch today, holding each other in the highest regard. Like any group of highly trained, competitive professionals, some had their differences and as a result lost touch over the years. Some have passed on, and in a tragic twist of fate, Charles Jones of the second MSE group would lose his life aboard American Airlines flight 11, at the hands of terrorists, on September 11, 2001.

Looking back on those early years of the space shuttle program and the military's involvement in it, those who had the chance to participate offer a wide range of opinions about its legacy. "The MSE program was probably an interesting way to try to get two large organizations to work together," offers Payton. "We ended up being a lightning rod to focus attention on the relationship between the air force and NASA." Ken Mattingly was once quoted as saying, "I sometimes thought the only people in the air force really interested in the shuttle were the MSEs." Loren Shriver, Mattingly's pilot on that first classified mission, suggests, "I think this expression may come from the situation the air force was in. They basically agreed that the shuttle would become the sole launcher of DOD payloads, and I think many in the air force were very uncomfortable with this arrangement. Their concerns were made real by *Challenger*. For over two and a half years, the air force was left without a launch vehicle for major national security payloads. Quite frankly, it would be hard to dream up a more serious blunder for national security than to limit their space launches to a single launch vehicle."

Pailes agrees that the decision itself turned out to be somewhat flawed. "I know the air force didn't want to have to use the shuttle for its launch vehicle, because it was more expensive, more complicated, a security nightmare, and, really, unnecessary," he offered. Looking back on the MSEs' viewpoint at the time, he often says that flying on the shuttle was something they would "get to" do, while the air force was told, "This was something you've *got to* do."

But once the directive was made clear, the two organizations made history by learning how to make the arrangement work. In Pailes's mind,

I think it's simply an example of a U.S. military service making the best of a situation after being directed to do something that, basically, made its job harder and not easier. And once committed, wanting to put its own officers on flights was a logical and reasonable idea. As far as the MSEs themselves are concerned, who can fault them for being motivated after being ordered to do something so exciting? Finally, and this probably is the most important part, without help from the DOD to pay for the shuttle program, perhaps the program wouldn't have been nearly as successful.

He would also point out that even though objectives didn't "mesh very smoothly all the time," most of the issues between the space agency and the air force were either resolved or nearly resolved when the program was brought to an end. "Probably half a dozen other MSEs, some in SD and some in SP, were programmed to fly," Pailes points out. "If it hadn't been for *Challenger*, I think the MSE program probably would have turned out to be a pretty good thing with a lot of successes, but we'll never know."

The culture clash between the DOD and NASA over the secrecy required of the classified flights still lingers in the memories of the astronauts. Mattingly related to NASA's Kevin Rusnak, "I still can't talk about what the missions were, but I can tell you that I've been around a lot of classified stuff, and most of it is overclassified by lots," he explained. But he shifts from that opinion somewhat when recalling the top secret shuttle missions. "What those programs did are spectacular. They are worth classifying, and when the books are written and somebody finally comes out and tells that chapter, everybody is going to be proud."

Payton's and Pailes's flights aboard the space shuttle were the vindication of decades of failed programs, interagency conflicts, technical challenges, and politics. The Manned Orbiting Laboratory and the X-20 Dyna-Soar never got off the drawing board, save for one unmanned test launch, and the space shuttle would never live up to the heady assumptions of NASA, the DOD, or the politicians who attempted to force them into an unwilling partnership.

The men assigned to cram their ultrasecretive national security payloads into a vehicle that wasn't designed to carry them faced hurdles not only in the hardware but also in a civilian organization with a strong heritage of doing things in its own way and in the full view of the public. However, the promise of ensuring the nation's security against an unpredictable Cold War enemy, and their dreams to see the planet from a vantage point where no borders exist, drove them to rise above all the challenges. Today, they all exude a sense of humble pride in being selected for such a pioneering experimental program. Payton sums up the entire era of the air force's long-held desire to put a military man in space as any good officer would and credits the work done by the team he was honored to serve with: "In that era, we were successful at getting shoulder to shoulder on getting the job done on each of the military flights that flew on the shuttle. I think a lot of that is due to the MSEs."

10. Space Walker

The goal of the program is to provide a commercial business
that utilizes the resource of space.

Charlie Walker

The maiden flight of *Discovery* carried the third payload specialist, Charles David Walker, into orbit on 30 August 1984. Unlike the Spacelab 1 mission, the prime focus of STS-41D was not strictly science. Three satellites were deployed, and a solar array was tested by the NASA astronauts. Walker, from Bedford, Indiana, brought the same enthusiasm for scientific research that Byron Lichtenberg and Ulf Merbold championed on STS-9 but perhaps for different motives. Walker was the first industrial payload specialist and operated a continuous flow electrophoresis (CFES, pronounced "see-fess") device on this mission, which created a product that held great promise to serve the needs of millions of people and for pharmaceutical companies to reap huge earnings.

Walker, an engineer employed by McDonnell Douglas, was not chosen in the same manner as the Spacelab payload specialists. Instead, he finagled a ride on *Discovery* via a change in NASA policy. According to the press kit, the policy allowed "major Space Shuttle customers to have one of their own people onboard to operate their payloads." Previously, a customer was required to pay for at least half a mission to be awarded the opportunity to place one of their own crewmen on the shuttle, but NASA eased the requirements to include any company that had a significant cargo on board.

Walker, born on 29 August 1948, took his bachelor of science degree in aeronautical and astronautical engineering from Purdue University in 1971. He held a variety of jobs—a civil engineering technician, land acquisition specialist, and U.S. Forest Service firefighter—prior to becoming a design engineer with the Bendix Aerospace Company. Following a stint with the Naval Sea Systems Command, he was employed in 1977 by the McDonnell Douglas Corporation, where he was assigned to test components of the shuttle OMS pods. Later, he moved to the space manufacturing group at McDonnell, which was investigating continuous flow electrophoresis, a purification process for biological cells and proteins. Walker eventually changed the group's name to Electrophoresis Operations in Space, which went by its acronym, EOS. Walker recalled thinking, "We need a name. I mean, electrophoresis, nobody can even spell it, much less pronounce it, so we've got to have something else that we can call this thing." He was the chief test engineer and payload specialist for the EOS project from 1979 to 1986.

Hank Hartsfield commanded this twelfth flight of a space shuttle with Michael Coats as his pilot. Mike Mullane, Steven Hawley, and Judy Resnik were mission specialists. Only Hartsfield had previously flown into space, as pilot on STS-4. McDonnell Douglas did not provide a backup to Walker for the STS-41D flight. Therefore, Resnik was assigned as Walker's backup, although Hartsfield had also been trained to operate the CFES equipment. According to Walker in February 2017, there were "limited knowledgeable personnel to choose from" at McDonnell Douglas. Additionally, the added complication to train another payload specialist played a role in not selecting a company backup. Ultimately, Walker was confident that the NASA "crew member backups were accepted by company management as able to provide the limited, basic payload functions on orbit if necessary."

The crew of STS-41D was known as the Zoo Crew, and each astronaut was given a nickname. For instance, Mullane was Tarzan, Hawley was Cheetah, and Resnik was Jane. The names were decided by the crew and chosen because of something unique and personal. The NASA crew didn't really know Walker very well, so they called him "CFES Charlie." With all due respect to Walker, that moniker sounds like an outcast carrying an infectious disease, accentuating the belief of many NASA astronauts that the payload specialists were different. Names aside, Walker would prove himself in orbit and earn the respect of the NASA astronauts.

The CFES device was the outcome of years of planning to take advantage of the shuttle program's capability for research in microgravity. Simple and smaller electrophoresis experiments had been carried out with success on the *Apollo 14* and *Apollo 16* missions to the moon and on the Apollo-Soyuz Test Project. McDonnell Douglas Astronautics and the materials lab at MSFC had worked together since 1975 to determine what research opportunities might exist in the microgravity environment. They looked at a variety of materials that could be "tested or produced in space" and then returned to Earth for the benefit of humankind and to turn a profit. They determined that pharmaceuticals were an area likely to fill this bill, and researchers concluded that electrophoresis held the greatest promise.

"Electrophoresis is simply a purification technique wherein a liquefied substance is purified using an electric field," Walker explained during a pre-mission press conference. "Electrophoresis, a big Greek word which is really applied to a pretty basic process as it's been used in laboratories around the world for the past hundred years, in which a compound like a gel or a liquid that has a[n] electrical conductive nature to it." For example, he explained that "blood is a complex mixture of proteins and cells, and every protein molecule has a resident electrical charge to it—very small, but it's different from every other chemical type of protein or a cellular body within that mixture." When an electric field is applied to fluids, the proteins "all move as a group toward the attracting electrical pole, and they'll move at different rates, and so if you expose that sample to an electric field for a period of time, when you shut the field off, you'll have groups of compounds all separated from one another," culminating in a purified product.

Walker would be using the same basic equipment that had already purified small amounts of the substance on four previous shuttle missions, and those four flights met 100 percent of the flight objectives. He speculated that through the process of electrophoresis, selected materials could be purified "hundreds of times more efficiently" in microgravity than on Earth.

For the STS-41D mission, the CFES equipment was modified to produce large enough quantities of a biological substance—a hormone—that Walker said could be used "to complete a testing program in the laboratory, animal testing and eventually clinical testing toward Food and Drug Administration approval to market materials which we hope to obtain beginning in 1987 from a large-scale automated system which will fly on the space shuttle in the cargo bay. So this flight is a very important step to us in seeing this program advance toward a commercial goal."

NASA was not staffed to pursue electrophoresis, which meant that McDonnell Douglas was left to progress the technology. According to Walker, they were confident that if all went as planned, they would have a product that could be marketed—with "purities of four and five times what could be done in the best processes here on Earth." They could potentially increase the amount of product by up to five hundred times. If successful, NASA would be able to tout their role in facilitating a medical breakthrough for the benefit of humankind; plus, they'd reap precious funding from McDonnell Douglas for ferrying their equipment into space and then back home again. McDonnell Douglas would turn a profit.

Sue Butler, representing *Time* magazine, asked Walker during a May 1984 preflight press conference if he could tell her the kinds of disorders that could be treated if his research were successful. Walker responded with a simple "No." Fielding a question by Harry Rosenthal with the Associated Press, Walker enlightened everyone by saying, "We can't or won't say at this point. The material we are working on falls back directly upon that word 'commercial.' The pharmaceutical industry is a very competitive industry, and as in any competitive business, you don't really want to let your competitors know what it is you're working on until the last possible moment."

Walker was happy to explain in 2005; the hormone they were evaluating was erythropoietin, which is produced in the adrenal glands of the kidneys. Human bone marrow uses the hormone to produce red blood cells, and "without this hormone, the disease condition known as anemia develops . . . a disorder which affects tens of millions of people on a chronic basis in this country."

The Ortho Pharmaceutical Company of the Johnson & Johnson companies was very interested in the opportunity, and in 1977 an arrangement was signed in which they and McDonnell Douglas would agree to develop the laboratory equipment on the ground to verify in a one-g environment this CFES process for pharmaceuticals purification. Johnson & Johnson happily invested their own money in what they believed to be a sound business venture, estimating in 1980 that there was a potential market of a billion dollars per year for a pure form of the hormone. It was at this time that Walker hired on with McDonnell Douglas.

Walker remembered years later that McDonnell Douglas was excited about the prospect of the shuttle being used to apply the process in space and invested significant capital in the venture, about $20 million from 1978 to 1986. Discussions were held with NASA for the test project, leading to McDonnell Douglas and NASA signing a joint endeavor agreement in 1980 with a quid pro quo arrangement whereby there would be no exchange of money.

The joint endeavor agreement provided for NASA to investigate sample concentration on STS-4 and to process two samples on STS-6 flown in April 1982. Additional samples were flown on STS-7 and STS-8 in 1983, building on previous results. Walker was assigned to train the astronauts on those missions to operate the experiment, notably working closely with Hartsfield on the STS-4 mission.

Walker and his CFES equipment were originally planned to fly on Spacelab 3, but that mission soon fell behind its launch schedule. McDonnell Douglas made it clear to Glynn Lunney, NASA's manager of the Shuttle Payload Integration and Development Program, that they could not tolerate continued delays. Lunney was sensitive to their problem and suggested that instead of flying the CFES on Spacelab, they might be able to fit the apparatus into the orbiter middeck on an earlier flight. As Walker recalled, "Glynn was very innovative in his idea. He knew the design of the systems and areas within the space shuttle orbiter very well, and his thinking was, 'There's a galley on the port side in the middeck of the crew compartment of the orbiter. That thing is about the same size as these electrophoresis program folks are telling me they're going to need to fly. Why don't we on a few flights . . . take the galley out, put in this electrophoresis materials processing device.' So it was Glynn Lunney that came up with the concept."

This innovative idea allowed the next CFES to be flown eight months earlier than would have been possible had they waited to fly it on Spacelab 3. Unfortunately, that left the crew without a galley to prepare their food; instead, they carried portable food warmers that seemed to work just fine.

But what Walker really wanted to do was operate the CFES equipment in orbit himself, a coup eventually realized from years of calculatedly planning a ride into space. About the same time he was seeking employment with McDonnell Douglas, Walker put in his application for NASA astronaut group 8, but he wasn't selected. "There was just the talk of maybe a dedicated scientist payload specialist that would be selected by peer groups of the researchers," but he realized, "I obviously don't work for a university. I'm not a PhD in any one specialty, so maybe the industrial part; maybe the private-sector researcher-engineer" might just provide a path to flying in space. So when Walker began interviewing with aerospace companies in 1977, he was "looking for that project that might actually produce in their design and development something that NASA would be willing to fly, in hopes that it might lead to the need for a researcher to fly with it." Electrophoresis fit the bill.

Walker didn't beat around the bush concerning his wish to work on an industrial project that could potentially get him a ride on the shuttle. While interviewing for a job, he responded to questions about career aspirations with his wish list: "technical work, design development for a few years, opportunity to move into management, and oh, by the way . . . if anything I'm working on has the opportunity to fly into space, I'd like the opportunity to approach NASA to go fly with it." Years later he marveled at his audacity: "Why didn't you kick me out the door?"

According to Walker the joint endeavor agreement held language that allowed, "at the discretion of NASA management in concurrence with McDonnell Douglas management, to fly a payload specialist if needed." The cost associated with the payload specialist on board as well as training costs was to be covered by McDonnell Douglas. This fee was expected to be marginal, because the cost to add one additional astronaut was minimal—additional food, water, oxygen, and other basic necessities. Plus, NASA already had trainers at JSC.

On the way to a meeting to update Glynn Lunney on the CFES results to date, Jim Rose of McDonnell Douglas indicated to Walker that if Lunney liked the results, he was going to petition for a payload specialist opportunity for Walker. Walker remembered that Rose asked him if he was "okay with that." Surely Rose knew what Walker's response would be. Walker had to be smiling inside; his plan was coming along nicely. Lunney liked the results, and according to Walker, Rose informed Lunney that they would learn more if they were able to fly their own payload specialist. Walker recalled, "Glynn chewed on his cigar a little bit and said something like, 'Well, we've been wanting to move into this payload specialist thing, so if you've got somebody that is qualified, can meet all the astronaut selection criteria, put in the application. We'll run it up individually as a special case, up through Headquarters, and it will obviously be Headquarters that will make the final determination. . . . Do you have somebody in mind?'" The rest is history. Walker would live his dream of flying into space!

The mission-independent training that Walker received began around June 1983, consisting of around 130 hours stretched over about eight months intended to familiarize him with orbiter and space shuttle systems. According to Walker, most of it focused on "how to live in a spaceflight environment: hygiene, food preparation, stowage, just how to live and work in zero-g." He also believed that much of the training was "just to allow me to work into this fantastic crew that I'm flying with. And they'll probably tell you that's probably been the hardest part of the whole training activity."

Although Walker didn't get the emergency water or survival training, he did "go through all the systems, orbiter systems, subsystems, the spacecraft systems training, both briefings as well as stand-alone simulator training, so I knew what systems did, like the electrical systems, like the control panels that controlled the electrical systems on board, environmental systems. I knew the computer interfaces."

Walker admitted, "I was there as a working passenger. I wasn't a full-fledged crew member." He also had to contend with some of the NASA astronauts who made it abundantly clear to him that he was an outsider. Astronauts are renowned for having a little fun at the expense of others, and a new payload specialist was ripe for picking. Hartsfield informed Walker that one of his assignments on STS-41D would be to prepare the meals for everyone. He was pulling Walker's chain, but Walker didn't pick up on the joke right away. Initially he thought that Hartsfield was serious, but he took it all in stride: "There was no belligerence, really, expressed openly, and no offense on my part taken."

Walker also trained Resnik to be his backup for the CFES project. "If I should have any problems in the flight, I know that she will be amply able to perform the functions that I would be performing in that eventuality," he said at the time. "And as a matter of fact, because of his extreme interest, Hank is, I think, equally capable."

Walker did a lot of classroom mission-dependent training, read the available training materials, and received one-on-one training by an instructor. Fortunately, Walker had access to a research payload simulator at the cape, a ground-based model of the equipment, and design and development personnel. Much of the mission-dependent preparation to operate the CFES equipment was done in St. Louis at the McDonnell Douglas facility, which Resnik often visited while being trained as Walker's backup.

27. STS-41D payload specialist Charlie Walker and his backup, Judy Resnik, train on the CFES equipment. Courtesy NASA/Retro Space Images.

Walker flew thirty to forty zero-g parabolas for the STS-41D flight in the KC-135 vomit comet and garnered a couple of backseat rides in the T-38 jet. With all the training costs plus the additional dollars for one more crewman on the shuttle, the approximate cost to cover Walker on this mission was a paltry $72,000—a pretty good deal for McDonnell Douglas.

Discovery was poised to make its first flight on 25 June 1984, but the launch was scrubbed due to technical problems and rescheduled for the next day. The next launch attempt, on 26 June, came ever so close to giving Walker his first ride into space, but again the stars were not aligned. Main shuttle engines 2 and 3 had already come to life, guzzling liquid oxygen and liquid hydrogen from the external fuel tank. The crew could feel the tremendous vibration caused by the powerful engines, each generating over four hundred thousand pounds of thrust at launch. Amid the anticipation of finally getting off the pad, a master caution alarm sounded, and the vibration ceased. Engine number 1 had failed to ignite, causing the other two engines to shut down in a matter of seconds. It only took about thirty seconds for the launch director to confirm that the vehicle was safe. If a persnickety main shuttle engine was not enough to give the crew pause—frighten the hell out of them—there was still cause for concern. Had the srbs been disabled, or were they going to suddenly light and tear the whole shuttle apart? Fortunately, the safeguards built into the shuttle had worked, and those giant boosters, each containing over a million pounds of explosive propellant, had been rendered impotent. If necessary the crew could now egress, cross over the service arm, and escape via the baskets located on the other side of the gantry. Fortunately, the wisdom of Hartsfield prevailed, and he told the crew to "sit sight," according to Walker.

The commander's decision to remain with *Discovery* proved to be one of the best decisions of the day. Walker explained, "The hydrogen and oxygen propellant that had gone unignited through the engines and out into the flame trench had been ignited by the one engine, and the fire of that engine-ignited propellant had ignited the rest of that, and there was literally a fire burning up and around the outside of the shuttle." Had the crew egressed from the shuttle and taken the route to the escape baskets, Walker said it likely would have been a bad day for them, "because it was a hydrogen fire, and hydrogen fire is invisible to the eye. It's very visible in the ultraviolet, but there weren't any ultraviolet fire sensors on the pad at that time. Needless to say, there have been on every launch since that time."

Discovery was rolled back to the Vehicle Assembly Building, where the faulty engine was replaced. The next launch attempt was on 29 August 1984 but again was scrubbed nine minutes before the scheduled launch due to a master events controller malfunction. The following day, *Discovery* finally made its majestic climb toward the heavens. Walker remembers the launch quite vividly. At T minus zero, "the vibration has started from those liquid-fuel engines firing." Then, once the solid rockets light, Walker recalls,

Suddenly this roar is exaggerated by ten times. I see the tower out there suddenly turn from a white gray in sunlight to—it looks like it's on fire. There's a golden blaze around it as the illumination from the solid rocket

boosters flares out there, and it's twice as bright as the sun, and it's yellowish, golden yellowish, and just as suddenly, instead of moving left and right, now the tower starts dropping away. I look out that porthole, and I could see the steel tower structure. It looked like the tower was moving. I'm sitting still. Whoa, boy, that is something to see, and that's the way it feels, although you're pushed back into your seat immediately with one and a half times the force of gravity.

Comparing liftoff to "driving a pickup truck with stiff shocks down a gravel country road at fifty miles an hour," he continued, "So there's this tremendous sensation of I'm not going up; the world is falling away from me out there, and now the world is spinning as the shuttle goes into its roll to the correct azimuth on flight path. And the window—I'm watching the tower structure go away. I'm watching central Florida and the VAB go by, and now the roll stops after a few seconds, and my window is looking south, and I can look down the Florida beaches to the south."

Just a few seconds later, he expounded, "the world is falling farther and farther beneath me, and within a few minutes I can see down the coast, and I can imagine I can even see the curve of the Florida coast around toward the keys. And I'm arcing up, and now it's disappearing out of sight. There's nothing but blue sky out there." Walker continued to pull superlatives from his engineering brain to describe what he was seeing, hearing, and feeling. He sounded more poet than engineer as he relived the launch experience, recalling that "a deep basal roar amplified through the vehicle. [It] sounds like a waterfall of air moving by the ship . . . the blackness starts eating the blue sky."

Walker readily shared in his 2005 NASA Oral History interview what his first few moments were like in the weightless environment. Although he intentionally consumed very little at breakfast, "about a minute after the engines stopped and we went weightless, my little bit of breakfast showed itself again. I could tell it was coming, so I had a bag in place. . . . It really didn't embarrass me too much or upset the rest of the crew too much, because I caught it." Walker experienced flu-like symptoms and felt poorly for about three days, remembering that "space adaptation syndrome had me by the neck, and the symptoms were occasional nausea and what the docs call episodic vomiting, and then once I threw something up, I felt fine again." Once in orbit, Walker was ready to vacate the confines of the middeck and take in the view from the best overlook on the shuttle—the flight deck. Someone asked, "You sure you feel okay?" Walker responded, "Ah, I'm feeling good enough. Let me go up and take a look." It was good enough for them. "Okay, okay . . . Clear the flight deck. Walker's coming up."

The sightseeing was fun, but they were in orbit to do work. Walker's CFES work was not the only game in town on this mission. The crew deployed three satellites: the Leasat 2 (Syncom IV-2) for Hughes Communications Services, the SBS-4 for Satellite Business Systems, and the Telstar 3 for American Telephone and Telegraph (AT&T). A 102-foot-tall, 13-foot-wide solar wing was also carried in the payload bay. It was "the first-time demonstration of large deployable solar power structures for future space stations." The wing was successfully extended to its full size and retracted several times by the mission specialists. There were also a handful of additional experiments on board, as well as an IMAX camera.

Perhaps it was the jolting launch or the weightless environment, but the CFES apparatus experienced some problems once Walker checked it out during the evening of 30 August. As flight director Randy Stone explained at the 31 August change-of-shift briefing, "Charlie performed an in-flight maintenance procedure which actually replaced [a component of] the device with a spare one . . . and the CFES started its activation on time even though we had to do that maintenance on it." It's likely that either Resnik or Hartsfield could have made the repair, but having the expert on board was a clear advantage.

Walker added, "In addition, there were some small anomalies in transducers, which are used to fine-tune the electrophoresis process. I also had indication that there was probably a programming [error] in terms of gain in the system; it was just that the software was not fine-tuned for operation in the spaceflight environment. But I think all of these things reflect back to my reason for being there." These adjustments came at a cost, as about 15 percent of the material was not processed. It's doubtful that Resnik or Hartsfield, as talented as they were, could have made these types of observations and modifications.

Walker ran the CFES continuously during the flight on days 2 through 5 and babysat it around the clock. During the 3 September change-of-shift briefing, Malcolm McConnell from *Reader's Digest* asked Stone about Walker's "watchkeeping on the CFES." Stone responded, "Charlie is sleeping with an earphone, so when he hears CFES alarms, it doesn't wake up the other crewmen. So, he is basically keeping a twenty-four-hour watch, but he's sleeping the normal sleep cycle. He did wake up last night with that one alarm." NASA is great at putting a positive spin on spaceflight. The device Walker had plugged into his ear while he slept allowed him to hear alarms from the CFES device, which would awaken him—all while orbiting Earth at over seventeen thousand miles per hour in a weightless environment—but he still maintained a normal sleep pattern.

Walker's dream flight was quickly coming to an end, and in spite of some minor contamination problems with his equipment, he proudly boasted, "The accomplishments, I think, were as we expected in flight for my research."

Discovery touched down at Edwards Air Force Base on 5 September 1984, rolling to a halt on runway 17. Later, James Fisher with the *Orlando Sentinel* asked Walker if he had experienced any surprises on orbit. Walker pondered, "Well, I think what I didn't expect was what is only natural. That is the detail. The actual experience of zero-g, of trying to work and adapt to everyday functions in zero-g. You talk about it; you have people give you advice on the ground. You practice procedures that are proven. But, until you do it, there is nothing like that experience. And so, just actually going and doing it and experiencing the entire situation."

Veteran space journalist Lynn Sherr posed a question to mission commander Hank Hartsfield at the preflight press conference: "Has there been any difference because there is someone flying who is for the first time not a NASA person?" Actually, Walker was not the first non-NASA person to fly on the shuttle; Lichtenberg and Merbold were the first, on STS-9. But Walker was the first private-sector and non-Spacelab payload specialist. Hartsfield made his position clear: "We haven't had a problem. I think in Charlie's case, since I've known Charlie since STS-4 and worked with the CFES at that time, he's no stranger. And most of the rest of the crew knew him because he had spent a good bit of time at Houston with the other crews that flew the CFES, so I think in this case it's been really easy for Charlie to fit right in with us." Postflight, Hartsfield maintained his stance that Walker was a valuable crew member.

Pilot Michael Coats had nothing but superlatives to describe Walker's contributions to the flight:

28. Charlie Walker with his CFES experiment (seen in the background) in the middeck of *Discovery* during the STS-41D mission. Courtesy NASA/Retro Space Images.

Well, Charlie worked really hard. We had no problem at all adopting Charlie, including him in the crew. . . . When we got up on orbit, he had lots of problems with the machine. . . . From the time he woke up until he went to sleep, [he] was downstairs working on that machine. We joked; I don't think he got upstairs to look out twice the whole mission, just working his tail off. We had an awful lot of respect for Charlie and how hard he worked. He wanted that thing to work. . . . He was just really easy to get along with. Still is. Nice guy. We stay in touch.

Walker would fly into space twice more with his CFES apparatus on STS-51D and STS-61B, working hard to fine-tune the CFES procedures and equipment so that McDonnell Douglas, Johnson & Johnson, and a handful of other pharmaceutical companies could provide a product that might one day help millions of people suffering from anemia. And turn a profit. And allow Walker what he started out to accomplish—flying into outer space on the shuttle!

11. First Passenger

But my hope that I will eventually be able to fly on
the shuttle myself is still alive.

Hans Mark, *The Space Station*

The fifth flight carrying payload specialists ushered in a new era in American spaceflight. On STS-51D, for the first time ever, a passenger—Utah senator Jake Garn—flew on the shuttle with no obvious reason to be on board, other than he wanted to be there. Garn held a hole card; his position in the United States Senate helped him grease the skids necessary for him to hitch a ride on the shuttle. Previously, only individuals with clearly defined skill sets that supported mission objectives had been selected to serve as payload specialists.

Payload specialist Garn flew aboard STS-51D primarily to observe. Granted, he also volunteered to serve as a guinea pig for a medical experiment and helped out on another investigation, but to many, these appeared to be merely add-ons to justify his ride on the shuttle at the taxpayers' expense. Several years later a similar level of criticism would also be applied to the STS-95 shuttle flight of legendary Mercury astronaut John Glenn (also a latter-day U.S. senator), who spent nearly nine days in orbit in October 1998 at the age of seventy-seven, which many perceived as nothing less than a nation's gold-ring reward to a spaceflight legend.

The announcement that Garn had been assigned to their flight was initially greeted with skepticism and disbelief by most of the NASA crew members on STS-51D. As Don Williams, pilot on the mission, reflected, "The day that happened, we all looked at each other and said, 'Oh, man, this is just what we need, a senator as part of this crew.'"

Mission specialist Rhea Seddon recalled learning about the addition of Garn to the crew from her commander: "We . . . were in the simulator when Mr. Abbey called Bo [Bobko] over. We all looked at each other, and we said, 'Hm, we think we know what this means.'" While the crew was waiting for another simulator training run, Bobko scribbled a message on a piece of paper bearing the news that Garn had been added to their mission. The savvy Dr. Seddon was the first to recognize that his addition might actually be a blessing in disguise. Williams recalled Seddon's wisdom: "This is a good deal. You guys aren't going to believe this right now today, but it's going to be a really good deal. We're going to get a lot of positive press out of it, a lot of publicity, and we're going to learn a lot." Initially, Williams was skeptical and confessed, "Hmm. I don't know. Maybe, maybe not." He later admitted that Seddon was spot on.

Mission specialist Jeff Hoffman recalled his reaction to the news. "Dave [Griggs] and I were just leaving the Orbiter Processing Facility, where we had been doing some tests, when we heard on the radio a rumor that NASA was thinking of flying a U.S. senator. We just cracked up. We thought this is never going to happen, this is crazy. Then we got home to Houston, and sure enough, not only was it going to happen, but he was going to be on our flight."

Commander Bo Bobko recently shared with the authors his reaction to the addition of Garn to the crew. "We were getting close to flight and George [Abbey, director of flight operations] said, 'We're wondering what you would do if you were going to train a payload specialist that was going to be put on at the last minute.'" Fearing where the conversation was going, Bobko responded, "[George], what are you going to do? Are you going to put a payload specialist on my flight?" Abbey, a manager either loved or hated by the astronauts, came back, "'Uh, yeah. It's gonna be Jake Garn.'" Abbey thrust the knife even deeper, "'And you've only got . . . ten or twelve weeks to flight.'"

Bobko confessed, "And so I wasn't too happy about that right then. I gave it a little bit of thought and came back to [George] and said, 'Hey, we're pretty close to flight, so what I'd like to do is have . . . a tutor for Jake.' And the tutor was [shuttle astronaut] Mike Smith. But once I got to know Jake and realize that he was a pilot and behaved like a very disciplined crew member, that I didn't have any problems with it."

Payload specialist Charlie Walker joined Garn and the crew of STS-51D. Having previously flown aboard STS-41D, Walker was making his second shuttle flight to carry out additional testing of his CFES apparatus. Rhea Seddon was assigned as Walker's backup; she was already quite knowledgeable of the CFES experiment from her support role on the STS-6 mission, which flew an early version of the CFES device.

Edwin Jacob (Jake) Garn was born in Richfield, Utah, on 12 October 1932 and received a bachelor of science degree in business and finance from the University of Utah in 1955. He devoted four years of his life to active duty in the U.S. Navy, during which he flew high-performance military aircraft. Following his separation from the navy, he continued his military career in the Utah Air National Guard—there was no navy in landlocked Utah—retiring in 1979 as a full colonel. Garn flew a variety of military and civilian aircraft, accumulating over ten thousand hours of flight time. He was elected to the U.S. Senate in 1974 and was reelected in 1980. Garn was a longtime supporter of America's space program, although he had been openly critical of the economic viability of the shuttle. He served on a plethora of committees in the Senate during his political career.

By the time late 1984 rolled around, NASA had built a fleet of three orbiters—*Columbia*, *Challenger*, and *Discovery*—that were considered operational. With fifteen successful shuttle flights under their belt, NASA had made space travel seem safe and commonplace, bringing forth a gaggle of wannabe astronauts, begging for a ride into the heavens on the shuttle. Comedian Bob Hope was hopeful of snatching a ride on the shuttle. NASA announced in 1984 that they were considering a citizen observers and participants program, whereby citizens—writers, poets, journalists, artists—could vie for a chance to travel into space on the shuttle. But Garn was a powerful U.S. senator, and he didn't need the observers-participants program to orchestrate his journey into space. He had an inside track. He just happened to be a member of the U.S. federal government's Senate Appropriations Committee and was chairman of a subcommittee that coincidentally controlled NASA's budget.

Garn had taken an interest in the exploration of space from his role on the Appropriations Committee. According to Jeff Bingham, Garn's chief of staff at that time, Garn made a trip to Houston around 1975, where he "flew" the Apollo-Soyuz simulator (loosely speaking it seems) with one of the Apollo astronauts. Bingham reflected, "He went down there and ended up flying with Tom Stafford in the Apollo-Soyuz simulator . . . totally destroying both capsules. He was a very accomplished pilot, but he was used to if you let off the throttle, you slow down. That didn't happen in space, so he wasn't able to reverse thrust and crashed everything."

Bingham explained that the senator's fascination with NASA peaked following the first shuttle mission, which launched on 12 April 1981, when Garn made it crystal clear to anyone who would listen that he wanted to fly on the shuttle. Bingham recalled that several days after *Columbia* returned to Earth from its first mission, NASA deputy administrator Alan Lovelace was presenting NASA's budget request, which would be presented to the Appropriations Committee, of which Garn was a member. During Garn's opening comments, he congratulated NASA on the success of the first shuttle mission and, according to Bingham, said, "One of the questions I have is one of the more serious ones I want you to think more carefully . . . in answering." Bingham recalled an intimidating Garn leaning forward with his "bald head and brooding eyebrows" and then playfully popping the question, "When do I go?" Lovelace brushed off the flippant remark with a chuckle, but the first seed of Garn's plan to get into space had been sown.

Continuing the story, Bingham shared that shortly after, in mid-1981, James Beggs and Hans Mark had been nominated to become the new NASA administrator and deputy administrator, and both stopped by Garn's office in Washington DC to pay him a courtesy call. Garn would have no vote on their nominations, but he wielded a pretty big stick in controlling the purse strings of NASA. Over small talk, Garn related to Beggs and Mark that he had told Lovelace of his brazen aspiration. Both men were already aware of Garn's audacious yearning, and Bingham recalled Mark's response: "But of course you should fly. The whole purpose of the space shuttle is to have routine access to space. What better way to demonstrate that than to fly a member of Congress?" What he likely meant was, How much more money can we get for NASA if we allow you to fly?

That, Bingham said, was all Garn needed to hear. "Up till that point, it had been kidding and wishful thinking and that sort of thing, playfulness." But now that Garn had his foot in the door, he planned to keep on pushing until it was wide open, even assigning one of his staffers to remind folks that he was serious about copping a ride on a shuttle. Shuttle crews often visited NASA Headquarters located in Washington DC following their missions. Afterward, Garn sometimes had the opportunity to speak with them. True to course, Garn would remind them that he expected to fly on the shuttle. Bingham confessed, "It became kind of a litany. Everybody knew that he had every intention at some point of trying to get on board the space shuttle."

Hans Mark became a champion of human-crewed spaceflight when he met and worked with the legendary Wernher von Braun in the 1970s, eventually coming to support the inclusion of ordinary people flying on the shuttle. Perhaps helping Garn secure a spot would open the door for other passengers, perhaps even him? According to Mark in *The Space Station: A Personal Journey*, as late as mid-1984, he harbored his own dreams of flying into space on the shuttle.

Garn admitted in his autobiography, *Why I Believe*, that he had persistently pestered Beggs for a spot on a shuttle mission shortly after the launch of STS-1. Bingham remembered that in 1984 Beggs began to investigate the possibility of ordinary citizens flying on the shuttle, which eventually led to the Teacher in Space Program. Shortly before the announcement proclaiming that a teacher (Christa McAuliffe) would fly on the shuttle, Bingham received a phone call from a staffer alerting him to an upcoming announcement that would declare that Garn was slated to fly on a shuttle mission and fly before the teacher. John Noble Wilford of the *New York Times* quoted a letter from James Beggs to Garn, clarifying that it was "appropriate for those with Congressional oversight to have flight opportunities to gain a personal awareness and familiarity." The *Times* announced on 7 November 1984 that Garn had accepted NASA's invitation and would become the first public official to fly aboard the space shuttle.

Beggs, in his 2002 NASA Oral History interview, recalled that Garn pestered him relentlessly about hitching a ride on the shuttle. Garn was adamant that when NASA finally decided to allow regular people access to space, he was going to be the first to go. NASA only had a few shuttle flights under their belt at the time, and Beggs informed Garn that they would give the idea consideration down the road, once they were confident that the shuttle was safe enough to fly passengers. Beggs recollected that whenever the two men crossed paths, Garn would make it perfectly clear that he was more than qualified to fly into space by virtue of his aviation background. Giving Garn his due, Beggs confided, "He was, too." Beggs believed that there was unique value in getting Garn into space, because he believed the good senator from Utah, as a member of the Senate Appropriations Committee, was certainly in a position to help NASA in a variety of ways, including budgetary considerations. Beggs got quite a kick out of Garn's reaction when he finally informed him that NASA had approved his request: "His jaw dropped open, his jaw slackened and his mouth dropped open, and he said, 'You're kidding.'"

News correspondent Jane Pauley interviewed Garn on the *Today Show* the morning following the announcement of his imminent journey into space. Pauley tried to paint Garn into a corner by suggesting that the only reason NASA had selected him to fly was because he was a member of the Appropriations Committee. Bingham remembered Garn's response to her accusation. "Of course," he replied. "Why would you invite the chairman of the Agriculture Committee?" Garn had cleverly turned the tables on Pauley. He was a seasoned senator accustomed to doing battle with cagey lifetime politicians and media heavyweights; a mere reporter was not about to derail his flight into space.

In January 1985 Garn and Bingham met with the crew that would shepherd the senator into space. Bingham recollected that Garn told them, "Look, I know how you must feel, being saddled with this senator, and I want you to know I'm going to do everything I can to be a contributing member of the crew. I've been in the military. I know chain of command. You're the commander, Bo. You tell me to jump, and I'll ask you how high. And I want to make it real clear my name is Jake and not Senator. I'm not a 'sir' when I'm here. I'm a payload specialist." Bobko responded, "Yes, sir," evoking a gregarious laugh from his crew.

One might not have realized that there was a second payload specialist on board by watching the news. Charlie Walker received little attention on this flight from the press while Garn stole the spotlight. Walker was on board to continue his electrophoresis research. The original concept for the payload specialist was that they would fly only one mission, but Walker was going to break that paradigm. McDonnell Douglas had hoped that Walker's STS-41D flight would provide a successful test of the CFES equipment, and Walker explained in his NASA Oral History interview that future missions would carry a "semiautomated apparatus that a NASA mission specialist could turn on, turn off, and we could conduct the last one or two research and development flights in our program that way." But a contamination problem experienced on STS-41D and a recognition that the device required much more attention than expected led to a major design change in the CFES equipment. Therefore, McDonnell Douglas management believed the complicated apparatus required their research and development engineer to accompany the device on STS-51D. Walker recalled NASA saying that he "seems to have made it back okay, and none of the crew really got ticked off at him on this flight, so maybe he can fly again." Walker had his second flight.

Don Williams recalled that Garn was back and forth between Cape Canaveral and Washington DC during training. Garn may have had senatorial duties that were more important to tend to, but he was determined to spend as much time with the crew as possible, as Williams acknowledged. "Jake, because he was a senator and a fairly senior one, used to be called back to Washington a number of times for critical votes and for committee meetings and for whole-Senate meetings. Almost every time that he came back to Houston and he'd join us in whatever simulation or training exercise or class or whatever it [was] we were [doing], he would almost invariably come in and sit down and look around in the simulator or the room and he'd say, 'You know, it's really nice to be back where people know what they're doing.'"

Jeff Bingham told Rebecca Wright in 2006 that astronaut Mike Smith was Garn's "mother hen" during training. Bo Bobko explained in December 2016 that Loren Shriver had been exposed to the measles during his training regimen for the STS-51C mission. As a precaution, NASA assigned Smith to train alongside Shriver just in case he became ill. A case of the measles would have disqualified him from flight duty. To Shriver's delight the measles never materialized, and he remained with the STS-51C crew. Smith was fully trained but without a mission, which made him available to become Garn's tutor on shuttle operations.

Bobko was adamant that the unorthodox training plan worked well. For example, if he had scheduled an afternoon training session, Smith would lead the senator through the exercise in the morning, and then a fully prepared Garn would join the rest of the crew in the afternoon, when they would all work together as a team. Most of Garn's training was mission independent; observing didn't require a whole lot of mission-dependent training. Not surprisingly, he learned the basic shuttle systems in a short time frame—just enough for him to survive for a week or so in orbit. He participated in many simulations on shuttle operations and learned how to carry out the few experiments that NASA politely tossed him. Bingham stressed that Garn made it his priority to participate in as much of the mission training as possible, contingent on his busy congressional schedule.

Seddon remembered that Garn volunteered to help out with the medical experiments, such as the echocardiograph, which pleased her. Garn was unyielding in his efforts to justify his ride into space any way he could; he would observe and also be a research subject. Reporter Storer Rowley with the *Chicago Tribune* wrote in a 24 February 1985 article titled "Senator Applied and Is Going to Heaven" that there were those who called Garn's upcoming expedition into space on the shuttle not only a junket but perhaps the greatest one in congressional history. On the contrary, Garn didn't feel any apologies were necessary; in addition to his duties to observe, he was going to carry out important experimentation that NASA had already been working on well before he wangled a ride into space.

Charlie Walker planned to implement procedures to eliminate the contamination problems with the samples collected on STS-41D in 1984. Those samples of hormones were unfit for animal testing due to a contagion. Software and temperature modifications were also implemented to improve the CFES process. Walker's mission-independent training for his second foray in space included flying as an observer with Bobko and Williams in the STA, exclaiming, "I got quite a kick out of that." With a mission under his belt, Walker already knew the basic shuttle operations and how to operate his equipment. However, not only did participation in the simulations help prepare him for the flight, but equally as important, the simulation runs fostered teamwork and allowed the crew to get to know him better. He also believed that NASA learned from him. He had spent two years training crews to carry out his CFES experiment, which gave him a lot of insight into how to best train the aviators and science-focused mission specialists.

The NASA astronauts welcomed Garn and Walker onto the crew with open arms. Regardless, at times, they were treated as second-class. For example, they were required to have an escort anytime they visited the Space Mission Simulation Facility located in building 5 at the JSC campus, which placed an unnecessary burden on the crew and wasted their precious time.

If a crew member was not available to escort the payload specialist into building 5, the "outsider" had to, as Bobko recalled, "search for an escort or risk a security violation."

Bobko was making his second journey into space; Williams was his pilot. Seddon, Griggs, and Hoffman served as mission specialists and, along with Williams and Garn, were space rookies. Walker's second flight no doubt miffed more than one of the NASA mission specialists—especially some who had not yet flown into space.

Walker nearly missed out on STS-51D due to a last-minute scare; his CFES device developed a leak on the launchpad. Walker lamented, "Right down to like twenty-four hours before flight or so, that thing was leaking out on the pad." If the problem couldn't be resolved, then he would have had nothing to do once in orbit, so why send him? Walker was in limbo for a while, but fortunately for him and McDonnell Douglas, the issue was settled, and he was soon on his way into space for the second time.

Discovery, all 250,891 pounds, thundered off launchpad 39A on 12 April 1985, twenty-four years to the day after Yuri Gagarin became the first human in space and four years—also to the day—after the first shuttle launch. At T minus seven seconds, Garn claims that his pulse rate shot up to a blistering 126 pulses per minute from his normal resting rate of 48. Once *Discovery* reached orbit, the crew began preparations to execute several major tasks; the most crucial being to insert two satellites into orbit.

First up, the crew was scheduled to deploy the Telesat I (Anik C-I) communications satellite, a Canadian venture owned and operated by Telesat. The second satellite, Syncom IV-3—built by Hughes Aircraft and also known as Leasat 3—would be leased by the DOD, replacing an older communications satellite. Also on board were the American flight echocardiograph, phase partitioning experiments, a couple of Shuttle Student Involvement Program experiments, and two getaway specials.

Seddon intended to collect data using the American flight echocardiograph, which would hopefully allow doctors and scientists to gain a better understanding of the effects weightlessness had on the cardiovascular system of astronauts. Garn, in addition to observing and helping out Seddon with the American flight echocardiograph, would conduct the phase partitioning experiment, which was designed to test the nonconvective effect of space on the separation of biological cells and macromolecules, a term he had likely never encountered on the Senate floor. The protein crystal growth experiment, which Walker planned to operate, was a device developed by MSFC in conjunction with academia and was intended to grow protein crystals large enough to examine their internal structures, using x-ray or neutron-diffraction analyses. Crystals grown on Earth in a gravitational environment were too small for such studies.

Seddon lamented about her first flight into space: "The flight itself, we took two satellites of the type that had been flown before. I was taking the echo [echocardiograph]. Jake was doing some experiments, and Charlie was growing crystals. It was a pretty ho-hum flight." Unbeknownst to the crew, fate was about to intervene and test their ability to overcome adversity.

Once in orbit, after having some fun enjoying the microgravity environment and figuring out who was vomiting and who wasn't, the crew deployed the Canadian communications satellite without a hitch. Later on, Seddon plunged into her work with the echocardiograph experiment before calling it a day.

Walker cranked up his CFES operations three hours and fifty minutes into the mission, intending "to process 1.1 liters of concentrated protein material" and on the last day of the flight conduct optimization tests. The project was slightly behind schedule, but McDonnell Douglas–Ortho was optimistic that commercial products would be ready to go to market by 1988.

Once Garn was in orbit, the media focused many of their questions on him: what was he doing, and had he gotten sick? During the change-of-shift briefing on the first day of the mission, Frank Seltzer, with CNN, asked if Garn had gotten sick. Flight director Randy Stone replied that he didn't have that information. Seltzer pressed, wanting to know if they would be informed if any of the astronauts became sick. Stone made it perfectly clear: "If any crewperson gets sick that impacts the mission, we'll tell you." The truth is Garn became quite sick once in orbit. According to Garn in a 2005 interview by John Hollenhorst, the malady took two days to run its course, but he did not vomit. He was extremely nauseous, and in a dubious honor following his flight, the Garn Scale was invented to gauge the severity of space sickness. According to Hollenhorst, a Garn 1 meant the astronaut was feeling pretty good, whereas a Garn 10 purported a very sick astronaut. Hollenhorst rumored that Garn reached the level of Garn

29. Senator and payload specialist Jake Garn in the middeck of *Discovery* during his STS-51D mission. Courtesy NASA/Retro Space Images.

13. Not until the second satellite went afoul after it was deployed did Garn get a respite from the press.

On day 2 the crew released the Syncom satellite out of the payload bay as planned, but in simple terms, it didn't work. A crucial antenna had not deployed. The Hughes engineers assessed the situation and decided that the only logical culprit was a separation switch that controlled activation of the satellite. They began thinking of ways to determine if the switch was fully in the on position and, if not, how to get it there. Ground control began looking for a solution with a similar fervor to that which brought the Apollo 13 crew home safely in April 1970. Finally, the mission with no pizazz became really interesting; for the first time in the space program's history, a shuttle crew would improvise a repair to a satellite they had just deployed. Jeff Hoffman and David Griggs were going to perform the first contingency EVA in NASA's history. Bobko and Williams would do some fancy flying; and Seddon, some slick manipulation of the remote manipulator system, or Canadarm. The mission was extended for two days so the crew could attempt the repair.

The solution dreamed up by the ground to fix the wayward satellite was to fashion several devices, fitted on the end of the Canadarm, that would be used to nudge the suspect switch on the spinning satellite and then toggle it to the on position. One of the two devices the crew would have to construct to hopefully coax the satellite to life resembled a flyswatter; and the other, a lacrosse stick. An EVA would be required to attach these devices to the end of the Canadarm, which made Hoffman and Griggs very happy. Once the devices had been attached to the end of the Canadarm, Bobko and Williams would have to perform an intricate rendezvous with the satellite to inch within reach of the Canadarm, essentially placing the satellite into the payload bay. Seddon would then have to ever so delicately use the devices that Hoffman and Griggs attached to the end of the Canadarm to swat the errant switch in an attempt to awaken the satellite.

The EVA may have excited Hoffman and Griggs, but it was going to cause problems for Walker. The EVA required the cabin to be depressurized to just a little over ten pounds per square inch, about four pounds per square inch below normal cabin pressure. As a result, oxygen partial pressure had to be increased inside the crew compartment. Walker bemoaned, "Well, that was really going to play hob with my electrophoresis process, so I had to shut down my process . . . and kind of secure the device before cabin depressurization, and then on the other side when we boosted the pressure up again after the EVA was done, to again reconfigure my device and turn it back on." Fortunately, the changes caused no anomalies with the CFES.

First, the devices intended to swat the errant switch had to be fabricated using only materials available on *Discovery*—book covers, pieces of metal, duct tape, whatever. Garn graciously jumped in and assisted in building the tools. Seddon recalled that Garn was most eager to help anywhere he could and provided a very valuable second pair of strong hands in building the flyswatter.

The plan to mend the satellite was a good one, and the crew carried it out to perfection. The repair attempt played out up close for the crew as they peered out the orbiter windows at the massive satellite hovering directly in front of their eyes while Seddon tried to swat the errant switch on the dead satellite. Ultimately, they were not able to activate the stubborn switch and had to admit defeat.

Reporter Bill Silcock, at a change-in-shift briefing, wanted to know if Garn was accomplishing what he was sent along to do—observe. Observing how the crew reacted to the failure of the Syncom satellite could not have been scripted any better—a perfect situation for Garn to carry out his primary objective on the flight.

The crew participated in an in-flight press conference on 18 April, giving the press the opportunity to ask the astronauts questions that ground control wouldn't answer. Lynn Sherr, from ABC News, asked Garn about SAS studies and cut to the chase: "Did you get sick, sir?" Garn responded,

> *Yes, I did. I told you that I would report that. And fortunately, like most of the reports that if you take medication, you are over it in two days, and if you don't, you are over it in two days. And I will be very honest with you, I didn't feel good for two days, but I have sure felt fine since. It has been a wonderful experience, absolutely fantastic. I'm sorry we have to come down tomorrow. I'm glad we got to stay two days longer. And I wish we could figure out some way to stay up longer. This weightlessness is—if they'd let me, I'd love to show you how I can do everything [gymnast] Mary Lou Retton can do up here.*

Mike Goldpien, from KUTV out of Salt Lake City, asked Garn if he had been able to help the crew accomplish their mission. Garn answered thoughtfully, "So I have been able to be helpful a lot of times just when they needed hands—sewing on the so-called flyswatter. It took a little bit of extra strength that I was able to add. I have taken photographs, I have done some cooking, and in general just trying to be helpful in the spacecraft in every way that I possibly could." In addition to his primary mission—to observe—Garn was doing all he could to contribute anyway possible.

During the in-flight briefing on 18 April, Jules Bergman, with ABC News, asked Garn if, after a week in space, he'd rather be a senator or an astronaut. Garn was quick to quip, "Jules, that's one of the easiest questions I have ever had to answer. If I were about ten years younger, I would choose the working astronaut over being a senator so fast it would make your head swim."

John Getter, from channel 11 in Houston, asked Garn to "put on your reporter cap a second please and tell us overall what's been going on up there and what you think of it." What a perfect question to ask a pontificating politician!

Well, I'd be happy to, because I have watched a fantastic crew do an incredibly good job under difficult circumstances. I have heard a lot over the years about the team in Houston trying to figure out what to do up here in space, where you can't send up mechanics, you can't send up repairmen. This is something new that none of this crew had ever tried before. But out of materials that were here aboard the spacecraft they were able to make the so-called lacrosse stick and the flyswatter. They spent an afternoon doing it, and they worked very well. Unfortunately, it didn't start the satellite operating. But it was really a remarkable performance up here on what they put together. And to see the rendezvous was just a masterful job done by Bo and the rest of the crew. To rendezvous with that satellite and it's a big piece of machinery, bring it down to within about ten feet over the cargo bay, see it spinning above us, and then Rhea working with the arm. I never will see a better performance than what was put on by this crew trying to save that satellite. Truly remarkable.

Seltzer was interested in learning what Garn had gained from the mission that would justify him risking his life to fly into space. Garn hinted that the NASA budget was an area that needed some scrutiny but did not offer any specifics. He assured Seltzer that a formal report would be made to the Senate once he returned to Earth. A reporter from the *Chicago Tribune* asked about the cost it took to train Garn. Jesse Moore, associate administrator for space-flight from NASA Headquarters, gave an estimate of $75,000 to $100,000, similar to what NASA had charged other companies to send up a payload specialist.

President Reagan made a call to *Discovery*'s crew, congratulating them for their ingenuity in constructing the necessary tools for the Syncom repair attempt. The president concluded the teleconference with, "God bless you. And, you know, Jake, maybe, in around four years or so, you could use your influence with NASA to get a certain retired politician a ride on the space shuttle." Had the *Challenger* disaster not changed the way the payload specialist program was managed, it is entirely possible that numerous celebrities, dignitaries, and politicians may have ended up flying on the shuttle.

Eight days after *Discovery* launched, the ship and its crew landed from where they came—the Kennedy Space Center—on 19 April 1985. The orbiter and its precious crew had traveled almost 3 million miles, and in spite of the faulty Syncom satellite and some flawed brakes, the mission had to be considered a success. The Canadian communications satellite had been successfully deployed, Walker had purified his prized payload, and Garn had observed.

Successful mission or not, Bobko was not keen on having his payload specialists join the crew so close to launch. He would have preferred to have them assigned no later than twelve weeks prior to launch. The last few months of training for shuttle missions were extremely busy and hectic, and the last thing the crew wanted to do was to take on an additional crew member that close to launch. Bobko believed that Garn's flight experience made a difference. Fortunately, Walker knew his CFES equipment inside and out, and because he had spaceflight experience under his belt, he required minimal training.

Garn was a respected Republican senator, and many of the astronauts who got to know him have nothing but respect and good words to say about the man. Some have even remained steadfast friends. Hoffman shared his thoughts about Garn after the mission, clarifying that the senator had become a good friend to him: "I have to say . . . he was a good crew member. I won't comment on the politics of flying politicians, but he had been on a World War II airplane crew, so he knew what it meant to be a member of a crew, and he didn't try to play the senator with us. So we really did get along very well."

Bobko complimented Garn: "I can certainly say having Jake Garn with us was a pleasure. He has fit in with the crew and has done everything that he possibly can. As I said, when an extra hand was needed, he was ready to lend his. . . . So I think it probably is going to depend on the individuals, but I certainly can say that this one has worked out very well with this crew."

Charlie Walker received few questions at the postflight press conference; most of the accolades went to Garn. Walker recalled, "Jake, from my experience, and here is an outsider talking about another outsider, but I think Jake accommodated himself extraordinarily well in the circumstances."

There were thirty-five astronauts selected in astronaut group 8, the group Walker applied for, and by the end of the STS-51D flight, only three of them—Sally Ride, Rick Hauck, and Dale Gardner—had flown twice, the same number of missions that Walker had to his credit. Another three—John Creighton, Steve Nagel, and Shannon Lucid—were still waiting for their first flight. Walker's decision to pursue a trip into space on the shuttle via the payload specialist program was paying off handsomely, and his star was to shine again.

Flying with a senator had its benefits. Hoffman shared that the crew enjoyed a number of enjoyable postflight trips. The world-renowned Mormon Tabernacle Choir from Garn's home state performed just for the crew while they sat on the stage alongside the choir. Following the mission, the crew visited the White House for a special dinner, at which Hoffman sat next to the celebrated Mercury astronaut John Glenn. Glenn leaned over and said to Hoffman, "I really envy you guys. Everybody knows what I did, but I only had three orbits around the earth. I don't even know what space is really like." Then he prophetically announced, "Someday I'd like to get back into space." Years later, Glenn would use the senator card along with his age to get a ride on the shuttle—as a payload specialist—on the very same orbiter that Garn rode into space. And he too had to endure some of the same space-junket criticism that was aimed at Garn.

Garn shared his spaceflight experiences with Jeff Bingham, who then wrote a report to be delivered to Congress. Bingham had completed a final draft of the report and was in the process of wrapping it all up into a neat package when *Challenger* broke apart in January 1986, killing the entire crew. His report never made it to Congress. "So it got lost in the dust of that tragic experience," he reflected.

There was an added benefit that came out of Garn's flight. He believed that by virtue of flying into space on the shuttle, when anyone testified about space following his flight, they consciously spoke more accurately, which allowed him to do his job much better. Many of his fellow senators would seek out Garn for clarity regarding testimony on space-related issues.

Jake Garn left the Senate in 1993, electing not to run for office again. He has since served as a partner in a lobbying and consulting firm, has served on the board of directors of a number of companies, and has stayed active in volunteer work. He unselfishly donated one of his kidneys to his daughter, who had suffered from diabetes since childhood. Garn was promoted to brigadier general following his spaceflight.

A very religious man, Garn is devoted to his family. In 1976 he tragically lost Hazel, his first wife of nineteen years, in an automobile accident, and he considered retiring from the Senate to raise his children. His mother, clinging to her faith in God, convinced him not to resign but, instead, to look forward in life. Garn continued on with his political life and eventually remarried. After his flight, many asked him if he had found God in space, but Garn made it clear that he knew God well before his venture into the heavens.

For a time, there was even a venture into writing. In 1989 Garn combined his literary talents with those of established author Stephen Paul Cohen to produce the fictional technothriller *Night Launch*, and in 1992 he released a book on his life, experiences, and deep personal beliefs called *Why I Believe*.

Garn is quoted in a 2006 *Deseret News* interview by Marc Haddock as saying that he is remembered more for his trek into space than for being a good senator. Rachel Trotter, with the *Standard-Examiner*, reported on 14 October 2014 that Garn was asked at a gathering at the Hill Aerospace Museum, located in Utah, what his thoughts were on the future of space exploration in light of the government's paltry financial support of the agency. Garn still retained his support of human spaceflight almost thirty years after his foray into space, making it clear he wasn't happy with the status quo. Trotter quoted Garn as saying, "I feel that as children of God we are meant to travel around spaceship Earth." He was adamant that it is time to set aside all the political differences and continue the exploration of space.

Garn's pioneering trail to a space shuttle flight was radically different than any previous payload specialist. His mission to orbit, while widely criticized in the press, served him well in his congressional duties for years after and blazed a path that other politicos would follow to space.

12. International Goodwill

On launch day, you will have 800 million Muslims, 155 million
Arabs glued to their television sets, to their radios, watching an
American space shuttle carrying one of their own out into space.
If that's not bringing America closer to that part of the
world, I don't know what will.

Prince Sultan Salman Abdulaziz Al-Saud

"I just didn't believe that we were launching until the last minute of it and
the engines started, and then that changed very quickly when the SRBs fired,"
recalled Saudi Arabian payload specialist Prince Sultan Salman Abdulaziz
Al-Saud. The ignition of the three space shuttle main engines six seconds
prior to liftoff definitely alerted the crew that something was happening
beneath them, but when the 5.3 million pounds of raw power generated by
the SRBs kicked in and the massive constraining bolts holding the shuttle
stack in place were simultaneously severed, the shuttle leaped off launchpad 39A and left the crew in no doubt that their journey had begun.

During his postmission technical crew debrief, Al-Saud explained that
the ascent to orbit was considerably smoother and much less noisy than
he had anticipated, although he distinctly recalled a slight increase in the
noise level as well as a noticeable jolt when the SRBs separated approximately two minutes after launch. He had no recollection of the external
fuel tank separating from the orbiter just before *Discovery* reached orbit,
quite understandable given the myriad of events the rookie astronaut was
trying to process. "I appreciated the commander and pilot's talk back to
us through the whole ascent and just sort of keeping us informed of what

was going on," he later reflected. "I thought the g-loading was much more than 3 g's through the acceleration."

The two and one-half months of mission-independent training NASA had given Al-Saud were inadequate to get him up to speed for a shuttle mission, especially since he was a foreigner unfamiliar with NASA's overall operations. Surprised that they were indeed launching on schedule, he explained that the terminal countdown demonstration tests that he and the crew had practiced relentlessly over the past several months were of tremendous benefit. However, he emphasized that at least six months of training would have been required to fully prepare him for spaceflight. Although he was confident that he was prepared, he later confessed that he did get nervous during the last few moments prior to launch.

French payload specialist Patrick Baudry—on board, according to the press kit, "as part of a cooperative project with the Centre National d'Etudes Spatiales (CNES) of France"—was the beneficiary of a slightly longer training regimen due to the shuffling of missions, which had become fairly common. Initially assigned to the STS-51E mission, Baudry was bumped to STS-51G when a faulty satellite led to STS-51E being canceled. The NASA crew of STS-51E was retained and moved to STS-51D. Specialized equipment required by McDonnell Douglas payload specialist Charlie Walker had already been installed in the middeck on *Discovery*, so there was no room to accommodate Baudry's research experiments, hence his move to STS-51G, where room was available. Baudry had extensive spaceflight-training experience as a backup cosmonaut to countryman Jean-Loup Chrétien on a Russian Soyuz flight, but the impending launch on the shuttle (for which Chrétien was serving as *his* backup) was going to be a brand-new experience for him. Like Al-Saud, Baudry was appreciative of the updates coming from the commander and pilot during the climb to orbit. He stressed that it was "important for the middeck to have some information from the flight deck about the speed because it's not only interesting but also, of course, prepares us."

Al-Saud and Baudry became the tenth and eleventh payload specialists to fly on a shuttle mission. The Arab League countries hired NASA to launch and deploy its $45 million Arabsat communications satellite, and NASA's standard customer agreement was that passengers were allowed to fly on the shuttle in exchange for purchasing satellite space. The inclusion of Al-Saud created quite a stir in the Arab countries, as this mission represented more than the deployment of a crucial communications satellite for the Arab world. The presence of the Saudi prince aboard *Discovery* promised to thrust them into the ever-growing technical world and change how the Arab countries were viewed by outsiders.

Dan Brandenstein served as commander on STS-51G, assisted by rookie pilot John Creighton. The remainder of the NASA crew was comprised of three mission specialists: John Fabian, Steve Nagel, and Shannon Lucid. Of these, only Brandenstein and Fabian had flown before.

STS-51G had an ambitious flight plan primarily dedicated to the deployment of three satellites. Morelos-A, Arabsat, and Telstar 3-D were all designed to improve communications in scattered parts of the world. A fourth satellite, Spartan 1, would be cast into orbit from *Discovery*'s payload bay, shadow the orbiter, and then be retrieved after seventeen hours of free flying. Its mission was to perform x-ray astronomy research. Neither Al-Saud nor Baudry would be involved in the deployment of any of the satellites; that job belonged to the NASA astronauts.

Baudry would be in charge of two life sciences experiments, the French echocardiograph experiment and the French postural experiment. These investigations were designed to assess the effects of weightlessness on the cardiovascular and sensorimotor systems, and were similar to investigations carried out on the Russian *Soyuz T-6* mission for which he had trained in 1982.

Patrick Pierre Roger Baudry, with a master of science degree in aeronautical engineering from the French Air Force Academy of Salon-de-Provence was born 6 March 1946 in Cameroon, West Africa, a French colony at that time. Baudry came ever so close to flying on a Russian spacecraft several years before STS-51G. The Soviet Union allowed foreigners the opportunity to become cosmonauts through their Intercosmos program, whose mission was to aid Soviet allies with their spaceflight aspirations. In April 1979, under a similar program, France was invited to have one of their countrymen join a Soviet crew on a flight, and CNES solicited candidates for a joint mission scheduled for 1982. Baudry applied and, along with Jean-Loup Chrétien, was one of two Frenchmen selected as CNES astronauts on 12 June 1980. He had earned his fighter pilot wings in 1970, flying F-100 and Jaguar strike aircraft at locations in France and Africa. In 1978 he was assigned to the Empire Test Pilot School located in Boscombe Down, England. He graduated following a year of learning how to push high-performance aircraft to their limits, earned the Patuxent Trophy, and then moved to the Flight Test Center in Brétigny-sur-Orge, France, in 1979, where he flew variations of Mirage, Jaguar, and Crusader jet aircraft. He accumulated over 3,300 hours of flight time in one hundred types of aircraft.

Jean-Loup Jacques Marie Chrétien was the first backup payload specialist to have already flown into space. Born in La Rochelle, France, on 20 August 1938, he attended the College Saint-Charles à Saint-Brieuc and the Lycee de Morlaix. In 1959 he enrolled at the École de l' Air—the French air force academy—located in Salon-de-Provence, earning a master of science degree in 1961 in aeronautical engineering. He was awarded his wings as a fighter pilot and pilot-engineer in 1962. He next served seven years in the Fifth Fighter Squadron in Orange, France, as a fighter pilot in an operational squadron where he flew Super Mystere B2 aircraft and then Mirage III interceptors. The next rung on the ladder was French test pilot school—École du Personnel Navigant d'Essais et de Réception (EPNER). Afterward, Chrétien served a seven-year stint as a test pilot at Istres Flight Test Center, where he had the fortune to supervise the flight test program for the Mirage F-1 fighter. From there he transferred to the South Air Defense Division in Aix en Provence, where he was deputy commander from 1977 to 1978. Chrétien had over eight thousand hours flight time in a variety of high-performance aircraft, including Russian-made jets.

Several months after their selection as CNES astronauts, Baudry and Chrétien began training at the Yuri Gagarin Cosmonaut Training Center, located in Star City, Russia. They both qualified as cosmonaut engineers on the Soyuz spacecraft and *Salyut 7* space station complex and trained for a variety of scientific endeavors, including physiology, biology, materials processing, and astronomy.

Chrétien was given the nod as the prime crew member for the *Soyuz T-6* mission; Baudry served as his backup. Commander Vladimir Aleksandrovich Dzhanibekov, flight engineer Aleksandr Sergeyevich Ivanchenkov, and research cosmonaut Chrétien launched on 24 June 1982 from the Baikonur Cosmodrome headed for the *Salyut 7* space station. After successfully docking with *Salyut 7* and its crew of Anatoli Berezovoy and Valentin Lebedev, the visitors spent almost seven days conducting joint Soviet-French experiments, including French echography cardiovascular

30. STS-51G backup payload specialist Jean-Loup Chrétien. Chrétien had already flown into space on the Russian *Soyuz T-6* mission, and later flew on STS-86 (*Atlantis*).
Courtesy NASA/Retro Space Images.

monitoring system experiments. *Soyuz T-6* and its crew departed the space station on 2 July 1982, landing a little over forty miles northeast of Arkalyk in northern Kazakhstan.

Chrétien gained much fame as the first Western European to make it into space. In honor of his achievements, following the mission, he was appointed to the lofty position of chief of the CNES Astronaut Office. By 1984 he had made his way to JSC in Houston with hopes of more space adventures.

The birth of Prince Sultan Salman Abdulaziz Al-Saud occurred in Riyahd, Saudi Arabia, on 27 June 1956. Born into the Saudi royal family as the nephew of King Fahd bin Abdulaziz Al-Saud, he received his early elementary and secondary education in his birth city. His next destination was the United States, where he earned a degree in mass communications from the University of Denver. He netted his private pilot's license in 1976.

Following college, he was appointed in 1982 to be a researcher in the Department of International Communications at the Ministry of Information in Saudi Arabia. The prince became involved in the 1984 Summer Olympics held in Los Angeles, California, as deputy director for the Saudi Arabian Olympic Information Committee. After completion of the Olympics, he was appointed acting director of the new Department of Advertising at the Saudi Arabia Ministry of Information.

Al-Saud's backup was Maj. Abdulmohsen Hamad Al-Bassam, a Royal Saudi Air Force fighter pilot born in Unayzah, Saudi Arabia, on 12 December 1948. He holds a bachelor of science degree in air science from King Faisal Air Academy located in Riyadh.

The concept of a communications satellite was initially brought forth by the Arab Telecommunication Union; the Arab Organization for Education, Science, and Culture; and the Arab States Broadcasting Union. In 1976 the Arab League endorsed the creation of an institution for satellite communications located in Riyadh, called the Arab Satellite Communications Organization (Arabsat), leading to a series of satellites to be named Arabsat. Dr. Ali Al-Mashat, managing director of Arabsat, explained that the Arab world was badly in need of a way to improve communications. Arabsat IA was launched in February 1985 but quickly encountered problems. The satellite was nursed to life, but it never lived up to the Arab League expectations. A replacement was desperately needed.

Al-Mashat recollected that the Arab League wanted to deploy Arabsat 1B through NASA, and following negotiations, an agreement was soon reached to carry the satellite into space on the shuttle, where it would be deployed to the desired orbit. An agreement was reached in 1984 to select an Arab astronaut—a payload specialist—to accompany the satellite. According to Al-Mashat, Saudi Arabia was behind this effort more than any other Arab nation—they even paid the way for some of the other Arab League countries to keep the project going. As the head of Arabsat, Saudi Arabia decided to nominate a payload specialist to accompany their satellite into space.

According to a documentary by SilverGrey Pictures, directed by Pierre Salloum, NASA requested that Saudi Arabia nominate twenty individuals for medical screening. Al-Saud did not become aware of the opportunity until late in the process but managed to beat the deadline for consideration. Abdulmohsen Hamad Al-Bassam recalled that he and his squadron mates were asked to consider volunteering for the payload specialist position by their squadron leader, Prince Mansour Bin Bandar. He had received information that one of them should volunteer to become an astronaut, but most of Al-Bassam's comrades shook their heads in disbelief, making light of the chance of a lifetime. Although skeptical of his chances, Al-Bassam was intrigued with the opportunity and did not hesitate to throw his hat into the ring.

Following a lengthy and demanding process by Saudi Arabia and NASA, Al-Saud was chosen as the prime payload specialist, with Al-Bassam as his backup. There were no experiments yet developed for Al-Saud to conduct while in space; that came later.

Initially, it appeared that Al-Saud might not get the chance to compete for the opportunity to represent Saudi Arabia on a mission into space. According to Al-Saud, his uncle, King Fahd, was not convinced that the twenty-eight-year-old prince was the right man for the job. Ben Evans reported in "'The Sultans of Space': The Multi-Cultural Mission of STS-51G" that King Fahd was worried that Al-Saud's selection might be viewed as nepotism. The king was also not convinced that his young nephew was up to such a demanding task. Al-Saud recalled that his father decided to talk to the king, making a case that his son was worthy of representing Saudi Arabia in this grand adventure. In the SilverGrey Pictures production, Al-Saud, based on his father's recollection of the incident, quoted the king as asking, "Is he strong willed? Is he up to the responsibility? Will he endure that tough training?" Al-Saud's father assured him that his son was up to the undertaking, and the king finally gave his wholehearted endorsement.

Al-Bassam believes that the royal blood of the prince could have played an important role if the decision had been made solely by the Saudis. But he did not believe that NASA would have been that naive. Instead, he insisted that the prince was chosen for his competence; he was the most qualified candidate.

Al-Saud informed reporters at a press conference that his flight had generated immense interest in the Arab world. "Look at your own experience when John Glenn or when the shuttle went up," he said. "You would not believe what's going on in the Middle East right now. It's just basically fired up the interest and enthusiasm among our generation, the older generation, and even the young kids. The enthusiasm that this trip will generate will be identical, I think, to that generated by the space program here in America." Because the launch would also coincide with the end of Ramadan, the holiest month in the Muslim year, Al-Saud said he had to seek religious guidance on fasting and prayer. "I asked religious leaders in Saudi Arabia, and I said, 'How do I pray to Mecca? By the time you find it, it's gone!' But as Muslims, God has told us that we can pray to him anywhere in the world facing any direction."

NASA and CNES had reached an agreement on 23 March 1984 to fly a Frenchman on the shuttle, and Baudry and Chrétien were given the nod. The experiments that the French had planned for the shuttle mission were almost identical to the ones that Chrétien had performed on the *Soyuz T-6* flight. Baudry backed up Chrétien on that mission, and he knew the experiments inside and out, so it seemed only fair and logical that Baudry should be chosen to fly with NASA. According to Chrétien, NASA administrator James Beggs saw it differently; flying Chrétien again would provide a much more accurate comparison of the scientific results. Chrétien felt it was a tricky situation, as NASA pushed hard for a long time to have it their way. The head of CNES asked Chrétien one day if he felt it was fair to deny Baudry the chance to fly, which he had earned with two years of diligent training with the Russians, and Chrétien said that he "could not tell him yes." CNES held their ground and, in the end, won out; Baudry was selected as the prime crewman on the shuttle flight, with Chrétien serving as his backup.

Baudry and Chrétien planned their arrival at JSC for an early 1985 launch on STS-51E, but the move to STS-51G awarded them more time—almost a year—to train. Most of that time was spent doing mission-dependent training in building 32 located at JSC, learning the experiments. Mission-independent training for the payload specialists lasted the normal two to three months just prior to the scheduled launch. Chrétien recalled, "So we spent almost one year here. But we are in building 32 with the experiments, and in close relation with the PI [principal investigator] and mostly the echograph PI and neurosensorial [investigations]. There [was] very, very little training on the shuttle as a payload specialist. Mostly, at that time, you spent very little time with your crew. That was the main difference with the formal training on the Soyuz."

Baudry loathed the abbreviated mission-independent training and, according to Chrétien, wanted no part of being a passenger. He wanted to "be on the flight deck" and learn how to fly the orbiter. The flight crew understood, and "they took him many times on the ascent-entry training." Ten years following the flight of STS-51G, Chrétien went through astronaut candidate training with NASA at JSC, eventually flying as a mission specialist on STS-86 in 1997. For him, that experience underscored the difference in the training for the payload and mission specialists, saying, "When you go through mission specialist training after, you understand what are the difference[s]."

Baudry would have been fully capable of replacing Chrétien on the *Soyuz T-6* flight had it become necessary. Conversely, Chrétien didn't believe the level of training that he received from NASA as a backup payload specialist was adequate for him to replace Baudry on STS-51G. There were two complete crews for the Soyuz mission, with the same training regimen. There was no backup shuttle crew for Chrétien to train with. Chrétien pointed out that if the crew was in "building 9 . . . and you have a session training, where is the backup guy?" In the NASA system, at least on the STS-51G mission, the backup was the odd man out. Chrétien described his mission-independent training on STS-51G as "mostly to follow, to look, and just get my own culture on the system here—the only real backup training that you get then is on the experiments."

Once Al-Saud was selected to represent Saudi Arabia, Dr. Abdallah E. Dabbagh, director of the Research Institute at the University of Petroleum and Minerals (UPM) in Dhahran, was directed to develop the scientific experiments for the prince to carry out once in orbit. Dabbagh traveled to JSC in March 1985 to meet with NASA payload integration personnel, who suggested several existing experiments, settling on four concepts. An ionized gas experiment was developed by a PhD candidate belonging to the Saudi royal family, which involved Al-Saud taking video shots of ionized gas clouds formed by the firing of the orbiter's engines. Another, the phase separation experiment, would assess how Saudi, Kuwaiti, and Algerian oil samples mixed with water in the microgravity environment. Al-Saud was also assigned to perform Earth observations and take extensive photographs of his homeland, which they expected to fly over forty-nine times. He would also participate in the French postural experiment that Baudry was scheduled to operate.

Al-Saud and Al-Bassam arrived at JSC on 1 April 1985, followed several days later by Dr. Manzour Nazer, assistant leader of the Arabsat scientific experiment team. Before the end of April, other Arabsat team members had joined them at JSC to prepare the scientific experiments and observations for flight and to train the Saudi Arabian payload specialists in how to operate them.

Being a wealthy member of a royal family also came with certain privileges for Al-Saud. During his training he stayed in a plush four-hundred-dollar-a-day hotel suite in Houston and was driven to and from work in a chauffeured limousine with two bodyguards.

The flight crew got along quite well with the payload specialists. Creighton felt that Baudry was "highly qualified" to fly into space because of his experience as a pilot. But initially, none of the flight crew knew how Al-Saud would fit into the mix. The French customs were similar to those of Americans, and although Al-Saud had spent considerable time in the United States and was accustomed to wearing Western attire, he had spent most of his life wearing the traditional Saudi Arabian robes and head scarf, or keffiyeh. Al-Saud was Muslim. Brandenstein confessed that "we'd been around Frenchmen before. I figured we knew and understood that enough, but the other was a total mystery to us." Thus, Brandenstein wished to learn about the culture of Al-Saud to reduce the likelihood that someone might say something offensive to him. Fortunately, the Saudi Arabian Oil Company—Aramco—had an office in Houston, so Brandenstein invited them over to teach the crew as much about Al-Saud's culture as possible. "We were told not to tell any camel jokes when Sultan showed up, and the first thing he did when he walked through the door was to say, 'I left my camel outside,'" John Fabian recalled, laughing. "So much for the public affairs part of the thing." Brandenstein needn't have worried; Al-Saud's American education had taught him American ways. Brandenstein explained that he was "more Americanized . . . than the Frenchman was. A lot of times we'd say . . . a subtle-type joke that the Frenchman didn't understand, and then Sultan would lean over and explain it to him. So it turned out to be a neat crew."

For his part, Al-Saud said that his experience flying American-made F-15 Eagles and F-5 fighter bombers helped a lot in his preparation for the seven-day mission, commenting, "I'm working over sixteen hours a day to be ready."

Creighton remembers that the flight crew was also very fond of Al-Saud's backup, who was equally impressed with Al-Saud. According to Creighton, Al-Bassam had never met anyone from the royal family. "It was obvious to all of us that Prince Sultan had grown up in different financial circles than the rest of the crew," he said with a laugh. He agreed with his commander that they all "got along pretty well."

Training progressed well for the payload specialists. However, there were several areas where the Saudi contingent was not pleased. The process for obtaining proper security clearances and approval for them to be admitted into JSC was inefficient, resulting in embarrassment, inconvenience, and loss of time. The office space allocated to them was too small for two payload specialists and two assistant team leaders, making it nearly impossible to hold team meetings in the cramped quarters. They also desired to have a full-time secretary, but JSC could not provide an extra office. Otherwise, the Saudi Arabian contingent was extremely complimentary of the JSC efforts to make their brief stay in Texas as pleasant as possible.

On launch day, a smiling Baudry sported a jaunty French beret as he and his crewmates sauntered out of the Operations and Checkout Building on their way to the launchpad. Baudry and Al-Saud were in a jovial mood, waiting in the White Room to be deposited inside *Discovery*, laughing, smiling, and shaking hands with the White Room technicians. Fabian, Al-Saud, and Baudry were seated in the middeck for launch; hence, they were the final three astronauts to enter the orbiter. Neither Baudry nor Al-

Saud displayed any outward signs of fear or nervousness, although they were fully aware that they were about to launch into space atop the equivalent of a bomb powerful enough to level the entire launch complex and then some. But on this day the rocket gods were with the crew.

On a hot and humid Florida morning, *Discovery* and its crew blazed a fiery trail into a blue cloudless sky a mere forty-two milliseconds late, beginning what would become a near-perfect mission. Baudry had carried out ascent-profile simulations during his training for the *Soyuz T-6* mission and expected the shuttle acceleration to be less than that of the Soyuz, although to him they surprisingly felt about the same. As Baudry said postmission, "I had to strap down again at the end of the ascent because of the upside component of the acceleration. And I think it's because of the seats and the position." He speculated that the inclination of the seat might have increased the g-forces. The sensation that he experienced was more likely due to the relationship of the thrust vector of the main engines and the centerline of the orbiter, instead of inclined seats. Regardless, the launch was much different than he had expected.

Discovery settled into an orbit approximately 217 miles high at an inclination to the equator of just a tad over twenty-eight degrees. While the flight crew quickly got down to work deploying satellites out of the payload bay, Baudry and Al-Saud began their assigned tasks. Incidentally, once in orbit, the side hatch was secured with a lock. As Fabian recalled, "We put a lock on the door of the side hatch. It was installed when we got into orbit so that the door could not be opened from the inside and commit hari kari [*sic*], kill the whole crew; that was not because of anybody we had on our flight but because of a concern about someone who had flown before 51G." Adding a lock to the orbiter side hatch became a fairly routine practice on flights carrying payload specialists.

Baudry, with help from Shannon Lucid, carried out the first French echocardiograph experiment assessment shortly after they reached orbit and then a second time on the first day of the mission. They would repeat the experiment at roughly the same time on each day of the flight. Data were also collected prior to the mission, and this would be collated once they were back on Earth, comparing it to the data Chrétien had collected on his Russian *Soyuz T-6* mission.

Baudry and Al-Saud took great pride in completing their assignments to the best of their abilities. As part of the French postural experiment, Baudry carried out investigations that tested an array of activities measuring the electrical activity of muscles based on a variety of well-orchestrated body movements. Following fifteen minutes spent retrieving all the necessary equipment from out of stowage compartments in the middeck and then hooking up the biochemical electronic sensors to his body, Baudry began to conduct one phase of the experiment. As he stood perfectly erect in the middeck, with both arms by his sides as if at military attention, he swiftly thrust his arms outward, perpendicular to the length of his body. The paraphernalia he had previously attached to his legs and face recorded the ensuing results. His crisp body movements and the stern expression on his face provided testimony of his commitment to doing the best job that he possibly could. The experiment took sixty-five minutes to conduct, including setup and calibration, all contingent on other activities planned for the crew.

Both French experiments worked as planned, with only minor problems, all of which were predictable, making the French team on the ground very happy. Flying the French echocardiograph experiment on *Discovery* was a huge advantage over the *Soyuz T-6* flight, on which Chrétien had to wait until he arrived at the *Salyut* space station to begin operating his experiments due to the cramped conditions on the Soyuz spacecraft. Baudry related that the scientists on the ground were elated by his efficiency. "I could start work with the [French echocardiograph experiment] one hour and fifty minutes after MECO [main engine cutoff]. And to have the first data recorded three hours and a few minutes after MECO, which was quite exceptional, and they did not expect so much. So they have exactly what they wanted and even more than what they wanted."

In spite of his enthusiasm over the spectacular beginning to his research, Baudry was not impressed with the orbiter as a research station.

Generally, the orbiter without Spacelab is not very good—[it] doesn't offer good space to make science . . . because there [are] too many people. You are all the time disturbed. And, for some experiments, it's very good to have good concentration. And, with the noise of the loudspeaker, with the movement around you . . . it's very difficult situation to work with on the mission. A good example is the cleaning of the filters. And that was a big surprise for me to see that to clean the filters was made twice on the mission and also that it took such a long time. And I did not realize at all that before the mission when you go in the middeck, you see somebody trying to work and you feel as if you don't want to disturb him, but you have to work. I'm not a scientist, but I tried to be one, and really that was the worst situation to work properly. But if the work could be done, it's because many of us really tried very hard to leave some peace during some periods.

Baudry believed steps could have been taken prior to the mission to make the situation more bearable and efficient. A crew activity plan developed early in the mission planning may have allowed the payload specialists to provide some input into how the scientific investigations were to be carried out. Clearly annoyed by the time required to clean filters and other disturbances, Baudry made it clear to NASA that "this kind of thing should appear in the [crew activity plan]." Al-Saud concurred with Baudry's view in his postmission report, citing the treadmill as one of the activities that disturbed his investigations. Consequently, the treadmill was hardly used during the mission, because it was excessively noisy, which disturbed crew members. Brandenstein agreed: "Several of the crewmen used it periodically, but there was not a great deal of use made by all crewmen due to conflicts with PS experiments." A more efficient crew activity plan may have allowed crew members to gain much-needed exercise at times when the payload specialists were not working in the middeck.

Al-Saud soon discovered that performing his traditional Muslim prayers in space was not going to be as easy as it is on Earth. In the weightless environment, he found it difficult to assume the proper prayer position. He also worried that an attempt to force himself into the proper configuration might induce the onset of SAS; therefore, he had to improvise.

Al-Saud planned to photograph Saudi Arabia from the overhead windows in the aft flight deck during daylight passes. He was primarily interested in the country's geology, including hydrological features, sand dune morphology, urban areas, forestry, and turbidity in the waters of the Red Sea. He humorously tried to broker a deal with Saudi Arabian geologists, saying, "If [there are] any mineral findings, the crew gets half, and they said no." Al-Saud's photography assignments from the aft flight deck proved to be much more difficult than expected. His training had taught him

31. Payload specialist Patrick Baudry enjoys the sensation of zero gravity inside the middeck of *Discovery* on his only flight into space on STS-51G. Courtesy NASA/Retro Space Images.

the expert use of the camera, and he was thoroughly knowledgeable of the landmarks he was to photograph. The problem was that the speedy orbiter moved so fast that he had difficulty locating landmarks in time to snap good pictures. He believed it was much easier to identify the features from the pilot's seat but not practical to move back and forth between the two locations. A crew member sitting in the pilot's seat to relay upcoming features would have vastly improved his photographic reconnaissance. He also advised that there was not enough detailed information provided in the payload specialist checklists and commented that geological features should have been better defined for his Earth observational work.

The phase separation experiment was designed to assess how different concentrations of oil mixed with water in the microgravity environment. Using a simple, transparent Plexiglas container comprised of fifteen chambers, which held the various oils and water, Al-Saud captured his observations and photographed the container after he had thoroughly shaken it. There were hopes that the experiment might provide results that could help engineers and geologists coax more of their prized oil out of the giant Saudi oil fields, as well as improve oil spill cleanup procedures.

32. STS-51G payload specialist Prince Sultan Salman Abdulaziz Al-Saud taking notes in *Discovery*'s middeck. Courtesy NASA/Retro Space Images.

In support of a Saudi Arabian PhD student at Stanford University, Al-Saud used *Discovery*'s TV cameras to take photographs of the orbiter's thruster plumes, so that experts could assess how the plumes affect operations measurements and communications associated with space vehicles. The data from this investigation would also be examined at the University of Petroleum and Minerals to assess the impact of gas particles on solid surfaces. As well, Al-Saud photographed the plumes emanating from the rocket engines of the Arabsat satellite when they were fired shortly after it was deployed.

Finally, Al-Saud carried out a controversial experiment associated with the end of the Muslim religious holiday Ramadan, designated by the first observance of the crescent of the moon with the unaided eye. His job was to locate the new moon while looking out the window of the orbiter following sunset on 17 or 18 June. Brandenstein had concerns that Al-Saud might take advantage of this opportunity to make a religious statement, which carried the potential for criticism from people around the world. Tactfully, Brandenstein talked to Al-Saud prior to the mission to make it clear that he was to keep religion out of his comments.

The Spacelab missions were loaded with a plethora of scientific investigations, requiring long days of work that kept the payload crews busy throughout most of the mission; rarely did they have time to float up to the flight deck and sightsee. Al-Saud had the opposite problem on sts-51g. He didn't have enough work to keep him busy and soon became inured to witnessing repeated sunrises and sunsets. Al-Saud now wished that nasa had developed a hefty schedule of additional tasks for him to carry out, some required and others optional, which would have given him something to do once he completed his regularly assigned tasks.

Al-Saud had one more recommendation for nasa regarding foreign payload specialists. His fellow citizens were immensely proud of his accomplishment, and they would be hungry to know more about his spaceflight once he returned home. Unfortunately, he had very little to bring back to show them, other than a few photographs and standard video taken as time permitted. He dearly wished that a crew member had been trained to produce high-quality video images of him in orbit, so that he could take it back to his home country for publicity reasons.

Al-Saud predicted at a 28 May 1985 news conference that his inclusion on sts-51g would have an incredibly positive effect on the relations between the United States and the entire Islamic world. Confident that the Arab world would be mesmerized by one of their own citizens flying into space on an American spaceship, Al-Saud was extremely optimistic of more space adventures for his own countrymen. With little surprise, his flight truly had a tremendous and positive influence on the Arab world countries, which he would quickly realize once he returned to his home country.

Brandenstein guided *Discovery* to a soft landing at Edwards Air Force Base in the early morning of 24 June 1985. Shortly afterward, the crew made trips to both France and Saudi Arabia. According to Ben Evans in "The Sultans of Space," Baudry was in the middle of a divorce at the time and even had a Russian girlfriend who was the daughter of a kgb agent; thus, tactfully the spouses were not invited to accompany the astronauts on their trip to France. Creighton recalled that it is still "a sore subject around my house to this day, because it was a wonderful trip." Laughing, he continued, "I mean, nobody wines and dines like the French."

Saudi Arabia was next on the postmission travel schedule. The crew flew into the capital, Riyadh, without Shannon Lucid, who was quite annoyed because Saudi Arabian women did not have the same civil rights as men, as Nagel recalled. The crew spent a few days in Riyadh; visited Al-Saud's family farm as well as the royal summer palace in the mountains, where they experienced the lavish lifestyle of the royal family; and spent a lot of time visiting and talking to children. Lucid was finally convinced to fly in for a short visit but didn't linger.

Neither Baudry nor Al-Saud flew into space again. Baudry was appointed in March 1986 as adviser to the chairman of the Aerospatiale Company. He next became advisor for manned spaceflight at the European Aeronautic Defense and Space Company, now Airbus Group NV, in 1993 until 2003, as well as a senior test pilot for Airbus. He participated in the early planning of the Hermes space plane, planned to be launched on a French Ariane rocket, but the project was cancelled in 1992 after a series of delays and funding problems. Baudry was later appointed as a UNESCO (United Educational, Scientific, and Cultural Organization) goodwill ambassador in September 1999 for his efforts to organize the European Space Camp for young people.

Jean-Loup Chrétien went on to fly into space twice more; his second flight came in 1988 with the Russians on the *Soyuz TM-7* mission, which included taking part in an EVA. From 1990 to 1993 he carried out pilot training for the Russian Buran spacecraft at the Moscow Joukovski Institute. Selected as part of NASA's astronaut group 15 in 1994, he flew his final space mission on STS-86 in 1997. Retiring from NASA in 2001 following a career-ending accident at a local hardware store, Chrétien entered the business world in the Houston area.

Al-Saud did not rest on his laurels following his return from space. He entered the Saudi Royal Air Force, where he qualified to fly several types of civilian and military aircraft, reaching the rank of colonel prior to retiring from military service. He accumulated over seven thousand hours of flight time, including jet aircraft, helicopters, and gliders. He also owns a commercial transport pilot certificate from the United States. In 1985 he was a founding member of the Association of Space Explorers—an international, nonprofit professional and educational organization. Fourteen years following his only flight into space, Al-Saud returned to the United

States, where he earned a master of science degree in social and political science at the Maxwell School of Citizenship and Public Affairs, Syracuse University, New York.

In 2008 he became the president and chairman of the Board of the Saudi Commission for Tourism and National Heritage. He has also been involved in a host of charitable and humanitarian organizations. Since his flight into space, he has been bestowed with an overabundance of medals, Orders of Honor, and other awards, including an honorary doctorate degree in science from the King Fahd University of Petroleum and Minerals in Saudi Arabia.

Al-Saud, a humble man, remains passionate about space exploration, including its history and his brief contribution on STS-51G. He contends that he has not been able to repay his country for the opportunity to travel into space, which changed not only his life but the lives of millions in the Arab world. He is honored to have met many astronauts and cosmonauts and has become friends with many. Al-Saud never imagined that he would one day join the space program and fly into orbit. While that flight lasted only eight days, for Al-Saud the real bonanza came after his flight, with the opportunity to use his experience in space to encourage children to dream and to aspire to do more with their lives. He still recalls the excitement in the faces of the people of Saudi Arabia when he returned home following his flight.

Following the STS-51G mission, Maj. Abdulmohsen Hamad Al-Bassam returned home to the world he had known before being selected to participate in the payload specialist program. He rose to the rank of general in the Royal Saudi Air Force before retiring from the service. Later, he was assigned the role of air force attaché at the Embassy of Saudi Arabia in London, England.

The deployment of satellites on STS-51G—its primary objective—went off without a hitch, causing many to call it a textbook flight, a much-needed success for NASA after a string of shuttle missions that had encountered a variety of pesky problems. Although Baudry and Al-Saud were not NASA astronauts, the entire crew worked as a team, and without a successful program by the payload specialists, the crew would not have considered the mission 100 percent successful. On orbit, Al-Saud and Baudry both received much-appreciated assistance from the NASA crew. Brandenstein gave the crew high marks, stating, "The crew that I took with me on 51G was superb."

Al-Saud reflected on his time in space shortly after his mission ended. "I think the Earth observation went very well," he reported. "Everyone had a special interest in keeping me in touch with the timeline, and we did all the passes we wanted to do. I think we got some pretty good pictures. So I think everybody had a vested interest in seeing that the PSS get their experiments done. And especially because the rest of the mission was going very well, they just wanted the rest of us to have a good mission too."

STS-51G was the fourth mission in 1985 to carry payload specialists, with four more coming down the pike before the end of the year. STS-51G may not have had the scientific audacity of Spacelab or the intrigue of a DOD mission, but the payload specialists on STS-51G were just as committed to pulling off a flawless mission. They had trained hard, formed a strong bond with the NASA crew, performed well on orbit, and made a significant contribution to a highly successful mission.

13. The Spaceman from Chilpancingo

From space I see myself as one more person among the millions
and millions who loved, live, and will live on Earth. Inevitably,
this makes one think about our existence and the way in which we
should live to enjoy, to share, our short lives as fully as possible.

Rodolfo Neri Vela

It was a strange homecoming for Dr. Rodolfo Neri Vela. A NASA Gulf-
stream jet had flown him to a dusty U.S. border town on the edge of his
home country, Mexico. Waiting for him were not dignitaries welcoming
their country's first space traveler home but rather a small band of Mexican border patrol officers. The men took him into one of their cars and
whisked him across the checkpoint to another waiting jet.

Several months prior to his flight aboard *Atlantis*, Neri happened by
the mail room in the Astronaut Office at JSC. There, as he recalled for the
authors, he learned of something he had not quite prepared himself for: "I
remember that the nice lady in charge of that office approached me, and
during our conversation she told me, 'You may not realize at this moment,
but your life is not going to be the same when you return home. You will
have no private life; you will be very popular. The same thing happened to
the Canadian astronaut when he returned home.' She spoke like a prophet
and was totally right."

When the Mexican-registered jet landed, it came to a stop in a remote
area of the airport. Its single passenger was deposited into another waiting
official car and was taken directly to Los Pinos, the office of the president
of Mexico, to report in person on the success of his mission. Days later, he
would be told by officials that the thousands of people who were expected

at any official arrival to celebrate his return might be difficult to control, hence the secretive transportation back to his home country.

Neri realized he was now in uncharted territory: "Maybe they were right, because everybody recognized me, everywhere, anytime. I was the most popular guy in Mexico for some time!" He had just been unwittingly thrust into the role of national celebrity, and on a scale rivaling that of the astronauts and cosmonauts of the early days of the space race. He had unexpectedly become his country's Yuri Gagarin, their Alan Shepard. He was their own son, and he was first of them to go into space.

Looking back today, his life had most certainly taken a strange turn after being off the planet for a week in 1985. That brief, fortuitous trip was something that did indeed change his life forever. It was an adventure beyond the wildest dreams of a young teenager who, in July 1969, found himself fascinated with an aspect of the historic American moon landing that would set him on a singularly unique path to space.

As Rodolfo Neri Vela grew up in Chilpancingo de los Bravo, a scenic town in southwestern Mexico, the thought of becoming an astronaut was the furthest thing from his young mind. While many space travelers traced their fascination with space to a childhood dream, Neri remembers, "In my case it was totally different. For a start, I was born at a time when astronauts still didn't exist, and when Yuri Gagarin became the first human being in space, I was nine."

On the historic evening at the climax of the Apollo program, Neri sat transfixed with nearly the rest of humanity watching the ghostly figures of two American astronauts taking mankind's first tentative steps on another world. But it wasn't the event itself that captured his imagination so much as the fact that he could bear witness to it as it happened, albeit on a small, 1960s-era black-and-white television. "I want to know how it is possible I can see on a screen what's going on there?" he would share with a young audience at KSC in January 2016. "They tell me those things happen because of microwaves, because the information travels invisibly through space and through the earth's atmosphere. That really made me dream." It was his first real awareness of the relatively new field of telecommunications, and while he was told it would be a difficult course of study, he was undeterred in his new dream to become a telecommunications engineer.

Entering the National Autonomous University of Mexico (UNAM), he found himself at a critical crossroads in his academic future. Although he was seriously considering going into chemistry, he decided to enroll in the faculty of engineering. "Without knowing it, of course, it was one of the best decisions in my life," Neri recalled, "because that paved the way to obtain my ticket to space fifteen years later."

Neri's chosen field of study was far from common for students in Mexico, and he excelled at it. Even before he graduated, he would be tapped to teach underclassmen courses on circuit theory, communications, mathematics, and control theory. He was very popular with his professors and classmates, and one of his most trusted advisors had recently returned from the United States with a PhD from Rice University in Houston. Neri recalled, "When I was a student, there were only a handful of doctors, and the only one specialized in communications was my tutor! He seemed to be very clever and inspired me to learn more about satellites. I told myself I had to be like him or better."

Like his mentor, Neri longed to study abroad. But to him the United States didn't seem to fit the bill: "I could visit it anytime. I needed to cross the ocean, to discover Europe, and to improve my English and knowledge of engineering in the United Kingdom." Fortunately, his early teaching experience helped him obtain the necessary grants, and immediately following graduation he left the only home he had known for a new life of discovery in England.

Neri would obtain his master's degree in telecommunications systems from the University of Essex in July 1976 and then go on to the University of Birmingham, earning his doctorate in electronic and electrical engineering three years later. He would return to Mexico with this coveted title in hand, putting his talents to work for the Institute of Electrical Research in the radio communications group. There, he performed research and systems planning on antennas and satellite communication systems. He would also work with the Ministry of Communications on the early planning stages of the Mexican satellite system known as Morelos.

All along, he never lost his passion for teaching others. He eventually returned to the National University of Mexico as a full-time lecturer. He had paid close attention to the American space shuttle program, watching with interest as a more diverse range of astronauts started going into space. Not only was NASA flying women and minorities, but the increasing number of foreign scientists and engineers allowed him to wonder if Mexico would ever be offered the opportunity. While mentoring students in the spring of 1985, he learned the answer:

> *The Mexican government made an announcement. An agreement with NASA had been signed to include a Mexican astronaut in one of the crews, specifically in the same mission that was scheduled to put in low orbit the Mexican satellite Morelos-[B]. When I read the list of requirements to participate in the contest, I had many doubts; I wondered if I had a slight chance of being selected. It seemed to be very difficult—something everybody wanted. Whoever was chosen would become the first Latin American citizen to represent his country in a NASA mission. It was so exciting, and I am very happy that I faced that challenge.*

Hundreds of applicants participated in the competition to be Mexico's first astronaut. PhDs in fields such as chemistry, biology, astrophysics, as well as engineering all sought the honor. After many rounds of eliminations, just five were selected as finalists to go to Houston for final examinations and interviews, and Neri found himself among them. When the entire process was complete and after weeks of nervous waiting, the results of competition were announced. At a 5 June 1985 press conference in Mexico City, Dr. Rodolfo Neri Vela was introduced to his countrymen as their first space emissary. Dr. Ricardo Peralta y Fabi, an aerospace engineer, would serve as his backup. "He was a very bright and independent guy," Neri recalled of his fellow payload specialist candidate.

Just days later, on 17 June, Neri was at KSC at the invitation of NASA to witness his very first space shuttle launch. Not only did the *Discovery* mission carry payload specialists from France and Saudi Arabia, but nestled in its payload bay with two other satellites was Mexico's Morelos-A, a spacecraft nearly identical to the one with which he would later fly. As Neri would write in his 1986 memoir *El Planeta Azul* (*The Blue Planet*), the liftoff left a visceral impression. "The whole spectacle affected me so deeply that my eyes filled with tears," he wrote. He could hardly believe that in just a few short months, he would be strapped into another orbiter, experiencing the same thrilling adventure himself.

Charlie Walker had just returned from STS-51D in April 1985, and he was already looking forward to flying again with his electrophoresis project.

When Brewster Shaw's crew was first assembled, they were targeted for a midsummer mission. McDonnell Douglas had at least one more flight manifested by its agreement with NASA, so it came as no surprise to Shaw when Walker was added to his crew. The company had no one else to offer to NASA who could operate the experiment as fluently as Walker, and having already flown with two crews, he had developed a solid reputation within the Astronaut Office as a compatible, competent crew member.

There was a promising future for the electrophoresis process, though, and the company was looking forward to utilizing the middeck unit many more times. McDonnell Douglas was also designing a larger production facility to be mounted in the payload bay. It would run with minimal crew member input and produce large quantities of purified, pharmaceutical-grade material for potential commercial use on Earth.

"I was actually thinking, my gosh, we could have our own astronaut corps, a private-industry astronaut corps," Walker shared with NASA's Sandra Johnson. "If we really are going to fly these things at the rate that we're talking about and we're going to continue to do R&D aboard shuttle in the middeck, then there's probably going to be somebody flying with this, and if NASA's really keen on it, then, yes, maybe that's what's going to happen."

On both of his previous missions, Walker had trained one of the mission specialists to back him up on his electrophoresis experiment responsibilities. Now, as the program matured and NASA management and astronauts got more comfortable with the payload specialists being on board, it was suggested that McDonnell Douglas provide its own backup crew member for this role. Walker recalled that his company thought, "Charlie Walker flying every seven months just seemed like a lot of pressure that maybe he didn't want and the rest of the company didn't want to impose."

As a result, McDonnell Douglas began an internal selection process for a backup payload specialist on the upcoming mission and presented Robert Wood to NASA to begin training with Shaw's crew. Wood—a twenty-eight-year-old MIT whiz kid from Fitchburg, Massachusetts, with a master's degree in physics—was described by Walker as "one of the computer gurus in our project at the time back in St. Louis." Munro Wood, one of his five children, recalled to the authors that his "transition from pure physics into more of the engineering side would have been in the early 1980s," and he

33. STS-61B payload specialist Charlie Walker (*right*) and his backup, Robert Wood. The mission marked the first time McDonnell Douglas Corporation provided a backup to potentially fly with its CFES experiment. Courtesy NASA/Retro Space Images.

could remember as a child his father describing some of the work he was doing programming the then-primitive machines.

Robert Wood reported to JSC in May 1985 and began shadowing Walker through training. But in Walker's recollection, there was never any question about who would fly the mission:

> *Brewster and the crew had to get to know two people, and of course, this is a backup situation. Nobody's expecting that I'm not going to be flying it, but you've got to be ready. I certainly expected and was desirous to fly myself, and quite frankly, I perceived at the time that the crew was sure hoping that nothing happened to me, because they were more comfortable with me, and they knew how I was going to respond in the space environment, having flown twice before. Robert Wood, they were just barely getting to know him and did not want to have to go through necessarily the dynamic of getting acquainted and feeling comfortable with him as a crew member.*

The space agency was still adapting to a new paradigm working with foreign and commercial non-NASA crew members as they had on STS-51G. Just when things seemed they couldn't get more complicated, Mexico's Morelos-B satellite dropped onto the manifest for Shaw's crew, and along with it came two more untested payload specialists.

Rodolfo Neri Vela could sense the mood of the Astronaut Office quite palpably when he began training with his crew for STS-61B. He and Peralta were assigned austere desks set off in a room designated for the visiting payload specialists. "I assume that most of the U.S. astronauts understood that for NASA it was important to have international partners," he says today, "although I heard occasionally that some of them were not very happy, because they thought a place in the spaceship was being given to 'a stranger' instead of to them, and they had to wait longer for an assigned spaceflight."

Fortunately for Neri, these opinions never manifested themselves on the part of his crewmates. He felt extremely lucky to have been paired with such a friendly, easygoing, and professional team that always made him feel welcomed. Commander Shaw, in particular, set the tone for the rest of the crew, and Neri remembers him as "very wise, patient, [and] protective—a real friend." Shaw, pilot Bryan O'Connor, and mission specialists

Jerry Ross, Sherwood (Woody) Spring, and Mary Cleave saw Neri as a de facto ambassador for Mexico. Neri vividly remembers his commander pulling him aside one day in the office and telling him, "You are the only one with a PhD in our crew, and you are representing your country. You are special in this mission." That one statement left Neri buoyant with a new confidence and enthusiasm for his role in the upcoming flight.

After all the manifest changes and the payloads were finalized, the mission was at last targeted for liftoff the day before the American Thanksgiving holiday. Several additional secondary payloads were added to the crew's activity plan, including some rather simple-to-perform experiments proposed by Mexican investigators. *Atlantis*'s autumn flight would also feature two spectacular EVAs, with Ross and Spring practicing space station construction techniques using two different types of structures towering high above the payload bay.

Charlie Walker now found himself in the unique position of being one of only two crew members with prior spaceflight experience. In fact, solely in terms of number of flights, he was the most experienced. Brewster Shaw had flown as pilot on STS-9; the rest of the crew were all space rookies. Walker took it on himself not only to look after his own backup, Wood, but to bring his Mexican crewmate up to speed as well.

Neri, as did several other payload specialists who came to NASA feeling like outsiders, regarded Walker as approachable and always willing to help a first-timer along. "We became very good friends," Neri recalled fondly. And their friendship remains over thirty years later. "I didn't have to ask him for help while training—he knew the ropes so well, and he always had the initiative to make sure I understood and did things right." In Neri's opinion, the training, while intensely crammed into just five short months, was more than adequate. But his most challenging training event was one even Walker could be of no help with.

Commander Shaw stopped by Neri's desk in the Astronaut Office one afternoon and dropped a bombshell announcement on him: "Tomorrow we are flying the T-38. See you at Ellington Field at nine o'clock." Neri could instantly feel his heart pounding out of his chest. "I have never been a pilot," he admitted. Although he was nervous, he realized this was an important part of his training.

I wondered if I would survive such a test, but I had to do it. At the same time, I felt as a kid who was going to receive a gift not everybody could get. It was indeed a test, to see if I wouldn't get frightened, start crying in despair. At the beginning I was quite nervous, but I was confident that Brewster knew the ropes and how to pilot that flying machine. We flew upside down, we fell rapidly, we did several turns in a few seconds, and I was just praying the cockpit glass on top of me wouldn't break or the seat belt wouldn't get loose. At the end, Brewster said, "Now you will control [the] plane with the joystick." . . . And so I did. . . . It was perhaps the most difficult test of my life, but I enjoyed it very much. I assume I passed!

With this evaluation by his commander behind him, Neri had another event in his training syllabus that involved going up in a jet aircraft. But the purpose of this flight wasn't to teach one anything about aviation; it was to provide a brief glimpse into the insanely strange environment of zero gravity. It would be a packed flight aboard the KC-135, with Woody Spring practicing his space suit donning and the rest of the mission's crew assisting him and looking after their trainee payload specialists. As Neri described in *The Blue Planet*, the experience was terrifying at the beginning. "My first reaction was astonishment; it was difficult to believe my body weighed absolutely nothing," he wrote. As he struggled to control his movements, he felt "like a leaf blowing in the wind," aimlessly flying around the padded cabin.

Forty times the jet climbed steeply and then pushed over until the aircraft and everyone inside it were falling at the same rate. All the while, Shaw, clad in a bright-orange flight suit, floated with the confidence of an experienced spaceman, watching over Neri as he gradually gained his own. After some time, Neri would even relax enough to be able to smile for a photograph. With the training complete, the slightly queasy payload specialist wobbled off the jet while trying to put on a happy if somewhat pale face for his crewmates.

Neri had jumped onto a speeding train of sorts, as his crew had been training for years in all the little things he was now learning for the first time. The seven participated in grueling twelve-hour simulations of the major portions of their mission in ground-based simulators. Neri and Walker practiced cabin stowage and meal preparation in the middeck and worked with some apparatus they would use to perform a handful of medical exper-

34. Mexico's Rodolfo Neri Vela braves zero gravity for the first time aboard NASA's KC-135 aircraft. "I felt so heavy and helpless every time the plane went up to regain altitude, and then all of a sudden the plane fell towards the sea making everybody inside weightless. Quite an experience." Courtesy NASA/Retro Space Images.

iments and other investigations that had been proposed by Mexican scientists. Neri's other main task would be to take photographs of his home country from orbit, so he spent many hours with NASA experts learning how to operate a large-format Hasselblad camera. His superiors reminded him before the flight, "If you come back without any pictures [of Mexico], we are not going to like you, Rodolfo. So you'd better be doing your job!"

The planet that Neri was going to study and photograph from space showed its ever-changing nature in a most violent way on 19 September 1985. A devastating 8.0 magnitude earthquake struck Mexico City and the surrounding country at 7:19 a.m., causing massive damage to the city's infrastructure and killing at least five thousand of his fellow citizens. The tragic quake was followed by two major aftershocks, and the worst-affected areas were plunged into chaos. Not only did the disaster bring more importance to the photographic documentation Neri was charged with, but the timing of his flight would bring much-needed uplifting news and pride to his country following eight weeks of despair and anxiety.

Atlantis's payload of three communications satellites—Australia's Aussat 2; RCA's Satcom KU-2; and the Morelos-B, which represented Neri's ticket to space—had been checked out in the orbiter's cavernous bay awaiting their launch. During the night of the final countdown for the mission, Charlie Walker's CFES experiment, as it had on his previous flight, threatened to postpone the launch. Crawling around inside the strange, upended world of the middeck, a technician noted a small amount of chemical fluid leaking from the refrigerator-sized unit mounted just above the crew access hatch. A problem report was generated, but after a quick analysis, it was determined that the leak rate was minimal and that any fluid would likely be "contained in the CFES structure, isolated from mid deck environment." Concerned that any repair performed on the pad might worsen the issue, the report was closed, declaring that the "leak rate is acceptable for flight as-is for 61B only."

However, this would not be the end of the potential problem. As the crew arrived at the launchpad in the early evening, one of the astronaut support personnel found a white crystalline residue on the emergency air pack attached to the seat just below the CFES rack. Obviously a result of the leaking fluid dripping from above, this required the support personnel to write another discrepancy, a "crew squawk," as the flight crew began clamoring into the upper cabin. Charlie Walker, assuming responsibility for his experimental equipment, accepted the previous evaluation of the leak as the authorized flight crew representative. The astronaut support personnel closed the squawk with the concurrence of Walker, but unfortunately no one thought to inform the commander or any of the other NASA crew members of the issue. It was an oversight that would come back to haunt Walker.

Atlantis was to be launched in darkness for only the second time in the space shuttle program. As O'Connor settled into the pilot's seat on the right side of the cockpit, he found the cabin bathed in the blinding blue-white xenon lights surrounding the launch complex. The rookie pilot vividly recalled the mood in the flight deck to NASA's Sandra Johnson: "[A] couple of times I looked over there to Brewster to see how he was doing, and I got the full confident business from him. He looked over at me and gives me a thumbs-up and this look like, 'Hey, no sweat. This is working out fine.'"

Once the count reached inside thirty seconds, just prior to main engine start, O'Connor glanced at Shaw again and saw that he had his gloves off, wiping his hands on the legs of his flight suit. "I didn't want to see somebody whose hands are sweating at this point. That was not good for me, and I took a deep dive in the confidence zone there of, 'Oh, my God. My commander—who's been through this before—his hands are sweating. Why aren't mine sweating? I think I need to be nervous now if he's nervous.'" But before he could dwell on it further, the vehicle rumbled to life. "I don't care if I'm nervous or not," thought O'Connor. "Here we go."

"Charlie . . . have we stopped?" Charlie Walker glanced over at the wide-eyed face of his crewmate in disbelief. The thought that immediately occurred to him was, "Where was this guy during *that* lecture?" *Atlantis* had not stopped—in fact, the ship had just shed the two enormous SRBs on either side of the external tank and would continue to accelerate toward space under the power of its three main engines. "No, Rodolfo, everything is fine," Walker reassured him. "We're still on our way—six more minutes." Neri would admit that the experience was somewhat unsettling for a first-time astronaut: "Charlie gave me confidence. It was quite exciting, and I felt a little nervous, but what could I do? Just pray that everything went on well. It was difficult to breathe while the structure made such a loud noise; it rumbled and shook like mad, and I was not sure how long it would last, since time, under such emotional pressure, seemed to pass very slowly. No simulator can get near the real feeling and sensation. I was not trained, nor ready, for that awful experience, but I survived."

Walker was less worried about his own mortality while riding a space shuttle for his third time, concerning himself more with the reactions of his rookie Mexican crewmate. "Rodolfo was not Jake Garn," he shared with NASA's Sandra Johnson, referring to the senator he had flown with on STS-51D in April 1985. "The last time this had happened to me, Jake was sitting there. Jake was a little more conversant. Rodolfo, I think, was nervous, as one would fully expect, but his nervousness kind of equated into, well, he didn't really say very much. Now, this whole time, the ascent, as it's been before, rocking and rolling and going uphill. Kind of occasionally I think I remember looking out the corner of my eye at Rodolfo, and he's holding onto his seat like I'm holding onto my seat and doing nothing else."

With the big brown external tank's supply of fuel nearly exhausted, *Atlantis*'s engines shut down, and the cabin was instantly transformed into a new world for the five crew members who were now in orbit for the first time.

Neri recalled the zero-g training flight on which he had flown, allowing a few brief seconds of weightless acrobatics, but this was different. "Instead of only a few minutes as in the KC-135," he found, "this time in space, in orbit, it was permanent. I was not surprised, but it took me some time to control all my movements."

At first, Neri stayed strapped in his seat, but when he took off his gloves and let go of them, they drifted slowly toward the lockers in front of him as if magically suspended. He admits to having a brief bout with the dreaded space adaptation syndrome, which he described as "very unpleasant but part of the ticket," but once it subsided, he marveled at how quickly the human body adapted to this strange environment. Before long, he was imagining himself as Superman, his childhood hero, soaring around the middeck.

After the crew stowed all their helmets, harnesses, and seats used for launch, Commander Shaw called Neri up to the flight deck. He floated gingerly up through the opening in the flight deck floor and found himself taken aback by the panoramic view through the twin overhead windows. "When I saw the blue surface of our planet, I couldn't say a word. I stayed motionless, speechless, and it was the greatest gift I had in the whole trip." He fully recognized the great privilege he had to see Earth from this vantage point. Over the course of the mission, he would view the planet as a dynamic, living body in a constant state of motion.

Meanwhile, as Walker was getting his postinsertion tasks completed below decks, he took notice of an unusual piece of gear on the orbiter's hatch handle. A padlock had been covertly installed by the mission's commander, unbeknownst to anyone else on the crew. "I don't remember any conversation in flight about it taking place or about it being there," Walker recalled. Shaw would later admit that he had some concern at the time about how unfamiliar they really were with their foreign crewmate. "I'm probably a paranoid kind of guy," Shaw would add. "I don't know if I was supposed to do that or not, but that's a decision I made as being responsible for my crew, and I just did it."

"To me it's perfectly rational," Walker reasoned. "I might have done the same thing if I had found myself in his shoes." Shaw would note that while his fellow NASA crewmates occasionally did a double take at the hatch and shot him an inquisitive look, no one uttered a word, and Neri likely never knew it to be a nonstandard fixture. But after a few days in orbit, with things humming along smoothly, the commander realized his fears were unfounded: "He turned out to be a great guy, and we had a lot of fun on that mission."

Morelos-B was a typical Hughes 376 satellite. With a cylindrical, telescoping body and stabilized dish antenna, it was externally identical to the Morelos-A and many other Hughes-produced spacecraft that had been spun out of shuttle payload bays since operational missions began. While the Mexican-owned satellite was the justification for Neri being aboard, mission specialist Spring would have the prime responsibility to deploy the payload from *Atlantis* on the sixth orbit of the flight.

"I would have loved to be involved in the deployment operations," Neri admits, "but by contract with the Mexican government, that task was the full responsibility of NASA and the assigned personnel." Mexico's first astronaut would float alongside Spring, looking over his shoulder and taking careful measure of the spacecraft's progress toward its deployment:

> *I was with him all the time, observing all the maneuvers, and feeling very excited when the satellite separated from the cargo bay, flying up like a rotating cylinder at fifty revolutions a minute, immediately after a spring mechanism holding it had been released. Then the orbiter carried out a maneuver that took us further away from the satellite, because forty-five minutes after deployment there would be an automatic ignition of its powerful PAM (payload assist module), which would propel it even higher. We had to be a safe distance away by then; otherwise the ignition explosion could probably damage the spaceship.*

Morelos-B would gradually, over two years, drift up to a high geosynchronous orbit parked over its homeland and become a backup for its previously launched sister satellite. Mexico had decided to launch the second spacecraft as a spare due to the rising cost of launch services worldwide, thereby having it in orbit and ready to go years ahead of projected price hikes. Neri later reflected on his great fortune to be so intimately involved in bringing his country into the age of satellite communications: "It was an unforgettable experience."

The crew slept dangling from every available surface in the topsy-turvy weightless world of *Atlantis*'s cabin. Neri later wrote that with his body inside his sleep restraint with head and arms sticking out, "we looked just like turtles." Sleep would come in fits and bursts that first night, and with the steady hum of the orbiter's fans and running equipment, it seemed all too brief of a time before they were all jolted out of bed by overly loud wake-up music piped up from mission control—a NASA tradition that Neri had not been warned about.

With the second day of the mission falling on Thanksgiving, Shaw and his company would be just the second crew to spend the holiday in orbit, following the Skylab 4 crew of twelve years earlier. The support people in NASA's food lab had made a valiant effort to provide the astronauts with space-approved turkey dinners. But by this point the crew had not sufficiently adapted to zero gravity, and their stomachs told them to leave much of the meals in their bags. Neri, however, busily cut open a flat, sealed pouch and extracted a Frisbee-like staple from his home country, recalling thirty years later, "I told NASA. . . , 'Look, NASA, I like you very much. You are very professional, you are very friendly, but you have to understand something. This is going to be the first time a Mexican goes to space, and a Mexican cannot leave Earth without his tortillas.'"

Surprisingly, the flat, circular bread quickly proved to be a great improvement over NASA's previous attempts to package sandwich-making ingredients. Tortillas were easy to handle in weightlessness and produced virtually no crumbs that could float around and get into sensitive equipment. It was an elegant, simple, and, in retrospect, obvious solution to the problem. "I think that this amounted to something of a minor revolution in the U.S. manned space program," Charlie Walker correctly summed up. "The crew saw Rodolfo flying with these flour tortillas and immediately thought, 'Ooh, this may be real good,'" and it was real good. Not only did they taste great, but the crew found it easy to spread whatever they wanted on the tortillas and roll them up to eat without anything floating away.

At one point later in the flight, Walker saw an opportunity that no one else did, tearing a Velcro-held camera from a forward locker. "I was eating my Mexican tortilla rolled as a taco, and he immediately took a photo of me," Neri remembered. "That photo makes all Mexican people very proud, and if it hadn't been for Charlie, who knew the importance of special photos for media and presentations on Earth, perhaps that photo wouldn't exist! Thank you, Charlie!" Mexico's first astronaut had unwittingly inspired the

35. "Something of a minor revolution in the U.S. manned space program." Neri brought tortillas to space for the first time, and the crew found them to be such an eloquent solution to floating crumbs that NASA has included them as a menu item on every manned mission to this day. Courtesy NASA/Retro Space Images.

future of space food. NASA would begin routinely packaging his tortillas on every space shuttle mission, and the practice continues to this day aboard the International Space Station.

The crew of *Atlantis* still had two more satellites to deploy. Aussat was an identical twin of Mexico's Hughes HS-376, but the Satcom K-2 was an ungainly, boxlike package of antennae and solar panels. Powered up to its high perch by the new, larger PAM D-2 solid motor, the RCA Americom satellite was also the first to be launched uninsured. The high costs of insurance after the losses of several spacecraft in recent years led RCA to cover the spacecraft with its own resources. Fortunately for the company, the deployment went off without a hitch, controlled by Spring and Ross, while Neri and Walker busily conducted their own experiments in the middeck.

One of these experiments involved electropuncture, a technique devised to combat space adaptation syndrome that was similar to acupuncture, only with the devilish addition of a low electrical current added. Other Mexican-sponsored experiments included the transportation of nutrients in bean plants from the roots to the stem and leaves; the germination and growth of amaranth, lentil, and wheat seeds; and the reproduction and growth of bacteria.

Neri would, of course, not miss any opportunity to make his way to the overhead flight deck windows when *Atlantis* was passing over his home country. "I took hundreds of photographs of the Mexican territory with a Hasselblad camera, for different studies and purposes," he explained. Not only would his work aid researchers and provide data in the study of the recent earthquake, but the photographs would also be used extensively to share his amazing journey with his countrymen for years afterward.

Commander Shaw unstrapped from his flight deck seat and gently pushed off into a tuck position as he floated headfirst down through the interdeck access way. Checking in on his two payload crewmates, he found Neri upside down as well, hands clasped behind his head, appearing relaxed and confident monitoring one of his experiments. On the far wall by the main hatch, Walker was busy as usual tending to his electrophoresis machine.

A potentially commercial market product, erythropoietin, was being purified in the production chamber by Walker, and it was hoped that this drug could someday be used to treat anemia patients. Samples of the material would be extracted at a panel near the top of the machine by the use of syringes, and Walker would then use a compact chemistry set to test the purity of the drug throughout the mission.

These syringes would be another source of concern for the crew's commander. Like many small objects used in zero gravity, the supersharp needles would often get away from Walker and drift to various places around the orbiter's cabin. "Syringes were found floating in the cabin," Shaw reported postflight. "One uncapped syringe was collected on the flight deck and another syringe was collected on the middeck after it had lost some of its fluid. Even with the aid of gravity, inadvertent inoculation is a very real problem in laboratories whenever syringes are utilized."

But the worst problem for Walker came several days into his routine of daily operations on the machine. Bubbles in the fluid flow had been a known issue over the course of previous CFES flight experiments, and when they started to show themselves this time, Walker was prepared. NASA had allotted a small forward locker for him to bring along spare parts for the experiment, and he had decided to include an extra deaerator pump, specifically to help move the fluid along while absorbing the bubbles out of the solution. While it could serve as a spare, should a pump fail, Walker also planned to plug the pump into the loop to augment the primary ones.

In order to attach the pump into the system, Walker would have to remove the side panel of the CFES unit by means of several dozen quick-release fasteners. With the concurrence of mission control and Shaw, he got started on the task, breaking a seal that was intended to keep any fluid from leaking into the cabin. With the panel removed, he found something quite unexpected—shimmering blobs of liquid sticking to the plumbing of the machine. The "acceptable leak" that had been found and dismissed on launch day now posed a real problem in the zero-g environment.

As he worked within the unit, making the necessary connections for the auxiliary pump, small, quivering spheres of fluid released themselves from the interior of the CFES and came floating out into the cabin. Walker recalled, "I think Mary [Cleave] was a little anxious about that and expressed, 'What's that? Can we keep that from happening again?'" Walker did not think the nontoxic fluid would pose any problem for the crew, but before long the commander took notice of visible white crystals in the shaft of sunlight coming through the side hatch window adjacent to the CFES.

Shaw later reported, "The leaking buffer fluid did indeed find its way into the cabin environment and temporarily incapacitated an eye of one crew member." Years later, Walker added his own mea culpa: "A couple of us afterwards noticed a little bit of an eye irritation, so there might have, in fact, been something, some solution, some salts, maybe from the solution that we were using, which had no toxicity to it as such; it was just a little bit of an irritant. But apparently that did happen after I opened the door and before I could seal the hatch again—or the side panel—with the connections having been made."

Shaw directly linked the potentially serious contamination to the launch-pad leak. "None of the NASA crew was made aware of the situation," he pointed out. "NASA should establish procedures whereby [payload specialists] are not authorized to close any crew squawks or problems that can, in any way, affect the orbiter, payload safety, cabin environment, or any crew member." Shaw wasn't angry at Walker personally; he was more perturbed that the organization's own policies allowed such a sequence of events to take place. Spaceflight is a complex undertaking, and decisions related to safety have to take a wide variety of seemingly unrelated factors into consideration, many of which couldn't possibly be identified by a single crew member.

The additional pump did the trick for Walker's CFES runs, though Shaw reported that the cabin's atmosphere never fully cleared for the remainder of the mission. Walker, on this flight in particular, demonstrated once again the advantages of having a dedicated expert aboard a space mission to operate complicated, specialized equipment. He came to the mission with the knowledge and experience of his previous two and had brought along the proper equipment and skills to adapt to the challenges of pioneering on-orbit pharmaceutical manufacturing.

Jerry Ross summed up his experience of flying with two crew members from outside NASA to Jennifer Ross-Nazzal: "The guys did a great job on orbit. They were always very helpful. They knew that if the operations on the flight deck were very hectic, they stayed out of the way, which is the right thing to do, frankly. But at other times, they would come up onto the flight deck and enjoy the view as well as any of the rest of the crew."

Jerry Ross and Woody Spring sounded like two typical, hard-hatted construction workers in the payload bay of *Atlantis*, working away at building up an open-frame structure of interconnected tubular struts. The experimental payload was devised to examine various construction techniques to be used in building the recently approved space station. The tower would be assembled one triangular bay at a time on rails and slid upward to repeat the procedure for the next section until the entire frame reached high above the shuttle's cargo hold like a foul pole at a baseball park.

Ross and Spring would then break the entire structure down and do the exercise again using different positioning and anchor points, to assess which worked best. Neri did his best to stay out of the way on the flight deck, but he was amazed to see his crewmates through the aft flight deck windows. Through four orbital days and four nights, they repeated the tower construction, and then they moved on to another pyramid structure made up of six much larger tubes connected at four nodes, attached upside down at its tip to the support structure in the bay. During the night passes, with their twin helmet-mounted lights switched on, Neri thought they looked "like glowworms working" in the blackness of space.

Walker also recalled to NASA's Sandra Johnson that it was exciting to watch for the rest of the crew as well:

> I'd just pop up and down through the interdeck to the flight deck and look outside every hour or so for a few minutes and then get back to my work in the middeck, but I can remember that Brewster was really excited. This was one of the not very many moments in flight when I registered the recognition that "Gosh, Brewster is really excited about this." Besides that, he's this kind of the hotshot, ho-hum pilot kind of guy and just taking things on the even keel. But God, he was like, "Wow, isn't that amazing to see them out there?" Yes, it is, Brewster; it really is.

Ross and Spring conducted a second EVA two days later, and this time when they built up the tower, they rode the arm up and topped the structure with an American flag, much like earthbound steelworkers on skyscrapers would. With their feet anchored to a foot restraint on the end of the arm, they would also take turns twirling the forty-five-foot-long structure around in their gloved hands to evaluate the mobility of large assemblies and the forces imparted on the arm and the orbiter.

Exhausted after completing two unprecedented EVAs, the spacewalking pair was helped out of the air lock by the rest of the crew. "Of course, they were received very warmly, and we all congratulated them on a job well done." Neri later wrote. "Dinner was ready and a good steak was waiting for them. They deserved it after doing such a good job." Removing their helmets, Ross and Spring could barely contain their excitement over the sights and experiences of working in open space. After helping the wide-eyed spacewalkers out of their suits and getting the meals prepared, the crew grouped together on the middeck as they did for most dinners. Walker then saw the exhaustion creep into the faces of his crewmates, as they drifted into silence after the big meal. "They just wilted," he remembers. "It was so physically draining that even in as good a shape as Jerry and Woody were in, that both the physical workout as well as, I guess, the emotion and the adrenaline of the experience, they just kind of ran up against a wall."

Astronaut Sally Ride, CAPCOM for much of the mission, took a moment to radio up to Walker, "The CFES people would like to send their congratulations to Charlie on finishing the sample separation, and they express the hope that now that he's not chained to the middeck anymore he can get some window time."

Like most astronauts, Rodolfo Neri Vela would for years after his flight be asked The Question: "How do you go to the bathroom in space?" It was the strangest thing—a question to be expected from children in youthful innocence yet just as often asked by grown adults. Many astronauts would shy away from the details; some would employ a quick, thoroughly rehearsed joke. It was as if the ordinary, earthbound people of the world were searching for something, well, ordinary to be able to relate to the person before them who had flown among the stars.

Neri wasn't thinking about how he might answer this question so many times over when he was squatted on a somewhat normal-looking toilet seat on the middeck of *Atlantis*. He was too busy trying to keep everything that he had just disposed of from getting away and drifting around the cabin like so many of Walker's eye-stinging water blobs. Fortunately, an ingeniously engineered flow of suction air drew his business end to a tight seal against the seat and usually prevented such a mishap.

"You take your trousers down. You try to sit down. You bounce back up," he bluntly explained. Then there was this "suspicious looking hose," to be used to relieve oneself. There was a checklist. There were restraint bars across the thighs. There were levers to push and pull to make the waste go where it needed to go. It could take quite some time to accomplish the whole process, but Neri admits today that it was still some of his most memorable time in space. This was because while he was afforded some privacy from the cabin by means of a tentlike setup of curtains, he had just to his left the small, round porthole of the orbiter's main hatch. "Well, wasn't it nice just to lean forward and look at the stars and think about the mysteries of the universe while you were doing your thing?" he recalls candidly. "Today the toilet is a very important thing on the space station, but they don't have a window with a view!"

He was still finding the effects of zero gravity to be quite funny. With all his crewmates experiencing the usual fluid shift in their bodies, they took on what he calls a "bird legs and moon face" appearance. It was several days into the mission before he started to look somewhat normal again, although he did take to growing a slight beard, which he had avoided back on the planet. Neri still found it odd how his body would orient itself in the absence of gravity—his arms and legs were always bent. As he describes in *The Blue Planet*, he felt like a baby in the "first months of gestation, floating around in our mother's womb."

On the flight day between the two EVA days, while the spacewalkers rested up, Neri had the opportunity to take a call from Mexico's president, Miguel de la Madrid. "The previous year, Marc Garneau, the first Canadian astronaut, had spoken from space with the prime minister of Canada, so in November 1985 it was my turn to have a conversation with the president of Mexico," he remembers. Referring to the exchange as a "very expensive long-distance call," the two countrymen spoke for about five minutes as *Atlantis* raced high above America's neighbor to the south.

The call began with de la Madrid addressing Commander Shaw, who responded fluently in Spanish. Walker took note of this and remembers feeling great pride in being part of what had become an international space program. After the greeting, Shaw floated aside and the president spoke to his emissary in space. The president went on to ask some detailed questions about the experiments Neri was performing and closed by wishing him a successful landing. With a subtle hint of the fame that lay ahead for their first astronaut, de la Madrid offered, "We Mexicans are all waiting for your safe return. We will welcome you home with a great deal of warmth and affection."

With the EVAs complete, the mission entered its final days as meteorologists and controllers kept a wary eye on the weather at Edwards Air Force Base. Unusually heavy rains and high winds were sweeping through high California desert, and even though they were forecast to pass through before landing day, the dry lake bed runways would be anything but dry when *Atlantis* returned to Earth. Ultimately, it was decided to utilize the concrete runway at Edwards rather than going to KSC. *Discovery* had been the last orbiter to land at the Florida launch site on STS-51D, and after suffering a blown tire during rollout, NASA had been cautiously returning shuttles to Edwards with its immense, natural overrun areas.

The crew took some time on their final full day in orbit to take questions from Mexican and American reporters. Neri, when asked if his flight represented the end of his country being considered "underdeveloped," offered that "what this trip really means . . . is that it is true that we can have cooperation with other countries. And in this case, Mexico and the United States have a joint effort to put a Mexican in space. But we must not forget that we still have to work hard to be able to develop properly and be equal, technologically speaking, as some other countries of the world. We just have to make use of all of these opportunities as much as we can."

Charlie Walker reported on the progress of his electrophoresis experiment and offered his view of the future: "The CFES work has been going well. I have gotten all of the primary sample processed; I have some development tests that I have fortunately completed. . . . The indications are here that we're going to have some good results. I think we're making tremendous progress, and we're soon going to be ready to go into the pharmaceutical manufacturing business using space as a major resource."

Rodolfo Neri Vela's arms drooped heavily to his sides. His legs no longer floated easily above the floor, and the tight clamshell helmet he wore for launch and entry made his head feel like a bowling ball on his shoulders. As *Atlantis* rocked to a stop at Edwards, Neri remembers vividly, "I knew we had left space and that the adventure had ended. I felt like a boy without his favorite toy." While he looked forward to the comforts of home, he compared the feeling to that of a tourist returning to "a life full of routine," all the while wondering if and when he might be afforded such an adventure again.

Shaw had settled the space shuttle onto the concrete runway so gently the crew could barely tell they were on the ground. "The landing was very smooth, but again I was taken by surprise when I tried to get up," recalled Neri. "I didn't think it would be so hard. I felt worried for a bit, but I turned round and saw that my crewmates were also having difficulties to get up and stand stable; I felt relieved." As they tried to regain their Earth legs, the crew wobbled around the cabin, steadying themselves against the middeck lockers while recovery crews worked to get the hatch open.

The transition back to life on Earth began with medical checks; hot showers; and fresh, clean flight suits for the crew. While awaiting their flight back to Houston, the seven relaxed over some real Earth food and several cold beers, happily proposing toasts to each other and the success of the mission. The NASA astronauts had no doubt that they would be flying again and looked forward to receiving their gold astronaut pins symbolizing that they had been to space. Walker knew he would return to space as well, after a well-deserved break, while his backup Robert Wood would get his chance to work in orbit.

Rodolfo Neri Vela had no idea what was in store for him upon his return to his home country, but the enormity of his mission would only begin to reveal itself as he was whisked away to his meeting with his president at Los Pinos.

Charlie Walker returned to McDonnell Douglas in St. Louis after the mission to continue working on the development of the large electrophoresis facility for the shuttle's cargo bay. Its first flight was projected for the following year, with Wood flying as payload specialist and Walker backing him up. A new joint-endeavor agreement was signed in early 1986 that would have seen more middeck-mounted CFES experiments, in addition to the large automated facility. Walker fully expected to be flying again with all the new research and development coming ahead and even looked ahead to the proposed space station and its potential as an orbiting factory of commercial pharmaceutical material. As he explained in his NASA Oral History interview, "The Space Station was going to be a platform for the production of pharmaceutical materials. We would launch via Shuttle exchangeable packages of tanks and whatever else, tanks of liquids in it, that would attach to our apparatus at the Space Station and we would be paying rent to the U.S. government or NASA for that part of the Space Station, the power, etc., that we would use, as a service for the medical, biomedical industry in this country or internationally."

But he could have no idea, at the end of 1985, that not only would *Atlantis*'s mission be the last for Charlie Walker; it would also be the last for the electrophoresis project from McDonnell Douglas. Both competitive industry pressures and technical advances in the process would conspire to bring the project to a halt. Ortho Pharmaceuticals had backed out of the program already, so the organization began courting other drug companies in the United States and abroad that might be interested in pursuing the erythropoietin product. As Walker continued his work on the technicalities of developing the zero-g processing equipment, the business case for the drug product was beginning to unravel.

There were tremendous advances throughout the eighties in genetic engineering, and new companies were coming along doing research and development in this arena. Using genetically engineered cell lines, new technology was allowing the same enzyme the CFES machine produced to be manufactured in large quantities on Earth, without the risk and expense of spaceflight. The industry was beginning to realize that this was the future and that one could use the process "with almost probably any other kind of cell that you could genetically modify to produce the hormone or the enzyme that you wanted to see produced," remembers Walker.

With the loss of *Challenger*, it would be years before the company could be able to get back into space and continue its research with electrophoresis. Even when the shuttle program began flying once again, Walker believed that experimental commercial projects were never given the priority they once had. After being one of the first companies to approach NASA with a proposal that could benefit their own business interests while bolstering utilization of the space shuttle, the two organizations were now on different paths. With the near-term shuttle manifest largely committed to the DOD and the backlog of shuttle-dedicated payloads such as the Hubble Space Telescope and Spacelab, McDonnell Douglas soon terminated the program.

Having spent a total of twenty days in space over an unprecedented three missions as a payload specialist, Walker moved into various management roles over the next two decades. Remaining with McDonnell Douglas through its merger with the Boeing Company, he retired in 2005. Since then, he has remained close to his spaceflight experiences and fellow astronauts through the Association of Space Explorers, the National Space Society, and the Challenger Center. Walker is a regular guest at various space memorabilia and autograph shows and is warmly received not only by his fellow space shuttle flyers but also by the legendary figures of the Apollo program.

Robert Wood, after losing his chance for a spaceflight, continued engineering work for the company and moved into critical management roles as well. Wood's son Munro reflected that while his father most certainly regretted not flying, he didn't spend precious time contemplating it: "There was a picture of him in the flight suit that NASA took that we had framed in the house, so certainly it wasn't something that was hidden away like 'Never speak of this' or anything like that. I guess it was one of those things like, 'Well, that was fun while it lasted, but now I'm going to move on and do something else with my life,' and he did."

While Wood could not discuss some of the classified defense projects he later became involved in at McDonnell Douglas and Boeing, he shared his fascination of science, computers, and space with his children frequently. In his forties, he found a new challenge in triathlon competition and would take his children along on ten- sometimes twenty-mile road bike treks while he trained. Wood regularly rose before dawn to swim laps around a small lake nearby their home, as Munro recalls: "By the time he turned fifty he was consistently placing at the top of his age group, so he pretty much got in the best shape of his life right around that age. He was never the fastest runner in the field during the triathlons, but he was so much faster than all of his competition on the bike that he was able to make up for his slow run. But he's always been that kind of person that when he sees something worth going for, he goes for it all the way."

Wood did keep one piece of memorabilia from his NASA days—the old powder-blue flight suit he was issued in training for STS-61B. "He would wear that to Halloween parties sometimes," his son recalled. "That was kind of cool. I think people got a kick out of it." While his father had a great sense of humor and zipped on the suit somewhat tongue in cheek, he did allow himself a bit of pride in wearing it. Munro Wood remembers a sense of, "Well, this is the best Halloween costume I can have, because it's not fake. This is the real thing."

Tragically, at the age of fifty-one, the father of five was killed in February 2009 when a drunk driver slammed into the back of his car on Interstate 70 near St. Louis. "He didn't make enemies where he went; he made friends," Munro reflected. "All of his children are very proud of him, and we're just hoping that we can leave behind a legacy as great as he left for us."

Even today, more than thirty years after his spaceflight, Dr. Rodolfo Neri Vela is a widely recognized and respected public figure in Mexico. He is routinely invited for interviews on television and radio, and having authored several textbooks in the subject of telecommunications, he is a regular guest lecturer at many universities. "I cannot complain, for I have received love and admiration from millions of my countrymen and countrywomen of all ages and several generations," he rationalizes. "And at the same time, this is a challenge for me, in the sense that I feel the responsibility to keep working, to be updated in the space technology field and do things in the education field." Still the only astronaut to have flown as a representative of Mexico, his image has been featured on postage stamps in the year of the flight and again in 2010, celebrating the twenty-fifth anniversary of his mission.

Upon his return to Earth, Neri put his newfound fame to use in an attempt to establish a formal Mexican space agency. That initial effort was unsuccessful, but several years later, he joined with a large group of engineers and scientists and was able to convince Congress to approve the proposal. But he still considers his major achievements to be in the field of education, teaching for many years at the National University of Mexico and doing research with his students. As he puts it, he has had the great responsibility of "being the national voice on space exploration, satellite technology, and motivating thousands and thousands of young people to continue their studies." Dr. Neri also sees an important legacy in his mission of over three decades ago:

> *The program opened the door to several countries that could start doing research in microgravity with their own national astronauts. Mexico gained a lot; in spite of some critics who are never absent when an individual or a nation thrive to explore new opportunities towards progress, especially in an underdeveloped country. Our Mexican mission, the only one so far, gave happiness and pride to the whole population, inspired millions of kids and young people to study harder, to learn more, and to*

dare to reach goals that apparently are difficult or impossible. Our trip to space opened the eyes of many Mexicans and they learnt about the benefits of space science and technology. It was very important in the history of Mexico, as it has also been in the history of all those countries that could have their first national astronaut.

Ricardo Peralta was very interested in furthering Mexico's space research after the STS-61B mission, but as the program was halted after the *Challenger* accident, the efforts faltered and were eventually abandoned. Neri and Peralta rarely crossed paths in the decades following Mexico's first spaceflight. Prior to his death in 2017, Peralta worked as a researcher at the Instituto de Ingeniería of the National University of Mexico, while Neri would eventually retire from the Facultad de Ingeniería. Although both bodies were within the university, they had separate directors and did not interact very often. As Neri reflected, "Looking back in time, I would have loved to share many impressions, thoughts, and ideas with Ricardo, as well as to give some presentations together, but the circumstances did not allow it."

Neri today expresses some frustration with the fact that he remains the only astronaut to have flown on behalf of Mexico. Blaming "ignorance and lack of political interest," he has been an outspoken critic of the fact that so many of his countrymen in technical fields are forced to leave the country for better opportunities, while denials of such an exodus of national talent come from the government. Neri has met countless young students through his teaching and public appearances, and many of them tell him they would love to be part of such an adventure.

He gives them all the encouragement he can while keeping to a hectic schedule discussing science, technology, and education policy wherever possible. Sometimes blunt, often controversial, Neri shares his story with childlike happiness and a self-deprecating sense of humor. He is eternally propelled by the unexpected, wondrous, terrifyingly unforgettable experience that came his way half a lifetime ago. Today, Rodolfo Neri Vela still holds great optimism that others will follow him. "I hope sometime soon we will have our second Mexican astronaut, wearing with pride on his or her space suit the Mexican national emblem," he says. "It is a privilege as a citizen but also a huge responsibility."

14. On the Way to Disney World

This is really tough on the families. The career guys, most
of the wives married test pilots, so they knew what they were
getting into. You look at the PSS, and they married engineers, not
this guy that's going to go sit on 4 million pounds of
explosives so they can light it!

Robert Cenker

At the RCA Astro Electronics division in East Windsor, New Jersey, Bob Cenker was shuffling through some mundane paperwork one afternoon in March 1985. He had just wrapped up his responsibilities managing the systems integration on the company's Satcom K-2 communication satellite and was looking forward to a few months of downtime before taking on a new assignment with the fledgling space station program.

An accomplished aerospace engineer, Cenker had joined RCA almost thirteen years earlier and worked closely with NASA engineers and astronauts on the Satcom series of communications satellites. He even leveraged this experience in applying to be an astronaut himself on two occasions. Both times, for reasons unknown to him, he was rejected early in the process. For now, he would live his dreams vicariously through his NASA colleagues, watching the fruits of his labor soar into orbit aboard the space shuttle in a few months' time.

As he shared with an audience at KSC in March 2015, "I enjoy being an engineer. I like to build things. But I need some fire and smoke in my life once in a while. I need a launch. So I've spent my career working on commercial communication satellites because we typically launch one every two, two and a half years. So every couple of years, I get an opportunity to do that."

As he busied himself, the phone rang. "Bob Cenker," he spoke quickly, as he pushed up his oversized glasses and immediately recognized the voice of the division's vice president of engineering. "Hey, Bob, remember that payload specialist slot we talked about? Well, we got it approved. Are you still interested in flying?" Stunned, Cenker blurted out, "Gee, let me think about that—yes!" Rather than explaining further, the voice on the other end of the phone left him with a cliff-hanger. "Okay, I'll get back to you" were his parting words as he hung up, leaving the bewildered engineer to wonder what exactly had just occurred.

"I was a wreck. I couldn't work," Cenker told the authors. Not yet fully comprehending the news, his mind spun with questions. He pushed aside the stack of reports on his desk, swiveled out of his chair, and marched up to the vice president's office. There he found the vice president's smiling secretary, who let on that she already knew why the young engineer was there. She sent him directly into the office, where it became immediately clear to Cenker how real the offer was. "Now what?" he asked his boss. "You can't just lay this on me. How long is the line? Who do I kill to get to the front of the line?" he joked. The VP's response shocked him once again. "But we haven't picked your backup yet," he told Cenker. "My backup? Are you telling me that as long as I pass the physical, I'm flying?" Cenker could barely contain himself. "Yeah," the boss said.

It finally dawned on him that the next "fire and smoke" he might experience was going to be propelling a space shuttle that *he* would be sitting atop. His work on the space station would have to wait. Bob Cenker, the twice-denied astronaut hopeful, was going into space.

Growing up near Uniontown, Pennsylvania, Robert J. Cenker was always fascinated by anything that flew. As a young boy, he would nail pieces of wood together in the rough shape of an airplane and toss them into the air. Lacking any semblance of aerodynamic stability or control, they would come crashing down to Earth, leaving him to ponder why his glider didn't fly. He later found that he had a good head for mathematics, and once he got settled on attending Pennsylvania State University, aerospace engineering seemed to suit his interests and abilities. This would, in his mind, fill one of the prerequisites to becoming an astronaut, the other being joining the military to become a jet pilot.

"I was not a genius, but I had good grades," he recalled. Despite his natural abilities and burning desire to pursue an aerospace career, one subject stood in his way:

> *The general consensus was that the "aero" courses—the fluid dynamics, were the weed-out courses. They were going to separate the men from the boys in aerospace engineering. And I poo-pooed that. Not gonna be a problem. I can learn anything I set my mind to. I almost flunked! And it wasn't for lack of effort—I actually felt badly for my professor because he spent a lot of time with me. The head of the aerospace engineering department had both of us in his office trying to explain what was going on that this guy was flunking an honors student. I came into the program as an honors student, and I literally got a D in the first course in aerodynamics. And God's honest truth, I think the reason they passed me was because we all knew I was going into the space program and that spacecraft dynamics, orbital mechanics, which is what I would wind up doing for a career, had nothing to do with fluid dynamics.*

Still drawn to the physical sensations of flight while at Penn State, Cenker spent his free time launching himself into the air by any means possible. He worked out on the pool's diving boards and introduce himself to bouncing and flipping high above the gym's trampolines, experiencing a precious few seconds of stomach butterfly–producing weightlessness. Cenker figured due to his imperfect eyesight that this was about as close to real flying as he would ever get, since the military would accept nothing less than twenty-twenty.

When graduation came in 1970, entry-level jobs for a young aerospace engineer were scarce. With his bulletin board wallpapered with rejection letters from all the big-name companies, Cenker eventually settled on a position with Westinghouse in Pittsburgh, Pennsylvania, designing nuclear reactors for the U.S. Navy. And he *hated* it. He spent a year in the job before he learned that with the coming space shuttle program, NASA might be looking for scientists and engineers for the astronaut corps. So he formulated another plan to make himself more attractive to the space agency when the time eventually came to apply. Since his eyesight would preclude him from becoming a military pilot, he figured that perhaps experience as a rear-seated flight officer or navigator might get him some time in the air, operating as an integral part of an aircrew.

Cenker took physicals for both the U.S. Air Force and the U.S. Navy flight, but when he went to talk to the navy recruiter, he could sense that the military had other ideas for him, given his experience. While they would be willing to grant his first choice of aviation, he was reluctant to sign up.

The navy wanted me to sign a document that says, "Oh by the way, if you flunk out of flight school for any reason, we can put you anywhere we want to." And I said, "No—hell no, that ain't happening—this is not flying by any stretch of the imagination." I'm thinking with a year of mechanical design in nuclear submarines? I know where they're going to put me, and I don't want to go there! Because I was realistic enough to know that you never know when something would come up that you wouldn't make it in flight school.

With the option of joining the military now far less attractive and still desperate to get out of the Westinghouse job, Cenker accepted an apprenticeship with his old advisor at Penn State working on spacecraft dynamics and orbital mechanics. Cenker would earn his masters in aerospace engineering by 1973 and was again having difficulty finding a job appropriate for his skills. Commiserating with his professor one day, he was asked if he had looked at RCA. "RCA builds TV sets!" Cenker responded incredulously. "I'm going to go from nuclear reactors to TV sets?"

In fact, the Astro Electronics division of the RCA Company also built satellites, going all the way back to the TIROS I weather platform launched in April 1960. The division, based near Princeton, New Jersey, was in the process of developing and building Satcom I, one of the world's first geosynchronous communications satellites. The project would open a whole new business line for RCA as a satellite manufacturing and operating company. "And so the fact that I had no experience meant nothing, because nobody did," remembers Cenker. "I interviewed for the position, I worked on Satcom I, and as the Satcom series and commercial communication satellite business exploded, my career just got sucked along with it. I couldn't have timed it any better."

While a number of Satcoms had been launched on expendable launch vehicles, RCA had booked two Satcom spacecraft for launch aboard the space shuttle missions in 1985, reimbursing NASA for "launch services associated with" each payload. One of those services associated with launch was the accommodation of an RCA payload specialist. Ironically, of the potential justifications for having a company representative on board, none of them included any responsibilities associated with the RCA-built satellites.

RCA's Advanced Technology Lab, the U.S. Air Force's Rome Air Development Center, and RCA Astro had worked together on a new infrared camera. "They came up with this staring focal plane," explains Cenker, "which you can now buy in your local camera shop, but it was brand new thirty-some years ago." The concept was a great advance over the current state of the art, in which infrared imagery was taken by a scanning method. This required the scanner to be ratcheted back and forth repeatedly, and if one were looking for a transient event, it could easily be missed, depending on where the device was in its sweep.

The new device was extremely sensitive. "The staring focal planes that they had—and I think this is about a thousand by thousand pixels—typically you could only see a difference of one degree Celsius from pixel to pixel," Cenker explained. "The one that the guys came up with would see one-tenth of a degree Celsius. When we played with it on the ground, if I held out my arm, you could see the blood vessels in my arm, because they were a different temperature than the rest of my arm. It was fascinating playing with it on the ground in training." The objective of flying the infrared camera was to observe various phenomena in space such as aurora, volcanoes, zodiacal light, and the moon to evaluate what the new invention was capable of seeing.

RCA had designed and built the payload bay television cameras for the space shuttle, and the labs were able to package the infrared camera into the standard camera housing, which would occupy the aft starboard corner of the cargo hold during the mission. While the technology did have potential military applications, the results of the test were considered to be RCA's proprietary information rather than anything classified. "At the time, any data that a NASA astronaut took was public information," surmises Cenker. "RCA didn't want this to be public information, so they wanted to send one of their engineers along to take the data."

And so when RCA Americom—the division that would own and operate the Satcom K series satellites—signed the launch agreement with NASA, they included the provision for the payload specialist. And once the word got out, Cenker would make it abundantly clear to anyone who would listen that he was interested in the job. "I used to joke with RCA management— joke nothing—I used to *tell* them," Cenker says with a chuckle, "if you guys were really serious about the space program, you'd be flying a payload specialist, and oh, by the way, I'll go." But unfortunately for him, RCA had already selected their man.

In December 1984 Cenker was sent to JSC to brief the flight crews on the Satcom satellites they would be deploying on their missions the following year. While there, he ran across another group of RCA employees, one of whom was a PhD physicist from the company's Advanced Technology Laboratory. He introduced himself to Cenker as RCA's designated payload specialist for the infrared camera. "Congratulations! I hate your guts!" Cenker retorted, only half kidding. Somewhat deflated by this introduction, he shared with his RCA peers that he had long dreamed of spaceflight, even confiding that he had applied to NASA without success. Before long, the awkward conversation concluded, leaving Cenker wondering how management could have overlooked him.

With the conclusion of his work on the systems integration on the latest Satcom, Cenker anticipated being transferred to work on RCA's slice of the newly announced space station project. The company was awarded a work package to develop both a coorbiting platform—a free-flying vehicle that would provide experiment support free of the manned environment of the station—and a polar-orbiting platform to host civilian and defense payloads launching from the Vandenberg launch site in California.

Not long after the trip to Houston, RCA's corporate headquarters placed an inquiry with the Americom division, asking about the pending flight of their company's representative. Being far removed from the day-to-day operations, they were curious what his role was at Astro Electronics. The problem was, unbeknownst to the management, their payload specialist worked at the Advanced Technology Laboratory, not at Astro. "No" was the answer from the company's leadership. "If RCA is flying somebody in space, that person has to work at the space center." Cenker later learned that a simple solution was proposed—RCA offered to transfer the researcher

36. RCA's payload specialist for STS-61C Bob Cenker. After applying to NASA's astronaut corps twice and being turned down, he jumped at the chance to fly with the company's Satcom satellite on the last mission before the *Challenger* disaster. Courtesy NASA/Retro Space Images.

into the Astro division for a year or two in order to satisfy this requirement. The researcher declined.

"Obviously, it must not have meant too much to him," assumes Cenker, "because if somebody had told me, 'You've got to transfer to Timbuktu for two years, and you'll fly on the shuttle,' I'd say, 'Where do I sign?' And I'm gone." Apparently, that one man's decision opened the door for Cenker. In many ways, Cenker was the ideal candidate: "I was manager of systems engineering on the satellite that was deployed, so if anything went wrong with that spacecraft on deployment, I was the logical choice. Because I was in systems, I can understand the infrared camera. I can understand its workings. And we had already delivered the Satcom satellite. My work on that program was essentially done. But I hadn't picked up any responsibilities yet on the space station, so if I disappeared for six months of training, nobody would know I was gone."

From that unforgettable day in March 1985 when he marched into the vice president's office and got the news, he became known throughout the company as the guy who was going to space. He could hardly believe the sequence of events that led him to a point in his life to realize his childhood dream. Once the company had announced his selection, along with fellow engineer Gerard (Jerry) Magilton as his backup, he would repeatedly be asked around Astro how he managed to be selected. On a few occasions, he would use the term "dumb luck." But after a while, RCA management came to him and insisted, "Please don't say dumb luck. We did not pull your name out of a hat! Say right place at the right time."

Payload specialist Bob Cenker would happily oblige them.

Robert "Hoot" Gibson was one of the best pilots to have ever come to NASA. A former navy combat and test pilot, he excelled at everything he undertook and had fun doing it with an infectious sense of humor. His crew of Charles Bolden, Steve Hawley, George "Pinky" Nelson, and Franklin Chang-Diaz were an extremely tight, fun-loving team, despite coming from a wide variety of backgrounds. Hawley and Nelson were both astronomers; Bolden, the mission's pilot, was a Marine Corps test pilot; and Chang-Diaz had earned a PhD in applied plasma physics. Gibson, Hawley, and Nelson each had one spaceflight under their belts, and Hawley had also been aboard *Discovery* when its engines shut down in the program's first launch abort.

Easygoing as he was, Gibson had one firm rule, the infamous Hoot's Law. As the seasoned navy pilot would instill into his crew, the law stated a simple observation based on his decades of flying air- and spacecraft—no matter how bad things are, one can always make them worse. "There are lots of ways that you can," explains Gibson, "but one of the easiest traps to fall into is rushing." He would impose strict cockpit discipline whenever a critical task needed to be accomplished, and if he were to throw a switch that might mean life or death, Gibson insisted that another crew member verified he had the correct switch first.

In addition to RCA's Satcom K-I satellite, NASA had originally manifested a Hughes Leasat spacecraft for deployment during the mission. Hughes engineer Greg Jarvis, who had previously been bumped from the STS-51D crew to accommodate Senator Jake Garn, would serve as payload specialist. Following unrelated failures of the two previous Leasats deployed from the space shuttle, the payload was removed from the mission, but NASA retained Jarvis on the crew to finally satisfy the Hughes launch agreement from the prior year. He would perform fluid-transfer experiments to test satellite fuel systems that his company was developing for future spacecraft.

Following a somewhat nerve-racking medical exam, both Cenker and Jerry Magilton settled into their training routine. "I think when I arrived, they gave me a stack of videotapes and books to read," Cenker said, "because before we can start training, you have to have all of this background information before you're smart enough to learn." But there was never a lack of support from his NASA colleagues in learning the basics of flying aboard the orbiter. In his recollection, those in the Astronaut Office welcomed them as part of the team almost immediately: "I was amazed how well I was accepted. I fully expected there to be some level of bad feelings but didn't find anything like that. You know they talked about the NASA family," Cenker recalled, "most of whom would have given their right arm to fly, all of whom knew that I had literally walked in off the street and was flying. And I didn't get one hint of resentment or hard feelings."

In many ways, Cenker's previous exposure to the people and facilities of JSC benefitted him as a trainee. Being an engineer from the satellite industry, he already understood many of the technical aspects of flying the mission, and his instructors found him to be highly qualified. "They told me that, if push came to shove, and they had somebody from within the space business, that they could probably train them in a month," he shares. "Because you're not learning to fly the orbiter, you have no vehicle responsibilities." He still laughs today at the memory of a reporter from his hometown calling the space center to discuss his upcoming flight. When the writer asked what his training was going to consist of, the NASA spokesperson replied, "Well, we're gonna teach him what not to touch."

One afternoon not long after they began working together, Cenker and Greg Jarvis joined Hoot Gibson and the others for the traditional crew photograph. The five NASA astronauts and their payload specialists posed in the light-blue flight suits they would wear on launch day. But within just a few days of having the official photo taken, Gibson received a call from George Abbey to bring his crew across the JSC campus to his office in building 1.

When he closed the door behind them and sat down in front of the stone-faced director of flight crew operations, Abbey wasted no time getting to the issue. One of his crew members would not be flying aboard *Columbia* with them in December.

Jake Garn had set the precedent, with his flight aboard *Discovery*, that a congressional observer indeed had the right and privilege to fly aboard a NASA spacecraft. Often derided by the press and therefore the public as "the ultimate government junket," these missions were not without their detractors both inside and outside the space agency. Don Fuqua, chairman of the House Science and Technology Committee, was notably outspoken against the practice of sending politicians aboard the shuttle. He had himself turned down an offer from NASA administrator James Beggs to fly, as he shared with NASA's Bill Harwood: "I said, 'Jim, I don't want to go. Even if you told me I could go, I don't want to go. And I'll tell you why. I don't think I have any business being there. This is still a very hostile environment. I'm not even sure you ought to have the Teacher in Space Program going. I don't think I ought to bump somebody to go take a ride in space. I would love to! But I don't think I have any business doing that.'" But once Garn had successfully navigated the media minefield in the run-up to his flight, others within the Capitol Hill hierarchy took notice and began to entertain their own desires to follow in his footsteps—in particular one junior congressman from Florida, Bill Nelson.

Nelson was a student at Melbourne High School in the fall of 1957 when the Soviet Union placed the tiny Sputnik satellite into orbit, and like most youth of the day, he followed the progress of the early space missions. Being just south of Cape Canaveral's launchpads, Nelson watched firsthand as his hometown transformed into the center stage of a great new technological endeavor, yet he never saw himself destined to be part of it.

Nelson earned a law degree from the University of Virginia and joined the U.S. Army Reserves in 1965. He would serve two of his six years in the military on active duty and left the army in 1971 with the rank of captain. After practicing law in Melbourne, he was elected by his constituents to a seat in the U.S. Congress in 1978. His district included the Cape Canaveral peninsula and the surrounding communities populated largely by space industry workers, many remaining from the Apollo days. As NASA began painting the picture throughout the 1970s that the shuttle would open the new frontier of space to ordinary citizens from all walks of life, Nelson took notice.

He attended the launch of STS-1 in April 1981 and curiously read a report from James Beggs detailing the requirements for flying "observers" aboard the shuttle. At the time, it seemed a bit of a stretch to suggest that a politician would fit the description of a communicator, whose sole purpose would be to enhance the public's understanding of manned spaceflight, but that did not deter Nelson.

The congressman rationalized that he indeed met all the basic requirements and set out to prepare himself as much as possible should the opportunity ever present itself. He exercised in the gym and ran daily. He devoured every source of information he could find on NASA's programs and the space shuttle system. He leveraged his position in Congress to garner familiarization flights in high-performance jet fighters such as the F-15 and F-16, pulling as many blood-draining g-forces as he could stand. He wrote directly to Beggs, taking a gamble by overtly requesting a flight. But after two years with no response, the congressman thought better of pushing too hard and let things play out for a time.

Nelson was single-minded in his desire to accomplish what he could not even dream of growing up around the cape in the 1960s. As was the case with Jake Garn, it was well known around Washington that Nelson was pressing for a spaceflight. In early 1985 he challenged a senior congressman for the chairmanship of the Space Subcommittee and won. This did not only solidify his influence over the concerns of his home community;

he also knew that only the respective House and Senate chairpersons were being considered for spaceflights.

Some in NASA leadership were dubious following some adverse public reaction over Garn's flight and his less-than-satisfactory reaction in adapting to microgravity. Nevertheless, the space agency could not ignore the influence that potential congressional participants could have on the future promotion and funding of space activities. As the head of the powerful NASA oversight committee, Nelson was ideally placed in the budget-authorization world for Beggs to reconsider the benefits of granting him his chance to fly. The two would meet face-to-face a few months after Jake Garn flew in April 1985, and Beggs seemed to imply that a formal offer was not far off. In Nelson's 1988 memoir, *Mission*, he shares the letter he received from the NASA administrator dated 6 September, reading in part, "Given your NASA oversight responsibilities, we think it appropriate that you consider an inspection tour and flight aboard the shuttle. While we will be flying quite often in the coming year, we will have to work out with you a mutually acceptable date. There will be a relatively short period of training which we can work out between your office and the Johnson Space Center to fit your schedule."

Later that month, Nelson was already in Houston to undergo the same medical tests Cenker and Magilton had endured. He was sealed up in "the bag," a pressurized fabric sphere that was, early in the program, presented as a rescue device for crew members stranded aboard a stricken orbiter. With a limited number of complete space suits on board, astronauts in shirtsleeves could be hauled across to a rescue shuttle for return to Earth, but the bag also proved to be a convenient test for claustrophobia. Nelson, sealed up in the warm, quiet sphere, happily drifted off to sleep.

The congressman would continue to split his time between Houston and Washington throughout his training. He had told NASA that given several important votes coming up, his preference would be to fly either on *Columbia*'s December mission or on *Challenger*'s January flight, STS-51L. Beggs wanted Nelson to have as much time to train as possible, so on 27 September he called and offered to have him fly on *Challenger* with schoolteacher Christa McAuliffe. Nelson accepted the decision of NASA's leadership yet had confidence that he could be ready for the December flight. Behind the

37. Florida Representative Bill Nelson in "the bag," a proposed rescue sphere intended to transfer crew members from a stricken orbiter to a rescue shuttle. Tolerating the close confines was one of many tests he needed to pass before being cleared for spaceflight. Courtesy NASA/Retro Space Images.

scenes, though, the decision makers at JSC had other concerns about flying the eager young politician.

When Gibson and his crew were summoned to Abbey's office, it quickly became apparent that the administrator had been overruled. The gruff astronaut boss informed them bluntly that they were going to take on Congressman Nelson and make the best of it. Greg Jarvis, with the Leasat satellite no longer aboard the mission, would be moved to STS-51L instead of the lawmaker. As Charlie Bolden shared in his NASA Oral History interview, "Mr. Abbey, in his infinite wisdom, decided that Hoot Gibson and his crew of merry men could better handle the congressman than most other people out there, so he switched us." However, Cenker recalls that the decision, as it was explained to him at the time, was made for more than just his crew's ability to accept Nelson into their fold:

> *McAuliffe was [assigned to STS-51L]. I think what happened was when they brought Bill on board, they had two non-aerospace professionals—*

Bill and the teacher. They had two aerospace engineers—me and Greg. Greg no longer has any attachment to 61C; there's no Hughes spacecraft on board, so it doesn't make any difference where he flies. On the other hand, if you flip-flop him and Bill Nelson, you would at least have Christa flying with another PS, but one that has an aerospace background, rather than having two total outsiders, and two reasonably well-trained individuals, being Greg and I, on the one flight and then those two on the other one. They just swapped those two around. It wasn't like Greg was bumped for Bill Nelson; it was a logical choice, the way it turned out.

Nelson was back in Washington DC on 4 October when Jesse Moore, NASA's head of the shuttle program, called to inform him that he would be flying aboard *Columbia* in December. Nelson took it on himself to place a call to his new commander and introduce himself, as Hoot Gibson recalled to NASA's Sandra Johnson, "We are 'yes sir-ing' each other and 'Mr. Congressman' and 'Mr. Commander.'" After a few minutes of this, Nelson asked formally if he could refer to him as "Hoot." Once that was agreed on, Nelson insisted, "You must call me Bill."

The congressman would continue to go out of his way to try to fit in with his NASA colleagues. More than anything, he really wanted to be considered "one of the boys." George "Pinky" Nelson, who would take a major role in watching over him throughout his training, would regard him as "a model payload specialist," being in better physical shape than many of them and displaying an eagerness to get in the middle of things and be helpful. Sometimes, though, his enthusiasm would get the best of him, and he might not have recognized the limits of his experience. Pinky Nelson remembers what he considered to be one of the most protective things he did for his same-name trainee—holding his two fellow mission specialists back from virtually strangling him.

"Every once in a while, when you're inexperienced—he would just kind of get in the way," Pinky recalled in his NASA Oral History interview. "And being the personality that Bill had, [he] wasn't very good at getting himself out of being in the way, so there were times when you just had to kind of get him out of the way, and you had to be a little careful about how you did that." Steve Hawley would usually lose his patience first and move in to relocate the rookie crew member, only to be restrained by Pinky or Franklin. "It's just not worth it Steve!" Chang-Diaz would warn him. After a few weeks of training with the congressman, "It's just not worth it Steve!" would be repeated many times over, to the laughter of everyone within earshot.

Bill Nelson found that the astronauts tended to keep their emotions to themselves, and discussions about personal beliefs or politics often took a back seat to technical issues. The inherent danger of flying in space had been long accepted by the professional astronauts who expected and even desired to take on multiple rides into orbit. They did, however, possess a wicked, sometimes even morbid, sense of humor, and Gibson's crew stood out among their peers in this regard.

Given that he came to the crew so late in their training cycle and the fact that he had so little to offer the mission in terms of technical knowledge or operational experience, Bill Nelson got ribbed, hazed, and tormented by this court of jesters more than any other payload specialist who had come along. On the day Gibson was to take him up for a training flight in a T-38, the rest of the crew would put in bids for his personal effects should he not return. Even Nelson's openness about his religious faith was not off-limits, and Gibson recalled a plan to fire a burst from one of the orbiter's big thrusters in space and joke to Nelson that they'd just hit an angel. "We'd say, 'Oh, Bill, don't look; we just hit one. There's feathers everywhere. It's horrible, don't look!'" Gibson laughed. Fortunately for Nelson, his crew-mates never had a chance to hatch the plot.

Bob Cenker approached Gibson and the crew one day with an unusual request—he wanted to go on a second KC-135 zero-g flight. The Vomit Comet was not a favorite training event of many of the NASA astronauts, let alone the neophyte payload specialists, but Cenker loved it. It was the very thing he had dreamed about all those years ago on the diving boards and tram-polines of his alma mater; only, the airplane did a better job of allowing him to float freely. His first flight aboard the jet had been cut short due to equipment malfunctions, and he only got thirty cycles of weightlessness, rather than the forty prescribed in the training syllabus.

"Oh yeah, Bob," his commander said, "We'd like you to get to the point so you're comfortable with that so that you all actually enjoy it!" Steve Hawley, who had been aboard that flight with Cenker, rolled his eyes and told Gibson, "If he had had any more fun, we would have had to have shot him to get him off the airplane!" And so it was that Cenker found himself aboard the old converted cargo plane once again, along with his backup Jerry Magilton, Bill Nelson, Greg Jarvis, and teacher-in-space selectees Christa McAuliffe and Barbara Morgan. Over the course of the flight, one of the most notable photos of this new age of "ordinary citizens" traveling into space was taken. Soaring through the long, padded cabin of the KC-135 that afternoon, five of the fledgling space flyers—two engineers, two teachers, and one congressman—all joined hands and flew in formation as the cameras caught their laughing, childlike faces in their new, weightless world.

As their training progressed, Bill Nelson took his oversight responsibilities as seriously as he took learning the mountain of new information being thrust his way daily. The congressman was constantly taking notes on various aspects of his training, the safety culture at the agency, and any concerns he could pry out of the tight-lipped professional astronauts. Always mindful of their desire to fly in space as many times as possible, he would occasionally find real issues behind their death-defying humor that they were afraid to bring forward. Other NASA people he came in contact with during their training would also express their opinions in subtle ways.

One of their training tasks was a firefighting drill. A silver-suited instructor ignited a large pool of jet fuel and told the crew he was going to show them how to walk through it. The firefighter gave Bill Nelson the hose and had him set it to "fog." As Nelson would later share in his book *Mission*, "Instantly, a great cloud of fog spewed out in front of me, and I was able to walk right up to the blazing inferno without being scorched." Then the instructor took things a step further, having the crew turn their hoses to a steady stream, parting the searing flames "just like the Red Sea was parted for Moses."

The fire chief would explain to the crew how to sweep the stream of water back and forth to provide an escape path through the pool of flames. Wondering for a moment what he might be told to do next, Nelson was relieved when the instructor allowed them to back off without actually attempting the daredevil maneuver. When the exercise ended, he approached the silver-clad fireman and asked how effective such a procedure would be on the 195-foot level of the launch gantry, and he was met with a roll of the eyes from the chief. The congressman would come to suspect that many of the emergency drills the crew practiced would only be of use in an extremely benign contingency, not a catastrophic failure on the launchpad involving millions of pounds of volatile rocket fuels.

Nelson had also settled on an appropriate experiment to work on during the mission, a cancer research project sponsored by the University of Alabama. This payload would join a multitude of experiments aboard *Columbia*, including three that were part of NASA's Shuttle Student Involvement Program. With the Leasat satellite removed from the manifest, the now nearly empty cargo bay was filled by a hodgepodge of experiments, including the second Materials Science Laboratory; a Hitchhiker payload; and thirteen getaway specials, all but one of which were mounted on a special bridge assembly spanning the aft end of the bay.

In the cabin of the orbiter, the astronauts would utilize an overhead window and attempt to photograph Halley's Comet with a special camera as part of the CHAMP experiment. This would be the first of several flights of the Comet Halley Active Monitoring Program, an effort to obtain photographs and spectral data of the comet as it swung by Earth in its cyclical, seventy-five-year orbit of the sun.

Columbia's flight, it was suggested, was something of a "year-end clearance" mission. In fact, as the preparations for the launch played out, there were real concerns that there was but one pressing need to fly it at all. "Here we are—we're left with just one satellite, with the Materials Science Laboratory," said Gibson. "[It] has been suggested that the reason we didn't get canceled outright was because we had Congressman Nelson on board." The RCA satellite could have easily been remanifested; and the various experiment payloads, spread among several future missions. At just minutes more than five scheduled flight days, it would be one of the program's shortest nonmilitary missions.

Cenker returned to JSC after the November 1985 Thanksgiving holiday and found a surprise that really brought home the fact that he was about to go to space. The payload specialists had always been set aside in separate offices from the rest of the astronauts, but with the return of *Atlantis* after STS-61B, Cenker and his crew were now located together and afforded all the luxuries of being the prime crew for the upcoming mission: "The next flight up always took priority [for a] parking slot outside the Astronaut Office—there were seven slots. Whoever was flying next had priority, by definition. It didn't make any difference—and PS—didn't matter. When we went back after Thanksgiving, I had a new office, and I had a parking slot right in front of the astronaut building. I had *arrived*!"

As it would turn out, the astronauts of *Columbia*'s mission would be the next flight up for far longer than anyone could have anticipated.

Hoot Gibson and Charlie Bolden wanted to be anywhere but here—lying on their backs on *Columbia*'s flight deck bolted to a gigantic tank of explosive rocket fuel while lightning flashed all around the vehicle. "We climbed in, and I'll never forget when I climbed into the commander's seat on *Columbia*. . . . I'm looking up at the window," recalled Gibson. "It's raining so hard, and the tiles stick up about two inches around the window, so they form a dam. I've got a pool of water in my windshield."

Bolden agreed, recalling to NASA's Sandra Johnson, "It was the worst thunderstorm I'd ever been in. We were really not happy about being there, because you could hear stuff crackling in the headset." They attempted to reassure their crew that the arrester system, an umbrella of cables strung out from the white mast atop of the launch tower, would prevent a direct hit on the external tank, but with every bright flash and thunderclap, their teeth clenched in anticipation.

This was the fourth time Gibson's crew had climbed aboard the orbiter for a launch attempt. On 19 December 1985 a false reading on an SRB hydraulic power unit stopped the countdown just fourteen seconds prior to launch. With extensive repairs needed, NASA management decided to stand down through the Christmas holidays and tried again on 6 January 1986. This time, thousands of pounds of liquid oxygen was inadvertently drained from the external tank due to a procedural error.

The next day, the crew would again be stuck on the planet when poor weather at both of the transoceanic abort sites was below launch criteria. In a fortunate turn of events, this scrub allowed for the discovery of a broken temperature sensor lodged in the number 2 engine prevalve. It had likely found its way there during the defueling after the previous launch attempt. "That would have been a bad day," recalled Bolden. "That would have been a catastrophic day, because the engine would have exploded had we launched."

After hours of hoping that the fickle Florida weather would clear in time to launch *Columbia* on a stormy 10 January, the team decided to scrub yet again. For Cenker the closeout crew couldn't get them out of there fast enough. "We had already aborted the launch, and so we got out of our seats, and we were sitting up on the backs of the seats," he recalled. Pinky Nelson came down from the flight deck and lounged on the lavatory door. Suddenly, another clap of thunder shook the vehicle and filled the cabin with pure, white light. "You can come and get us anytime guys!" one of the crew members called out.

For the astronauts, though, the delays served to further bond them together. Bill Nelson, immediately following the first scrub, had returned to Washington, trying to make the transition, albeit temporarily, back to congressman. But following the Christmas break, he spent a majority of his time with the crew in Houston and Florida. In between January launch attempts, the astronauts spent hours in the KSC crew quarters watching classic comedies courtesy of Steve Hawley, as Gibson remembered: "He had *Animal House*. I had never seen *Animal House* until we started going down to the cape. [There was] *Life of Brian*, and it was *The Holy Grail*, those two Monty Python [movies]. He's just a really funny guy." After multiple viewings, it wasn't unusual throughout their preparations to hear one crew member or another reciting lines from the films at opportune times.

The downtime also afforded an opportunity for the two payload specialists to approach some subjects with the experienced NASA astronauts that had, up to that point, been pushed to the background. During late-night conversations, Nelson and Cenker would pick the brains of the crewmates on some of the things that could go wrong and what the potential outcomes of these contingencies might be. The accidental opening of the orbiter hatch was brought forth, as was the failure of two main engines early in the ascent. Nelson gradually came to realize just how much of a calculated risk each launch was and the sheer number of catastrophic ways one could fail.

Cenker also clearly remembers a discussion that came up during the wait for the second launch attempt in early January in which the issue of flying payload specialists was broached:

> We wound up in isolation over New Year's Eve, between '85 and '86, and our spouses are gone, and we're sitting there and drinking. . . . We had a few glasses of champagne or wine, and we were talking. The conversation came around to PSs versus career astronauts, and somebody asked

the question, "What are you doing that we couldn't do?" And it's a per-
fectly legitimate question. And my answer—this goes back to the reason I
believe RCA wanted someone to fly—I said, "With one exception, you can
do anything I can. . . . I'm going back to RCA! Would you want to ride
in a car that had been designed by somebody who had never even ridden
in one? RCA wants somebody that's been there, working on the spacecraft
that are going to be a part of it. And that's the real difference." That was
the only time the conversation ever came up, and they just sort of, "Mm,
okay," like that's a perspective to think about. Nothing more was said. I
don't remember any response to that, positive or negative, but I never got
a hint of any negativity while I was there.

Finally, after weeks of launch attempts and many more months of training and anticipation, 12 January dawned crystal clear and chilly. For the
crew of *Columbia*, the wait was finally over.

People would often ask Hoot Gibson, "When you're sitting there on the
launchpad, are you scared? Are you nervous about something?" He typically answered, "Yes, I am nervous that something's going to go wrong,
and we're not going to get to launch today. You're on your way to Disney
World. You don't want to wait another day. You want to go now."

"Disney World" lay two hundred miles above and an eight-and-a-half-
minute rocket ride ahead for *Columbia*'s seven-man crew. As each astronaut waited to walk across the access arm into the White Room 195 feet
above the launchpad, Bill Nelson, now for the fifth time, contemplated the
hissing, creaking, black-and-white space plane standing on end in front of
him. He stepped aside on the gantry and checked the right-leg pocket of his
flight suit, ensuring that his pocket-sized Bible was not left behind. Kneel-
ing down on one knee on the chilly steel grate floor, he silently bowed his
head and said a prayer for his own safety and that of his crew.

Once he was strapped in on the middeck of the orbiter, Nelson glanced
to his left just as Steve Hawley ducked his head in to check the progress of
the payload specialists' boarding. Nelson couldn't contain a burst of laughter as he was greeted by a Groucho Marx–masked astronaut. Hawley, who
now had more scrubs than anyone, joked that he didn't want *Columbia* to
recognize him, for fear of yet another cancellation.

The space shuttle stack vented streams of white vapor into the cold pre-dawn air, bathed in blinding white columns of xenon light that stretched far into the sky above the pad. At T minus four minutes, the launch controller called for the crew to close and lock their visors. "When the visor comes down, it actually seats around that seal, and air comes from the shuttle's air supply and inflates the inside seal, and it essentially isolates your skull from the sound," Cenker explains. Bill Nelson pulled back the cuff of his glove, ready to punch his stopwatch at liftoff to keep up with the rapid sequence of events that was about to happen.

Gibson kept a running commentary for the benefit of his crewmates below deck, who had limited visibility into what was going on. "T minus ten . . . minus six . . . there go the engines." The three main engines came to life and focused three blue shock diamonds of translucent flame into the Niagara-like torrent of sound-suppressing water cascading into the flame trench below. "When they light the main engines, you *feel* the noise for six seconds before they light the solids," recalled Cenker.

As the two payload specialists craned their helmeted heads around to the left to peer through the orbiter hatch window, the solid rockets ignited. "Then you find out what noise is," said Cenker. "I looked out that window, and I watched the gantry move. I didn't know we were moving. If I hadn't watched the gantry go by, all I felt was the noise. Now since I started hanging on the wall, as the vehicle turns over and flies downrange, I'm hanging from the ceiling. Now because you're getting pressed into your seat, it doesn't necessarily feel like you're hanging upside down. I've got the seat belt and two shoulder straps on; you feel like you're sliding up in your seat. It's an interesting feeling."

As the orbiter cleared the launch tower, control of the mission officially passed to JSC, and Gibson greeted them with a confident, "Houston, *Columbia*'s with you in the roll!" He could hear the cheers of the launch team over his headset, as the pent-up emotions of so many delays were finally vented with a tremendous roar. "Roger roll, *Columbia*," came the response from CAPCOM Fred Gregory. Then all hell broke loose.

A series of alarms sounded in the cockpit. The most critical of the failures could have had dire consequences. *Columbia*'s commander would recall the ensuing events vividly even thirty years later: "We got a caution for helium usage on the center engine." Gibson explained, "What it looks like to the computer and what it looks like to us is a leak. Each engine of the three main engines on the shuttle has its own helium supply bottle. We've got to have helium on those engines because the helium is a pressure barrier in the turbopumps between the hydrogen and the oxygen. You've got to keep them separated, or you've got a bomb. If the helium gets down to a certain pressure, [the computer is] going to shut that engine down."

The simulator had shaken them but not like this. Bolden had every possible contingency checklist strategically Velcroed around the cockpit within easy reach should they be needed. Only, now his carefully arranged workspace was rocking so violently around him that he couldn't read any of them. He desperately grasped for what he hoped was the correct card and tried to hold it close to his visor to dampen vibrations of the blurred checklist. Just then, he remembered . . . *Hoot's Law.*

"There is nothing we can do right away, no matter how bad you think it is," Gibson had instilled in him. "Let's at least make sure there are two of us that agree on the procedure, and then we're going to start working it. And we're going to work it as a team." Gibson and Bolden wrestled with the abnormality throughout the ride to orbit. All the while, Cenker and Nelson listened in as the flight deck crew calmly went through the procedure to isolate the potential leak, while Nelson kept track of their progress through the various abort points. The srbs separated with a loud bang, and as they passed the seven-and-a-half-minute mark, the crew relaxed a bit, knowing that even with the loss of two engines, they could still abort successfully without ditching.

Bolden troubleshot the reported leak as a false indication, with little input from mission control. Things were happening so fast and this crew was so good that there was little they could add anyway. Gibson took pride in having such a sharp crew: "Those guys were so on top of everything that we couldn't do anything wrong." The final minute of the ascent pressed *Columbia*'s crew into their seats with a crushing 3 g's. "You feel like you weigh five hundred pounds," recalled Cenker. As the steady hum of the main engines fell silent, though, he immediately found himself weighing nothing at all.

The instantaneous transition to weightlessness was pleasantly shocking. *Columbia* had behaved like a vehicle on a shakedown flight during the climb to orbit, following a two-year refurbishment at its birthplace in Palmdale, California. One quick burn of the oms engines had boosted the ship into an elliptical orbit, and another, longer burn would circularize it once on the other side of the planet. In the meantime, Bob Cenker would have one of the most memorable experiences of his life.

Hoot called out, "Okay guys, everything looked clean. If you want to get out of your seats, don't start unpacking anything, because we still have to confirm everything, but if you want to just get your space legs, you can unstrap." And I undid my seat belt and my harness and I came up out of my seat and I was holding on to the seat belt and I was looking down at the seat—and I can picture this like it was yesterday—thinking, "I'm not going to use that seat for the next five days. This is not a carnival ride; this is not twenty seconds of zero-g. I am in space." And that was just bizarre.

Bill Nelson had his helmet off and his nose pressed up against the hatch window to get his first look at Earth from orbit. Marveling at the beauty of the curved, blue horizon, the congressman caught sight of a sparkling white object tumbling slowly away into the blackness of space—a small sliver of ice shed from someplace on the orbiter. As he watched, the sun set behind them as *Columbia* passed into the inky darkness of the nighttime hemisphere.

The crew had a lot of work to do configuring the cabin and preparing for the Satcom deployment, but it didn't take long before Cenker noticed a strange sensation. No matter how he oriented himself, he felt like he was constantly upside down. The heart takes time to recognize that it is in zero gravity and typically keeps pumping the same volume of blood to the head as it does on Earth. This causes fullness in the head and, coupled with the visual cues his eyes were flashing to the brain, made Cenker feel as though his senses were in complete disagreement. "Flight day 1, I was not a happy camper," he explained. "I didn't get physically ill but had many of the symptoms of space adaptation." At his KSC appearance in 2015, he expanded:

They suggested because I wasn't happy and I didn't like that feeling, "You might not want to look out the window because everything is upside down. The shuttle is actually flying upside down, so turn upside down in the cabin." If I turned upside down in the cabin on flight day 1, I thought I was gonna die, because now all of my visual cues are telling me, "You're upside down." Now, there is no up or down in zero-g. Visually, it's amazing how driven we are by what we see and what our per-

ceptions are. It's one of the things that they believe is a heavy part of the space adaptation process.

From *Columbia's* 201-mile perch above the planet, the four-thousand-pound Satcom K-I spacecraft would be boosted over 22,000 miles higher by the new, larger PAM D-2 rocket motor. Nine hours into the flight, the sunshade was retracted, and the glittering silver-and-gold box began spinning up to fifty revolutions per minute. Cenker took great pride watching the satellite he had shepherded through its birth push up out of the payload bay with an audible thump.

That pride was still evident decades later when he spoke of the satellite with the enthusiasm of a proud parent. "If you had the Primestar direct to your home TV between 1986 and 1998, it came to you courtesy of the Satcom K-I spacecraft that was deployed on our flight. We had a design life of nine years, and one of my professional accomplishments, if you will, which involves a bit of luck to get anything like this to go longer than its design life—we went twelve years on this spacecraft."

Bill Nelson struggled a bit getting his protein crystal growth experiment working in the middeck. Working with various proteins, including purine nucleoside phosphorylase, which held promise for cancer treatment, he had an extensive list of tasks to perform to get the gear operating. There were forty-eight chambers in which to mix the various chemical agents, followed by initial photography of the experiment. And all of this had to be done while Nelson was still adapting to space, where every activity seemed to take a lot longer than it did on the ground.

By the beginning of their first full day in space, both Cenker and Nelson felt well enough to start enjoying the experience of weightlessness, experimenting with various oddities the environment provided. Nelson took delight in tumbling slices of grapefruit into his mouth, a fruit he insisted on having aboard the mission that earlier had caused a small controversy. Being a Florida representative, he had specified that NASA pack grapefruit grown in his home state. Worried about the reaction of other states' citrus growers to this partisan preference, the agency nixed the idea altogether. But Rita Rapp, NASA's dietician who oversaw all the food selection for spaceflight, managed to get enough deidentified grapefruit aboard *Columbia* for Nelson to share with his crewmates. Nelson had no idea while he was in

38. Bill Nelson peels a grapefruit from an undisclosed state courtesy of NASA's space food pioneer Rita Rapp. Courtesy NASA/Retro Space Images.

space that the public flap had not been easily forgotten by some other parties on Earth, and he had not heard the last of it.

The flight plan for *Columbia*'s mission was packed with maneuvers to be performed by Gibson and Bolden for the benefit of two of the payloads aboard—the ultraviolet experiment (UVX) and the comet-observing CHAMP. UVX was contained in three of the getaway special cans on the bridge structure, two housing the ultraviolet telescopes and one housing the electronics. CHAMP was to be mounted in an overhead window in the cabin of the orbiter and operated directly by the crew.

Each of these astronomy experiments competed both for crew time and for vehicle attitude, as the orbiter's payload bay had to be pointed at particular spots in the sky in order for the intended target to be observed. That competition ended abruptly on flight day 2 when Pinky Nelson set up CHAMP, only to find that it had been left powered on since it was loaded aboard *Columbia*; its batteries were dead. And nobody had thought to pack spare batteries. "Hawley's Comet," as the crew came to call the dirty snowball orbiting the sun, would remain unstudied until CHAMP could be flown again on another mission.

Meanwhile, mission managers on the ground had already been considering their options for recovering some of the lost time caused by the multiple launch delays. The decision was eventually made to shorten *Columbia's* flight by one day in order to get ahead on processing for the next mission, given that the major objective of deploying Satcom was behind them. With one less day now available to work on all the diverse experiments, several activities had to be replanned. When not maneuvering to various targets in the sky for astronomical observations, the Materials Science Lab 2 required the orbiter to be in free drift to minimize vibrations on the delicate study of various molten materials. Two sets of furnaces mounted on a support structure in the payload bay would melt samples that would then be suspended by either acoustic or electromagnetic levitators. Once solidified, it was hoped the materials would exhibit more attractive properties than metals produced on the ground. Unfortunately, throughout the third flight day, both the electromagnetic levitator and one of the furnaces kept repeatedly powering down.

While the NASA crew members tended to their balky experiments, the payload specialists mainly worked in the middeck on a variety of medical supplementary objectives. Cenker took part in an experiment studying space adaptation syndrome. "This was a set of goggles that you actually strapped to your head," he explained. "It measured your eyeballs' motion while you were doing things, to try to understand how the mind changes its processing of visual data in zero-g." This device, too, would experience a failure during the mission, putting Cenker's engineering skills to work in an effort to repair it.

Bill Nelson continued to monitor his protein crystal growth experiment and assist with the medical tests as well. A man capable of deep observation and introspection, he would frequently pull his small tape recorder out of a pocket and find a quiet place to capture some of his thoughts. At one point, he would retreat to the air lock, where squeezed in between the empty, white space suits; he felt as if there were two astronauts behind the helmets listening in on his dictation.

When it came time for bed, Cenker had no problem at all getting to sleep: "I could sleep anywhere anytime, so I just literally stuck myself to these Velcro strips and fell asleep hanging on the wall." There was one night

39. Cenker puts his engineering and mechanical skills to work, attempting to repair a goggle-like biomedical experiment after it failed on orbit. Courtesy NASA/Retro Space Images.

when his fellow payload specialist had a little fun at his expense. "At some point in the night, I moved away from the wall, and I'm floating around the cabin," Cenker recalled. In the continuous flow of air that circulated throughout the cabin, Cenker drifted slowly around in an arched, baby-in-the-womb slump, until he bumped up against a drowsy Bill Nelson. "Bill pushed me away, and the air pushed me back. And Bill pushed me away, and apparently this happened a couple of times," laughed Cenker. After several interruptions, Nelson decided to put an end to this. He grabbed a nearby roll of duct tape and set about firmly securing his crewmate to a wall, where he would wake hours later struggling slightly to free himself.

On flight days 2 and 4, Cenker got to operate the payload he was primarily responsible for. From the aft window in the flight deck, he and Bolden would take turns maneuvering the camera housing in the payload bay to point the infrared device, recording video of auroras, volcanoes, and various cities as they orbited high above. "It was great. We got a lot of data," Cenker shared. "We were trying to see what we could see with this particular camera. The question is, Okay, what can you tell? Who knows? You won't know it until you try it, because nobody had done it before. So we took a lot of video, and that experiment worked very well."

By 16 January, after barely four days in space, the crew was packed up for the trip home. With the payload bay doors closed and the cabin floors crowded with crew seats once again, all seven were outfitted in their launch and entry coveralls, harnesses, and helmets. However, the weather at KSC was not lending itself to the possibility of a space shuttle landing, with low clouds and rain showers. Just five minutes before the burn that would set *Columbia* on the irreversible path back to Earth, mission control waved them off. Not only would they regain the day lost due to NASA management's decision to shorten the mission; they would end up setting another record—the number of delays in trying to bring a shuttle mission home.

Columbia's crew would get very good at stowing the cabin for a landing attempt over the next two days. Backing out of all those preparations was a time-consuming and tedious task. The payload bay doors were reopened, and all of the orbiter's systems were reconfigured for on-orbit operations. On the first wave-off, they decided to leave the seats installed and the air lock hatch closed to shorten their tasks up a bit. Having already been awake for over eight hours prior to the decision, Bill Nelson actually dozed off to sleep, floating upside down freely in the middeck.

With a few hours left before they were scheduled to prepare for a sleep period, Gibson radioed to mission control, asking if there was anything they could work on in the intervening hours. A few suggestions came up in response, but the final task took the crew by surprise. "Okay, we want to do another run of this . . . and another run of something, and CHAMP." As Gibson remembers, "Charlie keyed the mike, and he started to say, 'Okay, we copy.' From downstairs on the middeck, as Charlie has got the mike keyed, Pinky and Stevie—when they had heard 'CHAMP'—they spouted a line from . . . I guess it was Monty Python and *Life of Brian*. They both simultaneously from downstairs called out, 'Aw, piss off!' Charlie started laughing so hard he couldn't finish his statement."

Unfortunately for Bill Nelson, the shortened flight plan dictated that he deactivate his protein crystal growth gear a day earlier than planned. Now, rather than having additional days of microgravity to work with the experiment, he couldn't restart it once it had been shut down. He would have to return to Earth with the samples he had and hope for the best. As he would learn after the conclusion of the mission, the experimental crystals he had seeded continued to grow on their own, even after he had stopped monitoring them.

The next day, the crew awoke to find their cabin virtually ready to return to Earth, given that they had done minimal unpacking. Their flight suits were splayed out neatly on the forward lockers, with their pockets full of the necessary items for the return home. But once again, it was not to be. The unpredictable weather at the coastal launch site on the Florida coast was still not acceptable to attempt landing. Cenker knew this had to be their last day in space—tomorrow they would be back home, be it in Florida or at Edwards Air Force Base in California. So he made the most of it. Cenker went to work on the infrared camera again. "Because the mission got extended that extra day, everything else had been packed up," he explained. "So for that extra day, we had videotape. We got quite a bit of video of engine firings, thruster control engine firings, and scenes from the ground."

Now six days into what was originally scheduled to be a five-day mission, Gibson's crew was running short on many essential items. Bill Nelson's grapefruit was depleted, as was much of the rest of their food. Steve Hawley would offer a glimpse into just how bad it was getting: "We had run out of most everything, including film, and part of our training had been to look for spiral eddies near the equator, because the theory was, for whatever reason, you didn't see them near the equator, and Charlie was looking out the window and claimed to see one, and I told him, 'Well, you'd better draw a picture of it, because we don't have any film.'"

During one of their final television opportunities, the crew sent a special message down to Houston that had the flight controllers bewildered. When the camera was switched on, six of the crew members were all oriented vertically in the middeck, with Pinky Nelson floating horizontally across the foreground. But in the middle of the group was the unmistakable red-suited, white-bearded figure of Santa Claus! Small gift-wrapped boxes spun in the air in front of him as Gibson told them how surprised they were to get Christmas gifts so late. Gibson would later reveal just how the "jolly old elf" himself had managed to rendezvous with *Columbia* in space:

We were going to be in space, and we were going to land on Christmas Eve. We went and made up a video. We went into the mock-up in building 9. The seven of us and another astronaut dressed up in a Santa Claus suit made it look like we were weightless. We had a couple of presents that actually were hanging by black threads. We'd be spinning them, and they'd be spinning in midair. That astronaut was Sonny [Manley L.] Carter. He was our Santa Claus. So there were eight of us in the picture. We took that to space with us because we were going to land on Christmas Eve, so we were going to call and say, "Hey, we have a special visitor up here that dropped by to bring us some presents." We actually wound up using it when we did go to space, because we went to all that work to make up that video. Nobody on the ground even realized that there were eight people in the video. They said, "Who was in the Santa Claus suit? Which one of you guys was in it?" We said, "Did you guys count noses in that picture? There were eight people in that video." Nobody even noticed it.

"That's a great video," remembers Bob Cenker. "When the people on the ground first saw the video, they wondered how the hell we commandeered the KC-135 to get that kind of fidelity." And the crew had one more surprise for the folks on the ground. Gibson, Hawley, and Pinky Nelson were the founding members of the all-astronaut band Max-Q, named for the period of maximum dynamic air pressure on the orbiter as it rocketed into orbit. Gibson rewrote the lyrics for the song "Where or When," and when he keyed the mike again, the entire crew joined in for their own rendition of the song, lamenting their seemingly endless circling of the planet, to raucous applause from the flight controllers.

That night, on his final opportunity to enjoy the incomprehensible experience of spaceflight, Bob Cenker didn't waste a single moment on sleep. Rather, he floated quietly at the overhead windows on the flight deck and took in the majesty of the earth below:

I stayed up all night and looked out the window. Went around the world five times. It just boggled the mind. I watched a thunderstorm over Africa, and it looked like I was watching popcorn in a popper. You could just see the clouds lighting up—almost like you could hear it, it was that intense. A sunrise and a sunset in space were just amazing. Imagine the most col-

orful sunset you have ever seen. Imagine flying through all of those col-
ors in about five minutes, because that's what's happening, you're flying
through the sun's light as its being bent by the Earth's atmosphere. And I
had told people if I could take my wife and family and move into space,
I'd be gone tomorrow. That was the only part that was bad. Whenever I
travel on business—when I was traveling to Houston, there was The Gal-
leria—it was a big mall down there . . . "Barbara would love this place."
And you go by the Astrodome . . . "My son would love this place." When-
ever I travel on business, you make those connections. And that night I
stayed up all night, I remember thinking, "I'm never going to bring any-
body here," and that was tough. That was tough.

Bill Nelson put on a good face, but he was having an especially difficult
time readjusting to the crushing force of gravity, which, aside from the
past week, he had lived his entire life with. Wobbling his way up into the
transfer van, he found waiting for him a huge basket of oranges with a sign
reading, "Congressman Nelson, welcome to the state of California. Enjoy
a delicious California orange." His insistence on having Florida citrus on
board had become well known, and astronaut Dan Brandenstein arranged
one last prank at his expense. Nelson was less than amused.

Just a few hours before, *Columbia* had come screaming over Los Angeles at Mach 3, rattling windows for miles around in the predawn darkness.
The third opportunity to land back at KSC in Florida had once again been
waved off due to the ever-changing coastal weather, and the time had come
to bring the flight to an end at Edwards Air Force Base. Only the second
time the shuttle had been landed at night, the move not only added days
to the turnaround time for *Columbia*'s next flight but also ruined Nelson's
triumphant return to his home state.

Fortunately for the crew, Hoot Gibson had insisted that most of their
simulated landings be practiced at night for just such a circumstance.
Columbia once again showed its unique personality to the pilots during
reentry, with a series of failures that kept them busy throughout the long
glide home. After a ten-thousand-foot rollout on the concrete runway at
Edwards, the crew took their time readapting to 1 g. As Cenker recollected,
"We waited in the White Room for about twenty minutes to a half an hour

to get your legs back. We're okay coming down the stairs strengthwise, but if you should stumble, your mind's not going to catch you automatically. Your mind thinks you're going to float off into space. You need to hang on to something to give yourself a chance."

Their mission complete, the payload specialists of STS-61C would go their separate ways. Cenker returned to RCA with the anticipation of bringing his spaceflight experience to the company's work on the space station. Nelson returned to Congress, where he served until 1991. After several years away from the political scene, in 1995 he became treasurer, insurance commissioner, and fire marshal of Florida. In 2001 he once again returned to Washington, winning a Democratic Senate seat for Florida, where he continues to serve as of this writing. Just ten days after they stepped off their orbiter at Edwards, *Challenger* lifted off from launchpad 39B at Cape Canaveral on its ill-fated final flight.

Bob Cenker to this day has no idea what happened to the data from the infrared camera he operated aboard *Columbia*. It disappeared into the somewhat-secretive research lab side of RCA, and he never saw it again. "Somebody called me about looking for the hardware, because the hardware came back too, obviously, and they wanted to fly it on an expendable launch vehicle," he shared. But that too was nowhere to be found. "So, there was interest in it, but it wasn't really part of my engineering discipline. I operated it as a competent operator, I guess."

Following the *Challenger* accident and the subsequent cancellation of shuttle launches from Vandenberg, RCA's concept for a polar-orbiting platform was shelved. Even though there was a Satcom K-3 satellite coming down the line, Jerry Magilton lost any hope to fly his own mission for RCA with the removal of commercial payloads from the shuttle. "We didn't know which way RCA might go," Cenker explained, "whether they would fly the same guy twice, whether they would start with a whole new pair. He and I talked about it, and certainly he wanted to fly. But we never had any insight. And basically, quite frankly, it wouldn't surprise me if RCA hadn't contemplated beyond that one."

Cenker would go on to work on many other satellite projects for what became GE Astrospace, and for several years prior to his leaving the company in 1990, he was the manager of payload accommodations for the company's contribution to the space agency's new direction. "[NASA] had started the Mission to Planet Earth," he reflected. "So they just resurrected all of that old stuff and called it the Earth Observation System, the EOS platform. And I was payload accommodations because originally I had been part of the station program that was going to run those spacecraft."

Since leaving GE, Cenker has continued to consult with a range of aerospace companies, often leveraging his spaceflight experience yet still reluctant to refer to himself as an astronaut. He occasionally does public appearances in front of large audiences and seems quite comfortable in the role, sharing his story of a single flight to space over three decades ago. "I often refer to myself as a payload specialist astronaut," he says. And to children and young adults in the audience who line up for photos and autographs, the qualifier doesn't seem to matter in the least.

When attending functions such as the Association of Space Explorers meetings, however, he is keenly aware of the feelings of some of his fellow space travelers:

> I know there are still those with some resentment or questioning, if you will, the qualifications of those of us who did not help fly the vehicle but were merely passengers. And there are many guys who are quite comfortable with it. Some of the old guys treat us like we're one of them, no questions asked. But then you'll hear rumblings from other people, "Well, he's not an 'RA'—a real astronaut." It doesn't really matter to me because I got to fly. It was a dream come true. I've done something that the vast, vast, vast majority of the world can only dream about.

He certainly would never hear anything of the sort from his old crewmates. The astronauts of *Columbia*'s mission have remained exceptionally close over the years, having several reunions and other get-togethers. "We have been dear friends," Hoot Gibson candidly admits today. "We all dearly love each other." Having flown five times with astronauts and cosmonauts from all over the world, he still considers these men "by far the closest crew that I've ever been with, trained with, and kept up with over all these years."

Today, they often cross paths with the man Gibson now has to address as "Senator Nelson" in more formal settings. Nelson has continued to be a staunch supporter of NASA's programs, even throughout the contentious years of the Constellation lunar program's cancellation, the formulation of new national space goals, and the development of the Space Launch System. Charlie Bolden was named NASA administrator in 2009, and both he and his former commander have been called to testify on numerous occasions in front of the committee chaired by Nelson. Neither Gibson nor Bolden would pass up an opportunity to help shape an endeavor they so passionately believe in and want to see flourish.

Nelson has always favored an inspirational quote that hung on his office wall for years and sums up his motivations perfectly. Harkening back to the risks he took to step aboard a space shuttle in 1986, he sometimes concludes spaceflight-themed speeches with the words of Helen Keller. "Life," it reads, "is either a daring adventure or nothing at all."

15. Walking through Fire

In any event this has had very unfortunate consequences,
the most serious of which is to encourage ordinary citizens
to fly in such a dangerous machine.

Richard P. Feynman

When Brett Watterson joined NASA's Jet Propulsion Laboratory, managing system-safety programs, he became fascinated with a tiny period of time—the millisecond. Just before this incredibly brief moment, everything is normal; everything is as it should be. But then "in a millisecond, whether it's a car accident or an accidental shooting or a meteorite hitting you or a bolt from the blue, people's lives are irretrievably changed," he explained. "The ripples go out to their families. It's over before you know it."

On 28 January 1986 Watterson—a U.S. Air Force manned spaceflight engineer—was still in training for *Discovery*'s STS-62A mission from Vandenberg Air Force Base, California. He and the rest of the crew were in a laboratory near Albuquerque, New Mexico, learning about one of the sensor packages they would be responsible for on what they hoped would be their July mission. Capt. Robert Crippen had been assigned to command this first shuttle flight to be launched from Vandenberg, on what would be his fifth shuttle mission.

Challenger, after nearly a week of delays, was about to launch from an unusually frigid launchpad 39B at KSC, and while Crippen's crew continued with their lesson, a small television sat in one corner of the room with the volume turned down. Aboard the shuttle were veteran astronauts Francis "Dick" Scobee, Judy Resnik, Ellison Onizuka, and Ronald McNair. Joining the experienced flyers were pilot Michael J. Smith and payload specialists

Greg Jarvis and Sharon Christa McAuliffe, the New Hampshire school-teacher chosen from thousands of applicants as NASA's first "citizen in space."

The countdown proceeded smoothly to zero, and on the television screen, *Challenger* rose silently into the crystal clear blue skies and slowly pivoted around to its proper trajectory out over the Atlantic Ocean. For seventy-three seconds the ship climbed flawlessly under the power of the two SRBS and three main engines. Then, in that millisecond, at a mission elapsed time of T plus 73.162 seconds, everything suddenly, irretrievably changed, and the ripples were sent out into the space program, its astronaut ranks, the crew's families, and the millions of students watching live on television as *Challenger* was engulfed in a massive cloud of orange-and-white vapor. "What was that?" exclaimed Dale Gardner, his eyes suddenly riveted to the tiny television set.

Standing behind his crewmates watching the launch, then undersecretary of the air force Pete Aldridge recalled to NASA's Rebecca Wright, "Crippen was sitting in front. I was in the back of the room, and I saw this explosion and thought, Jesus. Then I was waiting for the orbiter, as we all were, to come out of the smoke. But as soon as that explosion occurred, Crippen obviously knew what it was. His head dropped. I remember this so distinctly. He knew exactly what happened, or anticipated it much more so, I think, than the rest of us did."

Jerry Ross was so intently focused on his training tasks that he didn't have his eyes on the muted television when the explosion occurred. As he related to NASA's Jennifer Ross-Nazzal, "We all turned around, and each of us had this different impression of what we were seeing. I can remember debris flying everywhere and the two solid rocket motors corkscrewing through the sky, and my first thought was, 'They're doing a return-to-launch-site abort.'"

It didn't take long to realize that there would be no heroic return-to-launch-site landing by Dick Scobee and his crew. *Challenger* was gone. While the shocked news reporters struggled to come to grips with what they had just witnessed and broadcast, they could only offer false hope that the crew could have somehow survived. But in that ever-so-brief millisecond, Bob Crippen and anyone else who had experienced the violent, bone-jarring ride aboard a paper airplane strapped to two SRBS knew the crew's fate was sealed. Seven souls—fellow space explorers—had been lost.

Even as ragged shards of debris continued to rain down over the deep-blue Atlantic waters, thousands of lives were changed. For a moment, it seemed, the world stopped. It was one of those tragic events following which every person recalls exactly where they were and what they were doing at the time, and those who didn't witness it firsthand would soon hear the news. Many other NASA astronauts and payload specialists who either had flown previously or were preparing to fly watched the event unfold live, and for all of them it was an unforgettably shocking sight.

In the immediate aftermath of the *Challenger* tragedy, nothing in NASA's future seemed to matter. Crippen's crew certainly wouldn't be flying from Vandenberg in July, and no one could guess that it would be nearly three years before any space shuttle would fly again. Back at JSC, flight director Jay Greene locked down the Mission Control Center and began the protocols for securing all the relevant flight data. Astronauts far and wide jumped into their cars or T-38 aircraft and raced for either the cape or Houston, doing whatever they could to assist the families and the organization. Nationwide, teachers in classrooms struggled to explain to their students the instant, violent deaths of the seven astronauts they had unexpectedly witnessed on live television.

In that millisecond, the innocence of NASA's manned spaceflight program was irreversibly wiped away. The American public, which had only recently turned its attention back to the shuttle program to watch McAuliffe's mission aboard *Challenger*, would mourn the loss of a new national icon and six other astronauts whose names they barely knew. NASA had become a victim of its own success, with shuttle flights becoming so frequent and seemingly routine that the country stopped watching. But in achieving that success, NASA had been accepting high levels of risk to its fleet of orbiters and their astronaut crews. With those risks now laid bare in the starkest of examples, the future of the payload specialist concept, the commercial and military uses of the shuttle, and the entire space program itself all seemed in jeopardy.

Among the professional and nonprofessional cadres of space flyers, memories of that cold January day of *Challenger*'s demise would linger for decades, leaving them to wonder just how close they might have come to suffering the same fate.

Greg Jarvis could barely believe what he was reading. A simple paper flyer, stuck to the memo board with thumb tacks, teased him with a basic drawing of a space shuttle in flight and exclaimed in bold font, "Wanted—Hughes Employees to Ride Space Shuttle."

It's the chance of a lifetime—or two. A Hughes selection committee is accepting applications for two SCG [Space Communications Group] or HC [Hughes Corporation] employees to fly on the space shuttle as payload specialists. The designated flights, in February and July 1985, will launch the third and fourth Leasat spacecraft.

To qualify for the payload specialist positions, a person must pass several NASA requirements: a medical examination for spaceflight; a background security investigation; and a nine month training session, three months of which will require full-time participation. If you're interested in taking advantage of this opportunity, pick up an application from Ralph Rhoads.

Aside from the opening statement, it was an amazingly matter-of-fact solicitation. It read as if the company were trying to organize an after-work softball team, rather than an extremely hazardous rocket ride into the hostile environment of space. From across the SCG and the HC at large, six hundred payload specialist hopefuls would volunteer to fly on the two anticipated missions. It was to be the first time a satellite customer of NASA would fly with their payload aboard the shuttle.

Gregory Bruce Jarvis, always an adventurer at heart, jumped at the opportunity to fly in space. Born in Detroit, Michigan, on 24 August 1944, he reveled in all manner of outdoor activities and sports. He played squash and racquetball, backpacked, and skied cross-country. But the one sport he was most avid about was bicycling. When he married his college sweetheart, Marcia Jarboe, in June 1968, he even purchased a tandem bike so they could both share their love of endurance cycling.

Jarvis studied electrical engineering at the State University of New York at Buffalo, known locally as "UB." He was remembered by friends as an outgoing, energetic personality who was usually seen with a stack of books headed somewhere to delve into his studies. While he was not as naturally gifted as some in academics, his work ethic paid off, and he became a member of the National Honor Society.

A member of the U.S. Air Force Reserve Officer Training Corps, Jarvis completed his undergraduate degree in 1967 and immediately enrolled in graduate studies at Northeastern University. While attending Northeastern, he took a job with Raytheon in Bedford, Massachusetts, where he learned the intricacies of circuit design on a surface-to-air missile system the company was developing. With a master's degree in electrical engineering, he entered active duty with the air force in the summer of 1969 and found himself on the opposite side of the country designing tactical communications satellites.

Jarvis was assigned to the Space Division in El Segundo, California, the same organization that a decade later would produce the second cadre of MSES. Detailed to the Satellite Communications Program Office, he served as a payload engineer responsible for the early design phase of the FLTSATCOM (Fleet Satellite Communications) system. Captain Jarvis left the air force in 1973 and moved to the Space Communications Group subsidiary of Hughes Aircraft, settling in the South Bay suburb of Los Angeles known as Hermosa Beach.

Recognized for his relentless drive and enthusiasm since joining the program, Jarvis was promoted to spacecraft test and integration manager for the Marisat F-3 satellite in 1975. Three years later he was involved with the initial proposal for Syncom IV, the first communication satellite series designed specifically to be launched by the space shuttle. A fourteen-foot-diameter barrel design, the Syncom spacecraft would be leased to the U.S. military, earning it the commercial moniker Leasat.

Throughout the early 1980s Jarvis shepherded the first three Leasat satellites through their construction and would be remembered by colleagues as an energetic, fast-talking manager who always took a personal interest in his engineers' concerns. With the conclusion of his responsibilities in the Leasat program, in 1983 Jarvis moved into a project manager role in the System Analysis and Design Lab at Hughes, where he was working when the payload specialist opportunity was announced.

After the exhaustive screening and evaluation process, Hughes and NASA agreed on a total of four of the company's employees to participate in training for missions, and Jarvis was one of them. Gerry Dutcher, an engineering friend of Jarvis at Hughes, observed to New York Times reporter Jon Nordheimer, "Other people had worked just as hard as Greg, but no one could match Greg's enthusiasm, fascination with the space program and excellent physical conditioning." Jarvis would be backed up by William Butter-

40. "The Hughes Astronauts": Bill Butterworth, Greg Jarvis, John Konrad, and Stephen Cunningham. Jarvis and Konrad, selected as prime payload specialists, both expected to fly on Leasat satellite deployment missions in 1985. Courtesy NASA/Retro Space Images.

worth. Prior to his selection as Jarvis's backup, Butterworth had been an assistant program manager for Hughes's Galileo atmospheric probe, part of a larger spacecraft that would be headed to Jupiter in 1986.

The June 1984 announcement also included Dr. John Konrad, from the company's Systems Engineering Lab, as a primary selectee. He, along with Stephen Cunningham, a Systems Analysis manager, would train to fly a subsequent mission with the second Hughes satellite.

CHARLIE WALKER, STS-41D, STS-51D, STS-61B (T+73.162 SECONDS)
I was aggravated with news services that would cover a launch up until about thirty seconds. And whatever network I was watching ended their coverage. It wasn't but what, ten seconds later, and I'm about to pick my bags up and just about to turn off the television and go out my room door when I hear, "We interrupt this program again to bring you this

*announcement. It looks like something has happened." I can remember
seeing the long-range tracker cameras following debris falling into the
ocean, and I can remember going to my knees at that point and saying
some prayers for the crew. Because I can remember the news reporter saying, "Well, we don't know what has happened at this point." I thought,
"Well, you don't know what has happened in detail, but anybody that
knows anything about it can tell that it was not at all good."*

Jarvis and Konrad were to fly on their respective missions in mid to late
1985, accompanying what the scg referred to as their "widebody" satellites.
Jarvis had been appointed the first to fly, aboard sts-51d, with Leasat f3.
In the weeks following their selection, the team were again sent to jsc for
further medical and psychological evaluations.

Returning to Houston in September for basic training, the Hughes engineers would also take part in altitude chamber testing, where they would
come to recognize their own individual reactions to hypoxia, a dangerous
aeromedical condition resulting from a lack of oxygen to the brain. Joined
by payload specialist candidates from France and Great Britain, Jarvis and
his teammates experienced air pressure in the chamber reduced to an equivalent altitude of twenty-two thousand feet.

The four were also fitted for the flight coveralls, g-suits, and helmets
that they would wear in training and in flight. After more safety training
and orientation at jsc, they were all flown to Cape Canaveral in September 1984 and allowed to tour launchpad 39a, where *Discovery* was poised
to launch with their Syncom f1 satellite on the sts-51a mission that would
also recover two satellites stranded in low Earth orbit. Jarvis and the team
returned to the cape in November to witness the launch, which was an
impressive event for an astronaut hopeful, as Jarvis related to Hughes's *Sig-
nal News*: "It was a moving experience to watch the shuttle carry the spacecraft I had worked on into orbit. And I was very taken aback by the sound
and by the feeling of the sound waves hitting my body. It just made me
want to fly in the shuttle all the more."

Jarvis would also conduct an experiment in the orbiter's middeck explor-
ing the behavior of rocket fuel in satellite fuel tanks. Given that Hughes's
satellites were getting larger by design, there were still unknowns about fluid
dynamics in zero gravity, and the Leasat's unique Frisbee-like deployment

method introduced more complexities that needed to be examined. This experiment would yield important data for the future design of both civilian and military satellites and was a common area of interest between Jarvis and several of the MSEs, including Frank Casserino, who recalls, "We developed models with different types of baffles in these fuel tanks to minimize the sloshing that goes on when satellites move. Because [as] you can imagine, some of the satellites that we were dealing with required some precise pointing. And sloshing of fluid would impact the precise pointing of these satellites. I spent a lot of time in the zero-g aircraft testing out the different tanks and the different baffles. Greg Jarvis was going to bring back his data. [We would] integrate the data and modify the tanks and use that for additional research on orbit."

Jarvis and Butterworth would host their NASA crewmates at Hughes to tour the high bay facility where Leasat 3 was being prepared for flight. Astronauts Dan Brandenstein, J. O. Creighton, John Fabian, Shannon Lucid, and Steve Nagel were briefed on the satellite payload and made a special effort to ensure the two engineers responsible for the satellite felt they were now part of their crew. But even as Jarvis was preparing to train full-time in Houston, NASA was still facing the challenges of flying an operational space shuttle program, and events were unfolding that would dramatically change Jarvis's plans for spaceflight.

BILL NELSON, STS-61C (T+73.162 SECONDS)
Suddenly I was no longer in Washington. I was with them—those seven souls I had grown to know and love. I was strapped in my seat in the shuttle, my back to the Earth and my face toward heaven. I could feel the vibrations, the roar, the surge of incredible energy. I fought back tears.

NASA's shuttle manifest was in a state of continuous flux. Several changes in payloads, orbiters, and crew assignments landed Jarvis on Robert "Hoot" Gibson's STS-61C crew. Ironically, the failed Leasat deployment on *Discovery*'s April mission may well have been a situation where a commercial payload specialist might have been the greatest asset to a crew on orbit. Joe Engle's STS-511 crew deployed the Leasat 4 and then chased down the failed Leasat 3. The rescue and redeployment of the satellite was a huge success, but their own payload failed after only twenty hours in orbit. This mission also flew without a Hughes payload specialist on board. Finally, Jarvis was swapped with Congressman Bill Nelson, which would place Jarvis aboard *Challenger* in late January.

FRANK CASSERINO (T+73.162 SECONDS)

I was at Sunnyvale Air Force Station working on some crew procedures for my mission. I flew into San Francisco airport, got in my rental car, turned on the radio, and heard about the Challenger. *I was flying into San Francisco to go down to Sunnyvale to work on these procedures and I was within two or three weeks of moving down to NASA, for my flight specific training. My wife was pregnant with our daughter—she would have come with me and lived in Houston. She was briefed by the Air Force public relations folks about how things were going to be, and this was a classified mission and so it wasn't going to be publicized. So we were ready to go.*

The shuttle had not even flown before the thought of flying ordinary citizens was first suggested by some within NASA. As early as 1982 an ad hoc group of advisors, calling themselves the Informal Task Force for the Study of Issues in Selecting Private Citizens for Space Shuttle Flight, convened to formalize the concept. By May 1983 this task force had released a preliminary report detailing many of the proposed requirements and raising many questions. Who should be allowed to go? How would they be selected? The idea was even floated to hold an open lottery. The group settled on a number of professionals who could better communicate the experience of spaceflight to the general public. At least for the first phase of the program, writers, broadcasters, poets, artists, and teachers were to be at the top of the list.

Administrator James Beggs would take the proposal under consideration for the better part of a year, as successful shuttle missions continued to build the confidence of NASA and the public. He would eventually take the proposal to the White House, where he found an agreeable Ronald Reagan in the midst of his reelection campaign. The state of education in America was a major issue during the election season, and the Reagan administration was already proposing sweeping changes during campaign stops.

Even though it was widely assumed at the time that a journalist would be the natural choice for the first citizen in space, Reagan and his advisors may have seen an opening to reach out to the teaching profession and further his education platform while still accomplishing the goals set out by Beggs. On 27 August 1984, after visiting a local high school and speaking to faculty and students, the president attended a ceremony at the J. W. Marriott Hotel in Washington DC honoring award-winning secondary schools. He delivered a lengthy speech on his view of education and some of the legislation he had pursued to help improve it. Near the end of his address, he revealed his choice of the first spaceflight participant: "One area where those wonders and benefits is most apparent is space. It's long been a goal of our space shuttle, the program, to someday carry citizen passengers into space. Until now, we hadn't decided who the first citizen passenger would be. But today I'm directing NASA to begin a search in all of our elementary and secondary schools and to choose as the first citizen passenger in the history of our space program one of America's finest—a teacher."

Although the decision only warranted two paragraphs in a day full of soaring public dialogue on the future of education in the country, it was not made in a vacuum. The space agency carried the speech live on NASA TV, and Beggs held a press conference of his own following the president's remarks, where he detailed some of the selection plans. He foresaw a windfall of candidates that would need to be winnowed down to ten, who would then come to Houston for physical exams and further evaluations. From five finalists, a primary and a backup participant would be chosen for the mission by Beggs himself.

In December 1984 a proposed rule for candidate selection was published in the *Federal Register* for public comment. At that time, Beggs was quoted as saying that he expected two or three citizen observers or participants to fly per year, possibly beginning as early as mid-1985. He also made a point reflected in the original report, emphasizing that the flyer would be expected to propose an activity that would make their journey worthwhile. In keeping with the political goals of the president, Beggs was quoted in NASA's *Space News Roundup* as stating that the choice of a teacher as the first citizen in space would "inspire young people to excellence. NASA will live or die depending on the quality of education our young people get. [A] good teacher can have a profound impact on youngsters."

Although some mention was made during the initial proposals of the potential risk this new class of payload specialist might pose to the mission, there was not yet any public consideration of the risk of the mission to the citizen astronaut's well-being. The first announcement of opportunity was released in October by the office of NASA's Space Flight Participant Program. By the closing date, NASA had received 11,146 application packages from teachers all across the country. One of those packages was submitted by a thirty-seven-year-old social studies teacher from Concord, New Hampshire—Sharon Christa McAuliffe.

RODOLFO NERI VELA, STS-61B (T+73.162 SECONDS)
It was terrible. I was already back in Mexico. That morning I was visiting my parents. Someone was watching the news in the living room and came running into the kitchen screaming and telling the bad news. I immediately got up and went to watch the TV. They kept repeating the same images, again and again, and I was horrified, and very sad. I automatically thought about the families and friends of the seven 51L astronauts. I felt so sorry for them. Perhaps I should have thought first of the crew, but for them everything was finished, so I thought of their loved living ones, and how much they were suffering at that time. I thanked God mentally and I realized I had been very lucky. It was as if I had been reborn. Then I thought about Christa, and about the millions of kids who were watching the launch and ready to get a few hours later the lessons that Christa had so carefully designed and practiced during her training. Nothing but sadness came to my heart and my mind.

Christa McAuliffe grew up and attended college in Framingham, Massachusetts, graduating in 1970 with her degree in education and history. After teaching for several years in the Maryland school system and earning a master's in education supervision and administration, she and her husband, Steve, settled in Concord, New Hampshire, with their growing family. There, at Concord High School, she earned the admiration of faculty and students alike for her enthusiastic, inspiring teaching style. She took her law class students on day trips to actual court proceedings so often that she earned the informal title Queen of the Field Trips.

In November 1984 she served as a New Hampshire state delegate to the National Council for the Social Studies Annual Conference in Washington DC. Attending the event with a close teacher friend, McAuliffe happened across a blue-and-silver-trimmed table stacked with information and application booklets for what had become known as the Teacher in Space Program. She scooped one up and set about the arduous task of filling out all the necessary information by hand.

In response to an essay question on the application, McAuliffe explained her perspective on being the first private citizen in space:

> *As a woman, I have been envious of those men who could participate in the space program and who were encouraged to excel in the areas of math and science. I felt that women had indeed been left outside of one of the most exciting careers available. When Sally Ride and other women began to train as astronauts, I could look among my students and see ahead of them an ever-increasing list of opportunities.*
>
> *I cannot join the space program and restart my life as an astronaut, but this opportunity to connect my abilities as an educator with my interests in history and space is a unique opportunity to fulfill my early fantasies. I watched the Space Age being born and I would like to participate.*

By the time she had completed the packet, time was running short. Her friend from the conference worked long nights editing McAuliffe's submission on a computer before typing it into a final application form. McAuliffe managed to get the stack of forms, recommendations, and credentials in the mail just before the 1 February 1985 deadline. As she would soon learn, her recent trip to Washington would not be her last.

ROBERT CENKER, STS-61C (T+73.162 SECONDS)

I was on an airplane for LA and contrary to the rules, because there was a launch, I had a transistor radio and I was listening on the radio. If I could have reached through the radio and throttled the radio announcer, I would have, because he said they were looking for parachutes and I'm thinking this guy clearly has absolutely no idea what he's talking about, these people are gone. And when I landed in LA, I called Barbara, and my neighbor answered the phone because there was [a] TV truck in my driveway. Apparently they had parked and they were trying to videotape through my living room window—my kids. It was a zoo.

On the afternoon of 26 June 1985 McAuliffe and 113 other nominees were ushered into the East Room of the White House to be greeted by President Reagan. With his typical humor, he began with, "Class will come to order," and was rewarded with polite laughter from the teachers. He went on to congratulate them all for making it that far in the competition and added, "When one of you blasts off from Cape Kennedy next January, you will be representing that hope and opportunity and possibility—you'll be the emissary to the next generation of American heroes. And your message will be that our progress, impressive as it is, is only just a beginning; that our achievements, as great as they are, are only a launching pad into the future. Flying up above the atmosphere, you'll be able to truly say that our horizons are not our limits, only new frontiers to be explored."

Over the course of the Washington trip, the candidates were welcomed by several astronauts in formal and informal settings, including a stern lecture from a recently flown shuttle pilot. According to McAuliffe's mother, Grace Corrigan, in her book *A Journal for Christa*, the subject of the risk to her life was finally breached for the first time. "She said that one could be intimidated thinking of all that he had said," she wrote, "until you realize that NASA employed the most sophisticated safety features, and they would never take any chances with their equipment, much less an astronaut's life."

McAuliffe left Washington full of enthusiasm and drove a short distance into Maryland to stay with old friends for the night, before returning to New Hampshire. Unbeknownst to her at the time, the selection board had already made its decision on the ten finalists, and NASA had been trying to reach her before she had even left DC. With virtually no time for her to take that piece of news in, the agency wanted McAuliffe to come back to Washington for the formal announcement on 1 July.

GARY PAYTON, STS-51C (T+73.162 SECONDS)
I'd gone into the job of helping the Air Force and NASA get ready for the Vandenberg flight. So I was getting ready for one of these ops integration meetings. I went in and somebody came in the room and [said], "The Challenger *has blown up during launch," and that a few people had seen parachutes come out. Well, okay. Blew up during launch? Yeah that's possible, but there were no parachutes that the crew could wear, in those days.*

Throughout the first half of July, the ten finalists were poked and prodded by the doctors, interviewed by more panels, and constantly thrown in front of the press. It was quickly becoming apparent that an otherwise-

41. Teacher-in-space Christa McAuliffe (*center*) and backup Barbara Morgan (*left*) meet the STS-51L crew in the Astronaut Office at Johnson Space Center on 9 September 1985. Courtesy NASA/Retro Space Images.

routine shuttle mission was going to be something of a national phenomenon. On 19 July McAuliffe and the other nine finalists were back at the White House for the formal announcement, where they learned of the winner just before entering the roomful of reporters. When the competition came to an end, it was McAuliffe who was selected by Beggs for the mission, with Barbara Morgan, a thirty-four-year-old second-grade teacher from Idaho, as her backup.

With President Reagan recovering from a recent surgery, Vice President George Bush stood in to make the public announcement: "And the winner—the teacher who will be going into space—Christa McAuliffe. She plans to keep a journal of her experiences in space. She said that 'just as the pioneer travelers of the Conestoga wagon days kept personal journals, I as a space traveler would do the same.' Well, I'm personally looking forward to reading that journal someday."

An emotional McAuliffe stepped to the microphone with her now trademark smile. "It's not often that a teacher is at a loss for words," she began. "I know my students wouldn't think so. I've made nine wonderful friends over the last two weeks. And when that shuttle goes, there might be one body . . ."—she put her finger to her lips as she began to choke up with tears—"but there's going to be ten souls that I'm taking with me."

STS-51L was the tenth planned mission for the orbiter *Challenger*. The primary payload was the long-awaited second Tracking and Data Relay Satellite (TDRS-B), which had been grounded for several months due to unresolved technical problems. In addition, the crew would take advantage of their orbital vantage point to observe Halley's Comet, deploying a suite of sensors on the Spartan Halley free-floating satellite, which would be retrieved using the shuttle's robotic arm after two days of study away from the orbiter's environment. They would also attempt more observations of the comet with the CHAMP experiment that had caused the previous crew so much frustration.

While Jarvis would operate his fluid dynamics experiment, McAuliffe, in keeping with her communicator role, was tasked with televising two classroom lessons from space on the fourth day of the flight. The first, titled *The Ultimate Field Trip*, would provide a guided tour of the orbiter's two decks with assistance from Scobee and Smith. The second lesson, to be broadcast three hours later, was called *Where We've Been, Where We're Going, Why?* and would feature Jarvis, focusing on the unique properties of the zero-g environment and its benefits for manufacturing and research. Barbara Morgan would be on hand as a commentator on the ground throughout the flight for a special mission-length program called *Mission Watch* and would enhance the student-oriented coverage of the Teacher in Space Program.

HOOT GIBSON, STS-41B, STS-61C (T+73.162 SECONDS)
We're in the big conference room in Building 4. Somebody stuck their head in the door and they said, "Hey, guys, Challenger *is getting ready to launch. You want to take a break and watch the launch?" We said, "Yes, let's do that." We went into one of the smaller conference rooms where we had all the com loops plugged in and a television. That's where I was watching* Challenger *go down. What a bleak, dreary day. You look at where we had been, where we were. I was on top of the world. I had just commanded my first Space Shuttle mission. We had our fourth Orbiter. We were going to fly seems like eight missions in 1986. We were on our way to having a really big year. We were really sailing. We went from that position to being absolutely in the deepest darkest black hole you could ever imagine, just in the space of [seventy-three] seconds.*

The NASA public relations machine was in high gear for the teacher-in-space mission, and McAuliffe was inundated with media wherever she went.

42. Barbara Morgan (*left*) and Christa McAuliffe pause for a photograph during training at the Johnson Space Center, Houston, in December 1985. Courtesy NASA/Retro Space Images.

Training sessions were covered by the press, public appearances were more and more frequent, and mail piled up in the Astronaut Office requesting an autograph from the first private-citizen space traveler.

McAuliffe shared an office with Barbara Morgan on the first floor of building 4 at JSC. Their two desks were set at an angle to the walls, with a large window looking out over a parking lot. As candidates rotated from freshman trainees to prime crew members, various other payload specialists would share the office as well, including Brett Watterson and Rodolfo Neri Vela, and they quickly became friends with the two teachers turned space flyers. As Watterson recalled of McAuliffe, "She was a darling. She and I were office mates, along with her backup Barbara Morgan, and she was so excited about going. She and Barbara were the nicest and most interesting people. She was from the Northeast, and she had kind of a Northeast nasal accent that—it was just fun working with them."

Neri shared the same sentiment, remembering, "I went along very well with Christa McAuliffe and Barbara Morgan, who years later went to space and I felt very happy for her at the time. Both of them were wonderful women." The most striking image Neri has to this day of McAuliffe occurred just after he returned from space himself:

I remember that one or two days after the end of my mission and my return to Houston, I was walking somewhere in the Johnson Space Center and heard a voice calling my name. It was Christa. She congratulated me and asked with a bright curiosity in her eyes how it had been. She wanted to know everything, and I was pleased to tell her about the wonderful trip I had just had and she was going to have a few weeks after that. She said I looked very happy and that it seemed I would never stop smiling. She was very right about my feelings.

Bob Cenker had rented an apartment near the space center while he was in training for his much-delayed mission in early January. When the teacher-in-space candidates were selected, McAuliffe and Morgan ended up in the same apartment complex, and the three would talk often and even do some training together aboard the Vomit Comet. Cenker had just returned from space on 18 January, and with McAuliffe's mission less than a week away, they had a chance meeting at their temporary home: "I had landed, and she was getting ready to leave for the cape. She was, in theory,

43. A curious Barbara Morgan (*left*) and Christa McAuliffe listen as Greg Jarvis discusses his fluid dynamics experiment. Congressman Bill Nelson joined his fellow payload specialists onboard the November 1985 KC-135 training flight. Courtesy NASA/Retro Space Images.

in isolation, but she had to come back to her apartment to get a couple of personal things, so you sort of bend the rules in some of those cases. And she just looked at me as I was driving out, and she said, 'You've got to tell me what it's like!' And I said, 'No, no . . . when you come back and we're both veterans, then we're gonna talk, and we're gonna talk a lot.' Obviously, that never happened."

At 11:38 a.m. on 28 January 1986, with a large portion of the country's schoolchildren watching on television, *Challenger* and its crew of seven were launched into the cold Florida skies. Unseen by the nationwide audience and network commentators, a small puff of oily-black smoke emanated from the lower right SRB and pulsed with the violent rhythm of the booster's dynamic frequency. Just over a minute later, in the briefest of milliseconds, everything changed—for the families of the crew members, for NASA's space shuttle program, and for the country. The scores of payload specialists, MSES, and potential citizen observers who were waiting in the wings to fly may not have realized at that moment, but for many of them their dreams of spaceflight had just ended.

The inquisition began almost immediately. How could this happen? How could the seemingly infallible NASA, an organization that not only put men on the moon but was able to save one lunar crew from almost certain death on *Apollo 13*, lose a space shuttle during launch? It was unprecedented, and the loss of McAuliffe, who had become something of a national celebrity, made it all the worse, given the attention that her presence attracted.

Just an hour or so after the tragedy, President Reagan was peppered with questions from an incredulous press corps in the Roosevelt Room of the White House: "Mr. President, do you think it raises questions about having citizens aboard the space shuttle? Do you think it was a mistake to put the teacher on board?" These were questions the president could only struggle to answer. That night, he was to give the State of the Union address to Congress, but the tragic event of the day foreshadowed any such political theater.

Instead, speechwriters went to work crafting one of the most heartbreaking and memorable speeches any president would ever deliver. Reagan would go on national television to try to assuage the grief of a nation and reassure the millions of schoolchildren that risk is the price of progress and that the program would continue. "The future doesn't belong to the fainthearted; it belongs to the brave," Reagan delivered emotionally. "The *Challenger* crew was pulling us into the future, and we'll continue to follow them."

Reagan appointed a presidential commission to investigate the accident, headed by William P. Rogers. Members of the panel included notable scientists and aerospace engineers, including astronauts Neil Armstrong and Sally Ride. After several months of intense work, the Rogers Commission formally determined the cause of the accident to be what many in the space shuttle program already knew—the unusually cold temperatures on 28 January had affected rubber O-rings that sealed the case segments of the SRBS.

The O-rings were not able to seat properly into the machined grooves of the poorly designed joints between the case segments, allowing hot exhaust gas to blow by both the primary and backup rings. The small puffs of black smoke seen on the lower right-hand SRB were the beginning of a breach that grew larger as the shuttle ascended.

CHARLIE WALKER, STS-41D, STS-51D, STS-61B

There were burns on the inner O-ring, the primary seal on at least one SRB in one segment on each of my three flights, including that last flight 61B, which was two missions before Challenger *[was lost]. But again, that was something that, in retrospect, I don't think the crews, and me as a payload specialist . . . I know I don't recall ever hearing anything about that during my training or crew briefings. Whether it was spoken and it was just like another one of the little details, or whether it wasn't spoken, I don't know, but I was not made aware of those as issues that really somebody should look into.*

The SRBS' O-rings had shown not only signs of "erosion," or thermal damage, on nearly half the flights prior to *Challenger*'s, but in several cases, the primary ring failed completely, allowing the incinerating flames to blow by and damage the secondary ring. One of the worst occurrences of this phenomenon was revealed on STS-51C, the first DOD mission, which launched the previous January and carried the air force's first MSE.

GARY PAYTON, STS-51C

We never got told this after the flight, but when they pulled our solid rocket boosters out of the Atlantic Ocean [and] took them apart to ship them back to Thiokol, we had hot gas blow-by on our O-ring seals also. In fact, it blew by the primary O-ring seal and hot gasses impinged on the secondary O-ring seal. And the original design of the solid rocket booster was such that no hot gas was supposed to get to any O-ring, but ours was a worst case of hot gas blow-by on O-rings that they had seen up until that time.

None of the astronauts were made aware of the concerns about the SRBS that were occurring with alarming regularity. Decades after the tragedy, that lack of knowledge is one of the more difficult aspects of the accident for them to deal with. "I personally did not know this information until well into the *Challenger* investigation, which was more than a year after STS-51C," Loren Shriver told the authors. "I do not consider this to be timely in any sense, and to this day continues to be an unacceptable situation."

Payton also recalls learning of the O-ring concerns, but just days after the accident. Speaking to STS-51L flight director Jay Greene at the memorial for the fallen crew in Houston, Greene shared his opinion that the orbiter fleet should have been grounded following Payton's near-disastrous DOD mission. "It was news to all of us in the crew," he recalls.

A critical comment was made in the course of the Rogers Commission report regarding the presence of large icicles on pad 39B the morning of the launch that might effectively sum up NASA's safety culture in the mid-1980s: "In this situation, NASA appeared to be requiring a contractor to prove that it was not safe to fly, rather than proving it was safe." The problems the agency faced in the rush to get the shuttle program up to its promised potential went far beyond Morton-Thiokol's flawed designs and decisions in regard to their SRBs.

NASA had published projected manifests in 1985 that called for as many as twenty-four missions—two per month—by 1990. *Challenger*'s mission was the second of the month, coming just ten days after *Columbia*'s delayed landing. If the experience of operating these two missions within such a close time span served as any example, it didn't bode well for the future success of the program. Two major anomalies were noted during the STS-61C mission, with Bill Nelson and Bob Cenker on board. One was worse-than-typical O-ring erosion on one of the SRBs, and the other was a severely damaged wheel brake, which nearly led to another tire blowing. After *Columbia*'s diversion to an Edwards Air Force Base landing, *Challenger* was to be the first to land at KSC since the STS-51D blown-tire incident, something NASA would have never considered had managers been aware of the brake problem. As the commission's report noted, "Because Shuttle flights were coming in fairly rapid succession, it was becoming difficult to analyze all the data from one flight before the next was scheduled to launch."

One of the most important reasons for the degraded safety culture at NASA in the 1980s was that since being declared operational, the space shuttle program had slashed safety and quality assurance personnel at its field centers and headquarters. The routine image of the space shuttle program that was heralded by NASA to the public and to Congress belied the very real fact that the orbiter was still, in essence, a developmental test vehicle. Continuous technical modifications, upgrades, computer software changes, and flight profiles interjected new unknowns on every mission. Just the SRBs alone had evolved over the course of twenty-five missions, with thinner case walls to reduce weight and smaller exhaust throats to increase thrust. These changes combined to cause more flexing of the boosters as the shuttle's off-center main engines ignited, and during the violent powered flight as well. Every flight was a test flight.

GARY PAYTON, STS-51C
We were kind of naïve. There were a lot of civilian guys in the astronaut business. I think they took Challenger *harder than the military guys did. I had spent four years at Cape Canaveral watching Atlases, Deltas and Titans turn into roman candles across the Atlantic Ocean, so I knew the design margins were thin. But there was a lot of redundancy also, especially on the orbiter. We spent basically a year going through all of those redundancies in each simulator ride, so I think we all were naïve that there was enough redundancy in the orbiter systems that if a computer failed, or the hydraulic system failed or something like that, that we could get home.*

Even as the operational shuttle flights were revealing serious O-ring and nozzle anomalies, Thiokol had been developing the lightweight, filament-wound SRB cases that would be used initially on the Vandenberg-launched DOD missions. STS-62A would be the first to fly the new boosters, and with them came many new engineering questions that had to be proved out on their maiden launch. NASA seemingly took no consideration of the potentially fatal consequences of the new boosters failing, when they accepted Undersecretary of the Air Force Pete Aldridge as a payload specialist aboard the mission.

Watterson and Randy Odle had been instrumental in the development of payload procedures for the flight, and being military officers, they were accustomed to accepting risks. But Aldridge had replaced Odle at the direction of James Beggs—a purely political move in the never-ending push to assure the continuance of the program. "It was Beggs who put so much pressure to amortize the cost of the shuttle, and that's why he got Jake Garn and [Bill Nelson] and Pete [Aldridge], and the teacher," Watterson observed. "It made it into people believing this was a routine flight, and it wasn't like that at all. The astronauts kept saying—and I paid attention to what they were saying—when you go from zero to eighteen thousand miles (per hour) in eight and a half minutes, something is going to go wrong."

The odds of something going wrong have been open to debate over the thirty-year lifetime of the space shuttle program, but recent studies have demonstrated that the odds have fluctuated widely from mission to mission. Following *Challenger*, it was often said that the next mission would be the safest ever flown, due in large part to the lessons learned from the accident. And the data show that, statistically, the odds did improve after major events—some failures but some simply revelations of potential failures.

In an American Institute of Aeronautics and Astronautics report titled *Shuttle Risk Progression: Use of the Shuttle Probabilistic Risk Assessment (PRA) to Show Reliability Growth*, a statistical sampling of missions over the thirty years of the program were analyzed, and key risks to the vehicle and crew were considered. Overall, the risk of a loss of crew and vehicle (LOCV) was determined to be one in twelve for the first flight, STS-1. The ejection seats that the flight test crews used were disabled for STS-5, leading to an increased potential for LOCV of one in ten, where it remained through *Challenger*'s final flight. The SRB failure and subsequent redesign, along with new Phase II main engines and better software, did indeed make STS-26, launched in September 1988, the safest mission to date, with the potential for LOCV at one in seventeen—still not great odds.

For STS-1 the most significant threat to the vehicle was assumed to be debris from somewhere on the external tank or SRBs breaking off and damaging the critical heat-protection tiles. Catastrophic failure of the SRBs came next, followed by micrometeoroid strikes in orbit and explosive "uncontained" main-engine failure. In all these scenarios, it was assumed the ejection seats would not save the crew. The top three scenarios held their ranking through STS-51L, but for the first mission after *Challenger*'s failure, SRB failure dropped to number 6 on the list.

Of course, this analysis was done with the benefit of hindsight, near the end of the space shuttle program, and did not effectively account for the organizational culture that led to the STS-51L accident. If the Thiokol engineers who knew about the SRB O-rings' susceptibility to failure were able to incorporate the required design changes prior to the loss of the STS-51L crew, the risk assessment would be completely different. But that would have required the program to be grounded for a period of time that was unthinkable in those days. NASA, the can-do, unfailing team that helped define America in the latter half of the twentieth century, was experiencing an agency-wide case of "go fever," a term coined in the 1960s to describe a launch team's unstoppable urge to get a rocket off the pad.

The Rogers Commission also made observations on the continuous remanifesting of payloads and the stress that put on the program. Along with many of these payload changes came the late removal or addition of the payload specialists assigned to them: "One small change does not come alone; it generates several others. A payload specialist [Nelson] was added to mission 61C only two months before its scheduled lift off. Because there were already seven crew members assigned to the flight, one had to be removed. The Hughes payload specialist [Jarvis] was moved from 61C to 51L just three months before 51L was scheduled to launch. His experiments were also added to 51L."

NASA's own rules for flight preparations dictated that all middeck payloads and all payload specialists were to be firmly assigned to a particular mission no later than five months prior to the planned launch. The commission reported, "That rule has not been enforced—in fact, it is more honored in the breach than in the observance." When investigators looked at shuttle missions going back to *Challenger*'s STS-41G mission with Marc Garneau and Paul Scully-Power, a total of sixteen payload specialists had been assigned, yet seven of those were added inside of the prescribed five-month cutoff.

Once the Rogers Commission report was released, NASA knew it had to get down to the business of making the shuttle as safe as was technically feasible before entrusting the lives of astronauts on it again. A major revamping of the management structure would be enacted, and a renewed emphasis on safety was manifested by including astronauts in several key operational and safety positions.

Many of the threat mitigations that had been in place since the beginning of the program were finally acknowledged as having little value. There was no getting around the fact that during SRB-powered flight, there simply was no conceivable way of successfully aborting the flight in a survivable scenario. Several abort profiles following separation of the boosters would leave the orbiter out of reach of a suitable runway, and the only option was a ditching at sea, which had been analyzed as being nonsurvivable. Both the impact loads on the forward fuselage and the likelihood that a payload in the cargo bay would break free and crush the crew cabin left the astronauts with no lifesaving options.

The slide-wire baskets that would be employed to whisk crew members away from a launchpad emergency had never been rated for human usage. No one had ever ridden the baskets down to the perimeter of the launch area to evaluate their effectiveness. Astronauts had not worn pressure suits since the end of the test-flight program, leaving them vulnerable to a decompression of the cabin during launch or entry. The orbiter's brakes had been an ongoing source of concern, and with the pressure to return every mission to the confines of the KSC runway, the potential existed for a loss of a vehicle due to a runway excursion.

Much like Bill Nelson's observation of the senselessness of his firefighting training, the agency had been walking through fire itself since the maiden launch of *Columbia* in 1981. Up until that fateful day in January 1986, it had just barely managed to keep the flames of failure at bay. There were so many issues that had lurked in the background for years, any one of which could lead to catastrophe, but there simply wasn't time to properly address them all, given NASA's self-imposed pressure to fly as often as possible.

GARY PAYTON, STS-51C

What it boiled down to is the realization that you have to trust in the folks who were working on the shuttle—the folks who put it all together down there in Florida, the folks who code the software. There was this certain philosophy that says "Yeah, eventually we'll lose an orbiter. It'll run off the end of the runway or something will go wrong. I'll work as hard as I can to make sure that doesn't happen on the next flight." So that's the mindset that everybody kind of had.

The accident had a profound impact on the future direction of the space shuttle program and the payload specialists who were preparing to fly. The decision was made to no longer carry commercial satellites aboard the orbiter—they would be launched only aboard new fleets of expendable rockets. With the memory of the *Challenger* crew fresh in their minds, NASA managers would only risk human lives when astronauts were critical to the success of the mission. No longer would engineers from satellite builders or foreign countries be invited to fly into space along with their communications satellite. Many in the program, even some who were in line to go, agreed with the new philosophy. As Brett Watterson told the authors, "After Greg Jarvis died, who was a friend of mine, and Christa McAuliffe, who was my officemate, it didn't make a lot of sense to me why anybody would want to be on a space shuttle watching a payload that they represent being deployed by a mission specialist."

Civilian payload specialists weren't the only ones to lose their dream of spaceflight following the accident, though. STS-62A, with its filament-wound composite boosters, was canceled, and Watterson and Pete Aldridge would never get to go into orbit. As the MSE group was being disbanded, air force officials claimed that the risk of flying on the space shuttle was the primary reason they were getting out of the program. For many of them, this was a less-than-straightforward justification. As Watterson asked himself, "If it was so unsafe, why would they send national celebrities as opposed to military guys who are, pardon the expression but, they're in the business of getting things broken and getting themselves hurt? That's part of what you sign up for when you sign up to the military it seems to me." Clearly, some in the MSE group saw themselves as something much more critical to the program.

ERIC SUNDBERG, MSE GROUP I

Well I think we understood [risk] entirely. That's why during the interview process the question was, "Are you terribly afraid of dying or being killed?" And I think if someone had said "Honestly, yes I am," that probably would have been a turnoff. Now, some people may have said "No, I'm not" and in reality when they were faced with the situation they probably would have been a little more upset. The risks were very real and they were very honest about them.

FRANK CASSERINO, MSE GROUP I

The decision was made after the accident not to fly MSEs any longer, and it was one of those things you kind of scratch your head about. One of the reasons that they gave for not flying us was that they didn't want to risk our lives on these missions. Well, I thought I joined the military knowing that someday I might have to go to battle or risk my life for something. That was just a bunch of nonsense in my opinion.

The risks associated with spaceflight were ever present and continued to be after *Challenger*. But the agency took action on a large number of safety-related issues in the nearly three years the orbiter fleet was grounded. Aside from the SRB redesign, numerous features were added to the shuttle to enhance crew safety to the extent possible. New pressure suits would protect the astronauts in the event of loss of cabin pressure, and a bailout capability was incorporated by means of a curved pole that extended after the hatch was explosively separated, theoretically allowing them to parachute to safety. Loren Shriver would share the opinion of many in the Astronaut Office that "the pressure suits were probably the most significant of the two, but in reality, neither could realistically add that much to safety in catastrophic situations."

Many other enhancements to equipment and procedures were implemented, including establishing human-rating certification for the slide-wire baskets at the two shuttle launchpads. In May 1992 *Endeavour*'s maiden voyage would feature a huge drag chute for the first time. Deployed as the shuttle rolled out after landing, the drag chute—with red, white, and blue rings—helped slow the vehicle from its two-hundred-mile-per-hour touchdown speed and ease the stress on the orbiter's tires and brakes.

The space shuttle was made to be as safe as it possibly could be, but once the program returned to flight in September 1988, only NASA astronauts would be aboard the first missions. For over two years and twelve space shuttle flights, no payload specialists were considered.

Bob Cenker takes an engineer's perspective on the subject of risk, given that he spent his entire professional career in the space business designing and building satellites. "We are in the risk-management business. We are not in the risk-elimination business," he explained to the KSC Visitor Complex audience in 2015. "There is no way to completely eliminate risk." With his office desk piled high with memos from various engineers requesting more studies or analysis on one concern or another, one of his responsibilities as a manager of satellite integration was to say it was time to quit and go launch the spacecraft.

"Now, in my case, lives didn't hang in the balance, but somebody still has to make that call," Cenker explained. Engineers always want to make things better, and given more time and more money, they will come up with an improved design. At some point, he had to put an end to it. "It's a very difficult call. It's never going to be safe, but somebody has to make that call," he said.

In January 1986 he had to make that call with his own life on the line. "One of the things that amazed me was this army of people that was looking out for me," he remembers of those days. "If you stop and think about it, all of those people have to get it right. That's not easy at all. And so it's not for the fainthearted. If it were easy, anyone could do it." There was nothing left to do but climb aboard *Columbia* and trust in the work of the people who put him there. But there was no second-guessing for Cenker. "I knew what I was getting into," he stated pointedly to the audience. "Christa McAuliffe knew what she was getting into."

> *When we were in training, we trained for failures. You don't train for things going well—going well is easy. And I can remember on one particular occasion Christa asked the question, "Well, what happens if this fails?" And her commander looked at her and said, "If that fails, it's a loss of vehicle." And it doesn't take a rocket scientist to make the jump that says if that's a loss of vehicle, that's a loss of crew. And it wasn't a flip response; it wasn't a macho "By God, I don't care, I'm gonna die" kind of thing, no. It was—this is the job that we're doing, this is the position that we have gotten ourselves into, and we all accept it. As one of the guys I flew with has always described it—you prepare yourself as best you can, and then you accept whatever risk is left.*

NASA would do just that for the next seventeen years, carrying the nation's space program into the twenty-first century with a manned space plane designed in the 1970s. Getting their stride back after a triumphant return to flight, the shuttles at long last would loft the Magellan probe to Venus, the Galileo spacecraft to Jupiter, and the Ulysses solar probe around the poles of the sun. In April 1990 the highly anticipated Hubble Space Telescope would be deployed into an orbit over 380 miles high, and numerous missions would return to carry out needed service calls.

Success became routine once again, and once again astronauts performed spectacular missions that were barely noticed by the press and public. But as one astronaut stated to the Rogers Commission back in 1986, "The lessons learned here will have to be learned all over again." Older, experienced space workers moved on, to be replaced by a newer generation of engineers and astronauts. Anyone close to NASA couldn't avoid the ever-present memories of both *Apollo 1* and *Challenger*. The images of the crews and their mission emblems were everywhere, and every January, the agency would pause to remember them.

NASA, as an organization, would once again be tested, as the monstrously complex International Space Station came to fruition, requiring high-frequency space shuttle construction missions in coordination with the launches from other participating countries. Gradually, unseen by engineers, flight controllers, and managers with their sleeves rolled up in the biggest engineering project ever attempted, the agency that was the pride of the nation was once again drifting toward failure.

Epilogue

If we do not consider Flight Safety First all the time at all levels of
NASA, this machinery and this program will NOT make it . . . Our
space machinery is not airline machinery.

John Young

Just prior to the first anniversary of the *Challenger* accident, NASA administrator James Fletcher, who had returned to head the agency for a second term in May 1986, was quoted by *USA Today* writer Jack Kelly as saying that civilians would not be riding on the space shuttle for "probably the first twenty missions, and maybe forever." He also suggested that the agency had a semicommitment to fly Barbara Morgan, Christa McAuliffe's backup, but that there was still much deliberation within the agency about how risky such a flight might be, in terms of both politics and her personal safety.

Bill Nelson, who had returned to Congress and penned a memoir of his experience flying on the shuttle, expressly stated that he was not in favor of continuing the citizen-in-space program in the near term. Yet he too would support Fletcher's intentions and agreed that the one notable exception should be Morgan. Nelson felt that it was important enough to the schoolchildren of the country to see the teacher-in-space mission successfully completed.

In addition to Aldridge and Watterson on STS-62A, at the time of the accident, many more payload specialists and their backups were training for upcoming missions. Samuel Durrance, an astrogeophysicist from Johns Hopkins University, and Ron Parise, an astronomer who had developed an ultraviolet imaging telescope, were slated to fly on STS-61E's Astro-1 flight in March 1986. Another multinational satellite deployment mission was planned for June aboard *Columbia*, including Britain's Nigel Wood with the Skynet 4A and Indonesian payload specialist Pratiwi Sudarmono with the Palapa B3.

Toward the end of 1986 Frank Casserino was targeted to fly his classified mission aboard *Discovery*, and Katherine Sparks Roberts was to represent the DOD for the second Vandenberg launch of the same orbiter on STS-62B, in late September. Byron Lichtenberg, Michael Lampton, and oceanographer Bob Stevenson were in line to fly, as was Hughes Corporation's John Konrad and Nagapathi Bhat of India. Group 2 MSE Chuck Jones would have rounded out the year with a classified mission in December aboard *Challenger*.

All these missions were either canceled outright with the removal of commercial payloads or remanifested in the years following *Discovery*'s return-to-flight mission in September 1988. With the exception of the scientist–payload specialists who would crew the Spacelab series of missions, none of the others would ever venture to space. Barbara Morgan lingered around the space agency for a time, still trying to help inspire schoolchildren after the horror of the accident. She too eventually returned to teaching in Idaho, yet she never let go of the dream to continue McAuliffe's mission.

Over a two-year period following the return to flight, twelve space shuttle missions would fly with only the essential NASA crew members aboard. It wasn't until December 1990 that *Columbia* once again lofted two payload specialists—Durrance and Parise—as part of the STS-35 crew. The Astro-1 Spacelab mission that was to immediately follow STS-51L spent years on the back burner, and several of the original crew members had moved to other roles or left the agency altogether.

From an altitude of 225 miles above the planet, Astro-1 employed a suite of four telescopes to study celestial targets in the x-ray and ultraviolet wavelengths. It was the second flight of the pallet-only configuration of Spacelab, utilizing the three-axis Instrument Pointing System and a two-axis pointing system for the x-ray telescope. As was done on Spacelab 2, the crew operated the telescopes remotely from the flight deck of the orbiter in round-the-clock split shifts.

The DOD undertook one final effort to fly a payload specialist when they assigned U.S. Army Chief Warrant Officer Thomas J. Hennen aboard STS-44 as part of the Terra Scout program. A military intelligence officer by

44. When *Challenger* disintegrated during ascent on 28 January 1986, payload specialists Sam Durrance (*left*), Ron Parise, and backup Ken Nordsieck were training for the Astro-1 Spacelab mission. Durrance and Parise would wait nearly five years before being the first payload specialists to fly after the tragedy. Courtesy NASA/Retro Space Images.

training, Hennen was selected as a payload specialist candidate in September 1998 and named the primary crew member for Terra Scout a year later. Throughout the week-long mission, Hennen operated several instruments, including the Spaceborne Direct-View Optical System and the M88-1 Military Man in Space experiment, to evaluate what kinds of observations of strategic value were possible from orbit.

STS-44 represented both the first flight of a noncommissioned officer and the final flight for a dedicated DOD crew member. While experiments for other programs such as Terra View and Terra Geode were carried out by NASA mission specialists on other flights, the Defense Department curtailed any further participation in the shuttle program and even canceled a Strategic Defense Initiative–dedicated Spacelab mission named Starlab, which had been scheduled for the end of 1990. MSEs Capt. Craig Puz and Capt. Maureen LaComb had initially been assigned to the project, but eventually it was shelved to provide funding to higher-priority military programs.

Ulf Merbold would fly again aboard the International Microgravity Laboratory Spacelab mission in January 1992 with Roberta Bondar of Canada. In March his former Spacelab 1 crewmate Byron Lichtenberg flew aboard the Atlas-1 mission, along with Dirk Frimout of Belgium. Payload specialists from Italy, Japan, Germany, Ukraine, France, and Canada flew primarily on Spacelab missions throughout the 1990s, providing practical experience for the future multinational operations aboard the ISS. Although several Russian cosmonauts flew on the space shuttle during the years of the joint Shuttle-Mir space station program, they were designated mission specialists by NASA, due to their extensive professional experience in spaceflight.

When *Columbia* reached orbit on 4 April 1997 carrying payload specialists Roger Crouch and Greg Linteris aboard the Microgravity Science Laboratory, problems with one of the three power-generating fuel cells almost immediately revealed themselves. As a result, the unit had to be shut down, and the mission would be cut short before any of the research could even get started. When *Columbia* returned to Earth after barely four days in orbit, NASA made an unprecedented decision—they would leave the Spacelab module in the payload bay, service the orbiter, and refly the mission. Three months later, on 1 July 1997, Crouch and Linteris had the rare opportunity to fly twice as payload specialists.

For the most part, these missions were undertaken without much of the public attention of the early shuttle program or, for that matter, many of the high-profile spectacles such as the Hubble Space Telescope repair missions or Shuttle-Mir dockings. Overfamiliarity with scenes of successive shuttle launches and landings and astronauts waving at TV cameras from orbit meant that the American people once again had lost interest in the routine, space-based research missions that most of the payload specialists risked their lives to undertake. That interest, however, would once again be reignited in the fall of 1998, when a payload specialist who was already a household name for generations of Americans would depart from a Florida launchpad under the most unlikely series of fortunate events.

"Dan, I want you to send me back to space." NASA administrator Daniel S. Goldin could not believe what he had just heard the American icon seated before him say. Senator and former Mercury astronaut John Glenn, at the healthy age of seventy-six, had marched into Goldin's office with binders full of medical journal data and presumably his own medical history going all the way back to his NASA days beginning in 1959. Goldin recalled in a 2016 op-ed contemplating for a moment the risks and potential political fallout of such an endeavor and immediately came to his conclusion. "Absolutely not," he stated flatly.

Glenn, once grounded from spaceflight by President Kennedy following his historic orbital flight in 1962, now faced a similar uphill battle for another mission in 1997. But his justification went far beyond that of a sentimental joyride for a retiring politician; throughout his career in public service, Glenn had been exposed to the plight of aging Americans in the nation's health-care system and maintained contacts at the National Institutes of Health. Glenn pointed out to Goldin that many of the effects of weightlessness on the human body were similar to the aging process on Earth and was convinced that this was an untapped area for new scientific research. The former Project Mercury astronaut felt that he would be the ideal subject for this research.

Glenn was relentless. He detailed several possible experiments that he could perform, backed them up with peer-reviewed medical papers that his doctor friends had collected for him, and pressed the idea with Goldin at every opportunity. The administrator finally relented and opened the door to the possibility, however remote, that Glenn's long-dreamed-of second spaceflight might—*might*—happen. In order to make sure the flight would pass muster with the press and the public, not to mention Goldin's own reservations, he imposed four strict conditions.

Most importantly, he wanted to hear directly from Glenn's wife, Annie, that she fully recognized the risk involved and approved of her husband's desire. In order to be fully committed to training for the mission in terms of time and attention, Goldin wanted to be assured that Glenn would not seek reelection for his Senate seat. The science had to be good, and he was not willing to take Glenn's word for it. Goldin had been around Washington DC long enough to know that you had to cover your bases, and he wanted to hear it right from the director of the National Institutes of Health. And last, Glenn had to be able to pass a standard NASA physical and be medically cleared for the flight—no exceptions. One thing the nation's first astronaut to orbit Earth could not foresee was that in pursuing his dream of a second spaceflight, he was opening the door for another to finally make her first.

On 16 January 1998 Goldin was joined by Glenn for the press conference that would reveal to the world that he was going to fly aboard STS-95, a mission that would feature the deployment and later retrieval of the Spartan free-flyer satellite. The orbiter *Discovery* would also carry a host of biomedical and materials processing research within Spacehab, a pressurized laboratory similar to a short Spacelab module in the payload bay. Of course, Glenn himself would be the subject of many of the experiments, as he had used the research as justification to pursue the mission. It was certain that he would be the most famous payload specialist ever to fly on the shuttle.

On that same day, Goldin announced that at long last, after twelve years of waiting and wondering, NASA was offering Barbara Morgan the opportunity to fulfill her dream of flying aboard the shuttle and finally completing the educational mission of her friend and fellow teacher, Christa McAuliffe. As the negotiations were taking place regarding the possibility of sending Glenn—at that point a private citizen with no official ties to the space agency—into orbit, Goldin decided that he could not in good conscience offer Glenn a flight without also considering his predecessor's commitment to Morgan. She would not, however, be flying as a payload specialist.

NASA had no intention of reviving the Teacher in Space Program, fearing renewed memories of 1986 and the questions regarding astronaut safety.

Rather, Morgan was offered the chance to come to Houston as a full-time educator–mission specialist, a newly contrived classification of astronaut consisting of accomplished professional teachers. The January announcement was merely the first day of a long journey for Morgan. She was named to astronaut group 17 on 4 June 1998, among a class consisting of eight pilots and seventeen other mission specialist candidates. She would have to wait more than nine additional years to finally make it to orbit.

Following weeks of nostalgic media coverage of John Glenn's return to orbit, the space shuttle *Discovery* leaped from launchpad 39B into a cloudless sky on 29 October 1998. The words of launch controller Lisa Malone, broadcast live to the nation, captured the spirit of the mission when she intoned, "Liftoff of *Discovery* with a crew of six astronaut heroes and one American hero." As *Discovery* ascended, cameras around the launchpad captured a rectangular white object falling from the orbiter through the blue engine exhaust of the three main engines. The object turned out to be the cover panel of the shuttle's huge drag chute, housed at the base of the vertical tail, leading to fears that the chute could inadvertently deploy during reentry or landing. Managers decided to disarm the drag chute and not attempt to use it for landing, and simulations later indicated that it would not likely deploy on its own.

During the nearly nine-day mission full of almost daily public relations television transmissions, the celebrity payload specialist repeatedly steered reporters' questions away from himself and back to the eighty-eight scientific research experiments being performed by him and the other six astronauts in the Spacehab science module. Mission specialist Scott Parazynski, a medical doctor by training, supervised many of the biomedical experiments performed on Glenn and ESA mission specialist Pedro Duque. Chiaki Mukai, a payload specialist from Japan, and mission specialist Steve Robinson conducted still more research in life sciences, materials processing, and student-sponsored experiments.

After two days of solar corona observations flying separately from *Discovery*, Parazynski retrieved the Spartan satellite and latched it firmly into the payload bay. Commander Curt Brown and pilot Steve Lindsey guided the orbiter back to a landing at KSC on 7 November 1998, and the crew was welcomed with a fanfare rarely accorded a returning space shuttle crew, thanks to their pioneering payload specialist who rekindled so many memories of NASA's glory days.

Since Glenn's 1962 orbital flight, the so-called Canyon of Heroes, the lower section of New York City's skyscraper-lined Broadway, had offered six ticker tape parades for returning astronauts. In a rare second trip down the famed thoroughfare on 19 November 1998, seated atop a vintage automobile with his wife, Annie, alongside, Glenn and his fellow STS-95 crewmates were showered with confetti and streamers from tens of thousands of appreciative New Yorkers. Glenn waved, smiled, and flashed his very familiar thumbs-up to the throngs of admirers. It was a fitting end to a public relations coup by the nation's space agency that would be moving into the daunting era of space station construction over the coming years.

With the space shuttle fleet at long last performing the task for which it was originally conceived, there was little opportunity for onboard research and subsequently no seats available for payload specialists. Glenn and Mukai would be the last to fly for more than four years, until the two-week-long STS-107 mission of *Columbia* in January 2003. In the intervening years, the NASA organization, while never publicly far removed from the lessons of the STS-51L tragedy, was gradually drifting further and further away from the very architectures it had put in place to prevent another disaster.

Although many factors and pressures contributed to the slow degradation of the safety culture within the space shuttle program during the late 1990s and into the early twenty-first century, perhaps none were more prevalent than the need for on-time launches to build, supply, and service the ISS. The ISS assembly required critically timed launches of vital hardware in a specific sequence in order to integrate the enormously complex structure successfully. Schedule pressure once again caused managers to make decisions based on orbiter turnaround time in order to keep the program on track and confirm NASA's commitments to their international partners. Once the first Russian and U.S. elements of the ISS were linked together in December 1998, the pressure was on to move forward and complete the project.

With NASA laser focused on the ISS assembly and eventual operations, it seemed unlikely that another shuttle-based research mission would be conducted before the new facility became operational. *Columbia* was too heavy to contribute much lift capacity to the effort without extensive weight-

45. NASA administrator Dan Goldin (*left*) greets Senator John Glenn upon his return from space aboard *Discovery* on 7 November 1998. Courtesy NASA.

reducing modifications, but before those were to be done, NASA decided to fly one more Spacehab science flight aboard the flagship orbiter.

Ilan Wolfermann knew he wanted to be a fighter pilot from the age of sixteen, when a coworker of his father took him up in a light Cessna airplane, even allowing him to manipulate the controls for a time. Growing up in Beersheva, Israel, he would from that day share a passion for flying with his father, and the two of them spent countless hours soaring up into the clouds in unpowered sailplanes. He was accepted into the Israeli air force in September of 1972.

As was customary for Israelis, Ilan would change his name to Hebrew as he began his military service, in honor of his home country. Taking a combination of the letters from his father's name, he came up with Ramon, as he would be known for the rest of his life. Ilan Ramon was a naturally gifted pilot and was even sent into combat while still a trainee, during the Yom Kippur War of 1973. He would go on to fly the American-built A-4 attack jet, the French Mirage IIIC, and eventually the General Dynamics F-16.

It was his expertise in the F-16 that would lead to his selection to participate in a daring top secret raid to destroy an Iraqi nuclear facility in Tuwaitha on 7 June 1981. A year later, Ramon would again distinguish himself in combat during the Lebanon War, in which the Israeli air force downed eighty-two Syrian MiG fighters in less than two days. He received his bachelor of science degree in electronics and computer engineering in 1987 and returned to the air force to fly the F-4 Phantom.

Promoted to colonel, he managed weapons systems procurement for the Israeli air force until 1997. As he neared retirement, his superiors unexpectedly offered him the chance to become his nation's first astronaut. Unbeknownst to Ramon, at a summit between President Bill Clinton and the Israeli prime minister Shimon Peres in 1996, Clinton proposed the mission in order to further good relations between the two allies, and a formal agreement had been executed between NASA and the Israeli Space Agency shortly thereafter. After Ramon accepted the offer with great enthusiasm, he and his backup Lt. Col. Yitzhak Mayo moved their families to Houston in June 1998 to begin training.

Ramon and mission specialists Michael P. Anderson, Kalpana Chawla, David M. Brown, and Laurel B. Clark were named to crew STS-107 in Sep-

46. Ilan Ramon, Israel's representative aboard STS-107, during emergency egress training in November of 2002. He would be the last payload specialist to fly aboard the space shuttle. Courtesy NASA.

tember 2000, with commander Rick Husband and pilot William (Willie) McCool being assigned in December. The mission was to fly in 2001, but due to additional wiring inspections on *Columbia*, it was delayed and then put off again when the heavy, old orbiter was called into service to save the Hubble Space Telescope in March 2002. By June, cracks found in *Discovery* prompted more inspections of the orbiter fleet, requiring the removal of *Columbia*'s three main engines.

Columbia and its tight-knit crew of seven finally lifted off from KSC on 16 January 2003, carrying the Spacehab double module stocked with seventy-seven different payloads in a wide variety of disciplines. During the ascent, a chunk of insulating foam roughly the size of a suitcase separated from the external tank into the violent supersonic slipstream, slamming into the leading edge of the orbiter's left wing in a brief spray of white vapor that could be seen on tracking cameras on the ground. Without any knowledge of a debris strike to their ship's wings that would glide them home through a hypersonic reentry, the crew went on to activate their orbital laboratory for the following sixteen days of microgravity research.

Over the course of the next several days, engineers on the ground analyzed the foam strike using high-speed photography from launch and computer simulations that were utilized to estimate debris size and potential damage to the orbiter. Insulating foam was known to have separated from the external tank on at least six previous missions, as far back as STS-7 in 1983. Given this history of foam loss without critical damage, mission managers mistakenly concluded not only that the event on *Columbia* was considered to be "in family" but also that it posed no safety-of-flight concern for the orbiter and crew.

On several occasions, informal requests were made between NASA personnel and DOD contacts to take images of the shuttle in orbit in order to ascertain the extent of any damage that may have occurred, but all these requests were retracted at the direction of NASA management. The conclusion had been made—and as one witness recalled later, the imagery "was no longer being pursued since even if we saw something, we couldn't do anything about it. The program didn't want to spend the resources."

On 23 January, the halfway point of *Columbia*'s mission, ground controllers sent Husband and McCool an email titled "Info: Possible PAO [Public Affairs Office] Event Question." In it NASA officials for the first time informed the commander of the debris impact and their analysis:

> There is one item that I would like to make you aware of for the upcoming PAO event. This item is not even worth mentioning other than wanting to make sure that you are not surprised by it in a question from a reporter.
>
> During ascent at approximately 80 seconds, photo analysis shows that some debris from the area of the Bipod Attach Point came loose and subsequently impacted the orbiter left wing, in the area of transition from chine to main wing, creating a shower of smaller particles. The impact appears to be totally on the lower surface and no particles are seen to traverse over the upper surface of the wing. Experts have reviewed the high speed photography and there is no concern for RCC [leading-edge reinforced carbon–carbon panels] or tile damage. We have seen this same phenomenon on several other flights and there is absolutely no concern for entry.

The analysis was wrong. The chunk of foam liberated from the external tank had in fact slammed into the wing with such force that it blasted a hole the size of a bowling ball in the critical reinforced carbon–carbon panels. The mortal damage to the ship had been inflicted in an area of the wing's leading edge that could not be seen from *Columbia*'s flight deck windows, and the mission carried no robotic arm with its TV cameras, which could have been used to image the critical wound.

On 21 January 2003 Barbara Morgan was seated at the CAPCOM console, working with the STS-107 crew on the sixth day of their mission. She had been named as a member of the STS-118 crew that would fly aboard *Columbia* in November after modifications that would allow flights to the ISS. NASA administrator Sean O'Keefe had called her personally the previous December to tell her the news.

On this day, with the space shuttle Morgan was to fly aboard orbiting the planet, O'Keefe held a press conference to publicly unveil his new plan to recruit additional teachers for future astronaut classes, beginning in 2004. "NASA has an unfinished mission," O'Keefe said. "It is time for NASA to complete the mission—to send an educator into space to inspire and teach our young people."

Morgan was thrilled that after a decade and a half, the day was finally coming when she could head into orbit and teach from space, as McAuliffe was to have done. But the excitement of that possibility was soon to be replaced by tragic sorrow for yet more lost friends.

On 1 February 2003 as *Columbia* streaked high above California on its way to a KSC landing, observers on the ground saw the first of several unusual flashes within the glowing trail of plasma the returning space shuttle left behind. As the blowtorch-hot gases blasted into the hole in the left wing, they began slowly destroying the orbiter from within. Flight controllers could only watch as critical temperature and pressure sensors located in the wing began fluctuating and failing.

Unlike *Challenger*, which was unmistakably destroyed in an instant with millions of people watching, *Columbia* came to an end over several horrifying minutes in a virtual world of telemetered data—and on the exasperated faces of the controllers as they were slowly realizing their greatest fears. Tire pressure indications on the left main landing gear spiked momentarily before dropping off-line, prompting the final communication with *Columbia*'s crew.

"*Columbia*, Houston, we see your tire pressure messages, and we did not copy your last call." Commander Rick Husband responded, "Roger, buh . . . ," and was suddenly cut off in a burst of garbled static. At that instant, America's flagship space shuttle lost its battle with the searing heat of hypersonic flight. Tumbling and spinning wildly out of control, *Columbia* broke up in the skies high over eastern Texas, raining meteor-like flaming debris over a large swath of the state. But all of this went unseen by mission control. Repeated calls by CAPCOM Charlie Hobaugh of "*Columbia*, Houston, comm check" went unanswered.

It wasn't until astronaut Ellen Ochoa, seated in the back row of the control room, received a phone call informing her of the eyewitness reports from Texas that the tragic reality set in. As STS-1 pilot Bob Crippen would later say of his beloved orbiter, "I'm sure that *Columbia*, which had traveled millions of miles and made that fiery reentry twenty-seven times before, struggled mightily to bring her crew home safely once again. She wasn't successful."

The findings of the *Columbia* Accident Investigation Board closely mirrored the observations of NASA from sixteen years before. Faxes and telegrams had long been replaced by emails and video conferences, but the human failures in decision-making were virtually the same. The evidence was there. The failure that led to *Columbia*'s demise had been identified, studied, and set aside as an "acceptable risk." Once again, NASA managers took the successes of the past to assume success in the future. They had literally dodged a foam bullet for more than one hundred ascents, until one slammed squarely into *Columbia*'s left wing on 16 January 2003. As the *Columbia* Accident Investigation Board report noted, "By the eve of the *Columbia* accident, institutional practices that were in effect at the time of the *Challenger* accident—such as inadequate concern over deviations from expected performance, a silent safety program, and schedule pressure—had returned to NASA."

NASA's payload specialist program, controversial since its conception yet ultimately an unqualified success, would end on this tragic note. Ilan Ramon was the last payload specialist to ever undertake the hazardous journey aboard America's space shuttle. Amazingly, during the exhaustive recovery effort of *Columbia*'s shattered body, searchers came across a small pile of torn, soaked pages of what turned out to be Ramon's personal diary that he kept during the flight.

The diary pages, which contained his notes and thoughts through the first six flight days of the mission, were painstakingly restored and deciphered. Within the heavily damaged, handwritten text was an entry from flight day 6, which read, "Today was the first day that I felt that I am truly living in space. I have become a man who lives and works in space."

In the wake of the *Columbia* tragedy, President George W. Bush directed a shift away from the dangerously complex, aging space planes. The shuttles would be used only for the essential missions to complete the space station and then be ushered into retirement to make way for a new manned-exploration program of the moon and Mars, while continuing ISS operations in low Earth orbit.

Barbara Morgan would finally make it to orbit on 8 August 2007. She flew aboard *Endeavour*, the space shuttle that was built to replace the lost *Challenger*, more than two decades after the tragedy that claimed the lives of her predecessor and six others. On the eve of her launch, NASA public affairs officer Eduardo Campion, who had worked closely with Morgan and McAuliffe throughout their selection and training in 1986, sent an email to his coworkers. Campion pointed out that over those 7,861 days, Morgan had, without fail, carried the teacher-in-space banner, because she "recognized the potential the program had for inspiring youth," and he urged them to stop what they were doing, turn on their televisions, and "watch an event that will hopefully remind you that there are still people like Barbara who can inspire all of us."

Morgan was an integral part of the STS-118 crew, having gone through so many years of training as a mission specialist. During the flight, she controlled the robotic arms of both the shuttle and the ISS, to help install a structural truss segment to the station and transfer an external stowage platform from *Endeavour*'s payload bay. Morgan also took several opportunities to speak with schoolchildren, from the orbiting space complex, including a ham radio call to students in her hometown of McCall, Idaho.

Morgan never missed an opportunity to remind people that the tragic loss of her friend Christa McAuliffe changed her life and the makeup of the nation's astronaut corps. "She was, is, and always will be our first teacher in space. And she did a fantastic job representing the best of our profession," she reflected in a December 2011 NASA interview. "I was lucky to get to help carry that on. And what I am most proud of for all of us is what Christa started has continued on."

47. A teacher in space. Astronaut Barbara Morgan, STS-118 mission specialist, floats in the mid-deck of the space shuttle *Endeavour* in August 2007. Courtesy NASA.

With the successful completion of her long-awaited flight, Morgan retired from NASA in August 2008 to become the Distinguished Educator in Residence at Boise State University. The mission that she and Christa McAuliffe began with their selection in 1985 lives on within NASA's astronaut corps, with three educators—Joe Acaba, Ricky Arnold, and Dottie Metcalf-Lindenburger—joining their ranks in the class of 2004. All three flew space shuttle missions to the ISS, and Acaba completed a four-month mission as part of the Expedition 31–32 crew in 2012. In September 2017 he headed for the station once more for a five-month stay. Following Acaba's return to Earth, Arnold launched aboard *Soyuz MS-08* in March 2018 as part of Expedition 55–56.

Manned spaceflight operations aboard the ISS are far different from the brief one- or two-week sorties of the space shuttle missions. NASA's astronauts and those from partner countries train for years for expeditions typically lasting from four to six months. ISS crew members have to be proficient in such a wide range of activities—from flying a spacecraft to onboard scientific research, in-flight maintenance, and spacewalking—that there is no place for a specialized scientific researcher to take one of a very limited number of Soyuz seats.

Even NASA's current corps of astronauts has shrunk from a high of 149 in 2000 down to 44 (at the time of this writing), all of whom compete, along with a handful of eligible astronauts from Canada, Japan, and Europe, for one of the half-year missions. The 2017 class of NASA astronauts only consisted of eight candidates, reflecting the limited flight opportunities in the foreseeable future, and the twelve-member 2018 class is just beginning their initial training before becoming eligible for a mission.

NASA spent the 1980s touting the benefits of the manned space program to people here on Earth in an effort to retain its political support after Apollo. Low Earth orbit was to be the place where the space station and a steady rotation of space shuttles would carry out cutting-edge research and manufacturing that would improve the lives of everyday people. While it is entirely possible that the payload specialist concept could have carried over to the ISS, the loss of two orbiters, the reliance on Russia's Soyuz three-seat crew vehicles, and the resultant limitation of a six-person onboard crew have sharply reduced the available manpower for research aboard the station. Developmental contracts for commercial crew transport were awarded to the Boeing Company and Elon Musk's SpaceX for more capable vehicles, but neither would fly before 2018, after arduous funding issues and technical delays.

However, there is great promise for scientists and engineers to be able to conduct space-based microgravity research in a coming age of suborbital—and even orbital—private spaceflight. Two aerospace companies—Virgin Galactic and Blue Origin—are developing two radically different designs for passenger-carrying spacecraft intended to (initially) launch fare-paying thrill seekers on brief suborbital flights above one hundred kilometers, which is the generally accepted definition of "space."

Virgin Galactic, owned by British entrepreneur Sir Richard Branson, partnered with Burt Rutan's Scaled Composites and the Spaceship Company of Mojave, California, to produce SpaceShipTwo. In 2004 Rutan and his team claimed the $10 million Ansari X-Prize, after successfully launching the prototype SpaceShipOne three times above the 328,000-foot mark utilizing an air-dropped, rocket-powered, composite-hulled airplane. The design featured a unique feathering mechanism of the twin-boomed tail that allowed a relatively benign, hands-off reentry into the atmosphere, with minimal frictional heating.

Blue Origin operated largely in secret for several years before publicly revealing the unmanned test flights of its New Shepard capsule design, which to date has been flown successfully six times and recovered under three main parachutes, much like the Apollo spacecraft. Blue Origin utilizes a more conventional ground-launched rocket for its passenger ship, which will ultimately carry up to five people on short spaceflights, and the booster rocket is fully reusable by means of a powered vertical landing to return it to Earth.

Both of these companies are looking to the possibilities of conducting space research as an additional source of revenue along with their primary space-tourist business model. Virgin Galactic and Blue Origin will be able to provide a brief but very pure microgravity environment lasting approximately three to five minutes and can also offer spaceborne atmospheric and astronomical scientific research.

According to Virgin Galactic's *SpaceShipTwo: An Introductory Guide for Payload Users*, SpaceShipTwo will eventually offer more than a one-thousand-pound payload capacity, five hundred cubic feet of shirtsleeve working space, frequent and responsive flight access for "science of opportunity," large observation windows, and payload mounting systems that can accommodate most current experiment designs. "We are currently taking refundable deposits for flights of autonomous payloads on SpaceShipTwo," the company states. "In limited cases, we may also accept reservations for the flight of tended payloads—that is to say, flights of both the research experiment and the researcher him or herself." The company is also taking a page from NASA's payload specialist program and offering that "educators interested in Science, Technology, Engineering, and Math (STEM) outreach" might fly into space with them.

"I get extremely excited thinking about what the scientists and researchers of the world will do with [launch aircraft] WhiteKnightTwo and SpaceShipTwo," Branson offers to potential applicants. "It is so critical that researchers have the opportunity to send payloads to space, or even to fly themselves. I can't wait to see what great new ideas emerge and which of life's biggest questions will be solved using data gathered onboard our vehicles."

Blue Origin has teamed with Nanoracks to offer customers two different-size payload lockers for scientific experiments aboard its suborbital spacecraft. According to the company's website, "Our frequent flight schedule will allow you to launch your experiment multiple times to iterate on findings, improve statistics, or rapidly collect data. As human flights begin, you'll also be able to fly with your payloads for hands-on experimentation."

Each of the designs has its own unique benefits in terms of flight environment and safety. Though these two competing projects have been in the works since the success of the X-Prize flights, they have been met with many challenges that have precluded the initiation of this new industry of private space travel. The first SpaceShipTwo built, christened VSS *Enterprise*, was lost in a tragic accident during a powered test flight on 31 October 2014, killing test pilot Michael Alsbury and critically injuring Pete Seibold, who miraculously survived after being hurled out of the disintegrating vehicle at supersonic speeds.

Virgin Galactic and Blue Origin both now stand at the threshold of completing their testing and finally beginning to open space to many more people than ever before possible. There will no doubt be more difficulties in the future, more accidents, and even more lives lost. But the same intense desire that drove the payload specialists of the space shuttle era will bring a new breed of researchers full of curiosity to accept the risks that come with manned spaceflight. As these new endeavors gain momentum and the commercial sector expands in low Earth orbit, Boeing and SpaceX could be ferrying scientists and engineers, tourists and teachers, and perhaps even the occasional politician to space destinations such as Bigelow Aerospace's twelve-thousand-cubic-foot BE-330 expandable space habitat. Virgin Galactic and Blue Origin may not be far behind, with exciting new orbital designs being conceived even today.

Perhaps, at last, the future of manned spaceflight for everyone that NASA promised throughout the latter quarter of the twentieth century might finally come to fruition. The invitation will once again go out to a larger section of the world's population than ever before: "Come fly with us!"

Today, the three remaining space shuttles no longer thunder from the Florida Space Coast on their blinding bright-orange tongues of flame. *Discovery* was retired to the Smithsonian's Udvar-Hazy annex at Dulles International Airport in 2012, now resting on its landing gear as if just returning from space. *Endeavour* resides at the Los Angeles Science Center, supported horizontally with its wheels retracted as it awaits a move to the vertical position when it will be mated to a flight-built external tank and solid rocket boosters. *Atlantis* remains at its home at KSC, spectacularly displayed with payload bay doors open and remote manipulator arm deployed, canted toward visitors at an angle of 43.21 degrees in homage to the countdowns that culminated in its thirty-three successful missions.

Their black tiles, white quilted thermal blankets, and fragile gray carbon-carbon wing leading edges still show the dings, dents, and scorching of millions of miles travelling to and from space. Subtle streaks of burned residue sweep dramatically from the noses of the ships, giving the stark impression of the fiercely hot plasma each endured through their combined ninety-seven reentries. Even to the young children who see the shuttles up close for the first time, the swooping lines of the vintage delta-winged space planes are an iconic shape. More often than not, the first word out of one's mouth when first coming face-to-face with a space shuttle is, quite simply, "Wow!"

Among the throngs of visitors who view the three orbiters in the various corners of the country, there is occasionally one in the crowd who lingers a bit longer than most, with a longing gaze and a slight smile. Maybe a little older today than the last time they met but unlike the tourists who are seeing *Discovery*, *Atlantis*, or *Endeavour* for the first time—appreciating their reunion with the retired ships as when seeing an old friend. With long-misplaced memories flooding back from more than three decades ago, a Charlie Walker, a Gary Payton, a Rodolfo Neri, or a Bob Cenker stand in awe of the magnificent flying machine that catapulted them violently into orbit and returned them safely to Earth.

Vibrant images of the friends they flew with, unimaginable views of planet Earth, and the surreal oddity of weightlessness come instantly back to reality. Undoubtedly, memories of friends lost undertaking that same great adventure come to mind as well. As life goes by and new experiences fill the years since those seemingly detached events, it is sometimes hard to believe that spaceflight was part of their reality—that someone found them worthy of undertaking a mission to space. They may well find themselves asking quietly, "Did *that* really happen to *me*?"

"Wow!"

Appendix

Summary of Missions Carrying Payload Specialists, 1983–86

Mission	Payload specialist(s)	Mission date	Payload specialist objective
STS-9	Ulf D. Merbold PS1 Byron K. Lichtenberg PS2	28 November–8 December 1983	Spacelab 1
STS-41D	Charles D. Walker PS1	30 August–5 September 1984	Continuous flow electrophoresis
STS-41G	Paul D. Scully-Power PS1 Marc Garneau PS2	5–13 October 1984	Oceanographic observation and Canadian experiment suite
STS-51C	Gary E. Payton PS1	24–27 January 1985	Department of Defense classified payload
STS-51D	Charles D. Walker PS1 E. Jacob Garn PS2	12–19 April 1985	Continuous flow electrophoresis and congressional oversight
STS-51B	Taylor G. Wang PS1 Lodewijk van den Berg PS2	29 April–6 May 1985	Spacelab 3
STS-51G	Sultan Salman Abdulaziz Al-Saud PS1 Patrick Baudry PS2	17–24 June 1985	International goodwill
STS-51F	Loren W. Acton PS1 John-David F. Bartoe PS2	29 July–6 August 1985	Spacelab 2
STS-51J	William A. Pailes PS1	3–7 October 1985	Department of Defense DSCS III satellites (2)
STS-61A	Reinhard Furrer PS1 Ernst W. Messerschmid PS2 Wubbo J. Ockels PS3	30 October–6 November 1985	Spacelab D1
STS-61B	Charles D. Walker PS1 Rodolfo Neri Vela PS2	26 November–3 December 1985	Continuous flow electrophoresis and Morelos-B satellite
STS-61C	Robert J. Cenker PS1 C. William Nelson PS2	12–18 January 1985	RCA Satcom K-1 and congressional oversight
STS-51L	Christa McAuliffe PS1 Gregory B. Jarvis PS2	28 January 1986	Teacher in Space Program and space fluid dynamics experiment

Sources

Books

Burgess, Colin. *Oceans to Orbit: The Story of Australia's First Man in Space: Dr Paul Scully-Power.* Sydney, Australia: Playwright Publishing, 1995.

Collins, Michael. *Carrying the Fire: An Astronaut's Journey.* New York: Farrar, Straus, and Giroux, 1974.

Cooper, Henry S. F., Jr. *Before Lift-Off: The Making of a Space Shuttle Crew.* Baltimore MD: Johns Hopkins University Press, 1987.

Corrigan, Grace George. *A Journal for Christa: Christa McAuliffe, Teacher in Space.* Lincoln: University of Nebraska Press, 1993.

Dunar, Andrew J., and Stephen P. Waring. *Power to Explore: History of Marshall Space Flight Center 1960–1990.* NASA Historical Series. Washington DC: NASA History Office, 1999.

Emond, J., ed. *The Spacelab Accomplishments Forum.* Huntsville AL: Marshall Space Flight Center, 2000.

Evans, Ben. *Space Shuttle Challenger: Ten Journeys into the Unknown.* Chichester, UK: Praxis Publishing, 2007.

———. *Space Shuttle Columbia: Her Missions and Crews.* Chichester, UK: Praxis Publishing, 2005.

Farrimond, Richard. *Britain and Human Space Flight.* London: British Interplanetary Society, 2013.

Froehlich, Walter. *Spacelab: An International Short-Stay Orbiting Laboratory.* Washington DC: NASA, 1982.

Garn, Jake. *Why I Believe.* Salt Lake City: Aspen Books, 1992.

Lord, Douglas R. *Spacelab: An International Success Story.* Washington DC: NASA Scientific and Technical Information Division, 1987.

Mark, Hans. *The Space Station: A Personal Journey.* Durham NC: Duke University Press, 1987.

Marshall Space Flight Center. *Science in Orbit: The Shuttle and Spacelab Experience: 1981–1986.* Huntsville AL: NASA History Office, 1988.

Massimino, Mike. *Spaceman: An Astronaut's Unlikely Journey to Unlock the Secrets of the Universe.* New York: Crown Archetype, 2016.

Mullane, Mike. *Riding Rockets: The Outrageous Tales of a Space Shuttle Astronaut.* New York: Scribner Books, 2007.

Nelson, Bill. *Mission: An American Congressman's Voyage to Space.* San Diego: Harcourt Brace Javanovich, 1988.

Neri Vela, Rodolfo. *The Blue Planet: A Trip to Space.* New York: Vantage Press, 1989.

Newberger Speregen, Devra. *Ilan Ramon: Jewish Star.* Philadelphia: Jewish Publication Society, 2004.

Peebles, Curtis. *High Frontier: The U.S. Air Force and the Military Space Program.* Washington DC: U.S. Government Printing Office, 1997. https://media.defense.gov/2010/Dec/02/2001329901/-1/-1/0/afd-101202-013.pdf.

Reichhardt, Tony, ed. *Space Shuttle: The First 20 Years; The Astronauts' Experiences in Their Own Words.* London: DK Publishing, 2002.

Seddon, Rhea. *Go for Orbit: One of America's First Women Astronauts Finds Her Space.* Murfreesboro TN: Your Space Press, 2015.

Shapland, David, and Michael Rycroft. *Spacelab: Research in Earth Orbit.* Cambridge: University of Cambridge Press, 1984.

Wells, H. G. *Anticipations of the Reaction of Mechanical and Scientific Progress upon Human Life and Thought.* New York: Harper Brothers, 1902.

Westenhoff, Charles M. *Military Airpower: A Revised Digest of Airpower Opinions and Thoughts.* Maxwell Air Force Base AL: Air University Press, 2007. http://www.au.af.mil/au/awc/awcgate/milquote.pdf.

Young, John. *Forever Young: A Life of Adventure in Air and Space.* Gainesville: University Press of Florida, 2013.

Periodicals and Online Articles

"About: Biography." John Denver official website. http://johndenver.com/about/biography/.

Aguirre, Jessica Camille. "The Story of the Most Successful Tunnel Escape in the History of the Berlin Wall." *Smithsonian,* 7 November 2014. https://www.smithsonianmag.com/history/most-successful-tunnel-escape-history-berlin-wall-180953268/.

Air Force News Service. "New Space Operations Center to Control Satellites." *The Missileer,* 18 October 1985. http://afspacemuseum.org/library/missileer/1985/10-18-85.pdf.

Aldridge, E. C. Pete, Jr. "Assured Access: 'The Bureaucratic Space War.'" https://ocw.mit.edu/courses/aeronautics-and-astronautics/16-885j-aircraft-systems-engineering-fall-2005/readings/aldrdg_space_war.pdf.

"All Aboard the Space Shuttle: NASA Announces That Citizen Voyagers Will Be Put Aboard in 1985–86." *Life* 7, no. 11 (October 1984).

Associated Press. "Mexican Engineer, 33, Selected as Astronaut." *New York Times*, 6 June 1985. http://www.nytimes.com/1985/06/06/us/mexican-engineer-33-selected-as-astronaut.html.

"Astronaut Considering 2018 Presidential Run: Shuttle Mission's Neri Vela Sees 'Same Old Mafia' in Political Class." *Mexico News Daily*, 19 June 2015. http://mexiconewsdaily.com/news/astronaut-considering-2018-presidential-run/#sthash.xP67malL.dpu.

Atqvi, Athar S. "Some Computational Studies on the Smallest Visible Phase of the Lunar Crescent by the Naked Eye." *Muslim Scientist* 10, no. 1 (1981).

Banke, Jim. "Mission Columbia: The Long and Winding Road to Space." Space.com, 13 January 2003. https://www.space.com/19431-space-shuttle-columbia-mission-history.html.

Biddle, Wayne. "Problems at Space Shuttle Site Touch Off Inquiry." *New York Times*, 22 August 1984. http://www.nytimes.com/1984/08/22/us/problems-at-space-shuttle-site-touch-off-inquiry.html.

Bilton, Ross. "Paul Scully-Power: The First Australian, and Hipster, in Space." *Weekend Australian*, 23 April 2016. http://www.theaustralian.com.au/life/weekend-australian-magazine/paul-scullypower-the-first-australian-and-hipster-in-space/news-story/8f7d9a9c0c3816cafa037d3f81f6ddfb.

Blakeslee, Sandra. "Astronauts Return from Secret." *New York Times*, 8 October 1985. http://www.nytimes.com/1985/10/08/science/astronauts-return-from-secret.html?&pagewanted=all.

Boffey, Philip. "First Shuttle Ride by Private Citizen to Go to Teacher." *New York Times*, 27 August 1985. http://www.nytimes.com/1984/08/28/science/first-shuttle-ride-by-private-citizen-to-go-to-teacher.html.

Broad, William J. "Pentagon Leaves the Shuttle Program." *New York Times*, 7 August 1989. http://www.nytimes.com/1989/08/07/us/pentagon-leaves-the-shuttle-program.html.

Buck, Geena. "Question and Astronaut: Marc Garneau." *Maclean's*, 23 August 2015. http://www.macleans.ca/society/science/question-and-astronaut-marc-garneau/.

"Canadian to Fly on 51-a in October." *Space News Roundup* 23, no. 3 (10 February 1984).

Cannon, Carl M. "Challenger, Reagan and a Powerful, Unplanned Speech." *Real Clear Politics*, 28 January 2014. http://www.realclearpolitics.com/articles /2014/01/28/challenger_reagan_and_an_unplanned_speech__121382 .html#ixzz4VIlrg3X5.

Carney, Emily. "A Deathblow to the Death Star: The Rise and Fall of NASA's Shuttle-Centaur." *Ars Technica*, 9 October 2015. https://arstechnica.com /science/2015/10/dispatches-from-the-death-star-the-rise-and-fall-of-nasas -shuttle-centaur/.

Cassutt, Michael. "The Manned Spaceflight Engineer Programme." *Spaceflight* 31 (January 1989). http://epizodsspace.no-ip.org/bibl/inostr-yazyki/spaceflight /1989/1/mse.html.

———. "Secret Space Shuttles." *Air and Space Magazine*, August 2009. http:// www.airspacemag.com/space/secret-space-shuttles-35318554/.

David, Leonard. "Yellow Light for Citizen Astronauts." *Space World*, T-8-9-236-237 (August–September 1983).

Day, Dwayne. "Secret Shuttle Mission Revealed." *Spaceflight* 40 (July 1998).

———. "The Spooks and the Turkey." *The Space Review*, 20 November 2006. http://www.thespacereview.com/article/748/1.

———. "Ugly Little Gem: The Teal Ruby Satellite." *The Space Review*, 15 September 2014. http://www.thespacereview.com/article/2599/1.

Debono, Mark. "Feet on the Ground but Still Flying High." Australian Broadcasting Corporation, 1 July 2013. http://www.abc.net.au/local/stories /2013/06/28/3792065.htm.

Doherty, Robert. "Congressman Picked for Shuttle Ride: He Won't Have Far to Go to Launch Site." *Los Angeles Times*, 17 November 1985. http://articles .latimes.com/1985-11-17/news/mn-6979_1_space-shuttle.

Dooling, Dave. "Spacelab 1." *Space World*, T-8-9-236-237 (August–September 1983).

———. "Spacelab 1-A Striking Success." *Space World*, March 1984.

"Dr. Paul Scully-Power AM, DSM, NSM." University of Sydney, Alumni and Friends. Last updated 21 July 2017. http://sydney.edu.au/arts/alumni_friends/profiles /scully-power.shtml.

"Educator to be First Shuttle Passenger." *Space News Roundup* 23, no. 16 (31 August 1984). https://www.jsc.nasa.gov/history/roundups/issues/84-08-31.pdf.

"Educator Will Finally Get Her Trip in Space." *Los Angeles Times*, 13 April 2002. http://articles.latimes.com/2002/apr/13/news/mn-37607.

Eleazer, Wayne. "Launch Failures: Titan Groundhog Day." *The Space Review*, 26 October 2015. http://thespacereview.com/article/2852/1.

Evans, Ben. "Into the Black: NASA's Secret Shuttle Missions—Part Five." *Amer-*

icaSpace, 3 February 2012. http://www.americaspace.com/2012/02/03
/into-the-black-nasas-secret-shuttle-missions-part-five/.

———. "Long Wait for Space: 30 Years since Mission 51B." *AmericaSpace*, 2 May
2015. http://www.americaspace.com/2015/05/02/a-long-wait-30-years
-since-mission-51b-part-1/.

———. "'The Sultans of Space': 30 Years Since the Multi-Cultural Mission of STS-
51G." *AmericaSpace*, 14 June 2015. http://www.americaspace.com/2015/06
/14/the-sultans-of-space-the-multi-cultural-mission-of-sts-51g-part-2/.

———. "'. . . T-9 Minutes and Counting . . .': NASA's First Secret Shuttle Flight."
AmericaSpace, 23 January 2014. http://www.americaspace.com/2014/01/18
/into-the-black-nasas-secret-shuttle-missions-t-9-minutes-and-counting/.

———. "'Up against a Wall': What 1986 Might Have Been." *AmericaSpace*, 8
February 2015. http://www.americaspace.com/2015/02/08/up-against-a
-wall-what-1986-might-have-been/.

———. "Wubbo Ockels, Holland's First Citizen in Space, Dies Aged 68." *AmericaSpace*, 18 May 2014. http://www.americaspace.com/2014/05/18/wubbo
-ockels-hollands-first-citizen-in-space-dies-aged-68/.

"FalconSAT Program." United States Air Force Academy Fact Sheets, 14 April
2009. http://www.usafa.af.mil/About-Us/Fact-Sheets/Display/Article
/428292/falconsat-program/.

"First Steps Taken to Fly Citizens." *Space News Roundup* 23, no. 1 (13 January
1984). https://www.jsc.nasa.gov/history/roundups/issues/84-01-13.pdf.

"First Vandenberg Flight Delayed." *Countdown* 3, no. 2 (February 1985).

Fisher, Jack, comp. "The Hughes Astronauts." *Our Space Heritage 1960–2000* (blog),
4 June 2013. http://www.hughesscgheritage.com/hc-payload-specialists
-signal-hughes-communications-newsletter/.

Fisher, James. "Germans Blaze Trail for Science Challenger: Flies Off for Week
of Study, Discovery." *Orlando Sentinel*, 31 October 1985.

———. "Spacesickness." *Orlando Sentinel*, 14 May 1985.

———. "Verdict Still Out on Biofeedback to Control Spacesickness." *Orlando
Sentinel*, 14 May 1985.

Friend, David. "Seeing beyond the Stars." *Life* 8, no. 13 (December 1985).

"Garn, Daughter in Good Condition after Transplant." *Los Angeles Times*, 12 September 1986.

Goldin, Daniel. "The Time 76-Year-Old John Glenn Walked into My Office and
Demanded I Send Him Back into Space." *Independent Journal Review*, 13
December 2016. http://ijr.com/opinion/2016/12/262561-time-john-glenn
-stormed-office-demanded-send-back-space/.

"Guidelines Released for Citizen-in-Space Program." *Space World*, U-7-247 (July 1984).

Haddock, Marc. "Garn Has Worn Many Hats in His Lifetime." *Deseret News*, 22 June 2009.

Harding, Pete. "Commercial Rotation Plans Firming Up as US Segment Crew to Increase Early." NASASpaceFlight.com, 26 February 2016. https://www.nasaspaceflight.com/2017/02/commercial-rotation-us-segment-crew-increase-early/.

Harwood, William. "Arab, Frenchman Join Discovery for Shuttle Flight." *San Francisco Chronicle*, 16 June 1985.

Healy, Patrick. "For John Glenn, a Rare Repeat Tour of the Canyon of Heroes." *New York Times*, 9 December, 2016. https://www.nytimes.com/2016/12/09/us/astronaut-john-glenn-death-nyc-parades-broadway.html?_r=0.

"History of the Canadian Astronaut Corps." Canadian Space Agency. Last updated 1 July 2017. http://www.asc-csa.gc.ca/eng/astronauts/canadian/history-of-the-canadian-astronaut-corps.asp.

"Hughes Selects Two Specialists." *Space News Roundup* 23, no. 13 (20 July 1984). https://www.jsc.nasa.gov/history/roundups/issues/84-07-20.pdf.

"International Flight No. 110 STS-61B." Space Facts. Last updated 2 January 2018. http://www.spacefacts.de/mission/english/sts-61b.htm.

"In Their Own Words: Barbara Morgan." NASA Podcasts, 14 December 2011. https://www.nasa.gov/multimedia/podcasting/morgan_itow.html.

Irving, Doug. "Looking Back: Greg Jarvis' Dream Remembered." *Daily Breeze*, 28 January 2011. http://www.dailybreeze.com/general-news/20110128/looking-back-greg-jarvis-dream-remembered.

Kelly, Jack. "Civilians in Space Grounded." *USA Today*, 23–25 January 1987.

Klesius, Mike. "Space Shuttle Jr." *Air and Space*, January 2010. http://www.airspacemag.com/space/space-shuttle-jr-9563914/?no-ist.

Kurle, David. "Ceremony Activates AF Reserve's First-Ever Space Wing." Air Force Reserve Command, 7 April 2008. http://www.afrc.af.mil/News/Article-Display/Article/158453/ceremony-activates-af-reserves-first-ever-space-wing/.

Larivee, Marie-Eve, and Patrick Bruskiewich. "Canada's First Man in Space (an Interview)." *Canadian Undergraduate Physics Journal*, January 2009. https://archive.org/stream/MarcGarneauCanadasFirstManInSpaceanInterview/Garneau_Interview_djvu.txt.

Lenorovitz, Jeffrey M. "Europeans Urge Science Astronaut Designation." *Aviation Week and Space Technology*, 11 November 1985.

Leon, Steven J. "West Coast Shuttle Operations." *Space World*, u-9-249 (September 1984).

"Major General Frank J. Casserino." U.S. Air Force Biographies. Last updated December 2011. http://www.af.mil/About-Us/Biographies/Display/Article /108162/major-general-frank-j-casserino/.

"Mission 15: Secrets Satisfactorily." *Countdown* 3, no. 3 (March 1985).

"Mission 24 Makes 'End of Year Clearance Flight.'" *Countdown* 4, no.1 (January 1986).

"NASA Revises Policy for Specialists." *Space News Roundup* 21, no. 21 (29 October 1982).

"1984: Marc Garneau Chosen as Canada's First Astronaut." CBC Digital Archives. http://www.cbc.ca/archives/entry/1984-marc-garneau-chosen-as-canadas -first-astronaut.

Nordheimer, John. "2 Space Novices with a Love of Knowledge; Gregory Jarvis." *New York Times*, 10 February 1986. http://www.nytimes.com/1986/02 /10/us/2-space-novices-with-a-love-of-knowledge-gregory-jarvis.html.

Oman, C. M., B. K. Lichtenberg, K. E. Money, and R. K. McCoy. "M.I.T./Canadian Vestibular Experiments on the Spacelab-1 Mission: 4. Space Motion Sickness: Symptoms, Stimuli, and Predictability." *Experimental Brain Research* 64, no. 2 (February 1986): 316–34.

"Preflight Guide to 51-E." *World Spaceflight News* 2, no. 6 (January 1985).

"Preflight Guide to 61-C." *World Spaceflight News* 3, no.4 (November 1985).

"RAN-Apollo Joint Operation—They Helped Make History." *Royal Australian Navy News* 18, no. 15 (1–15 August 1975). http://www.navy.gov.au/sites /default/files/documents/Navy_News-August-1-1975.pdf.

Ray, Justin. "'Slick 6': 30 Years after the Hopes of a West Coast Space Shuttle." *Spaceflight Now*, 8 February, 2016. https://spaceflightnow.com/2016/02 /08/astronaut-interview-30-years-after-the-hopes-of-a-west-coast-space -shuttle/.

"Rodolfo Neri Vela—The First Mexican Astronaut." International Space Hall of Fame, New Mexico Museum of Space History. http://www.nmspacemuseum .org/halloffame/detail.php?id=111.

Rogoway, Tyler. "The Space Shuttle's Military Launch Complex in California That Never Was." *Fox Trot Alpha* (blog), 10 June 2015. https://foxtrotalpha .jalopnik.com/the-space-shuttle-s-military-launch-complex-in-californ -1710303170.

Rowley, Storer. "Senator Applied and Is Going to Heaven." *Chicago Tribune*, 24 February 1985.

Sanger, David E. "Titan Rocket, after Two Failures, Launches Satellite from Air Base." *New York Times*, 13 February 1987. http://www.nytimes.com /1987/02/13/us/titan-rocket-after-two-failures-launches-satellite-from -air-base.html.

"Sharon Christa Corrigan McAuliffe—Teacher-in-Space Payload Specialist," s.v., "*Challenger* STS-51L Crew." Challenger Center. https://www.challenger .org/who-we-are/#history.

"Six People Reach Short List to Be First Canadian in Space." CBC Digital Archives. http://www.cbc.ca/archives/entry/marc-garneau-chosen-as-first-canadian -astronaut.

Skapars, Linda. "New and Improved Orbiter Wars." *Space World*, V-10-262 (October 1985).

"Space Teacher to Fly in November." United Press International, 12 December 2002. http://www.upi.com/Science_News/2002/12/12/Space-teacher-to -fly-in-November/55761039733312/.

"Teal Ruby." National Museum of the U.S. Air Force Fact Sheets, 14 March 2016. http://www.nationalmuseum.af.mil/Visit/Museum-Exhibits/Fact-Sheets /Display/Article/589823/teal-ruby/.

Trotter, Rachael. "Garn Unhappy with NASA Spending Cuts." *Standard-Examiner*, 14 October 2014.

Turner, Laura. "Maj. Gen. Frank Casserino." 310 Space Wing Photos, 1 April 2017. http://www.310sw.afrc.af.mil/News/Photos/igphoto/2001725902/.

Vogel, Charity. "Gregory Jarvis: Buffalo's Connection to the Challenger Disaster 30 Years Ago." *Buffalo News*, 27 January 2016. http://buffalonews .com/2016/01/27/gregory-jarvis-buffalos-connection-to-the-challenger -disaster-30-years-ago/.

Wang, Taylor. "A Scientist in Space." *Engineering Science*, 1 January 1986.

Wilford, John Noble. "Garn, Head of Senate Space Panel, Is Chosen to Fly aboard Shuttle." *New York Times*, 8 November 1984.

———. "Space Test Jolts Inner-Ear Theory." *New York Times*, 7 December 1983.

Young, L. R., C. M. Oman, D. G. D. Watt, K. E. Money, B. K. Lichtenberg, R. V. Kenyon, and A. P. Arrott. "M.I.T./Canadian Vestibular Experiments on the Spacelab-1 Mission: 1. Sensory Adaptation to Weightlessness and Readaptation to One-G; An Overview." *Experimental Brain Research* 64, no. 2 (October 1986): 291–98.

Interviews and Personal Communications

Aldridge, Edward C. JSC Oral History interview with Rebecca Wright, 29 May 2009.

Beggs, James M. NASA Headquarters Oral History interview with Kevin Rusnak, 7 March 2002.

Bingham, Jeff M. NASA Headquarters Oral History interview with Rebecca Wright, 9 November 2006.

Bobko, Karol J. JSC Oral History interview with Summer Chick Bergen, 12 February 2002.

———. Discussion with Melvin Croft, Astronaut Scholarship Space Rendezvous, 12 November 2016.

———. Telephone interview with John Youskauskas, 17 December 2016.

Bolden, Charles F. JSC Oral History interview with Sandra Johnson, 6 January 2004.

———. JSC Oral History interview with Sandra Johnson, 15 January 2004.

Brandenstein, Daniel C. JSC Oral History interview with Carol Butler, 19 January 1999.

Campion, Eduardo. "Completing the Mission after 21 Years." Email to NASA employees, 7 August 2007. https://www.nasa.gov/mission_pages/shuttle/main/campion_essay_070808.html.

Casserino, Frank. Telephone interview with John Youskauskas, 16 February 2016.

Cenker, Robert. Public presentations at the Kennedy Space Center, Cape Canaveral FL, 20 March 2015.

———. Telephone interview with John Youskauskas, 9 September 2016.

———. Email correspondence with John Youskauskas, 6 June 2017.

Chappell, Rick. Telephone interview with Melvin Croft, 20 July 2015.

———. Telephone interview with Melvin Croft, 3 August 2015.

Crippen, Robert L. JSC Oral History interview with Rebecca Wright, 26 May 2006.

Duffy, Brian. Discussion with Melvin Croft, Astronaut Scholarship Space Rendezvous, 12 November 2016.

Fuqua, Don. JSC Oral History interview with Catherine Harwood, 11 August 1999.

Furrer, Reinhard A. Interview by Lena Fuhrmann. German Aerospace Center, 11 February 2011. http://www.dlr.de/dlr/en/desktopdefault.aspx/tabid-10366/561_read-456/#/gallery/473.

Garriott, Owen K. JSC Oral History interview with Kevin M. Rusnak, 6 November 2000.

Gibson, Robert. JSC Oral History interview with Sandra Johnson, 22 January 2016.

Gooch, Larry. Telephone interview with John Youskauskas, 10 April 2017.

Gregory, Fred D. Discussion with Melvin Croft, Astronaut Scholarship Space Rendezvous, 12 November 2016.

Hard, Donald. Telephone interview with John Youskauskas, 11 April 2017.

Hartsfield, Henry W. "Hank," Jr. JSC Oral History interview with Carol L. Butler, 12 June 2001.

————. JSC Oral History interview with Carol L. Butler, 15 June 2001.

Hauck, Frederick H. Email correspondence with Melvin Croft, 10 January 2017.

————. Email correspondence with Melvin Croft, 11 January 2017.

Hawley, Steven A. JSC Oral History interview with Sandra Johnson, 4 December 2002.

Hoffman, Jeffrey A. JSC Oral History interview with Jennifer Ross-Nazzal, 2 April 2009.

Leestma, David C. JSC Oral History interview with Jennifer Ross-Nazzal, 26 November 2002.

Lovelace, Alan M. NASA Headquarters Oral History interview with Sandra Johnson, 14 July 2011.

Mark, Hans. NRO interview with Gerald Haines, 12 March 1997. http://www.nro.gov/foia/docs/Hans%20mark.pdf.

Mattingly, Thomas K. JSC Oral History interview with Rebecca Wright, 6 November 2001.

————. JSC Oral History interview with Kevin Rusnak, 22 April 2002.

Messerschmid, Ernst. "During the D1 Mission, We Were in the Driving Seat." By Manuela Braun. German Aerospace Center, 29 September 2010. http://www.dlr.de/iss/en/desktopdefault.aspx/tabid-6220/10231_read-26809/.

————. "Ernst Messerschmid: STS-61A Payload Specialist." European Space Agency, 26 October 2010. http://www.esa.int/About_Us/Welcome_to_ESA/ESA_history/Ernst_Messerschmid_STS-61A_Payload_Specialist.

Morgan, Barbara. "Preflight Interview 2: Barbara Morgan." By Brian Dunbar. NASA, 11 July 2007. https://www.nasa.gov/mission_pages/shuttle/shuttlemissions/sts118/interview2_morgan.html.

Mullane, Richard M. JSC Oral History interview with Rebecca Wright, 24 January 2003.

Nelson, George D. JSC Oral History interview with Jennifer Ross-Nazzal, 6 May 2004.

Neri Vela, Rodolfo. Public presentations at the Kennedy Space Center, Cape Canaveral FL, 15 January 2016.

————. Email correspondence with John Youskauskas, 21 July 2017.

Ockels, Wubbo. "Wubbo Ockels: STS-61A Payload Specialist." European Space Agency, 26 October 2010. http://www.esa.int/About_Us/Welcome_to_ESA/ESA_history/Wubbo_Ockels_STS-61A_Payload_Specialist.

————. Interview by Lonneke Engel, 21 May 2011. http://organiceyourlife.com/wubbo-ockels-interview-by-lonneke-engel/.

O'Connor, Bryan D. JSC Oral History interview with Sandra Johnson, 17 March 2004.

Pailes, William. Email correspondence with John Youskauskas, 30 March 2017.

———. Telephone interview with John Youskauskas, 31 March 2017.

———. Email correspondence with John Youskauskas, 2–8 May 2017.

Parker, Robert A. R. JSC Oral History interview with Jennifer Ross-Nazzal, 23 October 2002.

Payton, Gary. Telephone interview with John Youskauskas, 17 November 2015.

Rezac, Edward J. Email correspondence with Melvin Croft, 27 June 2016.

Ride, Sally. JSC Oral History interview with Rebecca Wright, 22 October 2002.

Ross, Jerry L. JSC Oral History interview with Jennifer Ross-Nazzal, 4 December 2003.

———. Discussion with Melvin Croft, Astronaut Scholarship Space Rendezvous, 12 November 2016.

Scully-Power, Paul. "Interview with Dr Sir Paul Scully-Power." *Perth News Today.* YouTube video, 7:54. Posted by ZebedeeAU, 21 May 2014. https://m .youtube.com/watch?v=np2j977lVss.

———. Email correspondence with Melvin Croft, 7 January 2015.

Seddon, Margaret Rhea. JSC Oral History interview with Jennifer Ross-Nazzal, 21 May 2010.

Shaw, Brewster H. JSC Oral History interview with Kevin W. Rusnak, 19 April 2002.

———. Discussion with Melvin Croft, Astronaut Scholarship Space Rendezvous, 12 November 2016.

Shriver, Loren J. JSC Oral History interview with Rebecca Wright, 16 December 2002.

———. Email correspondence with John Youskauskas, 14 November 2015.

Stich, J. S. Email correspondence with Rick Husband, 23 January 2003. https:// www.nasa.gov/pdf/45253main_email_foam_strike.pdf.

Sullivan, Kathryn D. JSC Oral History interview with Jennifer Ross-Nazzal, 10 May 2007.

———. JSC Oral History interview with Jennifer Ross-Nazzal, 12 March 2008.

Sundberg, Eric. Telephone interview with John Youskauskas, 5 May 2016.

———. Email correspondence with John Youskauskas, 6 May 2016.

———. Email correspondence with John Youskauskas, 1 April 2017.

———. Email correspondence with John Youskauskas, 22–23 May 2017.

Thornton, William E. Telephone interview with Melvin Croft, 6 January 2017.

Walker, Charles D. JSC Oral History interview with Sandra Johnson, 7 November 2006.

———. Discussion with Melvin Croft, Spacefest, 8 June 2016.

———. Email correspondence with Melvin Croft, 26 June 2016.

————. Email correspondence with Melvin Croft, 22 February 2017.

Watterson, Brett. Telephone interview with John Youskauskas, 18 February 2016.

————. Telephone interview with John Youskauskas, 19 April 2016.

Williams, Donald E. JSC Oral History interview with Rebecca Wright, 19 July 2002.

Wood, Munro. Telephone interview with John Youskauskas, 20 November 2016.

Other Sources

Abbey, George W. S. Memorandum to J. de Waard (ESA), "Comments to the European Space Agency / Spacelab Payload Integration and Coordination in Europe (ESA/SPICE), Payload Specialist Training Plan," 7 September 1978. University of Houston–Clear Lake Archives.

————. Memorandum to Marshall Space Flight Center, "Backup for Mission Specialist for ASSESS II," 15 March 1977. University of Houston–Clear Lake Archives.

"An Affordable, Customizable Platform for Getting Your Payload to Space Quickly." Blue Origin. https://www.blueorigin.com/payloads.

Agence France-Presse news bulletin, 10 June 1985.

Al-Saud, Prince Sultan Salman Abdulaziz, and Abdulmohsen Hamad al-Bassam. STS-51G: Untitled Post Mission Saudi Arabian Payload Specialist Report. University of Houston–Clear Lake Archives.

"Announcement by George Bush of the First Teacher to be on the Space Shuttle on July 19, 1985." Master tape #632. YouTube video, 7:54. Posted by Reagan Library, 10 January 2017. Courtesy Ronald Reagan Presidential Library. https://www.youtube.com/watch?v=04V8FNCJX0g.

"Aorounga Impact Crater, Chad." NASA Earth Observatory, 10 August 2009. https://earthobservatory.nasa.gov/iotd/view.php?id=39727.

"Atlantis STS 51-J / Atlantis Rising." NASA Spaceflight.com Forum. Started by Ares67, 11 February 2012. http://forum.nasaspaceflight.com/index.php?topic=28019.0.

"Atlantis STS 61-B / Looking for 'Freedom.'" NASA Spaceflight.com Forum. Started by Ares67, 18 February 2012. http://forum.nasaspaceflight.com/index.php?topic=28098.0.

"B-330 Space Station." Bigelow Aerospace. http://www.bigelowaerospace.com/b330/.

"Barbara Morgan: No Limits." Produced by Marcia Franklin. Idaho Public Television, 2008. Video, 56:48. http://www.pbs.org/program/barbara-morgan/.

Brown, Harold. Memorandum to the Deputy Secretary of Defense et al., "National Reconnaissance Office," 8 August 1977. http://www.nro.gov/foia/declass/nrostaffRecords/7.pdf.

"Challenger STS 51-L—Part 1/4 Teacher in Space." NASA Spaceflight.com Forum. Started by Ares67, 1 March 2012. http://forum.nasaspaceflight.com/index.php?topic=28219.0.

Charlesworth, C. E. (NASA HQ, Washington DC). Memorandum to NASA Headquarters, "Flight Dependent Training Concerns," 1 April 1977. University of Houston–Clear Lake Archives.

Christa Corrigan McAuliffe Papers, 1948–2000. Henry Whittemore Library, Framingham State College. https://web.archive.org/web/20100528041008/http://www.framingham.edu/henry-whittemore-library/curriculum-library-archives-and-special-collections/christa-mcauliffe.html.

"Columbia STS-61-C / Should I Stay or Should I Go?" NASA Spaceflight.com Forum. Started by Ares67, 25 February 2012. http://forum.nasaspaceflight.com/index.php?topic=28160.0.

Cremin, Joseph. Memorandum to W. R. Lucas, "Spacelab 3 Payload Specialists," 16 June 1983. University of Houston–Clear Lake Archives.

Culbertson, Phillip E. (NASA HQ, Washington DC). Memorandum to Johnson Space Center, 18 June 1976. University of Houston–Clear Lake Archives.

———. Memorandum to Johnson Space Center, "NMI on Procedure for Selection of Payload Specialists for NASA-Sponsored STS Missions," 29 September 1976. University of Houston–Clear Lake Archives.

D-1 Report: The First German Spacelab Mission. Washington DC: NASA, 1985. Originally published as D-1 Report: Erste Deutsche Spacelab Mission (Linder Höhe, West Germany: German Aerospace Research Establishment, 1984). https://ntrs.nasa.gov/archive/nasa/casi.ntrs.nasa.gov/19850014091.pdf.

Dirks, Leslie C. Memorandum to Howard P. Barfield, "Potential Space Shuttle Applications," 20 July 1972. http://nsarchive.gwu.edu/NSAEBB/NSAEBB509/docs/nasa_43.pdf.

"Discovery STS 51-C / The Spy Who Came in from the Cold." NASA Spaceflight.com Forum. Started by Ares67, 10 January 2012. http://forum.nasaspaceflight.com/index.php?topic=27736.0.

"8 Years of Planning-8 Days of Exhilaration." Naval Research Laboratory, NRL publication 78-2630, February 1988. http://wwwsolar.nrl.navy.mil/sl2_pub.html.

"Eulogy for Space Shuttle Columbia." YouTube video, 3:47. Posted by leonidas28, 19 April 2011. https://www.youtube.com/watch?v=z3U-ZMacN8k.

Fichtl, G. W., J. W. Cremin, C. K. Hill, O. H. Vaughn, J. S. Theon, and R. Schmitz. "Spacelab 3: Research in Microgravity." Conference paper N87-22104, NASA Marshall Space Flight Center, Huntsville AL, 1 February 1987.

Flight Systems Office. *The User's Guide to Spacelab Payload Processing.* Kennedy Space Center, October 1986.

Glaser, H. (NASA HQ, Washington DC). Memorandum to Associate Administrator for Space Science, "Solar Terrestrial Programs. Issues Regarding Payload Specialists and Mission Specialists," 10 February 1977. University of Houston–Clear Lake Archives.

Golden, Edmond J. (NASA HQ, Washington DC). Memorandum to Distribution, "Proposed NMI re Selection of Payload Specialists," 20 September 1977. University of Houston–Clear Lake Archives.

Henize, Karl G. (JSC). Memorandum, 23 January 1974. University of Houston–Clear Lake Archives.

Hinners, Noel W. (NASA HQ, Washington DC). Memorandum to Distribution, "Payload Specialist Selection Process," 3 October 1978. University of Houston–Clear Lake Archives.

——. Memorandum to Dr. Christopher C. Kraft Jr. (JSC), 9 September 1977. University of Houston–Clear Lake Archives.

——. Memorandum to Dr. Christopher C. Kraft Jr., 20 December 1977. University of Houston–Clear Lake Archives.

——. Memorandum to Dr. Christopher C. Kraft Jr., 26 December 1977. University of Houston–Clear Lake Archives.

Hooks, I. (JSC). Memorandum to Technical Assistant to the Director, "Payload Specialist Activities—A Recent History and Some Suggestions," 6 September 1977. University of Houston–Clear Lake Archives.

Hosenball, Neil (NASA HQ, Washington DC). Memorandum to Assistant for Payload Operations, Office of Planning and Program Integration, "Payload Specialists," 8 February 1977. University of Houston–Clear Lake Archives.

Kennedy, Robert A. (NASA HQ, Washington DC). Memorandum to Distribution, 25 July 1977. University of Houston–Clear Lake Archives.

Kerwin, Joseph (JSC). Memorandum to Director of Flight Operations, "Mission and Payload Specialist Functions," 6 August 1976. University of Houston–Clear Lake Archives.

Kohler, R. C. Memorandum to M. F. Brooks, "Payload Specialist Training," 11 March 1974. University of Houston–Clear Lake Archives.

Kraft, Christopher C., Jr. (JSC). Draft memorandum to NASA Headquarters, "Preliminary JSC evaluation of ASSESS II." University of Houston–Clear Lake Archives.

——. Memorandum to Dr. Allan M. Lovelace (NASA HQ, Washington DC), 10 May 1978. University of Houston–Clear Lake Archives.

————. Memorandum to Dr. George M. Low (NASA HQ, Washington DC), 19 July 1974. University of Houston–Clear Lake Archives.

————. Memorandum to Dr. James C. Fletcher (NASA HQ, Washington DC), 12 October 1976. University of Houston–Clear Lake Archives.

————. Memorandum to Dr. John E. Naugle (NASA Associate Administrator), 28 July 1976. University of Houston–Clear Lake Archives.

————. Memorandum to Dr. Noel W. Hinners (NASA HQ, Washington DC), 28 September 1977. University of Houston–Clear Lake Archives.

————. Memorandum to John Yardley (NASA HQ, Washington DC), "Air Force Payload Specialist Selection Process," 14 June 1979. University of Houston–Clear Lake Archives.

————. Memorandum to Mr. John F. Yardley (NASA HQ, Washington DC), 5 April 1976. University of Houston–Clear Lake Archives.

————. Memorandum to Mr. John F. Yardley (NASA HQ, Washington DC), 24 May 1979. University of Houston–Clear Lake Archives.

Lee, Chester (NASA HQ, Washington DC). Memorandum to Johnson Space Center, "Development of Payload Specialist Training," 23 July 1976. University of Houston–Clear Lake Archives.

Marshall Space Flight Center. *Spacelab 2*. EP217, 20M385, NASA, 1985.

Memorandum from Deputy Director (NASA HQ, Washington DC) to Robert G. Wilson, "Preparation of a Plan for the Selection of NASA Payload Specialists," 12 May 1976. University of Houston–Clear Lake Archives.

Memorandum from Director, Program Operations Division, to Herbert D. Brown (MSFC), "NASA Cost-Reimbursement Contracts for Payload Specialists," 9 May 1978. University of Houston–Clear Lake Archives.

Messidoro, Piero, and Emanuele Comandatore. "Columbus Pressurized Module Verification." https://ntrs.nasa.gov/archive/nasa/casi.ntrs.nasa.gov /19880001460.pdf.

Mossinghoff, Gerald J. (NASA HQ, Washington DC). Memorandum to Associate Administrator for Space Science, 6 July 1977. University of Houston–Clear Lake Archives.

NASA. *Role of the Payload Specialist in the Space Transportation System for NASA or NASA-Related Payloads*. Washington DC: NASA, 1978.

"NASA Active Astronauts." NASA. Last updated 5 March 2018. https://www.nasa .gov/astronauts/biographies/astronauts/active.

NASA George C. Marshall Space Flight Center. "Payload Specialists to Be Selected for Spacelab 1." News release MSFC 77-168, 12 September 1977.

————. "Spacelab 1 Science Crew Begins Training." News release MSFC 79-4, 12 January 1979.

———. "Spacelab 2 Scientists Continue Payload Development." News release MSFC 79-10, 19 January 1979.

———. "Spacelab Science Crew Finalists Named." News release MSCF 77-229, 22 December 1977.

NASA News. "Crews for First Vandenberg Mission, DOD Flight Named." Lyndon B. Johnson Space Center press release no. 85-009, 15 February 1985. https://www.nasa.gov/centers/johnson/pdf/83137main_1985.pdf.

———. "NASA Administrator Announces Out-of-This-World Opportunity for Teachers." News release H03-016, 21 January 2003. https://spaceflight.nasa.gov/spacenews/releases/2003/H03-016.html.

———. "NASA Names Astronaut Crew for Department of Defense Mission." Lyndon B. Johnson Space Center press release no. 85-053, 17 December 1985. https://www.nasa.gov/centers/johnson/pdf/83137main_1985.pdf.

———. "NASA Names Crews to Deploy Satellites in Year-End Flights." Lyndon B. Johnson Space Center press release no. 85-005, 29 January 1985. https://www.nasa.gov/centers/johnson/pdf/83137main_1985.pdf.

———. "NASA Names STS-10 Astronaut Crew." Lyndon B. Johnson Space Center press release no. 82-046, 20 October 1982. https://www.nasa.gov/centers/johnson/pdf/83134main_1982.pdf.

"NASA STS-61A Space Shuttle Post Flight Crew Mission Presentation." YouTube video, 24:32. Posted by Matthew Travis, 14 July 2013. https://www.youtube.com/watch?v=1deq3vtDZgM.

"National Security Decision Directive Number 164, National Security Launch Strategy February 25, 1985." National Security Decision Directives of President Ronald Reagan. Ronald Reagan Presidential Library. https://www.reaganlibrary.archives.gov/archives/reference/Scanned%20NSDDS/NSDD164.pdf.

Neutral Buoyancy Simulator (NBS) Facility. Historic American Engineering Record no. AL-129-B. Washington DC: U.S. Department of the Interior. http://lcweb2.loc.gov/master/pnp/habshaer/al/al1100/al1193/data/al1193data.pdf.

Nunn, Sam (United States Senate). Memorandum to James M. Beggs (NASA HQ, Washington DC), 27 June 1985. University of Houston–Clear Lake Archives.

Proceedings of the Space Shuttle Sortie Workshop. Vol. 1, *Policy and System Characteristics, 31 July–4 August 1972.* Greenbelt MD: NASA—Goddard Space Flight Center, 1972.

Reagan, Ronald. "Address to the Nation on the Explosion of the Space Shuttle Challenger." 28 January 1986. Online by Gerhard Peters and John T. Woolley, *The American Presidency Project.* http://www.presidency.ucsb.edu/ws/?pid=37646.

———. "Exchange with Reporters on the Explosion of the Space Shuttle Challenger." 28 January 1986. Online by Gerhard Peters and John T. Woolley, *The American Presidency Project*. http://www.presidency.ucsb.edu/ws/?pid=37635.

———. "Remarks at a Ceremony Honoring the 1983–1984 Winners in the Secondary School Recognition Program." 27 August 1984. Online by Gerhard Peters and John T. Woolley, *The American Presidency Project*. http://www.presidency.ucsb.edu/ws/?pid=40300.

"Report of Columbia Accident Investigation Board, Volume I." NASA. Last updated 5 March 2006. https://www.nasa.gov/columbia/home/CAIB_Vol1.html.

Rogers, William P., Neil A. Armstrong, David C. Acheson, Eugene E. Covert, Richard P. Feynman, Robert B. Hotz, Donald J. Kutyna, et al. *Report of the Presidential Commission on the Space Shuttle Challenger Accident.* Washington DC, 1986. https://history.nasa.gov/rogersrep/genindex.htm.

Salloum, Pierre. "STS-51G Feature English LR." Produced by Silvio Saadé. Jeddah, Saudi Arabia: SilverGrey Pictures. From the Archives of HRH Prince Sultan bin Salman bin Abdusaziz Al-Saud and NASA. YouTube video, 49:48. Posted by SilverGrey Picture & Sound, 3 November 2015. https://www.youtube.com/watch?v=UNGNeXySgI8.

Scully-Power, Paul. *Naval Oceanographer Shuttle Observations Mission Report.* Naval Underwater Systems Center technical doc. 7611, 26 March 1986.

Spacelab 1 Experiments. European Space Agency and National Aeronautics and Space Administration, 1983.

Spacelab 1 Technical Crew Debriefing. December 1983. University of Houston–Clear Lake Archives.

"Space Shuttle Flight 13 (STS-41G) Post Flight Presentation." YouTube video, 15:53. Posted by National Space Society, 21 May 2011. https://m.youtube.com/watch?v=HHlgEY8fXpI.

"Space Shuttle Flight 23 (STS-61B) Post Flight Presentation." YouTube video, 19:48. Posted by National Space Society, 4 June 2011. http://www.nss.org/resources/library/shuttlevideos/shuttle23.htm.

Space Shuttle Mission STS-9 Press Kit. NASA Release 83-173, Houston, November 1983. https://www.jsc.nasa.gov/history/shuttle_pk/pk/Flight_009_STS-009_Press_Kit.pdf.

Space Shuttle Mission STS-41D Press Kit. NASA Release 84-117, Houston, August 1984. https://www.jsc.nasa.gov/history/shuttle_pk/pk/Flight_012_STS-41D_Press_Kit.pdf.

Space Shuttle Mission STS-41G Press Kit. NASA, October 1984. https://www.jsc.nasa.gov/history/shuttle_pk/pk/Flight_013_STS-41G_Press_Kit.pdf.

Space Shuttle Mission STS-51B Press Kit. NASA Release 85-60, Houston, April 1985. https://www.jsc.nasa.gov/history/shuttle_pk/pk/Flight_017_STS -51B_Press_Kit.pdf.

Space Shuttle Mission STS-51D Press Kit. NASA Release 85-47, Houston, April 1985. https://www.jsc.nasa.gov/history/shuttle_pk/pk/Flight_016_STS -51D_Press_Kit.pdf.

Space Shuttle Mission STS-51F Press Kit. NASA Release 85-100, Houston, July 1985. https://www.jsc.nasa.gov/history/shuttle_pk/pk/Flight_019_STS -51F_Press_Kit.pdf.

Space Shuttle Mission STS-51G Press Kit. NASA Release 85-8, June 1985. https://www .jsc.nasa.gov/history/shuttle_pk/pk/Flight_018_STS-51G_Press_Kit.pdf.

Space Shuttle Mission STS-51L Press Kit. NASA Release 86-5, Houston, July 1986. https://history.nasa.gov/sts51lpresskithighres.pdf.

Space Shuttle Mission STS-61A Press Kit. NASA Release 85-145, Houston, October 1985. https://www.jsc.nasa.gov/history/shuttle_pk/pk/Flight_022_STS -61A_Press_Kit.pdf.

Space Shuttle Mission STS-61B Press Kit. NASA Release 85-153, November 1985. https://www.jsc.nasa.gov/history/shuttle_pk/pk/Flight_023_STS-61B _Press_Kit.pdf.

Space Shuttle Mission STS-61C Press Kit. NASA Release 85-167, December 1985. https://www.jsc.nasa.gov/history/shuttle_pk/pk/Flight_024_STS-61C _Press_Kit.pdf.

Space Shuttle Mission STS-95 Press Kit. NASA. Last updated 27 October 1998. https://www.jsc.nasa.gov/history/shuttle_pk/pk/Flight_092_STS-095 _Press_Kit.pdf.

"Space Shuttle System Baseline Reference Missions." Vol. 3, "Mission 3A and Mission 3B." JSC internal note no. 73-FM-47, 26 March 1973. Johnson Space Center, Mission Planning and Analysis Division, Houston.

STS-9: Change-of-Shift Briefing, 29, 30 November, 3, 4, and 5 December 1983. Lyndon B. Johnson Space Center, Houston. https://ia802707.us.archive .org/6/items/STS-9/Sts-9PcTranscript.pdf.

"STS-9 Columbia-Spacelab 1 Highlights 1983 NASA; Post Flight Press Conference Film; John Young." YouTube video, 18:36. Posted by Jeff Quitney, 26 November 2017. https://www.youtube.com/watch?v=l1kErrPZ49M.

STS-9: Flight Crew Report, 8 June 1984. Lyndon B. Johnson Space Center, Houston.

STS-9: Science Briefing, 29 November 1983. Lyndon B. Johnson Space Center, Houston. https://ia802707.us.archive.org/6/items/STS-9/Sts-9PcTranscript.pdf.

STS-41D: Flight Crew Report, 8 January 1985. CB-85-007. Lyndon B. Johnson Space Center, Houston.

STS-41D: Technical Crew Debriefing, October 1984. JSC-20536. Lyndon B. Johnson Space Center, Houston.

STS-41G: Flight Crew Report, 20 December 1984. Lyndon B. Johnson Space Center, Houston.

"STS-41G: Mission Highlights." YouTube video, 50:01. Posted by NASA STI Program, 25 October 2011. https://m.youtube.com/watch?v=mY22VLpmObY.

STS-51B: Change-of-Shift Briefing, 3 May 1985. Lyndon B. Johnson Space Center, Houston.

STS-51B: Transcript Profile. https://ia902700.us.archive.org/6/items/STS-51B-test /Sts-51bTranscriptProfile.pdf.

STS-51C: Flight Crew Report, n.d. Lyndon B. Johnson Space Center, Houston.

STS-51C: National Space Transportation System Program Mission Report, March 1985. JSC-20393. Lyndon B. Johnson Space Center, Houston.

STS-51C: Status Report No. 2, 25 January 1985. Lyndon B. Johnson Space Center, Houston.

STS-51D: Change-of-Shift Briefing, 12 April 1985. Lyndon B. Johnson Space Center, Houston. https://ia601408.us.archive.org/2/items/STS-51D/Sts -51dPcTranscript.pdf.

STS-51D: Flight Crew Report, 17 January 1985. Lyndon B. Johnson Space Center, Houston.

STS-51D: Technical Crew Debriefing, May 1985. JSC-20079. Lyndon B. Johnson Space Center, Houston.

STS-51F: Flight Crew Report, 5 December 1985. CB-85-419. Lyndon B. Johnson Space Center, Houston.

"STS-51F Launch, Abort & Landing (7-29-85)." YouTube video, 10:40. Posted by 3210andLiftoff, 31 July 2009. https://www.youtube.com/watch?v=JSbMs _OnE4c.

STS-51G: Technical Crew Debriefing, August 1985. JSC-20649. Lyndon B. Johnson Space Center, Houston.

STS-61A: Flight Crew Report, 8 June 1984. Lyndon B. Johnson Space Center, Houston.

STS-61B: Flight Crew Report, 14 March 1985. Lyndon B. Johnson Space Center, Houston.

"Sultan bin Salman Al Saud." Buzz Aldrin Enterprises, 2014. YouTube video, 3:03. Posted by Apollo45, 16 July 2014. https://www.youtube.com/watch ?v=dB3V50WgDh0.

"Teacher in Space Application—Christa McAuliffe." 1985. *Challenger STS 51-L: Ephemera.* Book 19. Framingham State University. http://digitalcommons .framingham.edu/challenger_ephemera/19.

Van den Berg, Lodewijk. "How a Crystal Growth Scientist Became an Astronaut." Filmed 7 November 2011 in Delft, Neth. TEDx video, 18:02. https://www.youtube.com/watch?v=DlvQh8CNUDA.

Virgin Galactic. "Research Flights." http://www.virgingalactic.com/human-spaceflight/research-flights/.

———. *SpaceShipTwo: An Introductory Guide for Payload Users*. Revision no. WEB005, 27 May 2016. http://www.virgingalactic.com/assets/uploads/2016/06/VG_PUG_WEB005_20160503.pdf.

Wilson, Robert G. Memorandum to the Assistant Administrator for Planning and Program Integration, "Payload Specialist Selection," 8 June 1976. University of Houston–Clear Lake Archives.

Wright, Mike. "Women Scientists and Engineers in the 1960s and 1970s at the Marshall Space Flight Center." Marshall Space Flight Center, 2000. https://history.msfc.nasa.gov/saturn_apollo/womensci.pdf (site discontinued).

Yardley, John (NASA HQ, Washington DC). Memorandum to Christopher C. Kraft (JSC), "Air Force Payload Specialist Selection Process," 26 June 1979. University of Houston–Clear Lake Archives.

Index

In the Outward Odyssey: A People's History of Spaceflight series

Into That Silent Sea: Trailblazers of the Space Era, 1961–1965
Francis French and Colin Burgess
Foreword by Paul Haney

In the Shadow of the Moon: A Challenging Journey to Tranquility, 1965–1969
Francis French and Colin Burgess
Foreword by Walter Cunningham

To a Distant Day: The Rocket Pioneers
Chris Gainor
Foreword by Alfred Worden

Homesteading Space: The Skylab Story
David Hitt, Owen Garriott, and Joe Kerwin
Foreword by Homer Hickam

Ambassadors from Earth: Pioneering Explorations with Unmanned Spacecraft
Jay Gallentine

Footprints in the Dust: The Epic Voyages of Apollo, 1969–1975
Edited by Colin Burgess
Foreword by Richard F. Gordon

Realizing Tomorrow: The Path to Private Spaceflight
Chris Dubbs and Emeline Paat-Dahlstrom
Foreword by Charles D. Walker

The X-15 Rocket Plane: Flying the First Wings into Space
Michelle Evans
Foreword by Joe H. Engle

Wheels Stop: The Tragedies and Triumphs of the Space Shuttle Program, 1986–2011
Rick Houston
Foreword by Jerry Ross